PHP & MySQL

the missing manual®

The book that should have been in the box®

Brett McLaughlin

O'REILLY®

Beijing | Cambridge | Farnham | Köln | Sebastopol | Tokyo

PHP and MySQL: The Missing Manual

by Brett McLaughlin

Copyright © 2012 Brett McLaughlin. All rights reserved.
Printed in the United States of America.

Published by O'Reilly Media, Inc.,
1005 Gravenstein Highway North, Sebastopol, CA 95472.

O'Reilly books may be purchased for educational, business, or sales promotional use. Online editions are also available for most titles (*http://my.safaribooksonline.com*). For more information, contact our corporate/institutional sales department: (800) 998-9938 or *corporate@oreilly.com*.

Printing History:

November 2011:   First Edition.

Revision History:

   2011-11-09   First release

See *http://oreilly.com/catalog/errata.csp?isbn=9780596515867* for release details.

ISBN-13: 978-0-596-51586-7

Contents

Part One: PHP and MySQL Basics

Part Two: Dynamic Web Pages

Part Three: From Web Pages to Web Applications

Part Four: **Security and the Real World**

The Missing Credits

ABOUT THE AUTHOR

Brett McLaughlin is a senior level technologist and strategist, active especially in web programming and data-driven customer-facing systems. Rarely focused on only one component of a system, he architects, designs, manages, and implements large-scale applications from start to finish with mission-critical implementations and deadlines.

Of course, that's all fancy-talk for saying that Brett's a geek, spending most of his day in front of a computer with his hands flying across a keyboard. Currently, he spends most of his current time working on NASA projects, which sounds much cooler than it actually is. But hey, maybe that satellite overhead really is controlled by PHP and MySQL…

ABOUT THE CREATIVE TEAM

Nan Barber (editor) has been working on the Missing Manual series since its inception. She lives in Boston with her husband and various electronic devices. Email: *nanbarber@oreilly.com.*

Jasmine Perez (production editor) spends her free time cooking vegetarian meals, listening to her favorite freeform radio station, WFMU, and going on adventures whenever possible. Email: *jperez@oreilly.com*

Nan Reinhardt (proofreader) is a freelancer copy editor and proofreader, who is also a writer of romantic fiction. She has two novels with her agent at Curtis Brown Literary Agency. In between editing gigs, she is busy working on her third book. She blogs thrice weekly at *www.nanreinhardt.com.* Email: *reinhardt8@comcast.net.*

Ron Strauss (indexer) lives with his wife in northern California at 2,300 feet. When not indexing Missing Manual books, he moonlights as a musician (viola and Native American flute).

Shelley Powers (technical reviewer) is a former HTML5 working group member and author of several O'Reilly books. She is also an animal welfare advocate, working to close down puppy mills in Missouri. Website: *www.burningbird.net.*

Steve Suehring (technical reviewer) is a technical architect with an extensive background finding simple solutions to complex problems. Steve plays several musical instruments (not at the same time) and can be reached through his website *www.braingia.org.*

ACKNOWLEDGMENTS

Acknowledgements are always nearly impossible to do well. Before you can think anyone of substance, the music swells and they're shuffling you off stage. Seriously, before the writing, there's my wife Leigh and my kids, Dean, Robbie, and Addie. Any energy or joy or relaxation that happens during the long writing process filters through those four, and there's never enough royalties to cover the time lost with them. I suppose it's a reflection of their love and support for me that they're OK with me writing anyway.

And then, there's certainly the writing. Brian Sawyer was the first guy to call me when I became available to write, and he called when I was really in need of just what he gave me: excitement about me writing and encouragement that I could write into the Missing Manual series. I won't forget that call anytime soon. And then Nan Barber IM-ed and emailed me through this whole thing. She showed a really unhealthy level of trust that wasn't earned, and I'm quite thankful, especially in the dark days of early August when I had hundreds of pages left to write in a few short weeks.

Shelley Powers and Steve Suehring were technical reviewers, and they were both picky and gentle. That's about all you can ask. Shelley helped me remember to keep the learner front and center, and if you like the longer code listings when things get hairy, she's the one to thank. And Steve...Steve filled out my PHP holes. He caught one particularly nasty issue that I think vastly improved the book. You don't realize this, but you owe him a real debt of thanks if this book helps you.

And then there's the vast machinery at O'Reilly. It all works, and I don't know how, really, and I'm OK with that. I imagine somewhere Sanders is pulling important levers and Courtney is badgering authors and Laura is angry and in heels and Laurie thinks this all costs too much and Tim is...well, Tim is thinking about something important. I'm glad for all of them.

—*Brett McLaughlin*

THE MISSING MANUAL SERIES

Missing Manuals are witty, superbly written guides to computer products that don't come with printed manuals (which is just about all of them). Each book features a handcrafted index and cross-references to specific pages (not just chapters).

Recent and upcoming titles include:

Access 2010: The Missing Manual by Matthew MacDonald

Buying a Home: The Missing Manual by Nancy Conner

CSS: The Missing Manual, Second Edition, by David Sawyer McFarland

Creating a Website: The Missing Manual, Third Edition, by Matthew MacDonald

David Pogue's Digital Photography: The Missing Manual by David Pogue

Dreamweaver CS5.5: The Missing Manual by David Sawyer McFarland

Droid 2: The Missing Manual by Preston Gralla

Droid X2: The Missing Manual by Preston Gralla

Excel 2010: The Missing Manual by Matthew MacDonald

Facebook: The Missing Manual, Third Edition by E.A. Vander Veer

FileMaker Pro 11: The Missing Manual by Susan Prosser and Stuart Gripman

Flash CS5.5: The Missing Manual by Chris Grover

Galaxy Tab: The Missing Manual by Preston Gralla

Google Apps: The Missing Manual by Nancy Conner

Google SketchUp: The Missing Manual by Chris Grover

iMovie '11 & iDVD: The Missing Manual by David Pogue and Aaron Miller

iPad 2: The Missing Manual by J.D. Biersdorfer

iPhone: The Missing Manual, Fourth Edition by David Pogue

iPhone App Development: The Missing Manual by Craig Hockenberry

iPhoto '11: The Missing Manual by David Pogue and Lesa Snider

iPod: The Missing Manual, Ninth Edition by J.D. Biersdorfer and David Pogue

JavaScript: The Missing Manual by David Sawyer McFarland

Living Green: The Missing Manual by Nancy Conner

Mac OS X Snow Leopard: The Missing Manual by David Pogue

Mac OS X Lion: The Missing Manual by David Pogue

Microsoft Project 2010: The Missing Manual by Bonnie Biafore

Motorola Xoom: The Missing Manual by Preston Gralla

Netbooks: The Missing Manual by J.D. Biersdorfer

Office 2010: The Missing Manual by Nancy Connor, Chris Grover, and Matthew MacDonald

Office 2011 for Macintosh: The Missing Manual by Chris Grover

Palm Pre: The Missing Manual by Ed Baig

Personal Investing: The Missing Manual by Bonnie Biafore

Photoshop CS5: The Missing Manual by Lesa Snider

Photoshop Elements 9: The Missing Manual by Barbara Brundage

PowerPoint 2007: The Missing Manual by E.A. Vander Veer

Premiere Elements 8: The Missing Manual by Chris Grover

QuickBase: The Missing Manual by Nancy Conner

QuickBooks 2011: The Missing Manual by Bonnie Biafore

Quicken 2009: The Missing Manual by Bonnie Biafore

Switching to the Mac: The Missing Manual, Snow Leopard Edition by David Pogue

Wikipedia: The Missing Manual by John Broughton

Windows Vista: The Missing Manual by David Pogue

Windows 7: The Missing Manual by David Pogue

Word 2007: The Missing Manual by Chris Grover

Your Body: The Missing Manual by Matthew MacDonald

Your Brain: The Missing Manual by Matthew MacDonald

Your Money: The Missing Manual by J.D. Roth

Introduction

You've built a web page in HTML. You've even styled it with Cascading Style Sheets (CSS) and written a little JavaScript to validate your custom-built web forms. But that wasn't enough, so you learned a lot more JavaScript, threw in some jQuery, and constructed a whole lot of web pages. You've even moved your JavaScript into external files, shared your CSS across your entire site, and validated your HTML with the latest standards.

But now you want more.

Maybe you've become frustrated with your website's inability to store user information in anything beyond cookies. Maybe you want a full-blown online store, complete with PayPal integration and details about what's in stock. Or maybe you've simply caught the programming bug, and want to go beyond what HTML, CSS, and JavaScript can easily give you.

If any of these are the case—and you may find that *all* these are the case!—then learning PHP and MySQL is a great way to take a giant programming step forward. Even if you've never heard of PHP, you'll find it's the best way to go from building web pages to creating full-fledged web applications that store all sorts of information in databases. This book shows you how to do just that.

◼ What Is PHP?

PHP is a programming language. It's like JavaScript in that you spend most of your time dealing with values and making decisions about which path through your code should be followed at any given time. But it's like HTML in that you deal with output—tags that your users view through the lens of their web browsers. In fact, PHP in the context of web programming is a bit of a mutt; it does lots of things pretty well, rather than just doing one single thing. (And if you've ever wondered *why* it's called PHP, see the box below.)

FREQUENTLY ASKED QUESTION

What Does PHP Stand For?

PHP is an acronym. Originally, PHP stood for *Personal Home Page*, because lots of programmers used it to build their websites, going much further than what was possible with HTML, CSS, and JavaScript. But in the last few years, "personal home page" tends to sound more like something that happens on one of those really cheap hosting sites, rather than a high-powered programming language.

So now PHP stands for *PHP: Hypertext Preprocessor.* If that sounds geeky, it is. In fact, it's a bit of a programmer joke: the acronym PHP stands for something that actually contains the acronym PHP within itself. That makes it a *recursive* acronym, or an acronym that references itself. You don't have to know what a recursive acronym is; that won't be on the quiz. Just be warned that PHP's recursive acronym won't be the last weird and slightly funny thing you'll run across in the PHP language.

PHP Is All About the Web

If you came here for web programming, you're in the right place. While you can write PHP programs that run from a command line (check out Figure I-1 for an example), that's not really where PHP excels.

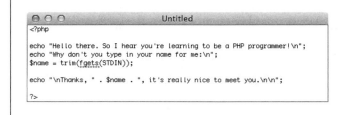

```php
<?php

echo "Hello there. So I hear you're learning to be a PHP programmer!\n";
echo "Why don't you type in your name for me:\n";
$name = trim(fgets(STDIN));

echo "\nThanks, " . $name . ", it's really nice to meet you.\n\n";

?>
```

FIGURE I-1

Sure, you can run PHP programs from a Terminal window or a command shell on Windows. But most of the time, you won't. PHP is perfectly suited to the Web, and that where you'll spend most of your time.

PHP comes ready to work with HTML forms and web sessions and browser cookies. It's great at integrating with your website's existing authentication system, or letting you create one of your own. You'll spend a lot of time not just handing off control to an HTML page, but actually writing the HTML you're already familiar with right into your PHP. Lots of times, you'll actually write some PHP, and then write some HTML, all in the same PHP file, as in the following example:

```php
<?php

require '../../scripts/database_connection.php';

// Get the user ID of the user to show
$user_id = $_REQUEST['user_id'];

// Build the SELECT statement
$select_query = "SELECT * FROM users WHERE user_id = " . $user_id;

// Run the query
$result = mysql_query($select_query);

// Assign values to variables
?>

<html>
  <!-- All your HTML and inline PHP -->
</html>
```

The result? Pages that are both full of HTML and have dynamic content, like Figure I-2.

FIGURE I-2

This page is as much PHP as HTML. It looks up your visitor's name in the database and displays it dynamically. The menu creates a Show Profile option specific to this user. But there's still lots and lots of HTML. This is PHP at its best: combining the HTML and even JavaScript that you know with the PHP you're about to learn.

JavaScript Is Loose, PHP Is...Less So

If you've written some JavaScript—and if you're checking out this book, that's probably the case—then you know that JavaScript lets you do just about anything you want. You can occasionally leave out semicolons; you can use brackets, or not; you can use the *var* keyword, or not. That sort of looseness is both great for getting things working quickly, and at the same time, frustrating. It makes finding bugs tricky at times, and working across browsers can be a nightmare.

PHP is not quite so loose as JavaScript, so it makes you learn a little more structure and tighten up your understanding of what's going on as your program is interpreted. That's a good thing, as it'll end up making you tighten up your JavaScript skills, too. And, perhaps best of all, PHP's stodgy consistency makes it easier to learn. It gives you firm rules to hang on to, rather than lots of "You can do this...or this...or this..."

So get ready. There's lots to learn, but everything you learn gives you something to build on. And PHP lets you know right away when there's a problem. You won't need to pop open an Error Console or keep an eye out for Internet Explorer's tiny yellow warning triangle like you do with JavaScript.

PHP Is Interpreted

PHP code comes in the form of *scripts*, which are plain text files you write. The PHP *interpreter* is a piece of software on your web server that reads that file and makes sense of it, giving the Web server HTML output and directions about where to go next, or how to interpret a user's form entry. Your text file is interpreted, one line at a time, every time that file is accessed.

This scheme is different from languages like Java or C++, which are *compiled*. In those languages, you write in text files, but then run a command that turns those text files into something else: class files, binary files, pieces of unreadable code that your computer uses.

The beauty of an interpreted language like PHP—and JavaScript, for that matter—is that you write your code and go. You don't need a bunch of tools or steps. You write PHP. Test it out in the browser. Write some more. It's fast, and that usually means it's pretty fun.

■ What Is MySQL?

MySQL is a database. It stores your information, your users' information, and anything else you want to stuff into it. There's actually a lot more nuance to MySQL—and SQL, the language in which you'll interact with MySQL (but better to save that for Chapter 3—when you've got a little PHP and context under your belt).

For now, think of MySQL as a warehouse where you can store things to be looked up later. Not only that, MySQL provides you a really fast little imp that runs around finding all that stuff you stuck in the warehouse whenever it's needed. By the time you're through this this book, you'll love that imp...er...MySQL. It'll do work that you could never do on your own, and it'll do that work tirelessly and quickly.

■ About This Book

PHP is a web-based language, not a program that comes in a box. And there are literally tens (hundreds?) of thousands of websites that have bits of PHP instruction on them. That's great, right? Well, not so much. Those websites aren't all current. Some are full of bugs. Some have more information in the comment trails—scattered amongst gripes, complaints, and lambasting from other programmers—as they do in the main page. It's no easy matter to find what you're looking for.

The purpose of this book, then, is to serve as the manual that should have been included when you download PHP. It's the missing PDF, if you will (or maybe the missing eBook, if you're a Kindle or Nook or iPad person). In this book's pages, you'll find step-by-step instructions for getting PHP running, writing your first program... and your second program...and eventually building a web application from scratch. In addition, you'll find clear evaluations of the absolutely critical parts of PHP that you'll use every day, whether you're building a personal weblog or a corporate intranet.

NOTE This book periodically recommends *other* books, covering topics that are too specialized or tangential for a manual about PHP and MySQL. Careful readers may notice that not every one of these titles is published by Missing Manual parent company O'Reilly Media. If there's a great book out there that doesn't happen to be published by O'Reilly, this book will still let you know about it.

PHP & MySQL: The Missing Manual is designed to accommodate readers at every technical level. The primary discussions are written for advanced-beginner or intermediate Web authors and programmers. Hopefully, you're comfortable with HTML and CSS, and maybe even know a bit of JavaScript. But if you're new to all this Web stuff, take heart: special boxes called "Up to Speed" provide the introductory information you need to understand the topic at hand. If you're an advanced user, on the other hand, keep your eye out for similar boxes called "Power Users' Clinic." They offer more technical tips, tricks, and shortcuts for the experienced computer fan.

Macintosh and Windows

PHP and MySQL work almost precisely the same in their Macintosh and Windows versions. And even more importantly, you'll do most of your work by uploading your scripts and running your database code against a web server. That means that your hosting provider gets to deal with operating system issues. You get to focus on your code and information.

In the first few chapters, you'll get your system set up to code and deal with PHP scripts. But you'll soon forget about whether you're on Mac or Windows. You'll just be writing code, the same way you write HTML and CSS.

FTP: It's Critical

One piece of software you *won't* forget you're using is a good FTP program. Most PHP programmers don't sit on a remote server typing into a command-line editor like *vi* or *emacs*.

AUTHOR'S NOTE Typing in a command-line editor is actually exactly how I work. But then, I'm a dinosaur, a throwback to days when you had to watch commercials to see primetime TV, and you'd miss emails because your pocket didn't buzz every time your boss whisked you a command through the ether.

Today, for most of you, a good text editor and a good graphical FTP client are much better choices. Seriously, my addiction owns me, and I so badly want to :wq! it.

Chapter 1 will point you at several great editors, and the fancier ones will have FTP built right in. But a program like Cyberduck (*www.cyberduck.ch*) is great, too. You can write a script, throw it online, and test it all with a few mouse clicks. So go ahead and get that FTP program downloaded, configured for your web server, and fired up. You're gonna need it.

About the Outline

PHP & MySQL: The Missing Manual is divided into four parts, each containing several chapters:

- **Part 1: PHP and MySQL Basics.** In the first three chapters, you'll install PHP, get it running on your computer, write your first few PHP programs, and learn to do a few basic things like collect user information via a web form and work with text. You'll also install MySQL and get thoroughly acquainted with the structure of a database.

- **Part 2: Dynamic Web Pages.** These are the chapters where you start to build the basics of a solid web application. You'll add a table in which you can store users and their information, and get a grasp of how easily you can manipulate text. From URLs and emails to Twitter handles, you'll use regular expressions and string handling to bend letters, numbers, and slashes to your will.

- **Part 3: From Web Pages to Web Applications.** With a solid foundation, you're ready to connect your web pages into a more cohesive unit. You'll add custom error handling so that your users won't get confused when things go wrong, and your own debugging to help you find problems. You'll also store references to users' images of themselves, store the images themselves in a database, and learn which approach is best in which situations.

- **Part 4: Security and the Real World.** In even the simplest of applications, logging in and logging out is critical. You'll build an authentication system, and then deal with passwords (which are important, but a bit of a pain). You'll then work with cookies and sessions, and use both to create a group-based authorization system for your web application.

At the Missing Manual website (*www.missingmanuals.com/cds/phpmysqlmm*), you'll find every single code example, from every chapter, in the state it was shown for that chapter.

■ About the Online Resources

As the owner of a Missing Manual, you've got more than just a book to read. Online, you'll find example files so you can get some hands-on experience, as well as tips, articles, and maybe even a video or two. You can also communicate with the Missing Manual team and tell us what you love (or hate) about the book. Head over to *www.missingmanuals.com*, or go directly to one of the following sections.

Missing CD

This book doesn't have a CD pasted inside the back cover, but you're not missing out on anything. Go to *www.missingmanuals.com/cds/phpmysqlmm* to download code samples, code samples, and also, some code samples. Yup, there are a lot of them. Every chapter has a section of code for that chapter. And you don't just get completed versions of the book's scripts. You'll get a version that matches up with each chapter, so you'll never get too confused about exactly how your version of a script or web page should look.

And so you don't wear down your fingers typing long web addresses, the Missing CD page also offers a list of clickable links to the websites mentioned in this book.

Registration

If you register this book at oreilly.com, you'll be eligible for special offers—like discounts on future editions of *PHP & MySQL: The Missing Manual*. Registering takes only a few clicks. To get started, type *www.oreilly.com/register* into your browser to hop directly to the Registration page.

Feedback

Got questions? Need more information? Fancy yourself a book reviewer? On our Feedback page, you can get expert answers to questions that come to you while reading, share your thoughts on this Missing Manual, and find groups for folks who share your interest in PHP, MySQL, and web applications in general. To have your say, go to *www.missingmanuals.com/feedback*.

Errata

In an effort to keep this book as up-to-date and accurate as possible, each time we print more copies, we'll make any confirmed corrections you've suggested. We also note such changes on the book's website, so you can mark important corrections into your own copy of the book, if you like. Go to *http://tinyurl.com/phpmysql-mm* to report an error and view existing corrections.

■ Safari® Books Online

 Safari® Books Online is an on-demand digital library that lets you easily search over 7,500 technology and creative reference books and videos to find the answers you need quickly.

With a subscription, you can read any page and watch any video from our library online. Read books on your cell phone and mobile devices. Access new titles before they are available for print, and get exclusive access to manuscripts in development and post feedback for the authors. Copy and paste code samples, organize your favorites, download chapters, bookmark key sections, create notes, print out pages, and benefit from tons of other time-saving features.

O'Reilly Media has uploaded this book to the Safari Books Online service. To have full digital access to this book and others on similar topics from O'Reilly and other publishers, sign up for free at *http://my.safaribooksonline.com.*

PHP and MySQL Basics

PHP: What, Why, and Where?

P HP is ultimately text, taken by your web server and turned into a set of commands and information for your web browser. And because you're just working in text, there's not a lot you have to do to get going as a PHP programmer. You need to get familiar with PHP itself—and the best way to do that is to install PHP on your own computer, even though most of your programs will run on a web server.

Then, you need to run an actual script. Don't worry; it's amazingly easy to write your first program in PHP, and you'll end up writing *more* than just one program before you hit Chapter 2.

And through it all? You'll begin taking control. PHP gives you the ability to be an active participant in your web pages. It lets you listen carefully to your users and say something back. So get going; no reason to leave you users with passive HTML pages any longer.

▨ Gathering Your Tools

You'll need to take just a few steps before you can start with PHP. You can't build a website without a web browser, and you can't write PHP without a few tools. But it won't take long before you've got your computer set up with your own customized PHP programming environment.

Although PHP isn't pre-loaded on every computer like web browsers are, you can easily download PHP from the Internet, get it working on your computer, and get up and running fast...all without spending a dime. On top of that, most of the easiest and best tools for writing PHP code are also free. All you need is your own copy of the PHP language on your computer, plus a plain old text editor. This section shows you where to find them.

PHP on the PC

PCs come with a lot of software pre-installed. Unfortunately, one program that most PCs *don't* come with is PHP. That's okay though: you can get PHP up and running in just a few minutes, as long as you have an Internet connection.

> **NOTE** If you have a Mac, you don't have to go through this installation process. Flip to page 9.

Open up your favorite Web browser and head to www.*php.net*. This site is PHP's online home, and it's where you'll download your own version of the PHP language, along with all the tools you need to write and run PHP programs. Look along the right side of the PHP home page for the Stable Releases heading; you can see it on the right of Figure 1-1.

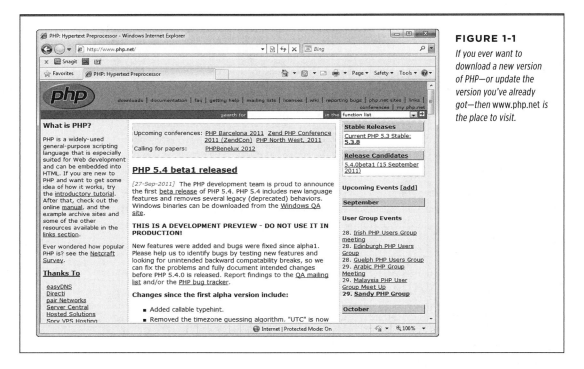

FIGURE 1-1

If you ever want to download a new version of PHP—or update the version you've already got—then www.php.net *is the place to visit.*

Click the link for the version with the highest number. (For more information on what all these versions mean, see the box on the next page.)

Once you've chosen a PHP version link, you'll see a screen like Figure 1-2, with links for the current version of PHP as well as at least one older version (which will have a lower version number than the most current version).

Before you download PHP, though, take a look further down the page. There's a heading titled Windows Binaries, and that's your ticket to getting PHP up and running fast on your Windows machine. Clicking this link takes you to another site, *http://windows.php.net/download*, which should look something like Figure 1-3.

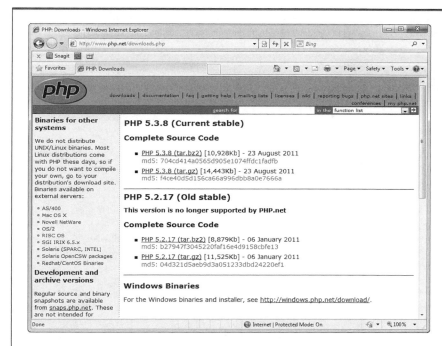

FIGURE 1-2

The PHP site always has at least the latest stable version, and the previous stable version available for download. Unless you've got a really good reason to do otherwise, always go with the latest stable version.

Release the Version Within

If you've never worked with software that comes in versions or releases, there's nothing to worry about. Both words mean pretty much the same thing when it comes to software: A *version* or *release* of software is just a way of saying that all the parts of that software are packaged together so that they work correctly for you, and with the other parts of that software.

Since software changes frequently, though, the folks that make software need a way to say, "Hey, our software has some new cool bells and whistles! There's a new package available!" The

software people (yes, they really exist) use *version numbers* (or *release numbers*) to do that. Generally, software begins at 1.0 and that number gets higher as the software adds new features. So version 2.2 of PHP is going to be newer than version 1.1, and probably will have some cool new features, too.

Sometimes, as on the PHP website, you'll see several different packages or downloads of a piece of software, each with a different version number. You can usually just download the latest version of the software you want and you'll be all set.

This page has options for the latest version and well as several older versions. For the newest version, there will be two big gray blocks: the first for the Non Thread Safe version, and the second for the Thread Safe version. You want to download the Non Thread Safe version, since it runs much faster. (For more detail on the difference between these two versions, see the box on page 7.)

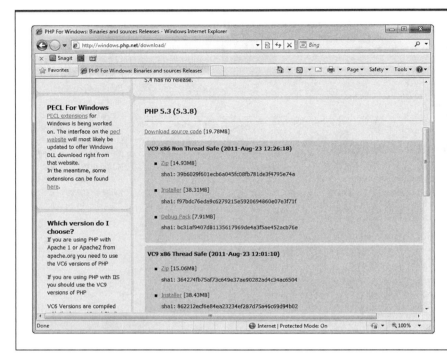

FIGURE 1-3

PHP has a page dedicated to Windows downloads. There are still a lot of options, but don't get too distracted by so many choices. You're looking for a single word: Installer.

Just look for the Installer option and click the link. The installer is usually a big download, but includes a nice Windows installer that will make getting PHP running a breeze. Click this link and then grab a cup of coffee while you're waiting for your download to complete.

NOTE If you're thinking you could have just gone directly to *http://windows.php.net/download/*, then you're right: You could have. But six months from now, you may forget that longer URL, but remember *www.php.net*. On top of that, a good old-fashioned Google search for PHP takes you to *www.php.net*, so it's a good idea to learn how to get to the Windows installer from the main PHP home page.

Once your download's done, find the downloaded file and double-click it. When Windows asks for permission to run the installer, click Allow, and then click Next on the pop-up screen to start the installation.

You'll have to accept a license agreement and then select an installation directory. Go with the suggested *C:\Program Files\PHP*, so you can always find PHP with all your other programs. Next, the installer asks about configuring a web server (see Figure 1-4). For now, you'll be using PHP on your machine to test programs, and then uploading those programs to a web server, so select "Do not setup a web server." If you want to add a web server later, you can always come back and change this option.

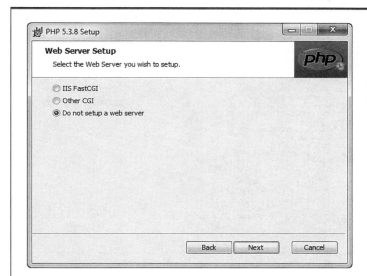

FIGURE 1-4

If you want to install a local web server to test your entire web applications on your machine, select the IIS FastCGI or Other CGI option. But for getting started, "Do not setup a web server" is the simplest option.

UNDER THE HOOD

PHP on Windows: Fast or Safe?

PHP was first released in a Windows-friendly version back in 2000. In those early releases, PHP was released only in one version: Thread Safe. While Mac OS X and Unix/Linux systems use something called *processes* to run multiple things at one time, Windows systems use *threads*. Those Windows threads can interact with each other, and so to prevent them from screwing each other up, PHP came in a version that was *thread safe*.

Unfortunately, keeping those threads out of each other's way takes a lot of time. The thread-safe version of PHP on Windows is slow, and PHP programmers flocked away from Windows whenever possible. A few clever PHP programmers figured out ways to recycle threads, and now a lot of web servers that run on Windows now come pre-installed with a PHP version that can recycle threads right from the start.

Still, not everyone liked installing PHP and then having to install a tweaked web server, or make manual changes to PHP, to get it running at tip-top speed. As a result, there's now a *non-thread safe* option. This option doesn't concern itself with other threads, and the result is a significant performance increase, ranging anywhere from 10 to 40 percent, depending on your applications.

Chances are, if you don't have a strong opinion or idea about which version of the PHP binaries you need, you'll do fine with the non-thread safe binaries, and you'll get a nice snappy performance. If you have real concerns about the non-thread safe version—perhaps you never want two users competing for the same piece of data, regardless of how fast or slow your application runs—then you can certainly choose the thread-safe binaries and tweak your own installation as you see fit.

The next screen asks you which items to install. The default options, shown in Figure 1-5, are fine for now. Just click Next to move on.

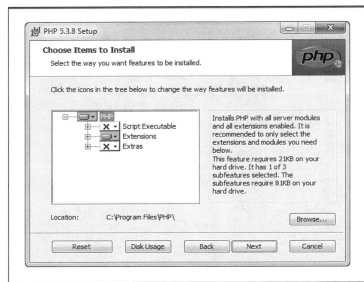

FIGURE 1-5

The Windows installer comes with the basic PHP installation, but you can also add several extras, which you can access by clicking the white box next to Extras and selecting individual features.

Finally, click Install and then let your progress indicator march to full. That's it! You've got PHP running on your machine.

To check out PHP, go to your Start menu and type *cmd* in the Search box. A command window opens, into which you can type commands like those that run PHP. Go ahead and type *php*, as you see in Figure 1-6.

Even though it doesn't look like much, that blank line and empty command prompt mean PHP is installed correctly. Now you're ready to get into your first program.

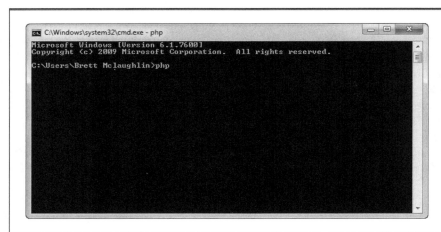

FIGURE 1-6

You won't spend a lot of time running PHP from the command prompt, but it's a nice quick way to test things out. The Windows installer makes sure you can run PHP from anywhere on the command line, from any directory.

PHP on the Mac

There's something downright sexy about Macs. All that metal and chrome...and, for the programmer, PHP! That's right, if you've got a Mac, you've already got PHP pre-installed. To prove it, open the Terminal application on your Mac.

If you've never used Terminal, don't worry; you'll get used to it quickly and find it's one of your best friends for working with PHP. Open your Applications folder (you can use Shift-⌘-A as a shortcut), and then look for the Utilities folder, shown in Figure 1-7.

WARNING Shift-⌘-A works only if your desktop or another file folder is active. If you're currently viewing this book in an e-reader or online, for example, click your desktop and then press Shift-⌘-A.

FIGURE 1-7

The Utilities folder hides all sorts of useful programs that come with Mac OS X. Look around, as there are all sorts of goodies you may want to use regularly.

POWER USERS' CLINIC

Opening Programs Without the Mouse

There's nothing wrong with opening a folder in the Finder and using your mouse to locate the Applications folder, and then the Utilities folder. But you'll find that programmers are impatient folks, and you can move a lot quicker if you don't have to take your hands off your keyboard so often. Keyboard shortcuts like Shift-⌘-A are perfect ways to do just that, so you may want

to take some time to learn these shortcuts as you run across them in software menus or these chapters.

This book will give you both the folder path and keyboard shortcut when one exists. You'll find folder paths expressed with arrow notation, as in Applications→Utilities.

Once you've found the Applications folder, open it and find the Terminal application. It looks like a computer monitor with black screen and a little white arrow, as you see in Figure 1-8.

FIGURE 1-8

The Terminal program lets you use a command line on Macs. A lot of your PHP coding will be done using Terminal, so you'll get used to this application pretty quickly.

TIP   You'll often use the Terminal application for testing out your PHP programs before you upload them to your server. To make it easier to launch Terminal, you may want to drag the icon into your dock so you can quickly launch Terminal in the future.

Double-click the Terminal icon, and you'll see a white rectangular screen with a little black cursor blinking, as in Figure 1-9. That little cursor is going to be one of your best friends on your journey to PHP nirvana.

FIGURE 1-9

When you first open Terminal, you won't be too impressed. You'll get a line that probably matches your computer's name, and then a weird dollar sign. Don't worry—this will all soon be old hat.

To make sure PHP is installed on your system, just type *php*, all in lowercase letters, and hit Enter. Unfortunately, the way to know things are working is if you *don't* see anything but that blank cursor, a little further down in Terminal. It won't even blink at you anymore; it's just a boring gray dark square.

Hit Control-C to stop that single eye from staying, and you'll get a blinking cursor again. This time, type *which php*. The *which* command tells you where on your computer the program you give it is located—*php* in this case. You'll probably get something back that looks like Figure 1-10; here, *php* is in the */usr/bin* directory. You'll probably get a similar result.

FIGURE 1-10

Lots of the programs you use in Terminal are scattered around your Mac's hard drive. The which *command lets you know exactly where a command really resides on your machine.*

Once you've seen exactly where *php* is, you're ready to go!

Take Control of Your PHP Installation

Like most of the programs on your computer, the PHP software package (which includes the *php* program you've been running) is updated fairly often. Most of the time, if you're keeping your computer updated with Apple's Software Update, you don't have to worry about updating PHP separately. But if you want to see what version of PHP you're actually running, you can type *php –version* into your Terminal window. You'll get back something like this:

```
Bretts-MacBook-Pro:~ bdm0509$ php -version
PHP 5.3.4 (cli) (built: Dec 15 2010
12:15:07)
Copyright (c) 1997-2010 The PHP Group
Zend Engine v2.3.0, Copyright (c) 1998-
2010 Zend Technologies
```

Look at the very first line that PHP spits out; it tells you you're running version 5.3.4. (See the box on page 5 for more detail on how version numbers work.)

If you want to get the very latest version of PHP, you can visit *www.php.net* and download the PHP source code. That's a little trickier than just using the version preinstalled on your Mac, though, so unless you're really into commands like *unzip* and *tar*, you can stick with what's already on your machine.

By the way, if you're *not* using your Mac's Software Update frequently, you may want to do so now. It'll keep your software current, without all the hassle of downloading programs on your own. Just choose →Software Update to find and install new software that's available for your Mac. And if your software is up to date, the dialog box lets you know.

Get Out Your Text Editor

All the programs you're going to write in PHP are plain old text files. In fact, writing PHP isn't much different from writing HTML or CSS or JavaScript. You'll type different things, but these are all just text files saved with a special extension. You use *.html* for HTML, *.css* for CSS, *.js* for JavaScript, and now *.php* for PHP files.

Since PHP is just text, you'll want a good text editor to work in. As simple as those programs are, they're perfect for coding in PHP. If you're on Windows, then you can use Notepad. If you're on a Mac, then TextEdit is a great choice. The good news is that each of these programs comes pre-installed on your computer, so you don't have to download anything, and you don't have to buy anything. The bad news is that none of these programs *knows* you're writing PHP, so you don't get much help spotting typos or organizing your files.

On the other hand, you'll find quite a few editors out there that are built to specifically handle PHP. For instance, on Windows, you can download NuSphere PhpED (*www.nusphere.com/products/phped.htm*), shown in Figure 1-11. You'll pay a bit for a program like NuSphere—usually between $50 and $100—but you'll get fancy color-coding, help with special language features, and in a lot of cases, some pretty nifty file organization and even the ability to upload your PHP directly to your web server, as discussed on page 20.

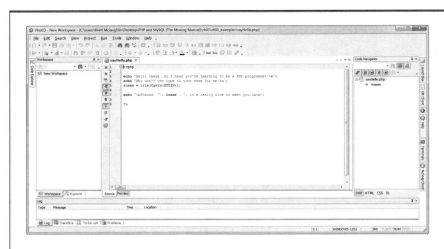

FIGURE 1-11

NuSphere PhpED gives you a ton of features, and supports JavaScript, CSS, and HTML, as well as PHP. It's also got great documentation for most of the PHP functions and libraries.

If you're on a Mac, then the two leading candidates for editors that do text plus lots of other cool things are BBEdit (*www.barebones.com/products/bbedit/index.html*) and TextMate (*www.macromates.com*). Both are Mac-only programs, and both offer similar features to what PhpED offers on Windows: color-coding, file management, help documentation, and support for HTML, CSS, JavaScript, and a lot more. You can see BBEdit in action in Figure 1-12; you'll need to drop $100 to get going with BBEdit.

You can see what TextMate looks like in Figure 1-13. It looks a little simpler than BBEdit, and if you've never used a programming editor, it might be a little easier to begin with. It's going to cost you about $60, slightly less than BBEdit.

FIGURE 1-12

BBEdit is supposed to be bare bones, but you'll find it's got more than adequate PHP support. It's tuned primarily for HTML, so there are a few oddities, but it's a great choice for PHP work on the Mac.

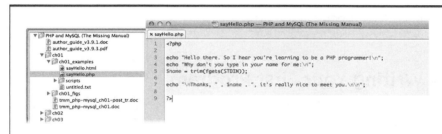

FIGURE 1-13

TextMate is an editor that seeks to provide color-coded editing and not much else. It does offer file management and FTP support, but it's best at letting you type code and staying out of the way.

UNDER THE HOOD

Text Editors: Mashing Up Programs

Although programs like PhpED, BBEdit, and TextMate are billed as text editors, they're really lots of programs rolled into one. Imagine having a text editor, a file management tool like Windows Explorer or the Mac's Finder, a telnet or terminal program, an FTP client, and then some glue to hold them all together. That's what these programs give you: a bunch of things all rolled into one single bit of software.

What's great about these "text editors plus" is that they offer you all sorts of features, and you don't need five or six icons in your Mac's dock or shortcuts on your Windows desktop. You've got access to almost everything you'll need for building web pages or programming in PHP at your fingertips.

What's not so great, though, is that generalized tools aren't often as full-featured as specific tools. In other words, a program that tries to do everything usually does lots of things decently, as opposed to lots of programs that only do one thing, but do that one thing really well.

Lots of the time, you're making a choice between convenience and features. If you only use FTP to upload files to a server on occasion, you almost never work with your computer's command line, and you get a kick out of color-coded text, then the bundled text editors with lots of extra features might be a really good fit.

Whether you use a more fully featured text editor or not, though, at some point you may need to ditch the editor and use the actual FTP or telnet programs. As long as you're comfortable diving into those programs *without* the use of an editor from time to time, then go forth and code in TextMate or PhpED without worry.

Once you're comfortable writing PHP code, spend some time playing with different enhanced editors to see which one is best for you. Or you may find that you're a Notepad or TextEdit programmer at heart after all. There's no one right option for PHP; all these choices work just fine.

Just starting out, though, try and use a simple text editor—Notepad on Windows or TextEdit on the Mac. You'll learn a lot more about PHP this way, even if you don't get all the bells and whistles of one of the editors that offer lots of extra features. Besides, once you really understand PHP and have learned to use its features manually, you'll appreciate and even be able to use the features of the other editors a lot more effectively.

> **NOTE** Once you've become familiar with PHP, you can also check out Eclipse PHP (*www.eclipse.org/ projects/project.php?id=tools.pdt*). The Eclipse IDE has long been a favorite for Java developers, and there are now enough plug-ins for PHP that it's a legitimate option for PHP programmers, too. However, there's a lot going on in Eclipse—tons of tools and gadgets—so you might want to wait a bit before you dive head first into Eclipse PHP. Come back to it later, though; it's well worth checking out.

■ Writing Your First Program

You've got PHP; you've got a text editor. Now all you need is a PHP program, which you'll create in the next few minutes. Open up your text editor, and type the following code, exactly as shown:

```php
<?php

echo "Hello there. So I hear you're learning to be a PHP programmer!\n";
echo "Why don't you type in your name for me:\n";
$name = trim(fgets(STDIN));

echo "\nThanks, " . $name . ", it's really nice to meet you.\n\n";

?>
```

A lot of this code may look weird to you, and that's OK. You'll understand every bit of it soon. Right now, just get used to looking at PHP, which is quite a bit different from HTML or JavaScript.

> **WARNING** Some of the editors you might use, like TextEdit, automatically create *rich text* documents. Rich text lets you use formatting, like bolding and underlining. You don't want that in your PHP code, so look for the option to use *plain text*, which doesn't allow formatting.
>
> If you're using TextEdit, choose Format→Make Plain Text. You won't have that option if you're already typing in plain text. If you're using Notepad, rich text isn't an option, so you've got nothing to worry about.

Once you're done, your editor should look something like Figure 1-14.

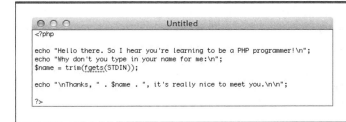

```php
<?php

echo "Hello there. So I hear you're learning to be a PHP programmer!\n";
echo "Why don't you type in your name for me:\n";
$name = trim(fgets(STDIN));

echo "\nThanks, " . $name . ", it's really nice to meet you.\n\n";

?>
```

FIGURE 1-14

PHP is just text, but it's got several weird characters. You'll want to start getting used to typing the dollar sign ($), angle brackets (< and >, just as in HTML), and the backslash (\). You'll be using those characters a whole lot.

This program does just a few simple things:

1. Identifies itself as PHP using *<?php*

2. Prints out a welcome message using the *echo* command

3. Asks the visitor for his name, again using *echo*

4. Gets the visitor's name and stores it in something called *$name*

5. Says hello by printing out a message followed by what's in *$name*

6. Finishes up with the *?>* characters

It's okay if a lot of this doesn't make sense, but you probably already could have figured out a lot of this, except maybe the weird line beginning with *$name =*. There are also some strange characters, like *\n*s and *STDIN*, that you'll learn about soon. Just see if you can follow the basic path of things: the opening *<?php*, the printing, the request for the user's name, another bit of printing, and the closing *?>*.

Now save this program. Name it *sayHello.php*, and make sure you add that *.php* extension. Otherwise you'll have problems down the line. Save the file some place handy, like on your desktop, in your home directory, or in a folder you're using to keep all your PHP programs in as you're learning.

NOTE Most programs on Windows and the Mac will supply you a default extension, like *.txt*. Make sure you replace that with *.php*. Windows especially tends to hide extensions, so make sure your full filename is *sayHello.php*, not something like *sayHello.php.txt*.

That's it; you've written your first PHP program!

Default to Plain Text

Most of the popular text editors let you change from rich text to plain text on a per-file basis, but they start out in rich text mode by default. That can become a pain, so you may want to change your editor to always start out in plain text mode.For

TextEdit on the Mac, open the Preferences menu. At the very top, under Format, you can set the default mode as Plain Text (as shown in Figure 1-15). On Windows, using Notepad lets you avoid this entire issue, so you've got nothing to worry about.

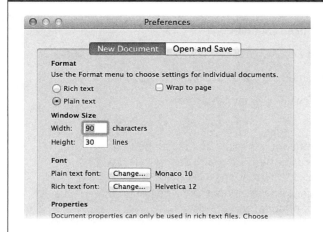

FIGURE 1-15

You can get to the TextEdit preferences under the Preferences menu, or with the shortcut combination ⌘-,. In the Preferences box, you've got lots of options, but the text format and font used for plain text are the most important for now.

Running Your First Program

What good is it to get all this code typed in if you can't see if it works? This particular program isn't ready to run on the Web yet, so you'll need to use the command line. You used the command line earlier to make sure PHP was installed correctly (page 8). Fire up your command line program again. If you're on a Mac, you've already opened up Terminal, and may even have a shortcut in your dock. Open Terminal again.

Now change into the directory in which you saved your program, *sayHello.php*. You can do a directory listing with *dir* (on Windows) or *ls* (on the Mac) to make sure you're in the right directory. Once you're in the right directory, type the following into your command line:

```
php sayHello.php
```

This tells the *php* program to run, and gives it your program, *sayHello.php*, as what to run. Pretty quickly, you should see the welcome message you typed, and then the program asks you for your name. Go ahead and type your name, and then hit Enter. The program should then greet you, just as shown in Figure 1-16.

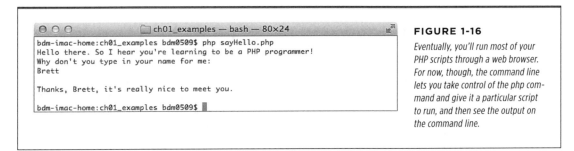

FIGURE 1-16

Eventually, you'll run most of your PHP scripts through a web browser. For now, though, the command line lets you take control of the php command and give it a particular script to run, and then see the output on the command line.

That's it! Your first program works, and you're ready to go deeper into PHP.

Writing Your Second Program

Why wait around before going a little further into PHP? You probably got interested in PHP because you wanted to make your web pages do a little more than is possible with JavaScript. If that's the case, PHP is a great language, and you need to learn how to get code like you've already written onto the Web. And because most PHP programs are accessed by web pages, you'll often start your PHP programming with an HTML page that will send information to your PHP scripts.

Start with an HTML Page

To get started, open up a new document in your text editor or favorite HTML editor, and create this HTML page:

```html
<html>
 <head>
  <link href="../css/phpMM.css" rel="stylesheet" type="text/css" />
 </head>

 <body>
  <div id="header"><h1>PHP & MySQL: The Missing Manual</h1></div>
  <div id="example">Example 1-1</div>

  <div id="content">
    <h1>Welcome!</h1>
    <p>Hello there. So I hear you're learning to be a PHP programmer!</p>
    <p>Why don't you type in your name for me:</p>
    <form action="scripts/sayHelloWeb.php" method="POST">
      <p>
```

```
            <i>Enter your name:</i> <input type="text" name="name" size="20" />
        </p>
        <p><input type="submit" value="Say Hello" /></p>
    </form>
  </div>

  <div id="footer"></div>
 </body>
</html>
```

NOTE   You can download this HTML, along with the rest of the book's sample files, from *www.missingmanuals.com/ cds/phpmysqlmm*. You can also get the CSS and images used by the samples, which let you give your programs a little extra visual pizzazz. Still, especially as you're just getting started, you'll learn a lot more if you'll type in the PHP code for these programs yourself.

Almost nothing about this page should be new to you. All it does is reference an external CSS style sheet, provide a text greeting like *sayHello.php* did, and then define a form into which users can type their names.

The only thing that should have caught your attention is this line, in the form definition:

```
<form action="scripts/sayHelloWeb.php" method="POST">
```

This code means that your form is going to submit its information to a program called *sayHelloWeb.php*, a new PHP program you're about to write. Once the form is submitted, *sayHelloWeb.php* takes over and prints out the welcome message.

Write a PHP Script

Now that you've got an HTML page sending information to *sayHelloWeb.php*, you need to actually write that code. When you write PHP to run on the Web, it's not much different from the program you've already written (page 14). You have to get information a little differently, because there's no command line that a user can type into. But other than that, things stay pretty much the same.

Open up a new text editor and type the PHP code shown here; it should look sort of like an HTML-ized version of the *sayHello.php* program:

```
<html>
 <head>
  <link href="../../css/phpMM.css" rel="stylesheet" type="text/css" />
 </head>

 <body>
  <div id="header"><h1>PHP & MySQL: The Missing Manual</h1></div>
  <div id="example">Example 1-1</div>

  <div id="content">
```

```
    <h1>Hello, <?php echo $_REQUEST['name']; ?></h1>
    <p>Great to meet you. Welcome to the beginning of your PHP programming
odyssey.</p>
    </form>
  </div>

  <div id="footer"></div>
 </body>
</html>
```

Save this program as *sayHelloWeb.php*, and be sure you've got your file in plain text with the right extension.

The first thing you probably noticed here is that this file looks a whole lot like HTML. In fact, compared to *sayHello.php*, the first PHP program you wrote, this version might look like a style of programming that's a lot easier to learn. That's because once you're using PHP to work and interact with web pages, a lot of what your PHP programs will do is insert data into existing web pages, which means you'll be working with HTML *a lot*. Of course, that's great news, because you already know HTML, so you'll be adding to what you know, rather than learning something completely new from scratch.

Once you realize that a lot of this program is just HTML, you can probably already guess what a lot of this program does. Here's a section-by-section breakdown:

- The page starts out with a normal *html* element and *head* section.

- The *body* section begins, and sets up the page heading and example number, just like the regular HTML page, *sayHello.html*.

- The page defines a heading with *h1*, and prints "Hello,."

- The *<?php* tells the browser some PHP code is coming. Then, then *$_REQUEST* variable is accessed, and a property called *name* within that variable is printed using echo.

- The end of the PHP code is indicated with *?>.*

- The rest of the HTML is output, just as in *sayHello.html*.

This program, like most PHP programs you'll write, accepts its input from a web page, either from one built in HTML like the pages you've created before, or from another PHP program. It's the job of that web page—*sayHello.html* in your case—to get the user to enter her information, and then send that information on to this program. The information from that HTML page is stored in *$_REQUEST*, which is a special variable in PHP.

Variables Vary

A variable in PHP, or any other programming language, is something that stores a value. Variables have names, and in PHP, those names can be almost anything you want. You can tell that something is a variable in PHP because the name starts with a $. So $myHeight is a variable called "myHeight," and $_REQUEST is a variable called "_REQUEST."

> **NOTE** Technically, the name of a PHP variable does not include the $, but most PHP programmers consider that $ a part of the variable itself. So you'll hear PHP programmers say things like "dollar my height" instead of just "myHeight" to refer to $myHeight.

Variables are not just names, though. They also have a value. So the value of $myHeight might be the number 68 (for 68 inches) or the text "68 inches." In PHP, though, you're not stuck with that value forever. You can change the value of a variable, which is where the word *variables* actually comes from: a variable *varies*, or changes.

In *sayHelloWeb.php*, you're using the special PHP variable $_REQUEST to get the user's name, which he entered into the form you built in *sayHello.html*. PHP gives you the ability to get to anything a user entered into a form using $_REQUEST and the name of the form entry field—in this case, "name." So $_REQUEST['name'] returns the information a user put into a web form, specifically into an input field called "name." If the user also entered in their phone number, say, into a form field called "phoneNumber," you could get that value in PHP with $_REQUEST['phoneNumber'].

> **NOTE** It's okay if you're still a little fuzzy on the details of how variables and $_REQUEST work. You'll learn a lot more about variables and in particular special variables in PHP like $_REQUEST in the next few chapters.

Once your PHP program grabs the value from the "name" form field, it prints that value out using *echo*, something you've already used in your first PHP program. That value gets dropped right into the HTML sent back to the browser...something you'll want to check out for yourself by running your new program.

◼ Upload Your HTML, CSS, and PHP

When you're running a PHP program on your own machine, using the command line, as soon as you've saved your PHP you can run it. But when you're working with web pages and web applications, things are a bit trickier.

When you're building a web page, you have to upload your HTML, CSS, and any JavaScript you've written to your own web server. Then, you access those files with a browser, through a web address like *www.yellowtagmedia.com/sayHello.html*. Typing that web address into your browser causes your server to supply your HTML to whatever web browser requested the page.

PHP works the same way. Once you've written your PHP programs, you upload them onto your web server with your HTML and CSS. Typically, you'll end up with files and directories like the following:

- **Root or home directory (/).** Your web root, where you put all your HTML. This usually is the location referenced by a URL like *yellowtagmedia.com/,* without any specific file after the web server name.

- **CSS directory (*css/*).** The directory where all your site's CSS is stored.

- **JavaScript directory (*js/*).** Your JavaScript files go here. You'll often see this directory also called *scripts/,* but since PHP programs are also called scripts, it's a good idea to be more explicit in your naming.

- **PHP directory (*scripts/*).** Here's where you put all your PHP programs. Again, you could call this something more specific like *php/* or *phpScripts/,* but more often than not, websites use *scripts/* for this directory, so following that lead is a good habit to get into.

- **Examples directory (*ch01/, ch02/,* and so forth).** As you're working through the examples, you're going to end up with a lot of PHP programs, and fast. To keep everything organized, you should have a separate directory for each chapter. So when you upload *sayHello.html* and *sayHelloWeb.php,* upload them into *ch01/sayHello.html* and *ch01/scripts/sayHelloWeb.php.*

> **NOTE** You don't have to organize things this way, but if you do, all the examples you download for this book will work without any changes. If you do change this directory structure, you'll need to change all the references in your HTML and PHP to CSS, JavaScript, and other PHP programs.

Now that you've got your HTML and PHP ready, you need to upload those files to the right directories on your web server. You should also download *phpMM.css* from the book's website at *www.missingmanuals.com/cds/phpmysqlmm,* and get the CSS in the right place as well.

Once you've got everything in place, your web server directory structure should look something like Figure 1-17.

■ Running Your Second Program

You've got your HTML and CSS in the right place, and your HTML form has your PHP program set as its action. You also should have *sayHelloWeb.php* in your *ch01/scripts/* directory. All that's left is to take your PHP for a spin. Open up a web browser and go to your web server, and then add *ch01/sayHello.html* to your server name. You should see the HTML you created in *sayHello.html,* just like in Figure 1-18.

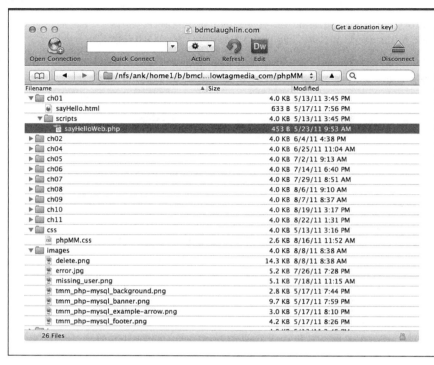

FIGURE 1-17

The HTML and PHP files you created are specific to this chapter, so they belong in ch01/. But phpMM.css is for all the book's examples you'll be building, so put it in css/ under the root of your web server.

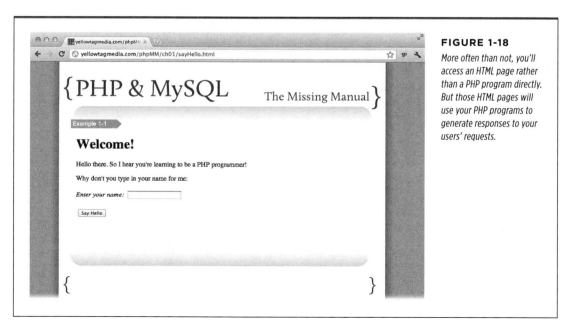

FIGURE 1-18

More often than not, you'll access an HTML page rather than a PHP program directly. But those HTML pages will use your PHP programs to generate responses to your users' requests.

Type your name, and then click the Submit button. The page sends your name as part of the form to the form's action, your *sayHelloWeb.php* program. That program runs on your web server, and then you should get a response back, something like Figure 1-19.

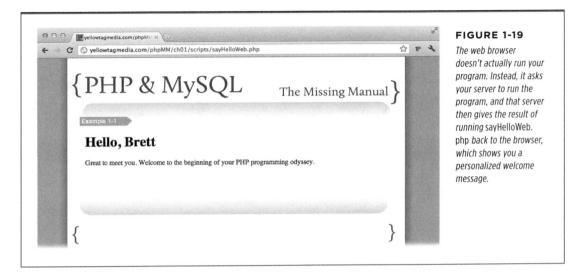

FIGURE 1-19

The web browser doesn't actually run your program. Instead, it asks your server to run the program, and that server then gives the result of running sayHelloWeb. php back to the browser, which shows you a personalized welcome message.

It may seem like you've done a lot of work just to have a web browser tell you your name. In fact, you could probably write the same program in JavaScript if you wanted. But now that you've created a few PHP programs, you should already see how easy it is to write this sort of code.

And before you know it, you'll be doing a lot more than telling users their names. You'll be talking to a database, doing advanced calculations, making decisions based on information the user gave you and what you have stored in a database, and more. But it all begins with a little HTML, a PHP program like the ones you've just written, and the directory structure you've got in place.

PHP Syntax: Weird and Wonderful

You've got a couple of PHP programs running, and one of them even works with an HTML form. But so far, you've just been typing code. Even though you've just gotten started with PHP, you're ready to dig deeper, and start to *understand* what's going on in that code. In this chapter, you're going to get comfortable with a lot of the PHP syntax: that means learning what special words you type into your programs, and what each one of those special words—usually called *keywords*—tells PHP to do.

Fortunately, this learning doesn't mean you can't still build interesting programs that run in a web browser. In fact, since almost everything that's done with PHP involves Web pages, all your scripts in this chapter will accept information from a Web form and work with that information. So you're not just learning PHP; you're learning to write Web applications.

■ Get Information from a Web Form

In *sayHelloWeb.php*, you used this line to get the value of a variable called "name" from the *sayHello.html* web form:

```
echo $_REQUEST['name'];
```

You may remember that *$_REQUEST* is a special PHP variable that lets you get information from a web request. You used it to get one particular piece of information—the user's name—but it can do a lot more.

Access Request Parameters Directly

In fact, to see just how handy *$_REQUEST* really is, open up your text editor. Type the code below, in which a visitor enters her name and several other important bits of contact information, like her Twitter handle, Facebook page URL, and email address.

```html
<html>
 <head>
  <link href="../css/phpMM.css" rel="stylesheet" type="text/css" />
 </head>

 <body>
  <div id="header"><h1>PHP & MySQL: The Missing Manual</h1></div>
  <div id="example">Example 2-1</div>

  <div id="content">
    <h1>Join the Missing Manual (Digital) Social Club</h1>
    <p>Please enter your online connections below:</p>
    <form action="scripts/getFormInfo.php" method="POST">
        <fieldset>
        <label for="first_name">First Name:</label>
        <input type="text" name="first_name" size="20" /><br />
        <label for="last_name">Last Name:</label>
        <input type="text" name="last_name" size="20" /><br />
        <label for="email">E-Mail Address:</label>
        <input type="text" name="email" size="50" /><br />
        <label for="facebook_url">Facebook URL:</label>
        <input type="text" name="facebook_url" size="50" /><br />
        <label for="twitter_handle">Twitter Handle:</label>
        <input type="text" name="twitter_handle" size="20" /><br />
      </fieldset>
      <br />
      <fieldset class="center">
        <input type="submit" value="Join the Club" />
        <input type="reset" value="Clear and Restart" />
      </fieldset>
    </form>
  </div>

  <div id="footer"></div>
 </body>
</html>
```

> **TIP** For more information on how HTML is used in this code, see the box below.

HTML Should Be Semantically Meaningful

You may have noticed some pretty big changes in this HTML from the simple form from Chapter 1 (page 18). In that chapter, the form used *<p>* tags to break up the form labels and input boxes, and manually formatted the form labels with *<i>* tags. That got the job done, but it's not a good use of HTML.

Anytime you're writing HTML, you're actually structuring your page. So a form tag doesn't really do anything visually; it just lets a browser know, "Hey, here's a form." When you use tags like *<i>*, though, you're not describing structure; you're telling the browser how something should *look*. That's really not what HTML is for, though; that's the job of CSS.

In this form, though, all the formatting has been pulled out. Instead, all the labels are identified with the *label* element, and a *for* attribute. That identifies the labels as labels—regardless of how those labels end up looking—and also connects each label with the specific input field to which it matches. There's also a *fieldset* element that surrounds the different blocks within the form: one for the labels and text fields, and a second for the form buttons. This arrangement also provides *semantic information*: information that has *meaning*.

By making the HTML mean something, a browser (and other HTML authors) know what things actually *are* in your form: labels are meant for, well, labeling things. Fields are grouped together with *fieldset*. And italic and bold are left to your CSS, just as they should be.

What's really cool here is that now your CSS can do an even better job of styling your form. Since you've gotten rid of formatting in the HTML, you can style all your form labels the same way—perhaps by bolding them, right-aligning them, and adding a right margin of 5 pixels. The same is true of your sets of fields; you might put a border around related fields, which is exactly what's going on in the CSS applied to this form. In fact, to see how the CSS affects these HTML elements, check out Figure 2-1.

Truthfully, if you're new to making your pages semantically meaningful, it may take you a little time to get used to using HTML just for structure, and keeping all your style in CSS. But stick with it; your pages will look better, and anyone who has to update your pages down the line will thank you.

Save this file as *socialEntryForm.html*. To make sure your HTML is just the way you want, go ahead and upload it to your server, in the *ch02/* directory. Make sure you've got the book's CSS in the right place—under *css/* in your server's root—and then open a browser and head over to your HTML form. You should see something like Figure 2-1.

In *sayHelloWeb.php*, you used *$_REQUEST* to get submitted form information, and then asked specifically for the "name" value. But with this new form, there's a lot more information being sent from the form.

To get all that information, you need to create a new script called *getFormInfo.php*, and enter in this code:

```
<html>
 <head>
  <link href="../../css/phpMM.css" rel="stylesheet" type="text/css" />
 </head>
```

```
<body>
  <div id="header"><h1>PHP & MySQL: The Missing Manual</h1></div>
  <div id="example">Example 2-1</div>

  <div id="content">
    <p>Here's a record of what information you submitted:</p>
    <p>
      First Name: <?php echo $_REQUEST['first_name']; ?><br />
      Last Name: <?php echo $_REQUEST['last_name']; ?><br />
      E-Mail Address: <?php echo $_REQUEST['email']; ?><br />
      Facebook URL: <?php echo $_REQUEST['facebook_url']; ?><br />
      Twitter Handle: <?php echo $_REQUEST['twitter_handle']; ?><br />
    </p>
  </div>

  <div id="footer"></div>
</body>
</html>
```

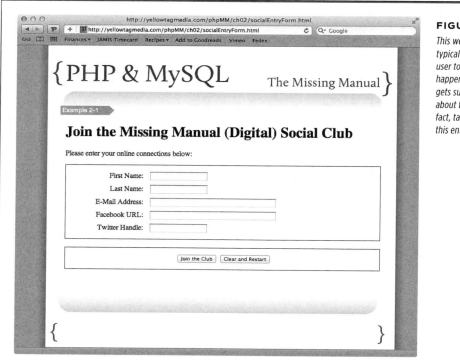

FIGURE 2-1

This web form is a pretty typical entry page for a user to fill in. But what happens when this form gets submitted? You're about to find out, and in fact, take control of all this entered information.

NOTE If you want to start taking a little more control of your scripts, you can name this program something other than *getFormInfo.php*. Just be sure that you also update *socialEntryForm.html* and change the form's *action* attribute value to match your own custom script name.

You can already see what's going on here. In addition to grabbing the value of the "first_name" and "last_name" fields—similar to getting the value of the "name" field in *sayHelloWeb.php*—you're using *$_REQUEST* to pull in the values the user entered into the other form fields.

Go back to your web form, and enter your information. Then submit the form, and you should see the result of *getFormInfo.php* running. Your browser should show you something like Figure 2-2.

In fact, this is the way you'll use the *$_REQUEST* variable in most of your PHP programs:

```
echo $_REQUEST['FORM_INPUT_FIELD_NAME'];
```

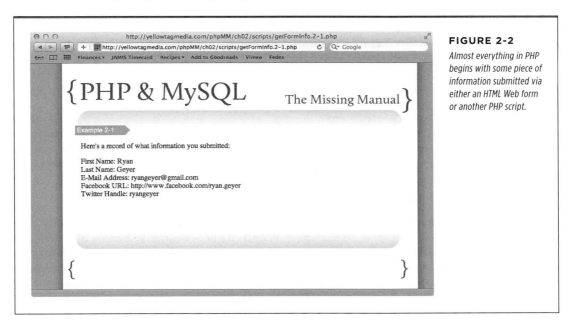

FIGURE 2-2

Almost everything in PHP begins with some piece of information submitted via either an HTML Web form or another PHP script.

Create Your Own Variables

You may have times where you don't want to just spit out the value of a field. Think back to your first program, *sayHello.php* (the version that didn't run on the Web). In that program, you created your own variable:

```
$name = trim(fgets(STDIN));
```

PHP lets you create all the variables you want. Just think of a descriptive name (for suggestions, see the box on page 31), and put a dollar sign before that name, like this:

```
$numberSix = 6;
$thisIsMyName = "Brett";
$carMake = "Honda";
```

With this chunk of code in mind, go back to your new program, *getFormInfo.php*. Instead of just using *echo* to print out the submitted information, store each piece of information in a variable. Then you can use that information however you want, and as many times as you want.

```php
<?php

$first_name = $_REQUEST['first_name'];
$last_name = $_REQUEST['last_name'];
$email = $_REQUEST['email'];
$facebook_url = $_REQUEST['facebook_url'];
$twitter_handle = $_REQUEST['twitter_handle'];

?>

<html>
 <head>
  <link href="../../css/phpMM.css" rel="stylesheet" type="text/css" />
 </head>

 <body>
    <!-- Existing HTML code -->
 </body>
</html>
```

Notice that you can create blocks of PHP code—beginning with *<?php* and ending with *?>*—anywhere you want. In this script, there's currently a block of PHP before any HTML, and then several small blocks of PHP within the big chunk of HTML. It's really up to you when and where your PHP goes, as long as it gets the job done. You could have put this block of PHP between the page's opening *html* and *head* element, or between the *head* and the *body* elements; that choice is up to you.

NOTE Just because you *can* do something doesn't mean you should. It's usually best to do as much of your PHP work as you can before you output any HTML, and then output as much of your HTML as you can in a single place. This system keeps most of your code in one place, and most of your HTML in another place. (For more advice on why it's important to keep your code well organized, see the box on page 32.)

Of course, you'll still have lots of times when you insert PHP into your HTML, as in *getFormInfo.php*, and that's okay. Those little bits of PHP fit into the HTML, and certainly don't mix things up as much as 20 or 30 lines of PHP stuck in the middle of your HTML.

You can check out your form in a browser, but you shouldn't see anything different from what you already saw, shown back in Figure 2-2. That's because your HTML—the part of the script that the browser displays to a user—hasn't changed at all.

But now there's a little bit of wasteful programming going on. You're getting the value of each form field through the *$_REQUEST* variable once, in the PHP block before all your HTML, and then you're getting all those variable values again in the HTML itself. Anytime you're doing something twice, you're wasting valuable web server resources.

Fortunately, it's easy to fix this problem. You have all the values you want, stored in your variables: *$first_name*, *$last_name*, and so on. So in the HTML part of *get-FormInfo.php*, you can just echo out those variables; you don't need to deal with *$_REQUEST* anymore. Here's the "content" *div* you'll want to update:

```
<div id="content">
  <p>Here's a record of what information you submitted:</p>
  <p>
    First Name: <?php echo $first_name; ?><br />
    Last Name: <?php echo $last_name; ?><br />
    E-Mail Address: <?php echo $email; ?><br />
    Facebook URL: <?php echo $facebook_url; ?><br />
    Twitter Handle: <?php echo $twitter_handle; ?><br />
  </p>
</div>
```

WORD TO THE WISE

What's in a Name? A Whole Lot!

PHP doesn't actually require you to use descriptive names. In fact, there are thousands of PHP programs on the Web with code that looks like this:

```
$x = $_REQUEST['username'];
$y = $_REQUEST['password'];
```

This code runs just as well as similar code that uses much more descriptive names:

```
$username = $_REQUEST['username'];
$password = $_REQUEST['password'];
```

So what's the big deal? Many programmers will try and convince you that it's a lot of extra work to type in these longer descriptive names. That's true, of course.

On the other hand, imagine how much work it would be when you've got to track down the username variable in a piece of code that you wrote three months ago—or someone else wrote? Suppose you've got a line much later in a script like this:

```
echo "Welcome back to the site, " . $y;
```

Suddenly, it's not so clear what *$x* is and what *$y* is. Was *$x* the username? Or was it *$y*? Better be careful...nobody wants his password printed out instead of his username!

Using descriptive names, even if they're longer and take a little extra time to type, makes your code easier to read, for you and anyone else who might need to look at it down the road.

You should submit values into your *socialEntryForm.html* again, and make sure your updated script works. You should see the exact same result as before (compare your results to Figure 2-2 again). It may surprise you that you've done all this work just to get the same result; but that's actually a big part of good programming. To learn more about this approach to programming, see the box below. This version has all the submitted values in variables, though, and that's an improvement.

Refactor as You Go

Any time you rearrange code, especially to better organize it, or separate different chunks of behavior, you're *refactoring*. So when you created a PHP block at the beginning of *getFormInfo.php* to grab all the information from the submitted form, and then just echoed out each variable within the HTML, you were refactoring your script.

Refactoring should be as much as part of your routine as saving your files. Anytime you can better organize your script—or, as you'll do later, better organize lots of scripts that all work together—do it. Even if you're not sure how your better organization might help your program, it's worth the effort. When you come back to your code a week from now, a month from now, or even a year from now, you'll have a much harder time remembering what everything does. Even worse, it's going to be tough to remember *where* things are in your script. (Your scripts are going to get a lot longer soon, too.)

By refactoring as you go, you ensure that it's easy to see what a script does from a quick look. It also means that when you

need to make changes, you can jump right to the spot in your script where those changes need to be made, get your work done, and go back to living the high life of a PHP programmer.

But be warned: refactoring isn't usually the most fun way to spend a Friday night. A lot of the time, the goal in refactoring is to *not* change how your code works, and especially to not change what it outputs in a browser. Since you're rearranging—and sometimes optimizing (making things run as smoothly as possible)—your goal is keep things looking the same.

That's the case with your refactoring of *getFormInfo.php*. You added some PHP, created a bunch of variables, and then used those variables in your HTML. The result? Exactly the same as your un-refactored version. But now your code's a lot easier to understand, and you're actually going to get some nice benefits by having those variables available, as you'll see on the next page.

But why put values into a variable? Right now, it may seem a little silly: all you're doing is changing the place within your script where you grab information from the *$_REQUEST* variable. That's not doing you any real good. So what can you do with these variables once you've got information in them? PHP gives you a lot of options, particularly when you have variables with text in them.

■ Working with Text in PHP

PHP sees all text the same: as just a collection of characters. Those characters can be letters, numbers, spaces, punctuation marks, or just about anything else. And in PHP, an English word like "caterpillar" is just as ordinary a piece of text as is something nonsensical like "!(gUHa8@m.@". To you, the first looks like a word, and the second like something QBert might have said. To PHP, though, it's all just text. In fact, PHP and most programming languages have a special word to refer to text, since it's such an important part of the language: a *string*. So a piece of text can also be called a string, and instead of text searching or text matching, you'll often hear programmers talk about *string searching* or *string matching*.

> **NOTE** If you don't need to Google QBert to find out what it is, take a moment to weep for your lost youth.

Combining Text

The good thing about PHP seeing all text the same is that you can do all sorts of interesting things with it, regardless of what that text is. So going back to your script, *getFormInfo.php*, you've got five variables, all of which are filled with text:

```php
$first_name = $_REQUEST['first_name'];
$last_name = $_REQUEST['last_name'];
$email = $_REQUEST['email'];
$facebook_url = $_REQUEST['facebook_url'];
$twitter_handle = $_REQUEST['twitter_handle'];
```

Two of these are related: *$first_name* and *$last_name*. It's pretty common to take in information this way—with the names separated—but it's just as *uncommon* to print them out separately. Imagine walking into your local Pier 1 Imports and being greeted by an old friend like this: "Hey there, First Name Brett, Last Name McLaughlin!" That's pretty awkward; and it's just as awkward on the Web.

There's no reason to settle for this separation, though. You can easily combine these two strings by using what's called *concatenation*. That's a fancy word that just means "combine," and in the case of strings in particular, combining two pieces of text end-to-end. So if you concatenate "my" and "girl", you'd get a new string, "mygirl."

In PHP, you concatenate with the period (.). In *getFormInfo.php*, then, find the two lines of HTML where you print out the first and last name:

```php
First Name: <?php echo $first_name; ?><br />
Last Name: <?php echo $last_name; ?><br />
```

Now change these to a single line, and concatenate the first and last names together:

```php
Name: <?php echo $first_name . $last_name; ?><br />
```

Go back to *socialEntryForm.html*, enter some information, and submit your form. You should see something like Figure 2-3.

That's all there is to it! Of course, there's a pretty obvious problem here: the first name and last name are smashed together. What you really need is a space between those two bits of text.

Here's where PHP treating all text the same really helps. You can add a space by simply putting it in quotes, like this: " ". PHP doesn't see that text as any different from the text in your variables. So you can just concatenate that string—the empty space—to *$first_name*, and then *$last_name* to that:

```php
Name: <?php echo $first_name . " " . $last_name; ?><br />
```

Try your form out again, and you should see a nice space between the first and last names. Check out Figure 2-4, which should match what your page now looks like.

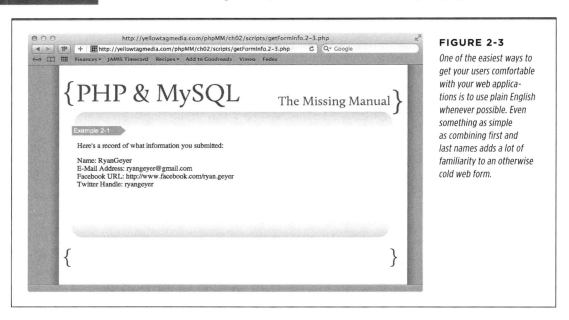

FIGURE 2-3

One of the easiest ways to get your users comfortable with your web applications is to use plain English whenever possible. Even something as simple as combining first and last names adds a lot of familiarity to an otherwise cold web form.

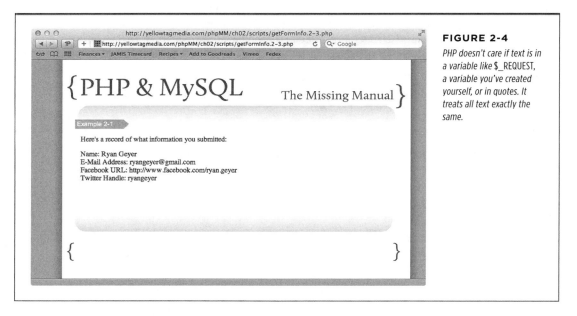

FIGURE 2-4

PHP doesn't care if text is in a variable like $_REQUEST, a variable you've created yourself, or in quotes. It treats all text exactly the same.

Searching Within Text

If all you could do with strings was to smash them together, that would be pretty boring. Thankfully, PHP gives you a lot more. One of the most common things you'll do with PHP text is search it. For example, take the *$facebook_url* variable you've got. Suppose you wanted to turn that into an actual link that people could click on:

```
<p>
  Name: <?php echo $first_name . " " . $last_name; ?><br />
  E-Mail Address: <?php echo $email; ?><br />
  <a href="<?php echo $facebook_url; ?>">Your Facebook page</a><br />
  Twitter Handle: <?php echo $twitter_handle; ?><br />
</p>
```

Now, instead of just showing the text of the URL, it's turned into an actual clickable link, like in Figure 2-5.

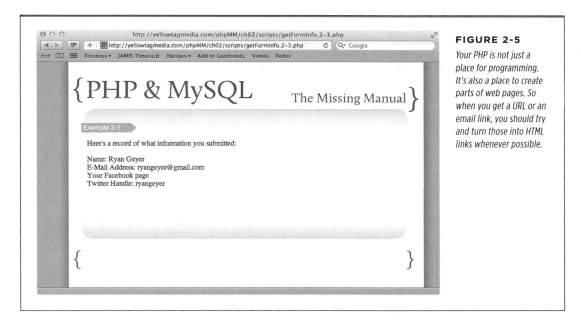

FIGURE 2-5

Your PHP is not just a place for programming. It's also a place to create parts of web pages. So when you get a URL or an email link, you should try and turn those into HTML links whenever possible.

But what happens if folks forget to put the *facebook.com* part of the URL in? Maybe they didn't read carefully, and they just threw in the part of the URL after *facebook. com*, like *ryan.geyer* or *profile.php?id=699186223*. Then, the link you create won't be of any use.

What you need, then, is a way to see if the text you've got in your *$facebook_url* variable contains *facebook.com*. If so, then it's probably safe to turn the text into a URL link. But if not, the link probably needs to have *http://www.facebook.com* added to the beginning of the variable's value.

The easiest way to do this in PHP is to look for the position of a piece of text inside a bigger piece of text. So you can see what the position of *facebook.com* is inside of *$facebook_url*, like this:

```
$first_name = $_REQUEST['first_name'];
$last_name = $_REQUEST['last_name'];
$email = $_REQUEST['email'];
$facebook_url = $_REQUEST['facebook_url'];
$position = strpos($facebook_url, "facebook.com");
$twitter_handle = $_REQUEST['twitter_handle'];
```

The *strpos()* function, which just stands for "string position," returns a number that tells you where in the search string the searched-for text exists. So if *$position* was 5, that would mean that *facebook.com* appeared at position 5 within *$facebook_url*. (And if you're wondering why that's 5 and not 6, see the box on the next page.)

But it's not enough to just get a position. You need to do something with it. Better, you need to figure out if it indicates a position within *$facebook_url*—which would mean that *$facebook_url* contains "facebook.com"—or if *$facebook_url* doesn't have *facebook.com* within it at all. You can do this by seeing if *$position* is false, something PHP defines for you using the keyword *false*. Otherwise, *strpos()* returns the position within *$facebook_url* where the searched-for string appears.

NOTE *strpos()*, like most functions in PHP, can return two totally different things: a number indicating a position within the search string, or the value *false*.

```
$first_name = $_REQUEST['first_name'];
$last_name = $_REQUEST['last_name'];
$email = $_REQUEST['email'];
$facebook_url = $_REQUEST['facebook_url'];
$position = strpos($facebook_url, "facebook.com");
if ($position === false) {
  $facebook_url = "http://www.facebook.com/" . $facebook_url;
}
$twitter_handle = $_REQUEST['twitter_handle'];
```

At first glance, it probably looks like there's a lot of new stuff going on here, but don't sweat it. You already understand almost all this code.

1. First, *strpos()* is used to see if *$facebook_url* has *facebook.com* within it. The value returned from *strpos()* is stuffed into a new variable, *$position*.

2. *$position* is compared to the special PHP value *false* using an *if* statement. You'll learn a lot more about *if* statements soon, but it does just what it looks like: if *$position* is *false*, then do the code within the curly brackets, { }.

3. The code that's within { } only gets run if the statement above is true—in this case, if *$position === false*. If that's true, then *$facebook_url* gets *http://www.facebook.com* smashed onto the front, to make a real link to Facebook.

4. This is really a hidden step: if *$position* is not *false*, then nothing happens. The line of code within { } gets completely skipped over.

Programming Languages Like Zeroes

The more you program in languages like PHP, or Java, or C, or Perl, the more you'll see some unusual uses of the number 0. In almost all these languages—and certainly in PHP—counting begins at 0, rather than 1. So if you were counting up the length of the text "That's weird," then the first letter—the capital "T"—would be at position 0, not position 1.

This system gets particularly tricky when you're searching for text within text, like in *getFormInfo.php*. Suppose someone types *facebook.com/michael.greenfield* into the Facebook URL text box. Then, in your code, you did something like this to see if the form value was a real URL:

```
if (strpos($facebook_url,
             "facebook.com") > 0) {
   $facebook_url =
         "http://www.facebook.com/" .
           $facebook_url;
}
```

On the face of it, this PHP looks good: if *facebook.com* doesn't appear in the first position or greater of *$facebook_url*, add *http://www.facebook.com/* to the front of *$facebook_url*.

But the result would not be good. You'd actually have a value like this in *$facebook_url: http://www.facebook.com/facebook.com/michael.greenfield*. So what happened?

Well, remember, PHP starts counting at 0, not 1. So position 0 is actually the first position in *$facebook_url*. And that position has an "f" in it. Position 1 has an "a", position 2 a "c", and so on. It turns out that the whole first part of *$facebook_url* is actually *facebook.com*, the string for which your code is searching. So *strpos()* returns a 0 to indicate that the searched-for string is in the first position of *$facebook_url*.

What this all means—besides the fact that programming languages count differently than real humans—is that you've got to be a zero-based thinker when you're writing code. So if you're searching for something within a string, a position of *0* or greater means the string was found, rather than 1 or greater. Remember that, and you'll save yourself a ton of bug hunting.

Now that you've got your changes made to your script, save it, and go back to your web form, *socialEntryForm.html*. This time, enter in a Facebook link without the *facebook.com* part of the URL, like *profile.php?id=100000039185327*. Then submit your form and see what your result looks like.

At first glance, nothing may look different. Your web page generated from your PHP probably still resembles Figure 2-5. But look at the source of your page (shown in Figure 2-6) or click the link itself (shown in Figure 2-7). In both cases, you can see that *profile.php?id=100000039185327* was turned into an actual URL, *http://www.facebook.com/profile.php?id=100000039185327*.

FIGURE 2-6

If you've not done a lot of web development, you may not be used to looking at your web page's source code. But you'll want to get comfortable viewing the source; it's one of your best ways to see what's really in the HTML your scripts generate.

FIGURE 2-7

It may seem like a small thing—and a lot of work—to take a partial URL and make it into a clickable link. But users are forgetful, and the more you can protect them from making a mistake without telling them about their problems, the better.

Changing Text

You've combined two pieces of text, you've searched within text, so what's left? Well, changing text, of course. And it turns out that you've already got a lot of the pieces you need to change text.

Take for example the Twitter handle people are entering into your web form. Most people put an @ before their Twitter handle, like this: @bdmclaughlin. But to see someone's Twitter profile on Twitter.com, you actually don't want that @. So if your Twitter handle is @phpGuy, then the Twitter URL to see your profile would be *http:// www.twitter.com/phpGuy*.

This means that to turn a Twitter handle into a clickable link, you have to take a few steps:

1. Create a new variable, *$twitter_url*, and start by giving it a value of "http:// www.twitter.com/".

2. Figure out of the Twitter handle has an @ sign in it.

3. If there's no @ in *$twitter_handle*, just add the handle to the back of *$twitter_url*.

4. If there is an @ in *$twitter_handle*, remove the @ from the handle, and add the handle to the end of *$twitter_url*.

5. Display the Twitter handle as part of an <a> link element in your script's HTML output.

You've done something similar to all these steps except for 4, so this program shouldn't be a big problem for you.

First, create a new variable to hold the Twitter URL you're building, and give it the first part of the Twitter URL:

```
$twitter_handle = $_REQUEST['twitter_handle'];
$twitter_url = "http://www.twitter.com/";
```

Then, you need to figure out if the Twitter handle—which you've got in the *$twitter_handle* variable—has the @ character anywhere in it. You can use *strpos()* again for this:

```
$twitter_handle = $_REQUEST['twitter_handle'];
$twitter_url = "http://www.twitter.com/";
$position = strpos($twitter_handle, "@");
```

In this case, you have to do something whether there's an @ in *$twitter_handle* or not. So you'll have an *if*, but also an *else*:

```
$twitter_handle = $_REQUEST['twitter_handle'];
$twitter_url = "http://www.twitter.com/";
$position = strpos($twitter_handle, "@");
if ($position === false) {
  $twitter_url = $twitter_url . $twitter_handle;
} else {
  // Do something to remove the @ from the Twitter handle
}
```

This should make perfect sense. If there's no @, just add the handle to the end of *$twitter_url*. If there is an @, you've got more work to do.

You've already seen that *strpos()* takes a string, and then another string to search for. PHP has a similar way to get just part of a string: *substr()*. *substr()* is short for "substring," which just means a part of a string. You give *substr()* a string, and then a position to start at.

So *substr("Hello", 2)* would give you "llo". That's because the "H" is at position 0, the "e" is at position 1, and the first "l" is at position 2. Since you gave *substr()* 2 as the position at which to start, you get the letters from that position to the end of the string: "llo".

> **WARNING** Remember, most PHP functions like *substr()* and *strpos()* start counting at zero. If you're still unsure about how that works, check out the box on page 37.

In the case of the Twitter handle, you can use *substr()* in a similar way. But you want to cut off everything up to and *including* the @ sign, which you already know is at the position stored in *$position*. So you can use *substr()*, and start your new string at the position after $position, or *$position + 1*.

What's With All the Angle Brackets?

Any time you're using PHP to show a lot of HTML, and then dropping little bits of PHP into that HTML, things can get pretty confusing. Take a look at one of the lines you've got in *getFormInfo.php*:

```
<a href="<?php echo $facebook_url; ?>">
  Your Facebook page
</a><br />
```

Some of that is strange, to say the least: you've got two opening angle brackets at the beginning, and then two at the end. On top of that, you've got all the PHP within quotation marks.

Unfortunately, this strangeness is one of the downsides to inserting PHP into HTML. It's a necessary evil, and it's something you'll get used to, but it can still trip you up. Anytime you have PHP code, you *really* should surround it in *<?php* and *?>*. (You don't have to, though; you can leave off *?>* if you're ending your script with PHP, but that's generally considered a lazy practice.) And if you're using PHP to insert something into an element that's already in brackets, you'll get this strange double-bracketed code.

It's also common to use PHP to generate a link, which in the case of an a element, becomes the value of an attribute. That means your entire PHP block will be surrounded by quotation marks.

That's okay—as long as your PHP doesn't *also* have quotation marks. If you do have a case where you need quotation marks within your PHP, and that PHP is *already* within quotes, you can alternate single- and double-quote marks, like this:

```
<a href="<?php echo
         'http://www.twitter.com/' .
          $twitter_handle; ?>">
  Your Facebook page
</a><br />
```

You can flip these around without a problem, too:

```
<a href='<?php echo
         "http://www.twitter.com/" .
          $twitter_handle; ?>'>
  Your Facebook page
</a><br />
```

Just be sure you don't open something with single quotes, and close it with double quotes, or vice versa. That will cause things to break, and nobody wants that.

There actually are some differences in how PHP handles double-quoted strings and single-quoted strings, but it's nothing you need to worry about right now.

```
$twitter_handle = $_REQUEST['twitter_handle'];
$twitter_url = "http://www.twitter.com/";
$position = strpos($twitter_handle, "@");
if ($position === false) {
  $twitter_url = $twitter_url . $twitter_handle;
} else {
  $twitter_url = $twitter_url . substr($twitter_handle, $position + 1);
}
```

> **NOTE** You're starting to see a lot of new code quickly, but don't worry if something confuses you at first glance. Just take a moment and look at each piece of the new code, bit by bit. As you understand each individual piece, you'll find the overall picture becomes really clear pretty fast.

Now all that's left is to update the part of your script that outputs HTML:

```
<p>
  Name: <?php echo $first_name . " " . $last_name; ?><br />
  E-Mail Address: <?php echo $email; ?><br />
  <a href="<?php echo $facebook_url; ?>">Your Facebook page</a><br />
  <a href="<?php echo $twitter_url; ?>">Check out your Twitter feed</a><br />
</p>
```

Hop back to your entry page, fill it up with information, and then submit the form to your updated script. Try it with and without an @ in your Twitter handle, and the results should be the same: a nice output page with links to your Facebook and Twitter page, with the @ correctly removed (see Figure 2-8).

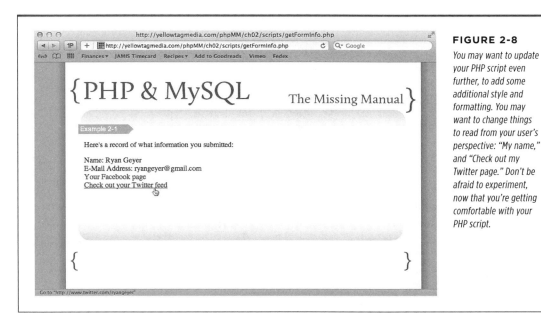

FIGURE 2-8

You may want to update your PHP script even further, to add some additional style and formatting. You may want to change things to read from your user's perspective: "My name," and "Check out my Twitter page." Don't be afraid to experiment, now that you're getting comfortable with your PHP script.

Trimming and Replacing Text

Once you start trying to help your users out with possible errors in their form entry, the world of PHP strings becomes a big toolkit at your disposal. Take two other common problems in web forms, especially web forms where users enter URLs:

- Users enter extra spaces around words, like " http://www.facebook.com/ryan. geyer " instead of "http://www.facebook.com/ryan.geyer".

- Users mix up .com and .org URLs, by putting in something like "http://www. facebook.org/profile.php?id=534643138" instead of "http://www.facebook. com/profile.php?id=534643138".

NOTE You'd be pretty surprised how often people mix up .com and .org. In fact, lots of companies that own *domain-name.com* will also buy *domain-name.org* and redirect anyone that goes to *domain-name.org* to *domain-name.com*, just because of this common problem.

You now how PHP strings work, and you've already used several PHP functions, so you just need to learn two more to handle these common problems.

■ REMOVE EXTRA WHITE SPACE WITH *TRIM()*

PHP's *trim()* function ditches any empty characters—what PHP calls *white space*—around a string. So trimming " I love my space bar. " gives you "I love my space bar." So with just a couple of simple additions to your script, you can make sure that extra spaces around your users' entries is a thing of the past:

NOTE PHP also gives you *rtrim()*, which trims just white space after a string (on its right side), and *ltrim()*, which trims whitespace before a string (on its left side).

```php
$first_name = trim($_REQUEST['first_name']);
$last_name = trim($_REQUEST['last_name']);
$email = trim($_REQUEST['email']);
$facebook_url = trim($_REQUEST['facebook_url']);
$position = strpos($facebook_url, "facebook.com");
if ($position === false) {
  $facebook_url = "http://www.facebook.com/" . $facebook_url;
}

$twitter_handle = trim($_REQUEST['twitter_handle']);
$twitter_url = "http://www.twitter.com/";
$position = strpos($twitter_handle, "@");
if ($position === false) {
  $twitter_url = $twitter_url . $twitter_handle;
} else {
  $twitter_url = $twitter_url . substr($twitter_handle, $position + 1);
}
```

The change is simple: every time you get a value from *$_REQUEST*, just wrap the value in *trim()*. You'll never have to worry about white space around your text again.

WARNING *trim()* (as well as *rtrim()* and *ltrim()*) remove only white space on the *outside* of your text. So *trim()* is great for dealing with something like " Way too much white space. " but won't help you at all with "Way too much white space."

■ REPLACE CHARACTERS IN TEXT WITH *STR_REPLACE()*

It's also easy to replace text in a string. You use *str_replace()*, and give it three things:

1. The text to search for. So if you're looking for facebook.org, the search text would be "facebook.org".

2. The replacement text. So if you want to replace every occurrence of facebook.org with facebook.com, your replacement text would be "facebook.com".

3. The string in which to search. In this case, the value the user types into your web form.

POWER USERS' CLINIC

Chain Your Methods (Or Not!)

You may have noticed that lots of times, what you can do in several separate steps, PHP lets you do in a single step. So look at this line in your PHP script:

```
$facebook_url =
   str_replace(
      "facebook.org",
      "facebook.com",
      trim($_REQUEST['facebook_url']));
```

This code actually combines several different things. You could rewrite this code like the following, to make all those separate things a little clearer:

```
$facebook_url = $_REQUEST['facebook_url'];
$facebook_url = trim($facebook_url);
$facebook_url =
   str_replace(
      "facebook.org", "facebook.com",
      $facebook_url);
```

Both of these code examples work the same, and from a performance and technical point of view, one isn't any better than the other. That means it's up to you which version you prefer. So how do you decide?

There are two basic schools of thought here. The first is common in programmer circles, and it's the "brevity is the soul of wit" approach to programming: "Why do in two, or three, or four lines, what you can get done in one line?" So with this approach, anytime you can combine steps, you should. The code is a lot shorter, and you don't have a lot of those in-between steps. The result is what's called *method chaining*: you do one thing to a piece of text, for example, and then the result of that one thing is sent to another thing. In other words, each step is a link in a chain, and the entire line is the chain, complete and ready to use.

The other school of thought is a little less popular among programmers, unless those programmers have to teach what they're doing to someone else. Above all else, this school of thought aims to make code easy to understand. So the more you can break down that chain of actions, the easier it is to quickly figure out what's going on. This takes a lot more code, but all that extra code is easier to understand, and (at least in theory) to fix if something goes wrong.

Realistically, you'll probably want to end up somewhere in the middle of these two approaches. For instance, your code in *getFormInfo.php* is still pretty clear, even though a few things are chained together. But if you end up lines that have 6, 7, even 10 things attached to each other, it might be time to split things up (and lay off the triple ventis from Starbucks!).

Put it all together, and you'll get something like this:

```
$facebook_url = str_replace("facebook.org", "facebook.com",
                            trim($_REQUEST['facebook_url']));
$position = strpos($facebook_url, "facebook.com");
if ($position === false) {
  $facebook_url = "http://www.facebook.com/" . $facebook_url;
}
```

NOTE For more information on why that *str_replace()* looks the way it does, see the box on page 43.

Make these changes, and then visit your web form again. Enter some information that might have been a problem for a less-skilled PHP programmer, with lots of spaces and a bad facebook.org URL, like in Figure 2-9.

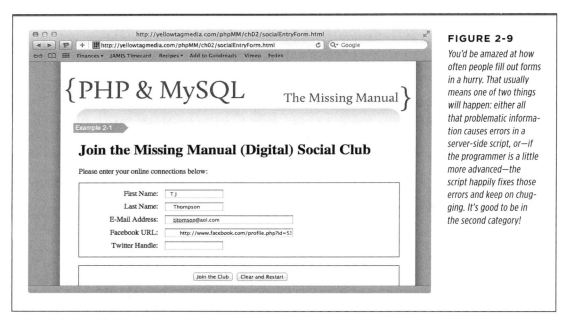

FIGURE 2-9

You'd be amazed at how often people fill out forms in a hurry. That usually means one of two things will happen: either all that problematic information causes errors in a server-side script, or—if the programmer is a little more advanced—the script happily fixes those errors and keep on chugging. It's good to be in the second category!

Submit this data, and you'll see in Figure 2-10 that *getFormInfo.php* doesn't miss a beat. It gets rid of all that extra space, and even fixes the bad Facebook URL (see Figure 2-11).

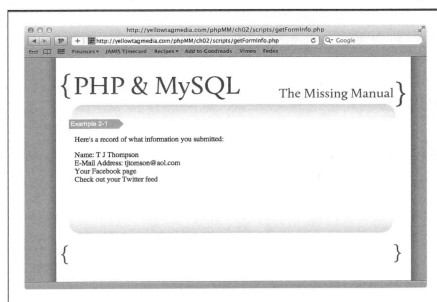

FIGURE 2-10

Using trim() and str_replace() and even strpos() is part of being a responsible PHP programmer. In fact, you may eventually build your own standard blocks of code that you run all your web form entries through, just to make sure they're formatted just the way you like.

FIGURE 2-11

Once again, View Source is your friend. In most browsers, this option is under the View menu, the Page menu, or available by right-clicking on your page. Make sure you can view your page's source; it's what's really getting sent to the browser, no matter how things actually look on your screen.

```
<html>
 <head>
  <link href="../../css/phpMM.css" rel="stylesheet" type="text/css" />
 </head>

 <body>
  <div id="header"><h1>PHP & MySQL: The Missing Manual</h1></div>
  <div id="example">Example 2-1</div>

  <div id="content">
    <p>Here's a record of what information you submitted:</p>
    <p>
      Name: T J Thompson<br />
      E-Mail Address: tjtomson@aol.com<br />
      <a href="http://www.facebook.com/profile.php?id=534643138">Your Facebook
page</a><br />
      <a href="http://www.twitter.com/">Check out your Twitter feed</a><br />
    </p>
  </div>

  <div id="footer"></div>
 </body>
</html>
```

■ The *$_REQUEST* Variable

PHP is a lot more than a way to work with text. You've been working with strings non-stop, but there are a lot more types of information you'll need to work with in your PHP scripts. As you might expect, there are all kinds of ways to work with numbers, and you'll work with numbers quite a bit before long.

But there's another really important type of information you need to understand; in fact, you've already been working with this type, as much as you've worked with text. This mystery type is an *array*: a sort of container that actually holds other values within it.

PHP Offers a Slew of String Functions

Believe it or not, you've really just scratched the surface of what PHP has to offer in dealing with strings and text. You can visit *www.php.net/manual/en/ref.strings.php* to get a complete list of what you can do with text in PHP. But get your high-resolution monitor out; this list won't even fit on a single screen for most web browsers.

But don't worry—you in no way have to memorize all these functions. Just bookmark this page—and the PHP manual, at *www.php.net/manual*—and know that it's there when you need it. If you run across a string you need to manipulate, just pull up your bookmarked PHP manual and search through it. That's what everybody else does. (Well, there may be some Dustin Hoffman lookalike out there rattling off all the PHP numerical functions in a monotone, all Rain-Manned up in his gray suit. But that guy is the exception.)

Instead of worrying about memorizing the odds and ends of every function in the PHP language, work on understanding the *patterns* of PHP, and how those patterns work. For instance, now you know that most string manipulation involves calling some function, passing it in a few pieces of information, and assigning the result to a variable. *That's* what's important, and now every time you do look up a string function in the PHP manual, you know exactly how to use that function correctly.

Arrays Can Hold Multiple Values

An array is a type of *data structure*. That's one of those terms that will gain you respect at a Google get together, but might get you some odd looks if you're having cocktails at a political fundraiser. But arrays aren't actually that hard to understand. Think of an array as a file cabinet of information, and you've got the idea.

So if you have a variable called, for example, *$file_cabinet,* that's an array, and it can store other information within it. You can stuff URLs, and first and last names, email addresses, and so on into that *$file_cabinet*. You fill up the file cabinet by telling PHP where you want your information using numbers in square brackets, right after the array variable name, like this:

```php
<?php

$file_cabinet[0] = "Derek";
$file_cabinet[1] = "Trucks";
```

```
$file_cabinet[2] = "derek@DerekTrucks.com";
$file_cabinet[3] = "http://www.facebook.com/DerekTrucks";
$file_cabinet[4] = "@derekandsusan";

?>
```

These numbers are like drawers in the file cabinet, or if you like things a little more compact, labels on file folders within the cabinet.

NOTE Any time you see a code example like this, you can type it, save it (using a name like *file_cabinet. php*), and run it with the *php* command. Go ahead and try it...you'll be changing things and making up your own programs in no time.

Then, you can get information out of *$file_cabinet* by using those same numbers within brackets:

```
$first_name = $file_cabinet[0];
$last_name = $file_cabinet[1];
$email = $file_cabinet[2];
$facebook_url = $file_cabinet[3];
$twitter_handle = $file_cabinet[4];
```

WARNING It's probably old hat to you by now, but remember that most things in PHP start counting at 0 (see the box on page 37). Arrays are no different. So the first item in *$file_cabinet* is *$file_cabinet[0]*, not *$file_cabinet[1]*.

And then you can do whatever you want with those values, including print them out. Here's a complete program that isn't very useful, but certainly puts an array through its paces. It fills an array, pulls information out of the array, and then does a little printing.

```
<?php

$file_cabinet[0] = "Derek";
$file_cabinet[1] = "Trucks";
$file_cabinet[2] = "derek@DerekTrucks.com";
$file_cabinet[3] = "http://www.facebook.com/DerekTrucks";
$file_cabinet[4] = "@derekandsusan";

$first_name = $file_cabinet[0];
$last_name = $file_cabinet[1];
$email = $file_cabinet[2];
$facebook_url = $file_cabinet[3];
$twitter_handle = $file_cabinet[4];
```

```
echo $first_name . " " . $last_name;
echo "\nEmail: " . $email;
echo "\nFacebook URL: " . $facebook_url;
echo "\nTwitter Handle: " . $twitter_url;
?>
```

Now, this is helpful—who doesn't like to file things away for use later?—but there's a bit of a problem here. Who's going to remember that at position 2, you've got a last name, and at position 4, you've got the Facebook URL? That's a disaster waiting to happen.

Fortunately, the wise folks that came up with PHP thought this through. PHP arrays are *associative*, which means you can associate labels with each item in the array. So going back to the idea of each number being a folder in a file cabinet, you can use an actual label on the folder. Better yet, that label can be anything you want.

So here's that same simple program; but this time it uses associative labels. You should make these changes to your own copy of this script if you're following along.

```
<?php

$file_cabinet['first_name'] = "Derek";$file_cabinet['last_name'] = "Trucks";
$file_cabinet['email'] = "derek@DerekTrucks.com";
$file_cabinet['facebook_url'] = "http://www.facebook.com/DerekTrucks";
$file_cabinet['twitter_handle'] = "@derekandsusan";

$first_name = $file_cabinet['first_name'];
$last_name = $file_cabinet['last_name'];
$email = $file_cabinet['email'];
$facebook_url = $file_cabinet['facebook_url'];
$twitter_handle = $file_cabinet['twitter_handle'];

echo $first_name . " " . $last_name;
echo "\nEmail: " . $email;
echo "\nFacebook URL: " . $facebook_url;
echo "\nTwitter Handle: " . $twitter_url;
?>
```

By now, though, this *$file_cabinet* should be looking a bit familiar. You've seen something that looks awfully similar...

Working with *$_REQUEST* as an Array

This special variable PHP gave you with all the information from a web form, called *$_REQUEST*, is also an array. And when you've written code like *$_REQUEST['first_name']*, you've just been grabbing a particular piece of information out of that array.

In fact, you've already seen that the most powerful way to use arrays is really behind the scenes. You (or a web browser) sticks information into the array, and then you pull that information back out, and work with it. It really doesn't matter that an array was involved; it's just a convenient way to hold things, as when a browser is sending a request to your PHP script.

You've seen that you can not only get to information in an array by a name—the label on a file folder—but by number (page 46). So you can do *$file_cabinet['first_name']*, but you can also do *$file_cabinet[0]*. The same is true of *$_REQUEST*; it's just an array, so doing *$_REQUEST[0]* is perfectly OK with PHP.

So what exactly is in *$_REQUEST*? Go ahead and create a new program, and you can see for yourself.

```
<html>
 <head>
  <link href="../../css/phpMM.css" rel="stylesheet" type="text/css" />
 </head>

 <body>
  <div id="header"><h1>PHP & MySQL: The Missing Manual</h1></div>
  <div id="example">Example 2-2</div>

  <div id="content">
    <p>Here's a record of everything in the $_REQUEST array:</p>
    <?php
      foreach($_REQUEST as $value) {
        echo "<p>" . $value . "</p>";
      }
    ?>
  </div>

  <div id="footer"></div>
 </body>
</html>
```

Here's another one of those scripts that may look intimidating at first, but it's really not bad at all. In fact, the only thing you've not seen before is the line with the *foreach* keyword, which you'll get into a lot more a bit later. For now, take a closer look at this line, which begins a PHP loop:

```
foreach($_REQUEST as $value) {
```

foreach is a nifty PHP creation that lets you quickly get at the values of an array. In this case, *foreach* takes an array—*$_REQUEST*—and then pulls each value out of that array, one at a time. Each time it pulls out a single value, it assigns that value to a new variable called *$value*; that's the *as $value* part of the *foreach* line. So inside the *foreach* loop, you'll have a *$value* variable that has a single value within the array.

Just as in the *if* statement you've used a few times, the curly braces—*{ }*—tell PHP where the beginning and the end of this loop are:

```
foreach($_REQUEST as $value) {
  echo "<p>" . $value . "</p>";
}
```

Everything between the *{ }* runs once for each time through the loop. So that means that for every item in *$_REQUEST*, this line is going to run one time:

```
echo "<p>" . $value . "</p>";
```

This line shouldn't be any big deal to you at all: it just prints out *$value* with some HTML formatting. But since each time through this loop, *$value* has a different value from *$_REQUEST*, it's a quick way to print out every value in *$_REQUEST*.

Now suppose that *$_REQUEST* has values within it like *Derek*, *Trucks*, and *@DerekAndSusan*. When PHP runs your code, it ends up doing something like this:

```
echo "<p>" . "Derek" . "</p>";
echo "<p>" . "Trucks" . "</p>";
echo "<p>" . "@DerekAndSusan" . "</p>";
```

Save this script as *showRequestInfo.php*. You'll also need to change where your *socialEntryForm.php* web form submits its information:

```
<form action="scripts/showRequestInfo.php" method="POST">
  <fieldset>
    <label for="first_name">First Name:</label>
    <input type="text" name="first_name" size="20" /><br />
    <label for="last_name">Last Name:</label>
    <input type="text" name="last_name" size="20" /><br />
    <label for="email">E-Mail Address:</label>
    <input type="text" name="email" size="50" /><br />
    <label for="facebook_url">Facebook URL:</label>
    <input type="text" name="facebook_url" size="50" /><br />
    <label for="twitter_handle">Twitter Handle:</label>
    <input type="text" name="twitter_handle" size="20" /><br />
  </fieldset>
  <br />
  <fieldset class="center">
    <input type="submit" value="Join the Club" />
    <input type="reset" value="Clear and Restart" />
  </fieldset>
</form>
```

> **NOTE** You may want to create a copy of *socialEntryForm.html*, and call it something else, like *socialEntryForm-2.html* or *enterInformation.html*. Then you can have two versions: one that sends information to *showRequestInfo.php*, and one that sends information to *getFormInfo.php*.

Now, visit your new web form, fill it out, and submit it. You'll get a pretty interesting web form back: the result of running your new *showRequestInfo.php* script. This finally tells you what's really being sent between your web browser and a web server, and you can see it all in Figure 2-12.

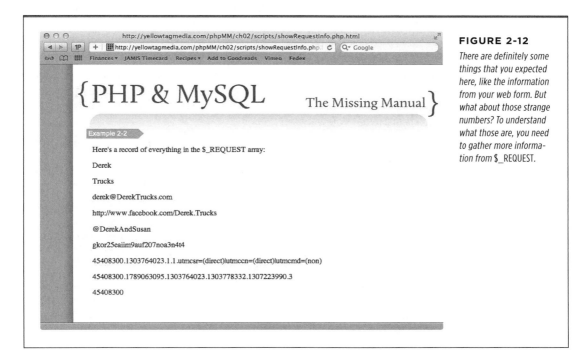

FIGURE 2-12

There are definitely some things that you expected here, like the information from your web form. But what about those strange numbers? To understand what those are, you need to gather more information from $_REQUEST.

So now you have the raw information, but what does it all mean? These results are like seeing all the files on a computer, but having none of those files' names. Or, if you like the file cabinet analogy, imagine having a cabinet of folders with all the labels torn off. It makes knowing what's going on a little trickier.

With the form data, you already know the labels: *first_name*, *last_name*, *email*, and so on. In an associative array like PHP uses, these are called the *keys*. So you can get the value of a particular "folder" in an array with code like this:

```
$value = $file_cabinet[$key];
```

This code gets the value from the array that's attached to whatever label the *$key* variable holds. If *$key* was *first_name*, then the code would basically be the same as this:

```
$value = $file_cabinet['first_name'];
```

So in *showRequestInfo.php*, you just need to also get the keys from the *$_REQUEST* array, instead of just the values. Then you can print out both the key *and* the value. And, wouldn't you know it, PHP makes that easy, again with *foreach*:

```
<div id="content">
  <p>Here's a record of everything in the $_REQUEST array:</p>
  <?php
    foreach($_REQUEST as $key => $value) {
      echo "<p>For " . $key . ", the value is '" . $value . "'.</p>";
    }
  ?>
</div>
```

This time, you're telling *foreach* to get both the key, as *$key*, and the value, as *$value*. That special => sign tells PHP you want the *$key* and then the *$value* attached to the key. In other words, you're grabbing a label and the folder that label is attached to, which is just what you want.

Fill out your form one more time, and check out the results of your updated PHP script, shown in Figure 2-13.

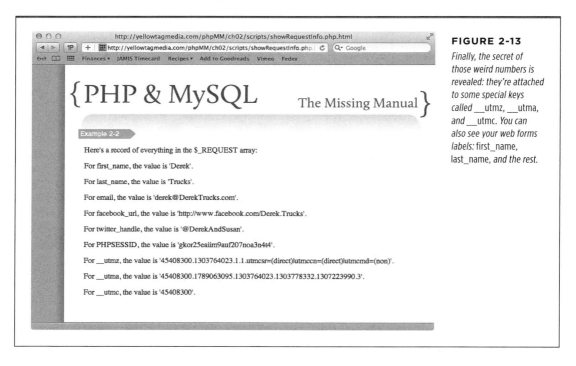

FIGURE 2-13

Finally, the secret of those weird numbers is revealed: they're attached to some special keys called __utmz, __utma, and __utmc. You can also see your web forms labels: first_name, last_name, *and the rest.*

NOTE You may see something similar to those weird things that *$_REQUEST* is storing: *__utmz* and *__utmc*, although that's largely dependent on your web server and your hosting provider. They're special HTTP variables that may get set by your server.

(These HTTP variables aren't anything you need to worry about, but if you're really interested, tweet *@missing-manuals* and tell them to get cracking on *HTTP: The Missing Manual.*)

■ What Do You Do with User Information?

At this point, you've got a lot of information stuffed into a lot of variables. In fact, your earlier web form, *socialEntryForm.html*, looks a lot like the signup forms you've probably filled out hundreds (or thousands!) of times online. But there's a problem, isn't there? In fact, you may have already run across it as you worked through all the changes to your *getFormInfo.php* script: none of that information ever got saved! You had to enter in your name and social information, over and over and over.

Good PHP programmers are able to solve just about any technical problem you throw at them. They know all the PHP string functions, they know about arrays, and a whole lot more. But *great* PHP programmers can solve a whole set of problems that those good PHP programmers never think about: user expectation problems. These are problems that really aren't technical—although you might need to be a good programmer to work around users.

Here's the million-dollar question: What does your user *expect* your pages and scripts to do? For instance, does your user expect to have to come back to your page and enter in the same information, over and over? Absolutely not. In fact, you'd probably stop visiting a site like that. So you've got a user expectation problem—and if you want users to hang around and use your site, you better solve this problem.

In fact, one of the best things you can do is actually *use* your own pages and programs. Get a cup of coffee, a notepad, and sit down at your computer. Close all your text editors and programming tools, and think, "I'm a user!" Then try out your web form, submit the form, enter weird information in, and see what happens. Take a few notes about things that bug you, but remember: you're just a user here.

> **TIP** You may be tempted to make all your notes in a text editor, or just start fixing things. Resist this urge. As soon as you start fixing things, or even getting immersed in your computer, you're not thinking like a user anymore, and you'll miss things.

You'll probably find all sorts of things you didn't even think about. So now what? Well, you've got to start fixing those things. And first up is this pesky issue of having to enter the same information into your page, over and over.

PHP & MYSQL: THE MISSING MANUAL

MySQL and SQL: Database and Language

W here does this thing go? It's probably one of the most common questions
you ask. Where does this sugar bowl go? Where do these shoes go? Where
does this new box of books go? Where do these receipts go? And since
that's such a common question, it shouldn't surprise you that when you're building
web applications, you've got to ask the same thing:

Where does my information go?

The answer, at least for the kinds of web applications you've been building with web
pages and PHP, is simple: in a database. Yes, a database is another tool to install and
another language you'll need to learn. But, as you'll see in this chapter, it's worth it.
If you're writing PHP code, you need a database, too.

▓ What Is a Database?

A database is any tool that lets you store information, grab that information when
needed, and organize the information you're storing. By definition, a metal file cabinet
is a type of database. You can toss things into it, pull things back out, and use files
and labels to keep your papers organized.

Databases Are Persistent

You've seen that PHP gives you arrays to serve as a sort of programmer's file cabinet
(page 46). So is an array a database? It fits the definition in the simplest possible
sense, but it's not going to serve your needs very long. For one thing, arrays and
their contents in PHP are trashed every time your program stops and starts again.
That's not a very helpful database. You'd be better off with an old metal file cabinet.

A good database can store information for the long term. So just because your program stops running—or your entire web server has to be restarted—a database doesn't lose your information. Imagine if every time your web server had to be shut down for an upgrade, your database lost every user's first name, last name, and email! Do you think your users would come back to your site just to type everything in again? Not a chance.

So a good database needs to store information more permanently. In programming terms, that's called *persisting* your information. In other words, if your web server goes down, or even if your database has to shut down and be restarted, the information you put in your database sticks around. (See the box below to find out how long this data really sticks around.)

Permanent Data Is Really Semipermanent

Even though databases store your information, and that storage lasts even when your computer or the database itself starts up and shuts down, your information is still not really permanent. Think about it: even if you write in ink, not pencil, you can still throw away the piece of paper you wrote on. That's the way databases work: they store information in a form that's harder to destroy, but that information still *can* be destroyed.

But databases do store information somewhere, usually on hard drives. If one of those hard drives crashes or becomes defective, your information is lost, no matter how good your database is. Additionally, threats to computers like overheating, or natural disasters, can wipe out your data by destroying the hard drives on which that data exists.

That's why most databases offer some form of backup and replication. *Backup* is just creating a copy of your database,

so if something goes wrong, you can restore the database from the backup, and get back all (or at least most) of the information that's been lost.

Replication is when an entire database is duplicated, and possibly that duplicated version is running, too. So in addition to having the main database and potentially a backup, you've got an entirely different copy of the database running, as well. With replication, you could have an entire database go down, but all your applications keep running because they can switch to using the replicated version.

Replication is expensive, because you need another server with another copy of your database software running. Still, if you've got an application that's used a lot, and earns money as long as it's running, replication is an important way to make sure information isn't lost in a disaster.

If you think about it, you're constantly working with something kind of like this on your computer: a system that stores your information long-term. It's your hard drive and file system. All files are on your computer are address files, email messages, financial documents, what level you've made it to on Angry Birds, and other pieces of information. And you can shut down your computer and start it back up, or even upgrade to a new computer, and keep all your information intact.

So a file system is really a sort of database. In fact, lots of databases actually use files much the way your computer does to do the persisting of its information. So why doesn't PHP just store information in files? After all, it has a whole set of tools for working with files, including creating, writing, and reading files. Isn't that enough? Not really. Read on to find out why.

NOTE You'll learn about how to use PHP to work with files on page 103.

Databases Are All About Structure

If you think about it, there's something pretty clunky about your computer's file system. Have you ever tried to remember the last time you sent an email to someone? You can't go to that person's address book card, because that's not connected to your email program. And your email program may not be much help if you can't remember the person's exact email address.

Then, even if you actually find that email message, you may need to reference some documents related to the email. And where are those? In another folder somewhere, probably in some organizing scheme about which you've long forgotten.

That's why your computer has all kinds of Search options. On Mac OS X, you can use Spotlight (see Figure 3-1) or something like QuickSilver (*http://quicksilver.en.softonic. com/mac*). Windows users can download Google's Desktop Search (*www.google. com/quicksearchbox*, shown in Figure 3-2). These programs look for all occurrences of a certain word or topic across your entire system.

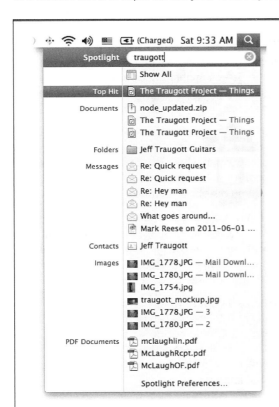

FIGURE 3-1

Mac OS X's Spotlight tries to relate files in different places by their name, the folder they're in, or their content. In other words, Spotlight seeks to determine the relationship between different files and folders.

In fact, these search programs are trying to do what databases do by nature: find and organize information. But if you've ever tried to make these sort of connections on your computer—whether you're using Spotlight or Google Search or doing it by hand—you know it's a hassle, and inconsistent at best. What you need is a better way to connect two, or three, or ten pieces of information together.

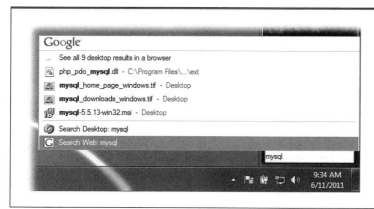

FIGURE 3-2

Google Desktop Search works on both Windows and Mac. It tries to index and connect files both on your machine and stored in Google Documents and Gmail. It actually builds its own database to create and remember these connections.

(Good) Databases Are Relational

What a file system and your hard drive lack, a database excels in: creating *relationships* between different pieces of information. So you might have a person, and that person has several email addresses, phone numbers, and mailing addresses. Your address book program already handles these sorts of relationships.

But a good database goes further. An email message is related to the sender's email address, and that email is related back to the person's name, phone numbers, and other contact information. And of course a map with streets connects those streets with the contact's street address. And the creator's name in a file description relates to that person, and his email address, and his phone number...and so on.

In a lot of ways, these relations are really a giant web of connections. And a good database both creates and manages all these relationships. In fact, MySQL and the other databases you most often run into are so keyed into relations that it's part of the name of this category of databases: *relational databases*. (For more information on the category of database that PHP fits into, see the box on page 59.)

So this means that in addition to telling a database what information you want it to store for you and your programs, you also tell the database how that information is connected to other pieces of information. You not only get to use this web of connections, but you also get to tell the database exactly how the web should be constructed. That's a lot of power, which is why you have to learn an entirely new language to work with these relational databases.

■ Installing MySQL

Before you can tackle this new language, though, you've got to install a database. As you can tell from the title of this book, you'll be working with the MySQL database, which is one of the most common databases used in web applications. That's because it's easy to get, easy to install, and easy to use.

NOTE As with most things in life, ease of use comes with some tradeoffs. There are some databases that cost a lot of money and are really complicated to use, like Oracle. But those databases typically offer features that programs like MySQL don't: higher-end tools for maintenance, and a whole slew of professional support options that go beyond what you get with MySQL.

Don't worry, though. Almost every single command, technique, and tool you'll learn for working with MySQL will work with *any* relational database, so even if you end up at a company or in a situation where Oracle (or an IBM product, or PostgreSQL, or something else entirely) is in use, you'll have no problems getting your PHP working with a database other than MySQL.

ALTERNATE REALITIES

Objects and Relations in Databases, Oh My!

For decades, the relational database has been the de facto standard for high-end applications, whether those applications are run on the Web or on an internal company network. These databases—often called RDBMS, or *relational database management systems*—are the best understood, and most data naturally fits into an RDBMS model. Not only that, but there are more stable and professional RDBMSes than any other type of database.

However, there are some competitors to RDBMSes these days. Most of these are *object-oriented database management systems*, or OODBMS for short. Although the OODBMS have been around since the 70s, it's really just in the last 10 years that these have gained popularity.

An RDBMS stores information in tables, rows, and columns. For example, you might have a table of users that has columns for their first name, last name, and email. Anything that's stored in the RDBMS involves some kind of mapping, so the information in your PHP script has to be mapped to particular tables and columns. You'd say, for example, the information

in *$_REQUEST['first_name']* needs to be stored in the *Users* table, and then in the *first_name* column. This mapping two-step isn't a big deal, but it is an extra step in working with relational databases.

In an OODBMS, you'd create an *object* in your code, which takes the place of a table with columns. So you might create a new *User* object, and assign its first name the value in *$_REQUEST['first_name']*. Then, when you want to store that user's information, you just hand the OODBMS your entire *User* object. In other words, the database figures out how to deal with an object instead of needing you to tell it where individual pieces of information go.

Of course, with an OODBMS, this means you have to have lots of objects in your code, so you're going to end up writing some code whether you're working with an RDBMS or an OODBMS. The RDBMS model, which is what MySQL uses, is far more common in web applications than OODBMS, so it's definitely what you want to focus on learning.

MySQL on Windows

Installing MySQL on Windows is pretty straightforward. You just need to know one thing: whether your computer is running Windows in 32-bit or a 64-bit version. You can find this out by clicking your Start Menu, right-clicking the Computer item, and then selecting Properties from the pop-up menu. You should see something like Figure 3-3.

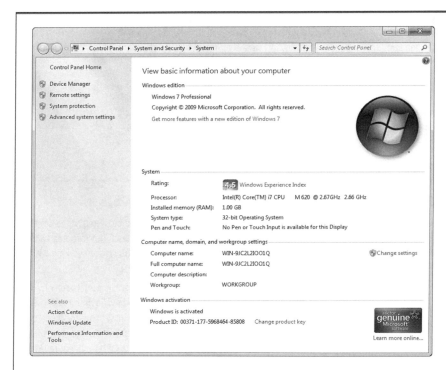

FIGURE 3-3

The machine shown here is a 32-bit system, running Windows 7 Professional. What you see in this window is determined partly by the Windows version you have installed, but also by what your computer is capable of. Both 32-bit and 64-bit systems can run MySQL with no problems.

NOTE If you have a Mac, flip to page 65.

Look for the line that says "System type." It should say either "32-bit Operating System" or "64-bit Operating System." Remember this bit of information, as you'll need it in just a minute.

Now visit *mysql.com* in your web browser. You get a page like that shown in Figure 3-4. This page has lots of introductory information about MySQL, which you can either read or skip. Click the big "Downloads (GA)" tab to get right to the software. You get a page that has information about a few different version of MySQL. You want the first one—MySQL Community Server—so click the Download link under that option.

The download page detects that you're running Windows and gives you several installer options (see Figure 3-5). You want the version that offers you an MSI installer, and matches your system type: 32-bit or 64-bit. After you select the correct version, you're asked to register on the MySQL website. You can skip this option, so if you're worried that the MySQL folks might one day use your physical address to stage a government coup, you can skip straight to the download servers.

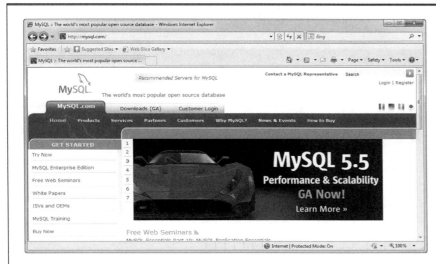

FIGURE 3-4

A few years back, MySQL moved from a completely open source project to a company-backed project. The database is still free, but there's now a lot more of a professional support system behind MySQL. That's much of what the mysql. com website offers: professional support and documentation.

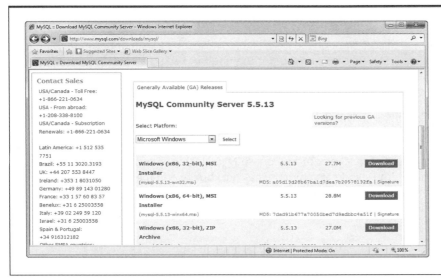

FIGURE 3-5

Just as with PHP, MySQL gives you lots of choices for versions and releases. Generally, the best option is the MSI Installer that matches your system. The Zip archive options aren't packed up nearly so nicely.

Finally, you get a list of servers from which you can download MySQL. Just select the one closest to you geographically (see Figure 3-6), choose a download location on your PC, and knock back an afternoon protein bar to keep your energy up; there's plenty of work left to do.

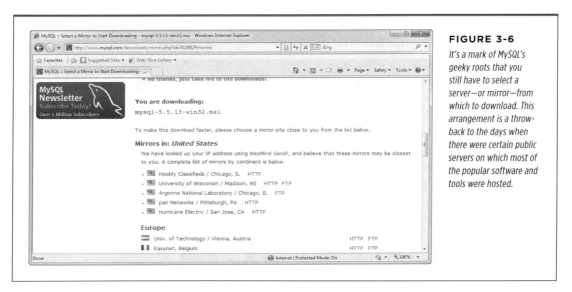

FIGURE 3-6

It's a mark of MySQL's geeky roots that you still have to select a server—or mirror—from which to download. This arrangement is a throwback to the days when there were certain public servers on which most of the popular software and tools were hosted.

Once your download is complete, you end up with a file called something like *mysql-5.5.13-win32.exe*. Double-click this file to run the installer. The installation wizard requires you to accept a license agreement, and then lets you choose the setup type. Select Typical, and then let the installation process whir along.

You have to click through the installation of a secondary set of programs, and then the installation finishes up. You get the option to run the MySQL Server Instance Configuration Wizard (shown in Figure 3-7) when installation is complete. Take the chance to get MySQL and your PC playing nicely together.

In the configuration wizard, select the standard configuration. Then, be sure you let MySQL set itself up as a Windows service, which means that Windows can access and control MySQL directly. You should also leave the "Launch the MySQL Server automatically" checkbox turned on, so MySQL starts up whenever you start your computer. You should also turn on the checkbox to add the MySQL bin directory to your Windows path (see Figure 3-8). This option ensures that when you start up a command prompt, you can run MySQL programs.

Next, you need to enter a *root password*, which is basically a master password. If this were a real database running on a server at Amazon.com or Zappo's, here's where you'd come up with some wild, 22-character password that the smartest computer couldn't crack. Of course, you're just running MySQL on your machine, so something a little less intimidating is fine; try *myqsl_root* if you're stumped. Finally, MySQL is ready to execute your setup. Click the Execute button and let it spin away.

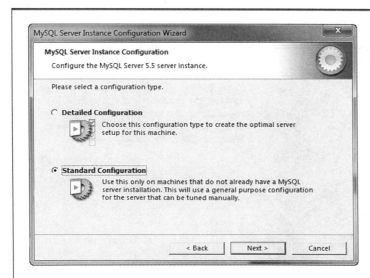

FIGURE 3-7

MySQL is worth a pretty thick book on its own. You can tweak literally hundreds of options to make it run better, faster, and with less strain on your system. For your purposes, though, you don't need all these complications: you just want a local database in which you can store information.

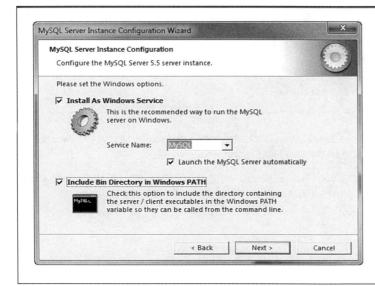

FIGURE 3-8

MySQL comes with several tools that let you start, stop, and interact with its databases. These are only easily available if you add the bin directory in your MySQL installation to your path. You're a programmer now, and definitely want access to these programs.

NOTE You're probably starting to see why most of the programmers you may have met are impatient, a bit jittery, and drink a lot of coffee. There's a lot of waiting around when it comes to installing software, and a lot more waiting when it comes to running your programs and making sure they behave the way they're supposed to.

Finally, the wizard should close, and your MySQL database is installed. If you click the Start menu, you should also see a new program available, the MySQL Command Line Client, as shown in Figure 3-9.

FIGURE 3-9

If you ever lose track of the MySQL command line client, you can just open up a command prompt and type mysql. This command opens up the command-line client, as long as you made sure to add the MySQL bin directory to your Windows PATH during installation of MySQL (Figure 3-8).

Open the MySQL Command Line Client, and type your super-secret password. You should get something that looks like Figure 3-10.

That's it: if you can log into MySQL, you've got a running database, and you're ready to start working with that database, and shoving information into it.

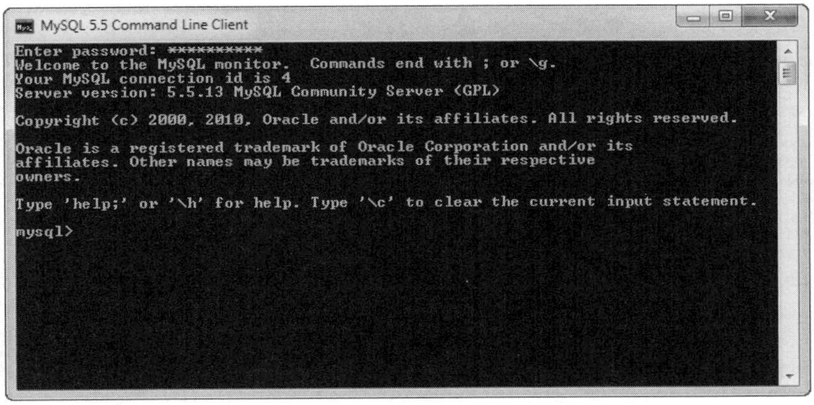

FIGURE 3-10

The command line program always starts by asking you your password. Password protection is important for this program, since it lets you do everything from creating and deleting structures to messing around with MySQL's data. It's like a direct line of access to MySQL, which is exactly what you need for testing out the PHP code you'll start writing in this chapter.

MySQL on Mac OS X

The MySQL installation process on Mac OS X is similar to the installation on Windows. Visit *www.mysql.com*, and select the "Downloads (GA)" tab near the top of the page. Then select the "MySQL Community Server" link to get to the downloads. The site detects that you're on Mac OS X and gives you options like those shown in Figure 3-11.

TIP   If you're on Windows, turn back to page 60.

Scroll down and find the DMG links. These are easy-to-install versions of MySQL that provide a nice setup interface. However, you're going to have to figure out whether you've got a 32-bit or 64-bit system, and that's a multi-step process on Macs.

First, go to → About This Mac, and then click the More Info button to get a window like Figure 3-12. Look for the Processor Name line.

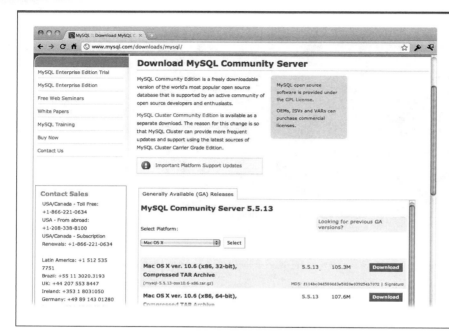

FIGURE 3-11

Like the Windows versions, MySQL for Mac gives you plenty of options from which to choose. The developers that work on MySQL tend to favor the Compressed TAR Archive options, since they give you the actual MySQL code itself. Since you're not planning on working on the actual MySQL code, that's a lot more than you need.

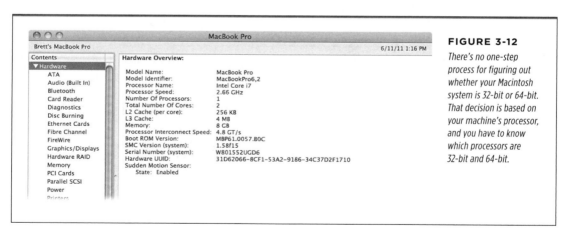

FIGURE 3-12

There's no one-step process for figuring out whether your Macintosh system is 32-bit or 64-bit. That decision is based on your machine's processor, and you have to know which processors are 32-bit and 64-bit.

Now you can compare your processor to Table 3-1, which will tell you whether your Mac is 32-bit or 64-bit.

TABLE 3-1 *Fortunately, you don't have to worry about tons of options. Macs have one choice (32-bit or 64-bit) for each processor.*

PROCESSOR NAME	32-BIT OR 64-BIT
Intel Core Solo	32-bit
Intel Core Duo	32-bit
Intel Core 2 Duo	64-bit
Intel Quad-Core Xeon	64-bit
Dual-Core Intel Xeon	64-bit
Quad-Core Intel Xeon	64-bit
Core i3	64-bit
Core i5	64-bit
Core i7	64-bit

NOTE Apple is constantly updating the Macintosh hardware choices. If you can't find your processor name in Table 3-1, visit *http://support.apple.com/kb/HT3696*, which usually has an updated list of processor names and whether they're 32-bit or 64-bit.

Select the DMG download for MySQL that matches your processor. You can then register (or skip it), select a download site, and start your download.

Once the DMG is downloaded, it will open automatically. You should see several files, as shown in Figure 3-13.

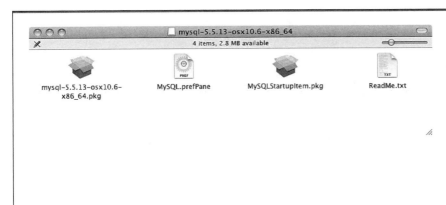

FIGURE 3-13

Most DMGs have a single file and, if you're lucky, some poorly written instructions. MySQL is a little more heavyweight, though, so in addition to the core installation, you get a preference pane (which you'll install in a few minutes), a program to handle automatic startup, and a helpful ReadMe.txt file.

Select the main file, which should be named something like *mysql-5.5.13-osx10.6-x86_64.pkg*. Double-click this file to begin installation. You have to agree to a license and select an install location. Then you need to type in an administrator password for your machine to launch the installation.

> **TIP** If you're on your own machine, this password is likely the password you normally log in with. Macs with only a single user set that user up as an administrator. Otherwise, bake some cookies and use them to bribe the computer's owner to let you turn his Mac OS X computer into a PHP and MySQL powerhouse.

Installation doesn't take very long (see Figure 3-14). Don't get too excited, though; you have a few more steps. Go back to the DMG, and if it's not still open, double-click to reopen it (look back to Figure 3-13 if you need to).

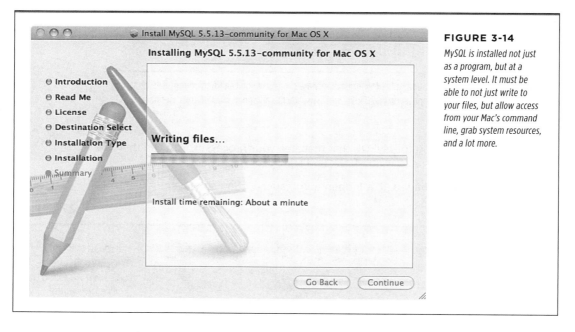

FIGURE 3-14

MySQL is installed not just as a program, but at a system level. It must be able to not just write to your files, but allow access from your Mac's command line, grab system resources, and a lot more.

Double-click the file named *MySQL.prefPane*. This installer adds a new control pane to your System Preferences. It also asks you whether you want to install this pane for you alone, or all users. You can probably keep the pane to yourself, unless there's a line behind you of other database-hungry users.

Once the pane is installed, it opens automatically, as shown in Figure 3-15. Go ahead and turn on the checkbox to have MySQL start up automatically; you get to enter your password one more time. Finally, start up MySQL now to make sure things are working as they should be.

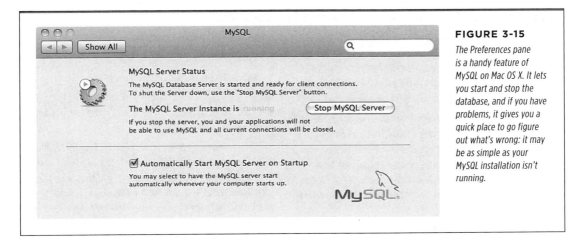

FIGURE 3-15

The Preferences pane is a handy feature of MySQL on Mac OS X. It lets you start and stop the database, and if you have problems, it gives you a quick place to go figure out what's wrong: it may be as simple as your MySQL installation isn't running.

And with that, you've got an installed, running database on your Mac. Now, open up a new Terminal window (go to *Applications→Utilities→Terminal;* if you haven't already, go ahead and drag the Terminal icon into your dock where it's easy to access). In the Terminal window, type the following command:

```
$ /usr/local/mysql/bin/mysql
```

This command is a bit on the long side, unfortunately. That's because one thing the installation *doesn't* do is set up your path so that you can easily call the MySQL tools and programs. (You'll probably do most of your MySQL work on your web server, so this isn't a huge deal, but you can make it so you can simply type the *mysql* part of that command; see the box on page 70.)

The command you just typed opens up the MySQL command prompt tool, and you should get output like in Figure 3-16.

Update Your PATH to Include the MySQL Programs

It's a bit disappointing that after you went to all the trouble of downloading MySQL and installing it on a Mac—including a handy Preferences pane—you still can't just type *mysql* into a Terminal window and be off to the races. Still, if you're not afraid of a little work, you can fix this problem yourself.

The secret to all these programs that run—and don't run—in your Terminal is your computer's *PATH*. That's a special variable (just like the variables you create in PHP) that tells your computer where to look when you enter a command. So when you type *mysql*, if your *PATH* includes */usr/local/mysql/bin*, your computer looks in that directory, sees a program called *mysql*, and runs it. Perfect!

But what about when your *PATH* doesn't include a directory you want it to? You can update the *PATH*, but it involves editing a file that's normally hidden. First, go back to Terminal and enter these two commands:

```
$ defaults write com.apple.finder Apple-
ShowAllFiles TRUE
```

```
$ killall Finder
```

The first line here tells the Finder—the program that shows you directories on a Mac—to show hidden files, like the one you need to edit. The second line restarts Finder and puts this change into action. Now open up a Finder window and go to your home directory. You'll see a bit of a weird view of your normal directory window; it probably looks something like Figure 3-17. There will be tons of files that are light gray, and seem faded, or nearly invisible. These are the files normally hidden from your view, and you may notice that most of them begin with a dot (.), which is why they're hidden.

Scroll until you find a file called *.profile*, and open up that file in a text editor like Mac OS X's TextEdit. If you've never worked with *PATH*s before, you may not have this file at all, and that's okay, too. Just open a new TextEdit file.

You want to add two lines to this file:

```
MYSQL_HOME=/usr/local/mysql
```

```
export PATH=$MYSQL_HOME/bin:$PATH
```

If you're creating a new file, just make these the first lines. If you already have a *.profile*, add these lines at the very bottom of whatever else is in the file.

The first line creates a new variable called *MYSQL_HOME*, and sets it to where you installed MySQL. This way, if you ever change your MySQL installation location, you simply update this variable, just as you updated the *$facebook_url* variable in your PHP script (page 44). The second line then sets the *PATH* variable to be the current *PATH*, but it adds the *bin* directory under *MYSQL_HOME* to the beginning of that path. The *export* keyword tells Mac OS X to make sure this updated *PATH* variable is available to all the programs on your machine.

Finally, save your file. If you're creating a new file, be careful to name it correctly, beginning the file name with a dot (.), and make sure it doesn't get a file extension. (If you accidentally save the file with an extension, simply remove that extension in the Finder.)

When you're done, you should have a file in your home directory called *.profile*. It should be grayed out, too, because it's hidden. Now you can open up a new Terminal, and type in *mysql*. You should see the MySQL command line program open right up.

Finally, before you hang up your new system-editing ninja skills, set Finder to hide all those files again:

```
$ defaults write com.apple.finder Apple-
ShowAllFiles TRUE
```

```
$ killall Finder
```

You can always unhide them if you need access later.

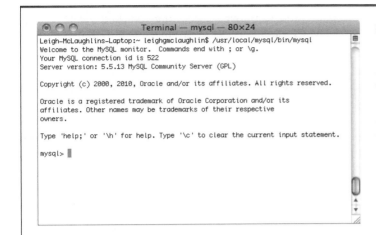

FIGURE 3-16

There are graphical tools for the Mac that let you work with your database, and you'll want to check those out. But for getting to the root of a tricky problem, or learning how to work with MySQL from PHP, nothing beats learning the commands that you can use from a MySQL command prompt to directly interact with your database.

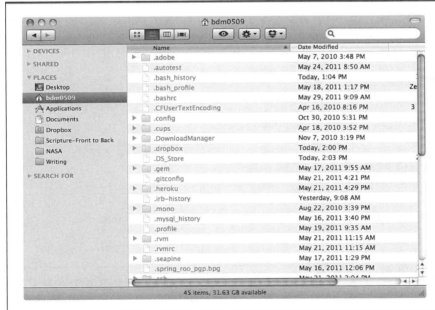

FIGURE 3-17

Most programs that update and work on your system create hidden files, all starting with a dot. So git, a version control system, creates .gitconfig, and DropBox, a popular file-sharing system, creates .dropbox.

If you're seeing something similar on your Mac, you've got a running installation of MySQL, and you're ready to start working with your database.

Running Your First SQL Query

Make sure you've got MySQL installed and running. On Mac OS X, you can check your Preferences pane (as shown earlier in Figure 3-15), and on Windows, you can go to your Control Panel, click Administrative Services, and then find Local Services. Scroll down until you see MySQL, double-click it, and make sure the status is Started (see Figure 3-18).

NOTE If you're already working on a web server, MySQL is probably both pre-installed and pre-started, so you're ready to go.

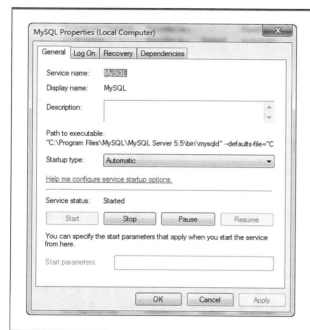

FIGURE 3-18

In Windows, you can find most of the programs that interact with your system in the Local Services section of your Administrative Services control panel. You can start and stop services, look for errors, and set a service to start automatically: all of which the MySQL installation so nicely handled for you.

Fire up your MySQL command line tool, and type this command:

```
show databases;
```

WARNING Be sure you end your line with a semicolon, or you'll get unexpected results. All your MySQL commands end with a semicolon, just like most of your PHP commands.

You should get a text response from MySQL that looks a bit like this:

```
mysql> show databases;
+--------------------+
| Database           |
+--------------------+
| information_schema |
| development        |
| eiat_testbed       |
| mysql              |
| nagios             |
| ops_dashboard      |
| performance_schema |
| test               |
+--------------------+
8 rows in set (0.25 sec)
```

You may not have as many databases that come back, or you may have different databases. The point here is that this shows you that MySQL has a number of pre-created databases sitting on your system.

But what was that *show* command? Well, *show* does just what you might expect: it shows you everything for a particular keyword, this case, *databases.* So it's just a way to ask MySQL to show you all the databases installed on your machine.

On top of that, now you know something really important: MySQL isn't so much a database as a piece of software that can store and create databases. In this example, *show databases; returns 8 rows*, so there are eight databases on that system, not just one. Before you're done, you'll have created several more databases, all running within MySQL.

For now, tell MySQL you want to work with the *mysql* database, which you have on your system even if you just installed MySQL. You do that with the *use* command, like this:

```
use mysql;
```

Now, you're "in" the *mysql* database. In other words, any commands you give to MySQL are run against just the *mysql* database.

You've already asked MySQL to show you all the databases it has; now tell it to show you all the tables in the database you're using:

```
show tables;
```

You should get a nice long list here:

```
mysql> show tables;
+---------------------------+
| Tables_in_mysql           |
+---------------------------+
| columns_priv              |
| db                        |
| event                     |
| func                      |
| general_log               |
| help_category             |
| help_keyword              |
| help_relation             |
| help_topic                |
| host                      |
| ndb_binlog_index          |
| plugin                    |
| proc                      |
| procs_priv                |
| proxies_priv              |
| servers                   |
| slow_log                  |
| tables_priv               |
| time_zone                 |
| time_zone_leap_second     |
| time_zone_name            |
| time_zone_transition      |
| time_zone_transition_type |
| user                      |
+---------------------------+
24 rows in set (0.00 sec)
```

A lot of these table names look pretty weird, but that's mostly because these are MySQL's internal tables. As you create new tables and users and set up your database, all that information is stored within another database: the *mysql* database.

To see some of this information, you have to *select* the information from a specific table. You can select all the information from the *user* table. Enter this command at your MySQL command prompt:

```
mysql> select * from user;
```

The *select* command is pretty self-explanatory: it selects information from a table. The asterisk (*) says, "Select everything." Then, *from* tells MySQL where to get the information you're selecting *from*: in this case, *user*, which is a table in your database.

Don't be surprised when you get a pretty confusing stream of information back from this command. In fact, it may look like something out of *The Matrix*; check out Figure 3-19 for an example.

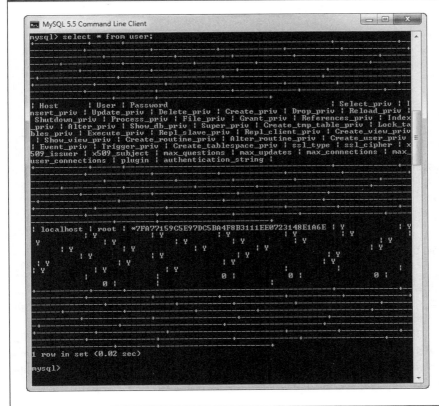

FIGURE 3-19

As you get more comfortable with MySQL and PHP, you'll learn to select just the information you want and clean up this messy response. There are also ways to format the response from MySQL, although you won't need to worry about formatting much, since you'll mostly be grabbing information from MySQL in a PHP script, where formatting isn't a big deal.

The problem here isn't in anything you typed. It's just that you told MySQL to select *everything* from the *user* table, and in this case, everything is a *lot* of information. In fact, it's so much information that it won't all nicely fit into your command-line window, which is why you got all the strange looking lines in your response.

To tame this beast a bit, you can select just a little information from a table. You do this by replacing the * with just the column names you want, separated by commas:

```
mysql> select Host, User, Password from user;
```

You'll get back just the three columns for which you asked:

```
mysql> select Host, User, Password from user;
+-------------------------+-------+-----------------------------------------
--+
| Host                    | User  | Password
|
+-------------------------+-------+-----------------------------------------
--+
| localhost               | root  | *62425DC34224DAABF6995B46CDCC63D92B03D7E9
|
+-------------------------+-------+-----------------------------------------
--+
1 row in set (0.00 sec)
```

This table shows that for your local machine (*localhost*), you have a single user named *root*. The password is encrypted, so don't see anything helpful there, but you can see that MySQL definitely has an entry for you. Since you only asked for three columns, this response is a lot more readable, and actually makes a little sense.

So what's a column? That's a *single category of information* in your table. So in a table that stored users, you might have a *first_name* and a *last_name* column.

NOTE   If your nose is bleeding from the rush of new terms, don't worry. You'll be working with tables, columns, and these MySQL statements over and over and over again as you build your PHP programs. You'll have all this new MySQL lingo under control in no time.

Now that you've got your feet dipped into the MySQL pool, it's time to get on your web server and start to create your own tables and columns, and fill those tables and columns with your own information.

■ SQL Is a Language for Talking to Databases

What you've been doing so far is using a program called MySQL, and you've been talking to that program using SQL, the *Structured Query Language*. And you've already written a couple of SQL queries:

```
mysql> select * from user;
...
mysql> select Host, User, Password from user;
...
```

Both of those commands are SQL queries, or just SQL. The "Structured" in SQL comes from the idea that you're accessing a relational database, something with a lot of structure, and you're using a language that itself is very structured. You'll soon see that SQL is very easy to learn, mostly because it's very predictable. That's why you can look at a command like this and figure out what it does:

```
mysql> select User, Password
         from users
       where first_name = 'Dirk'
         and country = 'Germany';
```

Even though you've never seen the *where* keyword, it's pretty obvious: this returns only the *User* and *Password* column, from the *users* table, where the user's *first_name* field is "Dirk" and the *country* field is "Germany."

FREQUENTLY ASKED QUESTION

Why Do I Need to Install MySQL on My Machine?

You saw it already in the first few chapters on PHP, and now you're about to see it again: most of your programming is meant to be run on a web server. You may pay a monthly fee for hosting to a place like *kattare.com* for your own domain; you may own your own server that's connected to the Internet; or you may deploy your code to your company's servers, housed in a room that's kept too cold for normal human beings and requires a key card to get through the door. In all these cases, though, your code ends up somewhere other than your own desktop or laptop.

But if that's the case—and it usually is—why go to the trouble to install PHP and MySQL on your own machine? Truth be told, you could ask a lot of PHP developers and they'd admit that they don't even have PHP (let alone MySQL) on their own machines. They live their programming lives through *telnet* and *ssh* sessions, writing code on a machine somewhere out on the Web.

Although your code will rarely ultimately run from your own machine, there are some good reasons to install your entire development setup on your own machine. First, you're not always in a place where you can connect to the Internet. You might be on a plane, in the back of a taxi, or lost in West Texas with nothing but an old leather-covered compass and a MacBook Pro. In all these cases, if you've got PHP and MySQL on your laptop, you can code away, testing your code against a real database, and never miss a beat.

Second, it's common to write a lot of code, run it, find out you messed up something (or a lot of somethings), rewrite code, and try again, and again, and again. The same is true when you start accessing a database, too. While you could do this on the server on which your code will ultimately live, that's a lot of time spent living through a network connection, using that machine's resources, and potentially adding and deleting and adding data to a database. It's much better to work on your own machine, and then at certain milestones, upload all your working code to your server.

And finally, you learn a lot by installing these programs from scratch. You get a better handle not only on the structure of your own machine, but also on how these programs work. If someone is getting a particular error, you might recognize that same error as something you got when a Windows service wasn't running, or the MySQL instance on a Mac OS X machine didn't have the right table permissions set up. Your computer can help you learn more about the tools you use, and that's always a good thing.

You can run the examples in this book on your own machine and on your web server, and learn by watching what happens. If you're working on your own machine, make sure you can get to your machine's code with a web browser. Otherwise, upload your code every time to make sure things are working correctly.

WARNING The pronunciation of SQL is more hotly contested than most presidential elections. Some folks say "sequel" while others insist on "S-Q-L," saying each letter individually. While you probably want to stick with the folks around you are using—it's tough being blue in a red state—both are perfectly fine.

You could buy a SQL book and start memorizing all the keywords, but it's a much better idea to simply begin buildings your own tables, and learn as you go. To do that, though, you need to get connected to the database you'll be letting all your PHP programs talk to.

Logging In to Your Web Server's Database

Now that you've got a basic lay of the MySQL landscape, it's time to get things set up on the database your web server uses. You'll probably need to use a tool like *telnet* or *ssh* to log in to your web server.

TIP If you've never used *telnet* or *ssh* before, Google either program's name, and you'll find a ton of resources. You may also want to call whoever hosts your domain, and ask them how you can best access your server. Many web providers now have a graphical version of SSH you can use right from the provider's online control panel. Most good hosting providers also have detailed online instructions to help you get logged in and started.

Once you're logged in, you should be able to use the MySQL command-line client, *mysql*. Almost every hosting provider that supports PHP supports MySQL, and that means that just typing *mysql* is usually the way to get started.

Unfortunately, you're likely to get an error like this right out of the gate:

```
bmclaugh@akila:~$ mysql
ERROR 2002 (HY000): Can't connect to local MySQL server through socket '/tmp/
mysql.sock' (2)
```

This kind of messages usually means that MySQL isn't installed on your server, or at least that it's not configured correctly. But that's probably by intention: most hosting providers will keep their MySQL installation either on a different machine, or at least make it only accessible through a different domain name, like *http://mysql.kattare. com*. That adds some protection, isolation, and security to the MySQL databases they host, all of which are good things.

NOTE If running *mysql* doesn't work, you might also try *mysql –hostname=localhost*. Some MySQL installations are configured to only answer to *localhost*, rather than what's called the local socket. That adds a bit of security to a MySQL installation, but isn't something you need to worry much about at this point. Just make sure you can get *mysql* running, one way or another.

Thankfully, having MySQL on a different server doesn't pose a problem. You can run *mysql* and give it some extra information to tell it exactly where to connect. The *--hostname=* option lets you give *mysql* the hostname of your MySQL database server, and *--user=* lets you give *mysql* your own username.

NOTE You'll almost certainly have a username other than *admin* or *root* for your domain provider's MySQL installation. You can ask them to give that to you when you find out about *telnet* or *ssh* access. Or, if you want to try something out on your own, start with the username and password you use for logging into your web server. Be cautious, though: good database systems will have different usernames and passwords than the web servers that talk to them.

Put all this together on the command line, and you get something like this:

```
bmclaugh@akila:~$ mysql --host=dc2-mysql-02.kattare.com
                        --user=bmclaugh --password
Enter password:
```

That last option, *--password*, tells MySQL to ask you for a password. You could put your password on the command itself, like *--password=this_is_not_very_secure*, but then your nosy cube-mate would be able to log in to your MySQL server.

Once you enter your password, you should get the standard MySQL welcome screen, shown in Figure 3-20.

Now you're ready to do something with this new SQL you've been learning.

USE a Database

On most MySQL installations that hosting providers give you, you don't have nearly as much freedom as on your own installation. For example, type in a SQL command you've used once before:

```
myqsl> show databases;
```

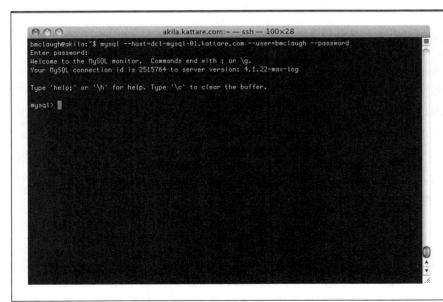

FIGURE 3-20

Once you're logged into MySQL, it really doesn't matter whether you're on Windows, Mac OS X, or a Linux or Unix machine on a hosting provider's network. It's all the same: you just enter in SQL, and get back responses.

The result may be a little surprising. It's sure not what you saw on your own machine:

```
myqsl> show databases;

+-----------+
| Database  |
+-----------+
| bmclaugh  |
+-----------+
1 row in set (0.09 sec)
```

The result is limited because you've got limited privileges on your hosting provider's server. The company certainly isn't going to let you log in to its *mysql* system databases and see what users are in its system's *user* table. What you probably do see is a single entry, a database named something like your login name. So if you log in to your system with the username "ljuber," you might see a database named *ljuber*, or perhaps *db-ljuber* or something else similar.

In fact, you're probably already set up within that specific database. Go ahead and tell MySQL that's the database within which you want to work:

```
mysql> use bmclaugh;
Database changed
```

> **WARNING** On some systems, you're automatically set up to use your user's database when you log in to MySQL. Still, the *use* command won't give you any problems if you tell it to use the current database, so it's always a good idea to begin your MySQL sessions with *use [your-database-name]*.

While you're acclimating yourself to your new MySQL environment, you also want to begin to get familiar with SQL commands being in all capital letters. So if you get an email from your database buddy and she suggests you use a *WHERE* clause or tells you your *SELECT* query is goofy, she's not actually yelling at you. She's talking (or really, writing) SQL commands in all uppercase letters, which is pretty typical.

In fact, the commands you've seen are more commonly written and typed like this:

```
mysql> SELECT * FROM user;
...
mysql> SELECT Host, User, Password FROM user;
...
mysql> SELECT User, Password
          FROM users
         WHERE first_name = 'Dirk'
           AND country = 'Germany';
```

This format creates a nice clear distinction between the SQL keywords like *SELECT*, *FROM*, *WHERE*, and *AND*, and the column and table names. As you've guessed, though, MySQL accepts keywords in upper- or lowercase letters.

NOTE   Although you don't *have* to use capital letters in MySQL for keywords like *SELECT* and *WHERE*, it creates a nice self-documenting effect. But in reality, lots of programmers get tired of all caps and just go straight for the lowercase letters.

Making Tables with *CREATE*

When you could get to and *USE* the *mysql* database, you had some tables all ready for you to *SELECT* from: the *users* table, for example. But now you're on a database server where you can't get to those tables. So before you can get back to working on your *SELECT* skills, you need to create a table.

As you may have already guessed, you can do that with another handy-dandy SQL keyword: *CREATE*. So what you need to do is create a table. You can then put data in it, get data out, and generally have all kinds of database fun.

Type this command in your MySQL command line:

```
CREATE TABLE users (
```

Be sure not to add a semicolon at the end. Then hit Enter, and you'll see something a little weird:

```
mysql> CREATE TABLE users (
    ->
```

What's going on? Remember, your MySQL commands should end in a semicolon. But here, you left that off. What that tells MySQL is "Hey, I'm writing a command, but I'm not done yet." In other words, you don't have to jam a really long line of SQL onto one line in your tool; you can split it up over several lines, and just keep hitting Enter. As long as you don't type that semicolon, MySQL won't try to do anything with your command. And that little arrow (->) lets you know that MySQL is waiting for you to keep typing.

So keep typing:

```
mysql> CREATE TABLE users (
    -> user_id int,
    -> first_name varchar(20),
    -> last_name varchar(30),
    -> email varchar(50),
    -> facebook_url varchar(100),
    -> twitter_handle varchar(20)
    -> );
```

Hit Enter after this last semicolon, and you get a very unimpressive response:

```
mysql> CREATE TABLE users (
    -> user_id int,
    -> first_name varchar(20),
    -> last_name varchar(30),
    -> email varchar(50),
    -> facebook_url varchar(100),
    -> twitter_handle varchar(20)
    -> );
Query OK, 0 rows affected (0.18 sec)
```

This last line is MySQL's modest way of saying, "I did what you asked."

You can probably tell at least a bit about what's going on in your *CREATE* command:

- *CREATE* tells MySQL you want to create a new structure in the database.

- *TABLE* tells MySQL what kind of structure. In this case, you want a table.

- *users* is the name of the table you're creating.

- The opening parenthesis—(—tells MySQL you're about to describe the table to create, one line at a time.

- Each line has a column name—like *user_id*—and a type—like *int* or *varchar(20)*.

- When you're done describing the table, you use a closing parenthesis—)—to let MySQL know, and then end the whole enchilada with a semicolon.

You'll learn a ton more about all the different types of columns you can have, but for now, there are just two to worry about: *int*, which is short for *integer*, and is just a whole number. So 1, 890, and 239402 are *int*s, but 1.293 and 3.1456 are not.

> **NOTE** MySQL is just as happy to accept *integer* as *int*. In fact, they're identical in MySQL.

The next type is a little less obvious: *varchar*. *varchar* stands for variable character, and just means it holds character data—strings—of variable lengths. So a *varchar(20)* can hold a string of length 1 all the way up to length 20.

The upshot of all these new terms is you've told MySQL to create a table with several new columns, one that's an *int* (*user_id*), and several that are *varchar*s of various maximum lengths.

How do you know whether the *CREATE* command worked? See for yourself using the *SHOW* command:

```
mysql> SHOW tables;
+-----------------------------------+
| Tables_in_bmclaugh                |
+-----------------------------------+
| users                             |
+-----------------------------------+
1 row in set (0.06 sec)
```

FREQUENTLY ASKED QUESTION

How Do I Fix a Typo?

Yes, even for PHP and MySQL wizards, typos are a problem. In fact, since programmers tend to type way too fast, typos are a real source of frustration in MySQL.

In some cases, MySQL simply gives you an error message and lets you try again:

```
mysql> use

ERROR:

USE must be followed by a database name
```

times, though, you'll make a mistake in the even worse, hit Enter:

```
    ->

    ->
```

There's an extraneous comma after the * in your *SELECT* line here. But MySQL is just giving you extra -> prompts every time you press Enter.

The problem is that in MySQL's eyes, you haven't ended the SQL command. So it isn't processing your command—including your mistake—and isn't giving you a chance to start over.

When you get into a situation like this, your best bet is to enter a semicolon (;), and then press Enter. The semicolon ends your current command—however broken that command may be—and tells MySQL to process that command. You'll usually get an error message, but at least you've got control again and can make fixes.

created a table. But what's actually in the table? To find out, you ew command: *DESCRIBE*. Try it out on your *users* table:

```
mysql> DESCRIBE users;
+----------------+--------------+------+-----+---------+-------+
| Field          | Type         | Null | Key | Default | Extra |
+----------------+--------------+------+-----+---------+-------+
| user_id        | int(11)      | YES  |     | NULL    |       |
| first_name     | varchar(20)  | YES  |     | NULL    |       |
| last_name      | varchar(30)  | YES  |     | NULL    |       |
| email          | varchar(50)  | YES  |     | NULL    |       |
| facebook_url   | varchar(100) | YES  |     | NULL    |       |
| twitter_handle | varchar(20)  | YES  |     | NULL    |       |
+----------------+--------------+------+-----+---------+-------+
6 rows in set (0.04 sec)
```

NOTE You can also use DESC (or desc) for DESCRIBE. So *DESCRIBE users;* is a perfectly acceptable SQL command, too.

Now you can see that MySQL did just what you told it to: created a table called *users* with all the columns you specified, using the types you gave it. There's a lot more information there, too, but you don't need to worry about that just yet.

DESIGN TIME

The Size of Your Columns Really Does Matter

When most people are creating tables, they spend a lot of time thinking about what they want to store in their database, and very little time thinking about things like how big the maximum length of a *varchar* field can get. So you'll see lots of tables that have 10 or 20 *varchar(100)* columns, even though those columns hold totally different pieces of information.

But it's better to stop and think about these things when you're designing your tables. Make your columns as long as they need to be—but not longer. Yes, it may seem safe to stick with overly long lengths, but then you're not doing a very good job of making your database look like the information it's going to store.

If you're storing a first name, there's really no way the maximum length of that first name is as long as, for example, a Facebook URL. A really, really long first name might be 15 characters (and that would be *really* long!). By contrast, you can

barely fit *www.facebook.com* into 20 characters. So it makes sense for your columns to have different maximum lengths.

But column sizing is about good design, not making your database hum. Your database uses only enough space for the information it holds, so you don't get penalized by wasted disk space or bad performance if all your *varchar* fields are super-long. What you do get, though, is a database that looks sloppy, and makes it appear that you didn't spend much time thinking about your information.

Take the time to do good design now, and it will pay off later. Make your *varchar* columns as long as they need to be, and maybe even a *little* bit longer, but always remember what information will go in those columns.

Deleting Tables with DROP

What goes up must come down, as the saying goes. For everything MySQL and SQL let you do, there's a way to undo those things. You've created a table, but you can also delete that table. However, *delete* isn't the command you want; instead, it's *DROP*.

So if you decide you no longer like that users table, or you want to practice that fancy *CREATE* command again, you can ditch users in a simple line of SQL:

```
mysql> DROP TABLE users;
Query OK, 0 rows affected (0.10 sec)
Boom! It's gone.

mysql> SHOW tables;
+------------------------------------+
| Tables_in_bmclaugh                 |
+------------------------------------+
0 rows in set (0.06 sec)
```

How simple is that? But wait...now you have no tables again, and nothing to *SELECT* from. It's back to creating tables again. Drop that *CREATE* statement into your MySQL tool one more time, and create the *users* table again.

NOTE　On many systems, you can hit the Up arrow and you'll get the last command you ran. Hit Up a few times, and it will cycle back through your command history. This move is a great way to quickly reuse a command you've already run.

INSERT a Few Rows

At this point, you've created, and dropped, and created the *users* table again. But it's still empty, and that's no good. Time to *INSERT* some data.

Try entering this command into your command line tool:

```
mysql> INSERT INTO users
    -> VALUES (1, "Mike", "Greenfield", "mike@greenfieldguitars.com",
    -> "http://www.facebook.com/profile.php?id=699186223",
    -> "@greenfieldguitars");
Query OK, 1 row affected (0.00 sec)
```

What a mouthful! Still, this is another case where you can just look at this SQL and figure out what's going on. You're inserting information into the *users* table, and then you're giving it that information, piece by piece.

You can actually trace each value and connect it to a column in your table. You might want to *DESCRIBE* your table again:

```
mysql> DESCRIBE users;
+----------------+--------------+------+-----+---------+-------+
| Field          | Type         | Null | Key | Default | Extra |
+----------------+--------------+------+-----+---------+-------+
| user_id        | int(11)      | YES  |     | NULL    |       |
| first_name     | varchar(20)  | YES  |     | NULL    |       |
| last_name      | varchar(30)  | YES  |     | NULL    |       |
| email          | varchar(50)  | YES  |     | NULL    |       |
| facebook_url   | varchar(100) | YES  |     | NULL    |       |
| twitter_handle | varchar(20)  | YES  |     | NULL    |       |
+----------------+--------------+------+-----+---------+-------+
6 rows in set (0.29 sec)
```

The first value, 1, goes to *user_id*; the second, "Mike", to *first_name*; and so on.

And that's all there is to it: you can insert as much into your table as you want, anytime you want. There are lots of ways to fancy up *INSERT*, and you'll learn about most of them as you start to work with *INSERT* in your *PHP*.

SELECT for the Grand Finale

Finally, you're back to where you can use good old *SELECT*. By now, that command should seem like ancient history, since you've used DROP and CREATE and INSERT and a few others since that first *SELECT * FROM users*. But now you've got your own *users* table, so try it out again:

```
mysql> SELECT * FROM users;
+---------+------------+------------+---------------------------+--
--------------------------------------------------+------------------
-+
| user_Id | first_name | last_name  | email                     |
facebook_url                                      | twitter_handle
  |
+---------+------------+------------+---------------------------+--
--------------------------------------------------+------------------
-+
|       1 | Mike       | Greenfield | mike@greenfieldguitars.com |
http://www.facebook.com/profile.php?id=699186223 | @greenfieldguitars
  |
+---------+------------+------------+---------------------------+-
-------------------------------------------------+-----------------
---+
1 row in set (0.00 sec)
```

No big surprises here; you got back the row you just inserted. But, just as earlier (page 76), this output is a bit of a mess. Too many columns make this hard to read.

To simplify things, grab just a few columns; you now how to do that:

```
mysql> SELECT first_name, last_name, twitter_handle FROM users;
+------------+------------+--------------------+
| first_name | last_name  | twitter_handle     |
+------------+------------+--------------------+
| Mike       | Greenfield | @greenfieldguitars |
+------------+------------+--------------------+
1 row in set (0.00 sec)
```

That output is a lot more readable. And once you're writing PHP to talk to MySQL, this formatting won't be such a problem. PHP doesn't care about fitting everything into a nice line or two. It's happy to take a big messy set of results and handle them without any problems.

If you like, take some time to insert a few more rows of users, and play with SELECT. If you want to get really fancy, try using a *WHERE* clause, like this:

```
mysql> SELECT facebook_url
    ->    FROM users
    ->   WHERE first_name = 'Mike';
+-------------------------------------------------+
| facebook_url                                    |
+-------------------------------------------------+
| http://www.facebook.com/profile.php?id=699186223 |
+-------------------------------------------------+
1 row in set (0.00 sec)
```

Don't worry if you don't completely understand *WHERE* yet. Just get a feel for it, play around, and see just how far you can get with all the SQL you've already picked up.

POWER USERS' CLINIC

SQL or MySQL? They're Not the Same

It's one thing to know what SQL stands for, and how to install MySQL. But it's something else altogether to know the difference between SQL and MySQL. Ask around at your local water cooler: You'd be surprised how many beginning programmers are not sure what the difference is between SQL the language, and MySQL the database program.

SQL is in fact a language. It's something that exists separately from MySQL or any other database, like PostgreSQL or Oracle. That means that SQL can change, or be updated, without your database automatically changing. In fact, the way it usually works is that SQL gets a new keyword or instruction, and then all the database programs release new versions to support that new keyword. Of course, SQL has been around for a long time, so this sort of thing doesn't happen a lot.

MySQL is a database program. It lets you create and work with databases, and those databases accept SQL commands. There are other database programs that don't accept SQL, and that doesn't make them any more or less SQL. In fact, MySQL could stop accepting SQL commands, and still be a database program (although the name wouldn't make much sense anymore).

If you can keep the difference between SQL and MySQL in your head, you're ahead of the game. That's because when you work with your PHP, you're connecting to a MySQL database, but you're writing SQL commands and queries. As a result, you can change to another database, and almost all of your SQL will work, as long as that database accepts SQL. That's the beauty of separating SQL from the database that you use, in this case MySQL. You can change one—moving to PostgreSQL or Oracle—without having to rewrite all your code.

Now, notice that the previous paragraph says *almost* all your SQL will keep working. Each database adds its own twists to how it implements the SQL standard. And most databases add some database-specific features to "add value." (You can read that as "to sell their product over another product.") So you can run into some problems moving from one database to another. But your understanding of SQL helps there, too. You'll be able to diagnose any issues, and quickly solve them.

So learn SQL, use MySQL, and end up with code that works on *any* SQL database.

Dynamic Web Pages

Connecting PHP to MySQL

N ow that you've seen a bit of the power both of PHP and MySQL, it's time to bring these two juggernauts together. With many programming languages, anytime you want to talk to a database, you have to download and install extra code, or install little plug-in models that give your programs support for talking to that database. PHP isn't like that though; it comes ready to connect to MySQL from the moment you run the *php* command.

Even though you've only recently begun your journey to PHP mastery, you're ready to use a database from your scripts. You just need to learn a few new commands and how to deal with the problems that can come up when you're working with a database. In fact, you're going to build a simple form that lets you enter SQL and run it against your MySQL database. When you're a PHP programmer you can go beyond the *mysql* command-line tool.

Then, to put a cherry on top of your towering sundae of PHP and MySQL goodness, you'll write another script. This script will take all the information from the forms you've built, add that information to a database, and then add one more form to let your users search for another user by name. All that in one chapter? Yes indeed.

■ Writing a Simple PHP Connection Script

No matter how simple or advanced your PHP scripts, if they talk to a database, they'll begin with the same few steps:

1. Connect to a MySQL installation.

2. *USE* the right MySQL database.

3. Send SQL to the database.

4. Get the results back.

5. Do something with the results.

Steps 3, 4, and 5 will change depending on what you're doing. A script that creates tables looks a little different from a script that searches through existing tables.

But those first couple of steps—connecting to MySQL and using the right database—are always the same, no matter how fancy your script. Just think, then: the code you're about to write is the same code that programmers making $150 or $200 an hour are writing somewhere. (They're just writing that code in much fancier houses with robots serving them iced tea as they lounge by the pool.)

Connecting to a MySQL Database

First, you have to tell your PHP script how to connect to a database. This process is basically telling PHP to do what you did when you started up your MySQL command-line client (page 69). When you connected to your web server's database, you probably used a command like the followng:

```
bmclaugh@akila:~$ mysql --host=dc2-mysql-02.kattare.com
                        --user=bmclaugh --password
```

You need those same pieces of information to give PHP so it can connect: your database host, your username, and a password.

Fire up your text editor and create a new script; call it *connect.php*. This script will be as simple as possible, because all you need it to do is connect to your database, *USE* the right database, and then run a sample SQL query to make sure things are working correctly.

In your script, type the following lines:

```
<?php
  mysql_connect("your.database.host",
               "your-username", "your-password")
    or die("<p>Error connecting to database: " .
          mysql_error() . "</p>");

  echo "<p>Connected to MySQL!</p>";
?>
```

> **NOTE** If you're running your database on the same machine as your PHP and web-serving files, your database hostname is usually *localhost*. *localhost* is just a way to say "the local machine."

It's really that simple! And like most of the other PHP scripts you've been writing, although there are some new commands, you probably already know almost exactly what's going on here.

First, there's a new command: *mysql_connect*. This command simply takes in a database host, a username, and a password, and connects. It's exactly as if you're running your *mysql* tool and connecting to a remote database.

NOTE Make sure you change *your.database.host*, *your-username*, and *your-password* to the values for your own database.

But what about the *die* bit? Sounds a little gruesome (like *Lord of the Flies* gruesome, not *Twilight* teen-angst gruesome). In fact, it is a bit nasty: you use *die* when something *may* go wrong in your script. Think of *die* as saying, "If my code dies, then do something less nasty than tossing out an error code to my user. In this case, *die* prints an error message that won't scare off your users.

But before you can understand *die*, you have to know a little bit about the inner workings of *mysql_connect*. When *mysql_connect* runs, it either creates or reuses an existing connection to your database. It then returns that connection to your PHP program, and makes available all the other PHP-to-MySQL commands you'll learn about soon. But if *mysql_connect* can't create that connection—for example, if your database isn't running or you've got a bad host or username—*mysql_connect* returns a very different value: *false*.

So what's really happening in your script is something like this:

```php
<?php
  // This isn't working code, but you get the idea
  if (i_can_connect_to_mysql_with("my.database.host",
                              "my-username", "my-password"))
    go_do_cool_database_stuff();
  else
    send_error_to_user_using_die
?>
```

But that's a lot of typing, so PHP lets you shorten it to the following:

```php
<?php
  mysql_connect("your.database.host",
              "your-username", "your-password")
    or die("<p>Error connecting to database: " .
          mysql_error() . "</p>");

  echo "<p>Connected to MySQL!</p>";
?>
```

Not only is this script shorter, but it flips things around a bit. It basically says, try to connect (using *mysql_connect*), and if the result isn't true (the *or* part of the code), then *die*. *die* prints out an error message, but it also "dies." In other words, it ends your script. So if *mysql_connect* returns *false*, and *die* runs, your script will exit. Your users won't ever see the "Connected to MySQL!" line because the script will have stopped running. It's dead on the server room floor, in search of a working database connection. (See the box on page 96 for more detail on the *die* command.)

Not only that, but *mysql_connect* sets up another function when it can't connect. It makes the errors it ran into in trying to connect available through another command, *mysql_error*. So you can call *mysql_error* as part of your *die* statement to show what really happened.

NOTE Technically, *mysql_connect*, *mysql_error*, and *die* are all examples of *functions*. A function is a block of code, usually with a name assigned to it, which you can call from your own code anytime you need that block. It's a lot quicker and better to call a function by name than to rewrite the block of code that function represents over and over again.

Don't worry about functions for now, though. Just use them like any old PHP command. Before long, not only will you understand functions better, but you'll be writing your own.

If *mysql_connect* connects without any problems, it returns that connection. PHP will skip the *die* line, and then execute this line:

```
echo "<p>Connected to MySQL!</p>";
```

To see this command in action, create a simple HTML form, and call it *connect.html*. You can use this HTML to get you going:

```
<html>
<head>
 <link href="../css/phpMM.css" rel="stylesheet" type="text/css" />
</head>

<body>
 <div id="header"><h1>PHP & MySQL: The Missing Manual</h1></div>
 <div id="example">Example 4-1</div>

 <div id="content">
   <h1>SQL Connection test</h1>
   <form action="scripts/connect.php" method="POST">
     <fieldset class="center">
       <input type="submit" value="Connect to MySQL" />
     </fieldset>
   </form>
 </div>
```

```
        <div id="footer"></div>
    </body>
</html>
```

This script is about as simple as it gets: it builds a form, drops a single button into place, and attaches that button to your new *connect.php* script. Load up your form in a browser (see Figure 4-1), and click "Connect to MySQL."

Hopefully, you see one of the simplest, happiest messages of your burgeoning PHP and MySQL programming career: you're connected! Check out Figure 4-2 for the sweet sight of success.

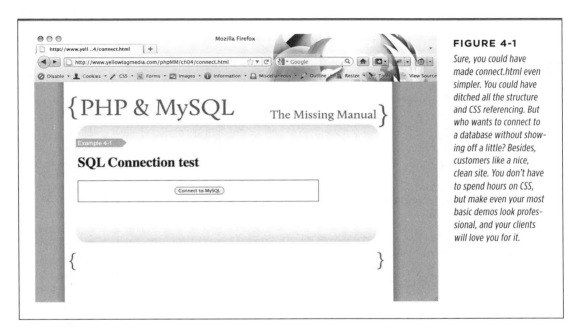

FIGURE 4-1

Sure, you could have made connect.html even simpler. You could have ditched all the structure and CSS referencing. But who wants to connect to a database without showing off a little? Besides, customers like a nice, clean site. You don't have to spend hours on CSS, but make even your most basic demos look professional, and your clients will love you for it.

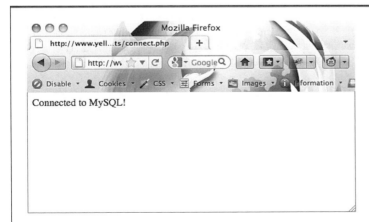

FIGURE 4-2

These three words mean that your PHP script now can do virtually anything you can imagine with your database. But there's something missing: how does MySQL know which database is yours? You still need to tell PHP which database to USE.

Selecting the Database to *USE*

There's something wonderful waiting around the programming corner now: almost all the *mysql_* family of functions works the same: you give them some values, and they return something useful. If something bad happens, you usually get back either *false* or a nonexistent object (something most programmers call *null* or *nil*).

So now you need to tell MySQL which database your PHP script wants to use. There's a function for that: *mysql_select_db*.

> **NOTE** There's an extended family of *mysql_* functions. You might want to bookmark their documentation page: *www.php.net/manual/en/ref.mysql.php*. If you ever get stuck, head over there and see if a function might do what you need.

POWER USERS' CLINIC

Everybody Dies at Some Point

It's frighteningly easy to forget to add those *die* statements to your PHP scripts. PHP doesn't require them, so it's perfectly happy to accept something like this:

```
mysql_connect("database.host.com",
    "username", "password");
```

That's the same code you've already written, except it just leaves off the *die* part.

But here's the thing: leave off that *die*, and when something goes wrong, your script is going to crash and provide something that's either a really useless error, or something so cryptic that you can't even tell *what* it is. For example, if you leave out *die*, and enter a wrong password, and run your script, you'll get an error similar to the following:

```
Can't connect to local MySQL server
    through socket '/tmp/mysql.sock' (2)
```

Believe it or not, this error message is actually a pretty informative one, as things go with missing *die* statements. Adding that one line of error handling can make a huge difference for a user when things go wrong.

In fact, as you begin to build much bigger, full-blown web applications, you might redirect your user to a nicely formatted error page, complete with contact information for an administrator and a CSS-styled error report. But none of that is possible without *die*.

Now, flush with PHP power, you may already think you make very few errors. You may think that *die* is for rank amateurs who don't write flawless code. Unfortunately, when you're up at 2 AM trying to hit a deadline so you can get paid, your brain starts to resemble, well...that of a rank amateur. Everyone makes mistakes, and *die* (along with other error handling techniques) is one of those lifesavers that helps you look prepared and professional when those inevitable mistakes do occur.

In fact, the highest-end, highest-paid programmers in the world are error-handling gurus. At the same time, they're probably *not* using *die*. They're more likely to use a more robust error-handling system; something like the error handling you'll use in Chapter 7. For now, though, a healthy and liberal use of *die* will help you get used to adding in a form of error handling.

You give *mysql_select_db* a database name, and—you guessed it—it *USEs* that database, or returns *false*. So update *connect.php* to *USE* the right database:

```php
<?php
  mysql_connect("your.database.host",
                "your-username", "your-password")
    or die("<p>Error connecting to database: " .
          mysql_error() . "</p>");

  echo "<p>Connected to MySQL!</p>";

  mysql_select_db("your-database-name")
    or die("<p>Error selecting the database bmclaugh: " .
          mysql_error() . "</p>");

  echo "<p>Connected to MySQL, using database bmclaugh.</p>";
?>
```

You should already see the pattern. *die* makes sure that if bad things happen, your script reports an error, your users read that error, and then the script exits. If things do go well, another happy message should get printed.

Try this new version out. Visit *connect.html* again and try and connect (and now *USE*) your database. You want to see something like Figure 4-3. Next up: talking SQL to your database.

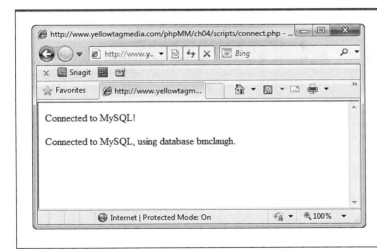

FIGURE 4-3

Once again, a few simple words, and major things are going on behind the scenes. Your script now has a connection to MySQL, and is USEing the right database.

SHOW Your Database's Tables

Now that you've got a connection, and you're tied in to the right database, you should see just what you've got to work with. In your MySQL tool, one of the first things you did was see what tables existed, and then start creating tables of your own. There's some more work to do in creating tables, and you'll do that in a bit, with a new HTML form and a new script.

But before diving into that, you can easily have your script see which tables are available in your database. Open up *connect.php* again, and add the following line:

```php
<?php
  // All your existing database connection code

  $result = mysql_query("SHOW TABLES;");
?>
```

Here's another new PHP-to-MySQL function: *mysql_query*. You'll become very, *very* familiar with this one; it's the key to passing SQL in to your database. This function takes in SQL, and you've given it some really simple SQL:

```
SHOW TABLES;
```

This command is *exactly* like typing SQL into your command-line tool.

■ HANDLING ERRORS BY SEEING IF YOUR RESULTS ARE *NOT*

But what about *die*? What about error handling? There's none of that, and by now, you know there should be. But there's something different about this line: whatever comes back from *mysql_query* is stuffed into a variable called *$result*.

So it's really *$result* that you want to examine. It should either have a list of tables, from *SHOW TABLES*, or it's reporting an error of some sort. And if it's reporting an error, then *$result* is false, because the *mysql_* functions return false when there's a problem.

You know how to check for a false value, though, so you can add this code to handle problems:

```php
<?php
  // All your existing database connection code

  $result = mysql_query("SHOW TABLES;");

  if ($result === false) {
    die("<p>Error in listing tables: " . mysql_error() . "</p>");
  }
?>
```

Now, this works, but it's really not how most PHP programmers do things. The === is a fairly unusual thing to use in PHP, at least for checking to see whether a variable is false. What's more common—and the way it's usually done in PHP—is to use the negation operator (also called the bang operator), which is an exclamation point: *!*. So if you want to see if a variable called *$some-variable* is false, you can say *if (!$some-variable)*. And that *!* says something like, "see whether *$some-variable* is false."

Even better, think of *!* as being "not." So what you really want to say in your code is, "If *not $result*, then die." Accordingly, you can rewrite your code to look like this:

```php
<?php
  // All your existing database connection code

  $result = mysql_query("SHOW TABLES;");

  if (!$result) {
    die("<p>Error in listing tables: " . mysql_error() . "</p>");
  }
?>
```

This kind of code is much better PHP, and now you've got any problems covered.

NOTE   It may seem weird to hear about "the way it's done in PHP." If code works, then it works, right? Well, yes...but have you ever heard someone who's just learning English speak? Often, their words are correct, but the order, usage, and idiom are wrong. Try and explain why more than one sheep is still just "sheep," and you've got the idea.

Programming languages are the same. There's writing code that works, and there's writing code that looks like you know the language. Sometimes this is called being *eloquent*. There are actually some great books for "speaking properly" in JavaScript and Ruby called *Eloquent JavaScript* (Marijn Haverbeke; No Starch Press) and *Eloquent Ruby* (Russ Olsen; Addison Wesley). It's worth learning not just how to write working PHP, but to write PHP that looks natural.

In fact, just to make sure your code deals with errors, change your SQL query to have a misspelling:

```php
<?php
  // All your existing database connection code

  $result = mysql_query("SHOWN TABLES;");

  if (!$result) {
    die("<p>Error in listing tables: " . mysql_error() . "</p>");
  }
?>
```

Now load up *connect.html* in a browser, and run your connection test. Figure 4-4 is similar to what you should see: still a little cryptic, but clearly a case where your code realized there was a problem and handled it with an error message rather than a massive meltdown.

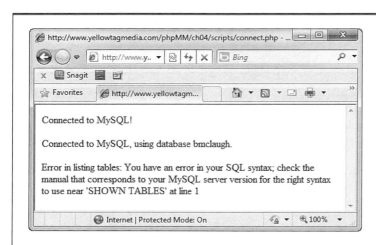

FIGURE 4-4

Deal with errors every step along the way. The better you handle errors, and the more specific your messages are, the easier it is to figure out what's gone wrong with your code. That means code that works well for your users, and that you can easily fix when bugs crop up.

■ PRINTING OUT YOUR SQL RESULTS

Errors are handled, problems are reported, and now you can finally deal with what's actually in *$result* when things don't go wrong. Unfortunately, things get a little trickier here. *$result* is actually not a PHP type you've used, or even one that you'll need to learn how to work with directly. It's something called a *resource*, which is PHP-speak for a special variable that's related to something outside of PHP.

Think about it like this: In the case of *mysql_query*, you've asked for the SQL results from running the query *SHOW TABLES*. But while PHP can talk to MySQL, it really doesn't know how to interpret SQL. So it can't know that *$result* should hold a list of rows, each of which with one value: a table name. All it knows is that something else—your MySQL database—is getting a query through the *mysql_query* function. And think about it: depending on what query you pass *mysql_query*, *$result* might hold rows with multiple pieces of information, like a first name and Facebook URL, or just an indication of whether a *CREATE TABLE* statement worked or not.

So in these cases, you usually end up with a PHP resource. That resource means *something*; it's just that PHP doesn't really know what that something is. So your PHP needs help. What it needs is something that knows about MySQL and can figure out how to work with *$result*. That's exactly what you get with another MySQL function, *mysql_fetch_row*. You pass this function in a resource returned from *mysql_query*, and it lets you cycle through each row in the results returned from your SQL query.

Here's the basic pattern:

1. Write your SQL query, and store it in a string or a variable.

2. Pass your query into *mysql_query* and get back a PHP resource.

3. Pass that resource into *mysql_fetch_row* to get back rows of results, one at a time.

4. Cycle through those rows and pull out the information you need.

5. Buy a really nice guitar with all the cash you're making.

NOTE That last step is optional, but highly recommended.

You've got a resource in *$result*, so now pass it in to *mysql_fetch_row*, like this:

```php
<?php
  // All your existing database connection code

  $result = mysql_query("SHOW TABLES;");

  if (!$result) {
    die("<p>Error in listing tables: " . mysql_error() . "</p>");
  }

  echo "<p>Tables in database:</p>";
  echo "<ul>";
  while ($row = mysql_fetch_row($result)) {
    // Do something with $row
  }
  echo "</ul>";

?>
```

WARNING If you changed your SQL to *SHOWN TABLES* to produce an error as described on page 99, be sure and change it back to working SQL: *SHOW TABLES*.

Even though PHP doesn't know what to do with the resource returned from *mysql_query*, *mysql_fetch_row* does. It takes in your *$result* resource and starts spitting out rows, one at a time, in an array.

And then there's that *while* loop, which is also new, but probably makes sense to you already. A *while* loop continues to loop as long as something is true. In this case, the loop keeps looping while *$row*—which is the next row of results from your SQL query—is getting a value from *mysql_fetch_row($result)*. When there are no more result rows, *mysql_fetch_row* doesn't return anything, so *$row* is empty, and the *while* loop says, "Ok, I'm done. I'll stop looping now."

And, you've got a nice unordered list (*ul*) ready to spit out each row, so there's just one thing left to add:

```php
<?php
  // All your existing database connection code

  $result = mysql_query("SHOW TABLES;");

  if (!$result) {
    die("<p>Error in listing tables: " . mysql_error() . "</p>");
  }

  echo "<p>Tables in database:</p>";
  echo "<ul>";
  while ($row = mysql_fetch_row($result)) {
    echo "<li>Table: {$row[0]}</li>";
  }
  echo "</ul>";

?>
```

This code should start looking familiar again. Each time *mysql_fetch_row* returns *$row*, it's actually returning an array, something you've see before (page 46). That array has all the different pieces of information from your SQL query. For *SHOW TABLES*, that's just one thing, at *$row[0]*: the table name. Pretty soon, you'll write some more complex queries, and you may need to grab the value in *$row[1]* or *$row[2]* or even *$row [10]*.

So in this case, you get back *$row*, you grab the table name by getting the first item in the array, at index 0, and then you print that with *echo*. There's just one other wrinkle here: those curly braces inside the string passed to echo. What's up with those?

Well, you could rewrite this line like this:

```php
  while ($row = mysql_fetch_row($result)) {
    echo "<li>Table: " . $row[0] . "</li>";
  }
```

Nothing wrong there, except all the extra quotation marks and period to stick strings together.

NOTE Major nerd points if you remembered that mashing strings together was called concatenation (page 33).

But PHP is pretty savvy, and the folks that wrote the language are programmers, too. They realized, like you, that you're constantly having to drop variables into the middle of strings. So instead of constantly ending a string and adding a variable, you can just wrap a variable inside of { }, and PHP will print the value of that variable instead of "$row[0]". It makes for a lot simpler code, and that's a good thing.

Save *connect.php*, revisit *connect.html* in your browser, and see what tables you've got in your database. Figure 4-5 is *connect.php* running against a database with a lot of tables. You may just have one or two, and that's fine. Just make sure you see a list of your tables.

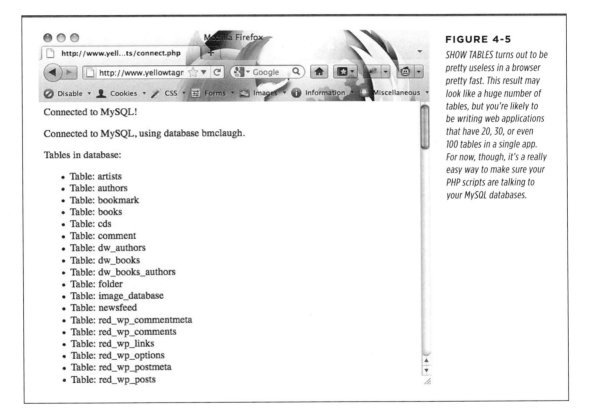

FIGURE 4-5

SHOW TABLES turns out to be pretty useless in a browser pretty fast. This result may look like a huge number of tables, but you're likely to be writing web applications that have 20, 30, or even 100 tables in a single app. For now, though, it's a really easy way to make sure your PHP scripts are talking to your MySQL databases.

Cleaning Up Your Code with Multiple Files

Even if you don't realize it yet, there's something problematic about your *connect. php* script. Look at the first few MySQL calls you make:

```php
<?php
  mysql_connect("your.database.host",
                "your-username", "your-password")
    or die("<p>Error connecting to database: " .
          mysql_error() . "</p>");

  echo "<p>Connected to MySQL!</p>";

  mysql_select_db("your-database-name")
    or die("<p>Error selecting the database bmclaugh: " .
          mysql_error() . "</p>");

  echo "<p>Connected to MySQL, using database bmclaugh.</p>";

  // And so on...
?>
```

You're manually typing your database host, your username, your password, and your database name into your script. Now suppose you have 10 scripts and you're typing that 10 times. The chance of a typo is pretty high.

Not only that, what happens when you change your password? Or you upgrade to a better hosting plan to handle all the web traffic your apps are generating, and you need to change your database host? You've got to track down every place you put that information, in every PHP script. That's a nightmare, and keeps you from actually writing new code and making more cash. Not good.

You need a way to *abstract out* those pieces of information. Abstraction is a programming term that means hiding the implementation, the way something (like a password) works, from the programs that uses it. You basically have a symbol, or a name, and that name refers to something else with a lot more detail. And even if that detail changes, the name still points to the right thing.

It's like saying "Leigh," and meaning my wife, without having to say, "that hot 34-year old woman with short blond hair and great legs." And the beauty of "Leigh" is that every birthday, you can keep saying, "Leigh," instead of changing your description.

Replacing Hand-Typed Values with Variables

So suppose you want your code to look more like this (actually, you really *do* want it to look more like this):

```php
<?php
  mysql_connect($database_host, $username, $password)
    or die("<p>Error connecting to database: " .
          mysql_error() . "</p>");

  echo "<p>Connected to MySQL!</p>";
```

```
mysql_select_db($database_name)
  or die("<p>Error selecting the database bmclaugh: " .
      mysql_error() . "</p>");

echo "<p>Connected to MySQL, using database bmclaugh.</p>";

// And so on...
?>
```

All you're doing is writing something that looks a bit like a variable in place of hand-typing the username or database name. Now you can define those variables up above your connection code:

```
<?php
$database_host = "your.database.host";
$username = "your-username";
$password = "your-password";
$database_name = "your-database-name";

// Database connection code
?>
```

But is this really that much better? Not yet; you've still got these same values hand-typed into your script. You want to stick the values in a file so no human has to type them. Read on.

Abstracting Important Values into a Separate File

Your goal is to get these values out of *connect.php*, into some place that all your PHP scripts can access them with no typing from you. Open up a new file, and call it *app_config.php*. Now drop your variables into this new file:

```
<?php
// Database connection constants
$database_host = "your.database.host";
$username = "your-username";
$password = "your-password";
$database_name = "your-database-name";

?>
```

NOTE   Be sure and save *app_config.php* somewhere that makes sense for all your application's scripts to access it. In this book's examples, *app_config.php* is in the root of the site, under *scripts/*. So if you're in the *ch04/ scripts/* directory, you'd access this file at *../../scripts/app_config.php*, or *[site_root]/scripts/app_config.php*. You can save the file wherever you want, as long as you get the path right in your PHP scripts that reference it.

When you move to a production version of your application, you probably want to place this file outside of the site root. That way, web users can't simply type the path to your configuration script and get all your passwords. Alternatively, you could add security to this directory, although simply getting it out of the web-serving directories altogether is usually easiest.

Now, you can have all your different PHP scripts use these shared variables. Change a variable here in *app_config.php*, and that change affects all your PHP scripts that use these shared variables.

But how do you actually access these variables? Go back to *connect.php*, and remove where you defined these variables yourself. If you try and access *connect.php* through *connect.html* now, though, you'll get a nasty error, as shown in see Figure 4-6.

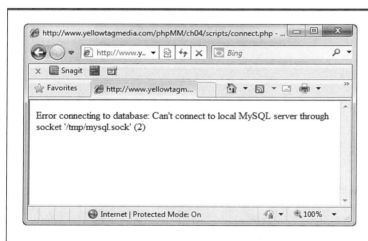

FIGURE 4-6

You defined your variables in app_config. php, *but* connect.php *doesn't know this. You need to tell your connection script that it shouldn't run until it loads* app_config.php. *Then things will behave, because the variables* connect.php *uses will be set properly.*

The error occurs because *connect.php* now has no idea what *$username* or *$password* refers to. You need to inform PHP that before it tries to do anything in *connect.php*, it's required to load *app_config.php*. And that's (almost) exactly what you type in your script:

```php
<?php

require '../../scripts/app_config.php';

// Database connection code
?>
```

Now, PHP loads the file *../../scripts/app_config.php before* it runs your *mysql_connect* function. In effect, *require* says, "Hey PHP, if you can't load the file I'm giving, then throw a nasty error, because nothing else is going to work."

WARNING Make sure the path and filename you give *require* matches where you actually put *app_config. php*, or you'll see the error that *require* produces up close and personal.

Try and run your connection script again, and you should see your table listing, which means things are working well again.

Require or Include?

There's another command in PHP that's very similar to *require*: *include*. *include* does exactly what *require* does in terms of telling PHP to load another file. The difference is that if that file can't be loaded, *include* just issues a warning and lets PHP keep running the later commands in your script. In other words, *require* completely shuts things down, but *include* lets your script keep going.

But here's the thing. Are you *really* going to bother including a file if you don't need that file? In most cases, probably not. And you're including that file because you need it; you *require* that file to run. So in almost every situation, you should use *require* to grab another file, not *include*. If something goes wrong, you want to know about it. You don't want the rest of your code running, because it's probably just going to error out anyway.

Variables Vary, But Constants Stay Constant

There's just one more nagging little problem with your code: you're still using variables for your username and password, along with the database host and database name. And what's a variable? Something that varies or changes. Accordingly, PHP happily lets you write the following code in *connect.php*:

```
mysql_connect($database_host, $username, $password)
    or die("<p>Error connecting to database: " . mysql_error() . "</p>");

// This is allowed, but some bad mojo
$password = "hijinks";
```

So what happens when some other script—which also requires *app_config.php*—tries to connect with *mysql_connect*? It's going to use *$password*, but now *$password* isn't correct anymore. It's set to "hijinks," and chaos will ensue.

What you really want is for those values in *app_config.php* to be constant, and never change. You can do this with the special *define* function. Open up *app_config.php* and change your code:

```
<?php
// Database connection constants
define("DATABASE_HOST", "your.database.host");
define("DATABASE_USERNAME", "your-username");
define("DATABASE_PASSWORD", "your-password");
define("DATABASE_NAME", "your-database-name");
?>
```

You define the name of a constant and the value for that constant, and PHP creates a new constant. That way, you can type *DATABASE_HOST* into your code, and PHP *really* sees "your.database.host". Perfect! And since this is a constant, it can't be changed anywhere along the line.

Constants are typed in all-uppercase letters. Caps aren't required, but it's another one of those "speak like a PHP programmer" things. You want constants to look different from variables, and using all uppercase names is one way to do that. Constants also don't have the *$* before their name, which is yet another way to differentiate a constant from a variable.

Now you need to make some quick changes to *connect.php* to use these new capitalized names of constants:

```php
<?php
  require '../../scripts/app_config.php';

  mysql_connect(DATABASE_HOST, DATABASE_USERNAME, DATABASE_PASSWORD)
    or die("<p>Error connecting to database: " .
          mysql_error() . "</p>");

  echo "<p>Connected to MySQL!</p>";

  mysql_select_db(DATABASE_NAME)
    or die("<p>Error selecting the database " . DATABASE_NAME .
          mysql_error() . "</p>");

  echo "<p>Connected to MySQL, using database " . DATABASE_NAME . "</p>";

  // SQL query-running goodness proceeds...
?>
```

> **WARNING** You can't use the { } inside your quotes to print constants. It's only when you surround a variable (which starts with *$*) with { } that PHP prints the value of that variable. Instead, use the normal string concatenation approach where you end your string and add the constants using the dot (.), as discussed on page 33.

Try *connect.php* again. You should get a perfectly good list of table names. But this time, you've got constants for your important information, safely tucked away in a file separated out of *connect.php*.

> **NOTE** It's also a good idea to add some additional security to *app_config.php*, and any other scripts that contain special values like passwords. You can set the permissions on the file to be more restrictive, or move the file to some place your PHP script can access, but your web users can't. Ask your web or server admin for help if you're not sure how to do that.

Start Small, Add Small, Finish Small

You may be wondering why you couldn't have just started with *app_config.php*, and the completed, working version of *connect.php*. Or, at a minimum, you could have just dropped all the database connection code into *connect.php* at once, and then done the printing code all at once. Isn't that how real developers write code?

Well, yes and no. Lots of developers do write code like that. They type 10 or 20 or 50 lines of code into their script, and then try it out. Lots of things will break, because developers type too fast and make mistakes. But then they'll fix each problem, one by one by one. And for lots of developers, that's just fine.

But here's the thing: that's not a very efficient way of working. On top of that, you're usually focused on the last step (like printing out the tables), and so you may not spend much time figuring out the best way to handle the in-between steps. You might not use *{ }* to simplify the statement that prints *$row[0]*, or you may skip a *die* because you're thinking about HTML output, not handling the case where the database password isn't right.

The best developers work on really, really small chunks of code at a time. They test that code, and then they move on to something else. In fact—and this goes a bit beyond this book,

but it's still important—a lot of really elite developers actually write tests *before* they write anything else. They write those tests, and the tests obviously fail, because they haven't written any code. Then they write just enough code to pass their test, and then they write another test.

This method may not make much sense at first. Why write tests for code that doesn't exist? Here's what's really nuts: often, this approach results in more test code than actual application code! It's a lot of work, and it's all based on the idea that you should write just enough code to get one thing working at a time.

But here's the big reveal, and why these elite developers are elite: this test-first approach results in better code. Working small, from start to finish, means you're focusing on one thing, and doing that one thing really well. You aren't rushing on to something else. And that means what you're working on is solid and works. This approach does take more time in the beginning, but it results in rock-solid code that breaks a lot less often.

So take your time, and work small. Your code will be better, and your customers will love you because your code is still running while they're on the phone trying to get help with a broken app from "the other guys."

■ Building a Basic SQL Query Runner

Now that you can connect to SQL, you're ready to take on something more ambitious: building your own version of a MySQL command-line tool. Of course, you're a PHP developer and programmer now, so mentally scratch out "command-line" and replace it with "web-based."

It turns out that you've already got most of the tools you need. You can easily build an HTML form that lets you and your users enter in a SQL query, you know how to connect to MySQL and select a database, and you can run a query. All that's left is to figure out how to interpret that PHP resource that *mysql_query* returns when it's not a list of table names.

Creating an HTML Form with a Big Empty Box

Before getting to *mysql_query* and its results, though, start with what you know: an HTML form. Keep things simple for now, and just create a form with a single text area into which you can type queries, and a few basic buttons.

Open up your text editor, and create *queryRunner.html*:

```
<html>
 <head>
  <link href="../css/phpMM.css" rel="stylesheet" type="text/css" />
 </head>

 <body>
  <div id="header"><h1>PHP & MySQL: The Missing Manual</h1></div>
  <div id="example">Example 4-2</div>

  <div id="content">
    <h1>SQL Query Runner</h1>
    <p>Enter your SQL query in the box below:</p>
    <form action="scripts/run_query.php" method="POST">
      <fieldset>
        <textarea id="query_text" name="query"
                  cols="65" rows="8"></textarea>
      </fieldset>
      <br />
      <fieldset class="center">
        <input type="submit" value="Run Query" />
        <input type="reset" value="Clear and Restart" />
      </fieldset>
    </form>
  </div>

  <div id="footer"></div>
 </body>
</html>
```

Fire up your favorite browser, and make sure things look like Figure 4-7.

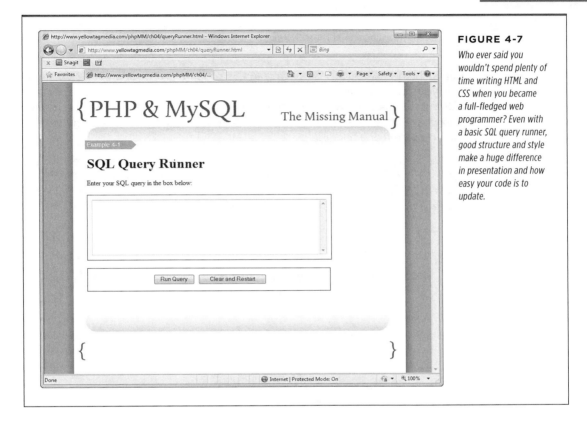

FIGURE 4-7

Who ever said you wouldn't spend plenty of time writing HTML and CSS when you became a full-fledged web programmer? Even with a basic SQL query runner, good structure and style make a huge difference in presentation and how easy your code is to update.

Connecting to Your Database (Again)

You know what's next: you need to connect to MySQL and then *USE* your database. This code should be pretty familiar by now; open up *run_query.php* and go to work:

```php
<?php
require '../../scripts/app_config.php';

mysql_connect(DATABASE_HOST, DATABASE_USERNAME, DATABASE_PASSWORD)
  or die("<p>Error connecting to database: " .
       mysql_error() . "</p>");

echo "<p>Connected to MySQL!</p>";
```

```
mysql_select_db(DATABASE_NAME)
    or die("<p>Error selecting the database " . DATABASE_NAME .
        mysql_error() . "</p>");

echo "<p>Connected to MySQL, using database " . DATABASE_NAME . "</p>";
?>
```

But wait...this *is* familiar. You've written this code before, back on page 97, and in fact, you have to write it every single time you connect to MySQL. That sort of duplication isn't good. That's why you moved your database constants into *app_config. php*: you wanted to be able to keep code that is always the same in a single place, rather than ten or a hundred places.

You've seen how easy it is to *require* a file (page 106), and pull in some constant values. You can do the same thing with your database connection code. Open up a new file, and call it *database_connection.php*. Save this new script right alongside *app_config.php*, and type the following code:

```
<?php
require 'app_config.php';

mysql_connect(DATABASE_HOST, DATABASE_USERNAME, DATABASE_PASSWORD)
    or die("<p>Error connecting to database: " .
        mysql_error() . "</p>");

echo "<p>Connected to MySQL!</p>";

mysql_select_db(DATABASE_NAME)
    or die("<p>Error selecting the database " .
        DATABASE_NAME . mysql_error() . "</p>");

echo "<p>Connected to MySQL, using database " .
    DATABASE_NAME . ".</p>";
?>
```

NOTE   Make sure your path to *app_config.php* matches where you stored that file. If you're saving *database_connection.php* in the same directory as *app_config.php*, you just need the file name, without any directory paths.

Now you've got all your database code tucked nicely away, which means you can radically overhaul *run_query.php*:

```
<?php
require '../../scripts/database_connection.php';
?>
```

How's that for short code? Also notice that you no longer have a reason to require *app_config.php*. Your script requires *database_connection.php*, and it's *database_connection.php* that handles bringing in *app_config.php*. Your code is much nicer and neater now.

Just to make sure this works, you should visit your *queryRunner.html* page and click Run Query. You should get something like Figure 4-8—all without anything but a single *require* in your main script!

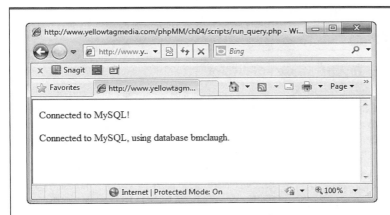

FIGURE 4-8

It may seem strange to write a script that (at least so far) does nothing more than require another script. Actually, the more comfortable you get coding, the more you'll favor this sort of reuse. You want to write just enough new code to get the job done. If you can reuse 100, or 1,000, lines of existing code, then you should.

Running Your User's SQL Query (Again)

At this point, you finally get to combine what you know about PHP and what you know about SQL. You already have anything the user puts into the big text area on your form through the *$REQUEST* variable, which as you remember is an array (page 46). And you also can use *mysql_query* to run a query.

You just need to put those two things together:

```php
<?php
require '../../scripts/database_connection.php';

$query_text = $_REQUEST['query'];
$result = mysql_query($query_text);

if (!$result) {
  die("<p>Error in executing the SQL query " . $query_text . ": " .
      mysql_error() . "</p>");
}

echo "<p>Results from your query:</p>";
echo "<ul>";
```

```
    while ($row = mysql_fetch_row($result)) {
      echo "<li>{$row[0]}</li>";
    }
    echo "</ul>";
?>
```

Just grab the appropriate field from the input from your HTML form, pass it to *mysql_query*, and you're good to go. You can then pass in the returned PHP resource, *$result*, to an error-handling *if* statement, and finally to *mysql_fetch_row* to print out the results from the query.

Why Not Abstract Out the *mysql_query* Function?

You may have noticed that just as you are constantly connecting to MySQL—with the same username and password, over and over—and selecting a database—often the same database, over and over—you'll be calling *mysql_query*, over and over and over. So why not place that in another file, and require that file?

The reason is right there in the code you wrote on page 113: what you pass to *mysql_query* is going to change almost every time you call it. For example, in *connect.php* (page 92), you passed the query *SHOW TABLES* to it; now you're passing it a query from the form field in *queryRunner.html*. Even though you're calling *mysql_query* over and over, what you're giving that function is changing, so it's not going to help you pull out that function from your main scripts.

You could move *mysql_query* out of your main script and pass to it the part of the statement that keeps changing—the SQL query. You'd need to create a custom function that takes in your query from your main script and hands that query to *mysql_query*. Then, when *mysql_query* finished running, the custom function would need to pass back anything it returned to your main script.

That may sound like a mouthful, and a lot of work. It's actually pretty easy, though, and once you start writing your own functions—something you'll be doing in Chapter 8—you'd have no problem doing it. But what would you gain? You'd still have to pass in a query, and get back a response. You'd not actually gain anything from building your own function; it would basically replace *mysql_query*, but you wouldn't get any extra functionality, and it wouldn't add any protection from changes or anything like that to your code.

Now, before you go thinking you shouldn't worry about this sort of thing, take a minute. Thinking, "Could I pull this code out into another general file? Should I make this a custom function?" is a very good thing! You want to think like that, even if you decide—as is the case here—that it's *not* a good thing. The more you roll around new ideas and ways to approach your code, the better a programmer you'll be. So keep asking yourself these questions; just don't be afraid to answer your own questions with a, "No, that's not such a great idea in *this* case."

The script looks pretty good, so now you're ready to actually try things out.

Entering Your First Web-Based Query

You probably don't have much in your database at this point, so start by creating a new table called *urls*. Here's the SQL you'll need:

```
CREATE TABLE urls (id int, url varchar(100), description varchar(100));
```

Of course, since you've got a nice big text area, you could also spread that out:

```
CREATE TABLE urls (
  id int,
  url varchar(100),
  description varchar(100)
)
```

Either way, you want a form that looks something like Figure 4-9.

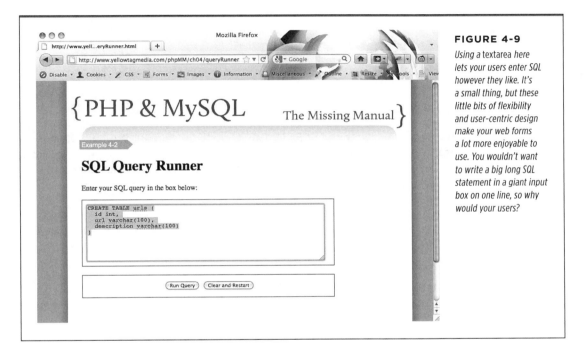

FIGURE 4-9

Using a textarea here lets your users enter SQL however they like. It's a small thing, but these little bits of flexibility and user-centric design make your web forms a lot more enjoyable to use. You wouldn't want to write a big long SQL statement in a giant input box on one line, so why would your users?

Now click Run Query. What did you get? Well, you're probably staring at a surprising screen, sort of like the one shown in Figure 4-10.

FIGURE 4-10

Sometimes the worst possible error message is not an error message. Nothing here helps you see what went wrong with your script. In cases like this, an error message would help, not cause frustration.

Well, what happened? If you want to really get confused, click the Back button on your browser, and run your *CREATE* query again. You'll see a message like the one shown in Figure 4-11.

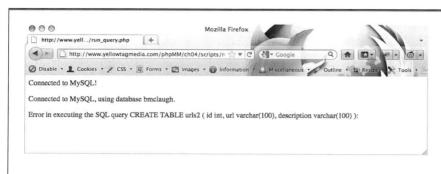

FIGURE 4-11

First, you had nothing, and now an error. What's going on? Even worse, although you know you have an error, what is the actual problem? There's still plenty of work to do here.

The first time you ran the *CREATE TABLE* query on page 81, you got nothing—no results at all. The next time, MySQL tells you the *urls* table already exists! In fact, if you hop to your command-line tool, you see that, yes, the table *does* exist in your database:

```
mysql> describe urls;
+-------------+--------------+------+-----+---------+-------+
| Field       | Type         | Null | Key | Default | Extra |
+-------------+--------------+------+-----+---------+-------+
| id          | int(11)      | YES  |     | NULL    |       |
| url         | varchar(100) | YES  |     | NULL    |       |
| description | varchar(100) | YES  |     | NULL    |       |
+-------------+--------------+------+-----+---------+-------+
3 rows in set (0.00 sec)
```

Look carefully at your code again:

```php
<?php
  require '../../scripts/database_connection.php';

  $query_text = $_REQUEST['query'];
  $result = mysql_query($query_text);

  if (!$result) {
    die("<p>Error in executing the SQL query " . $query_text . ": " .
        mysql_error() . "</p>");
  }

  echo "<p>Results from your query:</p>";
  echo "<ul>";
  while ($row = mysql_fetch_row($result)) {
```

```
    echo "<li>{$row[0]}</li>";
  }
  echo "</ul>";
?>
```

The *if (!$result)* code block is not running, so clearly *$result* came back as something other than false. But the *while* loop never ran; you never saw any results.

But wait a second. Your query was a *CREATE* query. What rows would be returned from that sort of query? There wouldn't be any rows, because you weren't asking for rows. You were just asking MySQL to create a table; in fact, a place to *put* rows.

Handling Queries That Don't *SELECT* Information

The secret here is that *mysql_query* is happy to take in a *CREATE* statement. It even does what you asked, which is why the second time you entered that query, MySQL gave you an error, saying that the *urls* table was already created. When *mysql_query* gets a CREATE statement, it returns *false* if there was an error—which your script handles—but true if there's not an error. And if there's not an error, *it doesn't return any rows*. You get a *true* value in *$result*, but nothing else. And that's where things went wrong.

When *mysql_query* gets most of the SQL statements that don't select data, like CREATE, INSERT, UPDATE, DELETE, DROP, and a few others, it just returns *true* (if things worked) or *false* (if they didn't).

NOTE   A few of those SQL commands, like *UPDATE* and *DELETE*, may look new to you. Don't worry, though. They do just what they look like they do: *UPDATE* updates information in a table, and *DELETE* removes it. And when you need to use those functions in this book, you'll get a lot more detail about exactly how to use each of them.

Fortunately, now that you know what's going on, it's not too hard to deal with the problem. You just need your script to find out whether the SQL query string the user supplied has one of these special words. If so, you must handle it differently. And it just so happens you're plenty comfortable with searching through strings.

So think this through; what you really want is something like this:

1. Grab the user's query from the HTML form.

2. Pass the query into *mysql_query*, and store the result in a variable.

3. Determine whether the result is false, which is bad no matter what type of SQL got passed in.

4. If the result is not false, see whether the query has one of the special keywords in it: CREATE, INSERT, UPDATE, DELETE, or DROP. (There are others, but these are the most common ones to check for.)

5. If the query has one of these special words, see whether the result of running the query was true, and let the user know things went well.

6. If the query does not have one of these words, try and print out the result rows like you've already been doing.

You've already got a lot of this code, so you need to only add an *if* (or maybe a few *if*s, actually), and some searching:

```
$return_rows = false;
$location = strpos($query_text, "CREATE");
if ($location === false) {
  $location = strpos($query_text, "INSERT");
  if ($location === false) {
    $location = strpos($query_text, "UPDATE");
    if ($location === false) {
      $location = strpos($query_text, "DELETE");
      if ($location === false) {
        $location = strpos($query_text, "DROP");
        if ($location === false) {
          // If we got here, it's not a CREATE, INSERT, UPDATE,
          //   DELETE, or DROP query. It should return rows.
          $return_rows = true;
        }
      }
    }
  }
}
```

> **WARNING** Be sure to use that triple-equals sign (===) in your *if* statements to check whether *$location* is *false*.

This code may appear tricky, but it's straightforward if you walk through it line by line. Basically, you have the same *if* statement, repeated over and over, with each of those having another nested *if* statement:

```
$location = strpos($query_text, "SEARCH_STRING");
if ($location === false) {
  // Try again with another SEARCH_STRING
}
```

Finally, if all the *if* statements fail, then you don't have *CREATE, INSERT, UPDATE, DELETE,* or *DROP* anywhere in the query string:

```
// This is the innermost if statement
if ($location === false) {
  // If we got here, it's not a CREATE, INSERT, UPDATE,
  //   DELETE, or DROP query. It should return rows.
  $return_rows = true;
}
```

But why is this so complex? The problem here is that you really want to search the user's query string, not just for a single matching word, like *CREATE* or *INSERT*, but for several matching words. That's a little tricky, so you've got to work with one call to *strpos* at a time.

NOTE Make sure you understand this code, but don't get too attached to it. It's really ugly, and in the next chapter, you're going to add an extremely new tool to your PHP programming kit, and rework this code to be a *lot* slimmer and sleeker.

At each step, if the search string is found, the user has put in one of those special SQL keywords that doesn't return rows, so the variable *$return_rows* is set to *false*, different from its original value, *true*.

Finally, at the end of this curly-brace love fest, the *if* statements unwind back to the main program, and either *$returns_rows* has a value of *true* because none of the searches matched, or *false* because one of them did.

Now you're ready to use *$returns_rows* to print a result:

```php
<?php
  // require and database connection code

  // run the query

  // handle errors in the result

  // see if the query has result rows or not

  if ($return_rows) {
    // We have rows to show from the query
    echo "<p>Results from your query:</p>";
    echo "<ul>";
    while ($row = mysql_fetch_row($result)) {
      echo "<li>{$row[0]}</li>";
    }
    echo "</ul>";
  } else {
    // No rows. Just report if the query ran or not
    if ($result) {
      echo "<p>Your query was processed successfully.</p>"
      echo "<p>{$query_text}</p>";
    }
  }
?>
```

NOTE   Remember that *if ($return_rows)* is just the same as *if ($return_rows === true)*. The same goes for *if ($result)*.

Most of this script is familiar. All the code you've been using to print out rows stays the same. That code just moves inside the *if ($return_rows)* block, because it only applies if the user put in something like a *SELECT* that returns (potentially) lots of results.

Then, in the *else* to that *if*, your script just reports whether or not things went OK. As an additional help, this section of the *if* prints out the original query so the user can know what was executed.

Now, technically, you don't really need that *if ($result)*. Since you tested earlier to see if *$result* is false, if your script gets to this last bit, you know that *$result* is *true*, so you can simplify things at the end a bit:

```
if ($return_rows) {
  // We have rows to show from the query
  echo "<p>Results from your query:</p>";
  echo "<ul>";
  while ($row = mysql_fetch_row($result)) {
    echo "<li>{$row[0]}</li>";
  }
  echo "</ul>";
} else {
  // No rows. Just report if the query ran or not
  echo "<p>Your query was processed successfully.</p>"
  echo "<p>{$query_text}</p>";
}
```

This script is getting to be a little long, but you know what every single line is doing at this point. Go ahead and try it out.

You probably created the *urls* table (page 116)—even though your PHP script didn't let you know that. So try entering *DROP TABLE urls;* as your SQL query. Then run your query, and this time, you should get a helpful message back, specific to your rowless query, as you can see in Figure 4-12.

Dealing with Humans

Unfortunately, there's still a problem in one of the lines in the code in the previous section. Right now, if your user types the following query, what happens?

```
DROP TABLE urls;
```

Your set of *if* statements understands that *DROP* is part of the query, realizes it has no return rows, and does the right thing: reports that the query either ran without problems, or that an error occurred.

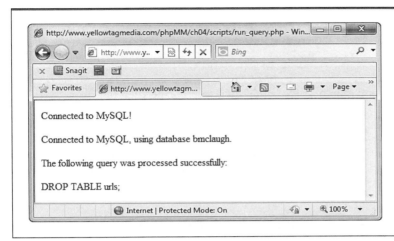

FIGURE 4-12

Now run_query.php, *as shown on page 119, figures out whether it's been passed a query with one of the keywords that indicates there aren't any return rows. The message when things go well is still a little terse, but at least there's no blank space from trying to show result rows when there aren't any result rows to show.*

But what about this query? Do you see where the problem is?

```
drop table urls;
```

Here's the statement that should indicate a match:

```
$location = strpos($query_text, "DROP");
if ($location === false) {
  // this should return true, and so there are no return rows
}
```

But that line searches for *DROP*, which doesn't match "drop" at all. *strpos* searches for strings, but it sees a lowercase letter, like "d", as a different letter from an uppercase "D". So that search finds "DROP" but not "drop" or "dRoP".

And, as always, you've got humans using your app, not robots. You can't just assume that those humans will be good SQL citizens and always use capital letters. You could put a little message on the form: *Please type your SQL in all capital letters,* but humans will be humans, and they tend to ignore instructions like this.

You'll spend *at least* as much of your time dealing with the human factor in your code as writing code that handles the so-called normal flow of operation. In fact, once you add real people to your line of thinking, you'll realize that "normal" isn't a very useful concept. Instead, your code simply has to deal with as many possibilities as you can imagine (and some you can't).

Fixing the lowercase and uppercase issue turns out to be fairly simple: you can sim-ply convert *$query_string* to all capital letters before starting to search through it:

```
$return_rows = false;
$query_text = strtoupper($query_text);
$location = strpos($query_text, "CREATE");
// All the nested if blocks.
```

Now, if a user types *drop table urls* or *DROP table UrLS*, the search string is *DROP TABLE URLS*, and searching for "DROP" will return a match.

But there's another problem! Before you read on, see if you can figure out what it is.

> **NOTE** Yes, there really are this many wrinkles and problems with just one simple program. That's why there are lots of programmers, but so few really great programmers: the difference is handling all these little details without throwing your iPhone through a nearby wall.

Avoid Changing User Input Whenever Possible

To spot this potential problem with your query script, take a look at the last bit of your code that's run if the user enters a rowless query like DROP or INSERT:

```
// No rows. Just report if the query ran or not
echo "<p>Your query was processed successfully.</p>"
echo "<p>{$query_text}</p>";
```

Run this code, and you'll get something like you see in Figure 4-13.

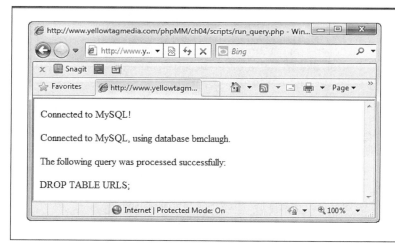

FIGURE 4-13

Sometimes the best problem you can solve is the problem that hasn't yet occurred. Look closely at the SQL query here, and compare it to the query in Figure 4-12. This sort of tedious detective work takes hours, but it's absolutely critical for getting web applications to work in the real world.

Carefully compare the code in Figure 4-12 and Figure 4-13. In Figure 4-13, you'll notice everything is in uppercase. That makes sense, because to make searching easier, you added this line to your script:

```
$query_text = strtoupper($query_text);
```

Then, when you output *$query_text* at the end, the output is shown in all uppercase letters. Is this a big deal? Well, it doesn't seem to be, at least not here. But it does reveal something: after that *$query_text* string is converted to uppercase, any time it's used, it's coming back with all uppercase letters. So suppose the original query was something like this:

```
SELECT *
  FROM users
 WHERE last_name = "MacLachlan";
```

Now consider this same query, turned into all uppercase letters:

```
SELECT *
  FROM USERS
 WHERE LAST_NAME = "MACLACHLAN";
```

Believe it or not, these are not the same query. *SELECT*—and most of the other SQL queries—are going to treat a last name of "MacLachlan" as being totally different from "MACLACHLAN." So those two queries are not identical at all.

At the moment, this doesn't create any trouble. Your script never re-runs the query, and *mysql_query* runs with *$query_text* before its turned into its uppercase version. But this is a problem waiting to happen.

In general, you want to try to avoid directly changing input from a user. That's because you get exactly this sort of problem: you may need to use that input again, and once you've changed it, you can't go back.

Luckily, the remedy is simple: instead of changing the user's input, you instead use a new variable to store the uppercase version of the query:

```
$return_rows = false;
$uppercase_query_text = strtoupper($query_text);
$location = strpos($query_text, "CREATE");
```

You should use this new variable in all your string comparisons:

```
$return_rows = false;
$uppercase_query_text = strtoupper($query_text);
$location = strpos($uppercase_query_text, "CREATE");
if ($location === false) {
  $location = strpos($uppercase_query_text, "INSERT");
  if ($location === false) {
    $location = strpos($uppercase_query_text, "UPDATE");
    if ($location === false) {
      $location = strpos($uppercase_query_text, "DELETE");
      if ($location === false) {
        $location = strpos($uppercase_query_text, "DROP");
        if ($location === false) {
          // If we got here, it's not a CREATE, INSERT, UPDATE,
          //   DELETE, or DROP query. It should return rows.
          $return_rows = true;
        }
      }
    }
  }
}
```

As small a change as that is, it protects you in case you ever need to use that query string again.

And just like that you've actually got a tool that will execute any SQL query you throw at it. But there's work still to do. All that search code really does clutter up your script, and there's just no getting around it: your script is pretty hard to understand at first (and even second) glance. In the next chapter, you'll tackle all this, taking your form from a basic handy form to a really nice exercise of your PHP muscle.

Get Specific with Position and Whitespace Trimming

In this chapter, you've definitely making *run_query.php* a lot better, but there are still some problems. Suppose someone wrote SQL like this:

```
SELECT *
  FROM registrar_activities
WHERE name = 'Update GPA'
   OR name = 'Drop a class'
```

This is a *SELECT* statement, so *run_query.php* should run the SQL and print out all the rows returned from this query. But there's a nasty little problem, isn't there?

Yup. Your code that searches for "update" and "drop" will report that this query has both words in it, and simply return "Your SQL was run without any problems." But that *is* a problem!

To solve the problem, think about the structure of SQL. Those special keywords—*CREATE, INSERT*, and their friends—all are the *first* word in the query. So you need to get the position of the match, and see if that position is position 0. You can do that by adding to your *if* conditions and using the or operator in PHP:

```
if ($location === false ||
    $location > 0) {
```

The double-pipe (||) means "or" to PHP. So line of code says, if there's no match at all (*$location === false*) or the match isn't starting at the first position (position 0), then look for the next keyword. Of course, you'd have to change all your *if* statements,

which is even messier. So this fix is an improvement, although one that really clutters up your code even further.

But it gets worse! You're dealing with real humans, and humans do funny things. Suppose someone enters this SQL into your form:

```
CREATE TABLE urls (
    id int,
    url varchar(100),
    description varchar(100)
);
```

Now you've got a new problem: this isn't a *SELECT*, but your search code won't find one of those special words at the beginning. The first character is just a space: " ".

But you can solve this problem, too, using another familiar function: *trim. trim* gets rid of whitespace, and if you do that before you search, then you should be in good shape:

```
$uppercase_query_text =
        trim(strtoupper($query_text));
```

That probably seems like a ton of work for a really simple, one-textarea form. But when you're working with user input, you want to constantly think about what would users might do. And how you can help avoid them seeing something weird or making a mistake. Think like that, and you're going to build better, more stable, more enjoyable web applications.

Better Searching with Regular Expressions

In the last chapter, you did one of the most common things programmers do: Write code that solves a problem, but is ugly, messy, and a little hard to understand. Unfortunately, most programmers *leave* code in that state because...well, it works.

Bad code is like sloppy plumbing or a poorly constructed house framing. At some point, things are going to go bad, and someone is going to have to fix problems. And, if you've ever had an electrician tell you what they've got to charge you because of the guy who did it wrong *before* him, then you know how expensive it is to fix someone else's mistakes.

But here's the thing: even good code is going to fail at some point. Anytime you've got a system where humans are involved, someone will eventually do something unexpected, or maybe just something you never thought about dealing with when you wrote your code. And that's when *you're* the electrician, trying to fix things when the customer's unhappy—but there's nobody else to blame.

So writing ugly code that works really isn't an option. And the code in *run_query. php* right now is very ugly. It's all those *if* statements, trying to figure out whether the user entered a *CREATE* or an *UPDATE* or an *INSERT*, or maybe a *SELECT*...or who knows what else? What you really need is a way to search the incoming query for all those keywords at one time. And then there's converting things to uppercase, and dealing with whitespace, and making sure the SQL keyword you want is at the beginning of the query, it gets complicated, fast.

Unfortunately, there's no elegant way to solve this problem with *strpos* and the string manipulation you've done so far. Fortunately, you've got another option: *regular expressions*. Regular expressions are like a giant keg of gunpowder: extremely powerful, and perfectly capable of blowing up your program and creating hours of frustration. There's no way to get the power without the danger.

That's okay, though, because you're not running off to battle just yet. Before you're done with *run_query.php*, you'll have introduced regular expressions, and cut out all but one of those annoying if statements around searching through *$query_text*. Most important, your program will make more sense and thus be easier to troubleshoot when problems occur down the line.

> **WARNING** It's pretty common knowledge that most people—and even most programmers—see regular expressions in particular as a complicated, difficult, black art of programming. That's okay; you're more than ready to tackle regular expressions. And once you understand how they work, you'll wonder why anyone wouldn't want to use them all over the place.

■ String Matching, Double-Time

So far, you've been using *strpos* to do string searching (page 36), and you've been passing your string into that function and then some additional characters or strings to look for. The problem is that using *strpos* in this way limits you to a single search string at a time. So you can search for *UPDATE* and you can search for *DROP*, but not at the same time.

Here's where regular expressions come into the picture. A *regular expression* is just what it sounds like: a regular sequence of characters or numbers or some other pattern—an expression—you want to search for. So if you had a string like "abcdefghijklmnopqrstuvwxyz," then you could search for the pattern, or regular expression, "abc." It would show up once, so of course that doesn't seem too regular.

But suppose you had an entire web page, and you wanted to search for links. You might use an expression like "<a" to find all the link elements. You might find none, or one, or ten; but with a regular expression, you can search for practically anything you want. But it does get a bit murky, so the best place to start is at the beginning.

A Simple String Searcher

Just about the simplest regular expression you can come up with is a single simple letter, like "a" or "m." So the regular expression "a" will match any "a." Doesn't sound too difficult, does it?

In PHP, if you want to search using regular expressions, you use the *preg_match* function. While that sounds related to childbirth, it actually stands for "p-reg," as in "PHP regular (expressions)." However you say it, you use it like this:

```php
<?php
$string_to_search = "Martin OMC-28LJ";
$regex = "/OM/";
$num_matches = preg_match($regex, $string_to_search);
```

```
  if ($num_matches > 0) {
    echo "Found a match!";
  } else {
    echo "No match. Sorry.";
  }
  ?>
```

WARNING Be sure that the first thing you give to *preg_match* is the regular expression, *not* the string in which you want to search. This arrangement might seem backward from how you've been working, but you'll soon be using the *preg_match* and related functions so often, putting the search string will start to feel odd.

So there you go. Save that program as *regex.php*, and run it from the command line. You should get a result like this:

```
--(08:25 $)-> php regex.php
Found a match!
```

Admittedly, this isn't very exciting. Before you can walk, though, you gotta crawl. And one of those crawling steps is understanding just how you write a regular expression.

First, regular expressions are just strings, so you wrap them in quotes. You'll typically use double quotes (") rather than single quotes (') because you'll need to do some funny escape characters, and PHP doesn't do as much helpful processing on single-quoted strings as double-quoted ones.

Additionally, regular expressions begin and end with a forward slash. It's then everything between those slashes that makes up the meat of the expression. So *"/OM/"* is a regular expression that searches for OM.

More specifically, *"/OM/"* searches for exactly OM. So it won't match "om" or "Om" or "OhM." It's got to be a capital O followed by a capital M. In other words, at least so far, this is just like the string matching you've already done.

And *preg_match* has some wrinkles, too. First, as you've seen, it takes a regular expression first, and then the string in which to search. Then, it returns the number of matches, rather than the position at which a match was found. And here's the first real wrinkle: *preg_match* will *never return anything other than 0 or 1*. It returns 0 if there are no matches, 1 on the first match, and then it simply stops searching.

If you want to find all the matches, you can use *preg_match_all*. So *preg_match("/Mr/", "Mr. Mranity")* returns 1, but *preg_match_all("/Mr/", "Mr. Mranity")* returns 2.

NOTE The re are also several additional things you can pass into—and get out of—*preg_match* and *preg_match_all*. You can find out about all this online at *www.php.net/manual/en/function.preg-match.php*. For now, though, just get comfortable with regular expressions.

Search for One String...Or Another

So far, there's not a lot that regular expressions seem to offer that you don't already have with *strpos*. But there's a lot more that you can do, and one of the coolest is searching for one string *or* another. To do this, you use a special character called the pipe. The pipe looks like a vertical line: |. (It's usually above the backslash character, over on the right side of your keyboard.)

Which Quote is the Best Quote?

Almost every programming language seemingly treats single-quoted strings ('My name is Bob') and double-quoted strings ("I am a carpenter") the same. However, also in almost every programming language, there's a lot more going on than you may realize, all based upon which quotation mark you use.

In general, *less* processing is performed on single-quoted strings. But what processing occurs in the first place? Take the statement *I'm going to the bank*. If you put that in a single-quoted string, you get *'I'm going to the bank'*. But PHP is going to bark at you, because the single-quote in *I'm* looks like it's ending the simple string *'I'*, and all the rest—*m going to the bank*—must be something else. Of course that's not what you mean, so you do one of two things: you either switch to double quotes and move on, or you *escape* the single quote.

Escaping something means telling the programming language *not* to treat something as part of the language; it's just part of the string. Typically, you escape characters by throwing a backslash (\) in front of the potentially problematic character. So in the string *I'm going to the bank.*, you'd write it in single quotes like this: *'I\'m going to the bank'*. That \ tells PHP to ignore both it and the thing that follows.

What if you want to actually write a backslash? Suppose you're writing a program for your great-great-great granddad, the one that still runs DOS on his 286? You might want to say, 'Never, ever, ever type in \'del C:*.*\' and hit Return!' Well,

you handled the single-quotes handily, but now PHP is trying to escape the character following that in-string backslash: *. That just confuses PHP, which can't figure out why it's being asked to escape an asterisk. In this case, you need to escape the backslash itself. So you just put in the escape character—the backslash—and then the character to be escaped: another backslash. The result is 'Never, ever, ever type in \'del C:*.*\'

Other than the single quote (') and the backslash (\), PHP doesn't do any other processing to your single-quoted strings. But there are lots of other things you might need processing for: a new line (\n), a tab (\t), or that slick way of inserting variables right into a string with *{$variable}* or just using *$variable*.

So with a single-quoted string, you get very little. With a double-quoted string, you get all the extra processing. As a result, most programmers tend to use double quotes. That way, they don't have to think, "Now do I need extra processing on this string? Or can I use single quotes?"

One last note: extra processing really isn't a performance issue in 99 percent of the applications you write. The processing involved in handling those extra escape characters and variables isn't going to frustrate your customers or send server hard drives or RAM chips into a frenzy. You can happily use double-quoted strings all the time, and you'll probably never notice any issues at all.

Anytime you want to search for one thing or another, you put those two things together inside of parentheses, separated by the pipe:

```
/(Mr|Dr)\. Smith/
```

First, though, notice a wrinkle: the backward slash (\). This character is escaping the period, as that period usually means, in a regular expression, "match any single character." But in this case, you want to match an actual period, not anything. So \. will match a period, and nothing but a period.

/Mr. Smith/ will match "Mr. Smith" but will skip right over "Dr. Smith." But */(Mr|Dr). Smith/* would match either "Mr. Smith" or "Dr. Smith".

Therefore, this little code snippet would find a match in both cases:

```
// This will match
echo "Matches: " . preg_match("/(Mr|Dr). Smith/", "Mr. Smith");

// So will this
echo "Matches: " . preg_match("/(Mr|Dr). Smith/", "Dr. Smith");
```

With this new wrinkle, you should be able to make some extensive changes to the *run_query.php* script from the last chapter (page 110). Open that file and take a look. Here's the old version:

```php
<?php
  require '../../scripts/database_connection.php';

  $query_text = $_REQUEST['query'];
  $result = mysql_query($query_text);

  if (!$result) {
    die("<p>Error in executing the SQL query " . $query_text . ": " .
        mysql_error() . "</p>");
  }

  $return_rows = false;
  $uppercase_query_text = strtoupper($query_text);
  $location = strpos($uppercase_query_text, "CREATE");
  if ($location === false) {
    $location = strpos($uppercase_query_text, "INSERT");
    if ($location === false) {
      $location = strpos($uppercase_query_text, "UPDATE");
      if ($location === false) {
        $location = strpos($uppercase_query_text, "DELETE");
        if ($location === false) {
          $location = strpos($uppercase_query_text, "DROP");
          if ($location === false) {
            // If we got here, it's not a CREATE, INSERT, UPDATE,
            //   DELETE, or DROP query. It should return rows.
            $return_rows = true;
```

```
            }
          }
        }
      }
    }

    if ($return_rows) {
      // We have rows to show from the query
      echo "<p>Results from your query:</p>";
      echo "<ul>";
      while ($row = mysql_fetch_row($result)) {
        echo "<li>{$row[0]}</li>";
      }
      echo "</ul>";
    } else {
      // No rows. Just report if the query ran or not
      echo "<p>The following query was processed successfully:</p>";
      echo "<p>{$query_text}</p>";
    }
?>
```

All that *if* stuff is what makes it messy. But with regular expressions, you can make some pretty spectacular changes:

```
<?php
  // require and database connection code

  $return_rows = true;
  if (preg_match("/(CREATE|INSERT|UPDATE|DELETE|DROP)/",
                 strtoupper($query_text))) {
    $return_rows = false;
  }

  if ($return_rows) {
    // display code
  }
?>
```

NOTE   You may want to save this version as another file, or in another directory, so you can go back and see what you started with. In this book's examples, you'll find the original version of *run_query.php* in the Chapter 4 examples directory, and this new version in the Chapter 5 examples directory.

Take a close look here, especially at the fairly long condition for the *if* statement. here's the breakdown of what's going on:

1. You start with setting *$return_rows* to *true*, instead of false. That's because your regular expression search is checking whether you *don't* have return rows. This version is easier to read than the older one, where you're constantly doing a comparison, and then if there's *not* a match, setting *$return_rows* to *true*.

2. Then, the *if* condition: it begins with *preg_match*. There's no need to use *preg_match_all*, since you only care if the search strings are found at all, not if they're found more than once.

3. The regular expression is actually pretty simple: it's each keyword for a SQL statement that doesn't return any rows, all separated by that pipe symbol. So it's basically an expression for matching a string that contains CREATE *or* INSERT *or* UPDATE *or* DELETE *or* DROP.

4. This expression is evaluated against the uppercase version of *$query_text*. Not only do you not change the value of *$query_text*, but you don't even really need to save the uppercase version. If you need an uppercase version again later, you can just call *strtoupper* again.

5. You know that *preg_match* returns 0 if there's no match, and PHP sees 0 as *false*. *preg_match* returns 1 if there's a match, which PHP sees as *true*. So you can just drop the whole *preg_match* in as your *if* statement's condition, and know that if there's a match, the *if* statement code will run; if there's not a match, it won't.

6. Inside the *if*, *$return_rows* is set to *false*, because a match means this is a query that doesn't have return rows.

Not only is this code easier to read, and makes more sense to a human brain, but you cut 20 lines of code down to 4.

WARNING It's not always good to have less lines of code. Sometimes you can sacrifice readability and clarity to save a few lines, and that's not helpful. But if you can condense four or five conditions into one or two, that usually *is* a good thing.

Get into Position

One of the problems with even this streamlined version of *run_query.php* is it looks for a match anywhere within the input query. If you read the box on page 125, you know there are still problems. You need to trim your user's query string, and that's pretty simple:

```php
if (preg_match("/(CREATE|INSERT|UPDATE|DELETE|DROP)/",
               trim(strtoupper($query_text)))) {
    $return_rows = false;

}
```

But there's another trickier problem: you really only want to search for those special keywords at the beginning of the query string. That prevents a query like this...

```
SELECT *
  FROM registrar_activities
 WHERE name = 'Update GPA'
    OR name = 'Drop a class'
```

...from being mistaken as an *UPDATE* or *DROP* query. This query, a *SELECT*, returns rows, but if it's interpreted as an *UPDATE* or *DROP*, your script will not show return rows.

It took some additional *if* conditions to get this to work before, but that was in the dark days before regular expressions. Now, it's no problem to tell PHP, "I want this expression, but only at the *beginning* of the search string."

To accomplish this feat of wizardry, just add the carat (^) to the beginning of your search string. ^ says, "At the beginning."

```
// Matches
echo "Matches: " . preg_match("/^(Mr|Dr). Smith/",
                              "Dr. Smith") . "\n";
// Does NOT match
echo "Matches: " . preg_match("/^(Mr|Dr). Smith/",
                              "  Dr. Smith") . "\n";
```

So in the first case, */^(Mr|Dr). Smith/* matches "Dr. Smith" because the string begins with "Dr. Smith" ("Mr. Smith" would be okay, too). But the second string does not match, because the ^ rejects the leading spaces.

Taking this back to your query runner, you'd do something like this:

```
if (preg_match("/^(CREATE|INSERT|UPDATE|DELETE|DROP)/",
                trim(strtoupper($query_text)))) {
  $return_rows = false;
}
```

That one little carat character makes all the difference. You can do the same thing with $ at the end of a string: it requires matches not at the beginning, but at the end of the search string:

```
// Does NOT match
echo "Matches: " . preg_match("/^(Mr|Dr). Smith$/",
                              "Dr. Smith  ") . "\n";
// Matches
echo "Matches: " . preg_match("/^(Mr|Dr). Smith$/",
                              "Dr. Smith") . "\n";
```

WARNING Make sure that your ^ and $ are inside the opening / and closing /. If you were to put, for example, /^(Mr|Dr). Smith/$, PHP would complain about that last $, saying that $ is an unknown modifier. This error is an easy to make, and it can be pretty frustrating to track down if you don't realize what you've done.

So in the first case, there's no match because the regular expression, which uses $, doesn't allow for the trailing spaces in "Dr. Smith ". The second check does match, though, because there's no leading space (which matches the ^(Mr|Dr) part) and no trailing space (which matches the Smith$ part).

In fact, when you have a ^ at the beginning of your expression and a $ at the end, you're requiring an exact match not just within the search string but to the string itself. It's like you're saying that the search string should equal the regular expression. Of course if you were doing a real equals in PHP (with == or ===), you couldn't have those nifty *or* statements with |, or any of the other cool things regular expressions offer.

Ditching *trim* and *strtoupper*

As long as you're simplifying your code with some regular expression goodness, take things further. Right now, you're converting *$query_text* to all uppercase with *strtoupper*, and then searching for CREATE, INSERT, and the like within that uppercase version of the query.

But regular expressions are happy to be case-insensitive, and not care about whether they match upper or lowercase versions of a word. Just add an "i" to the end of your expression, *after* the closing forward slash:

```
// Matches
echo "Matches: " . preg_match("/^(MR|DR). sMiTH$/i",
                              "Dr. Smith") . "\n";
```

This expression produces a match, despite the case of the expression and the search string not matching. So you can change your search in *run_query.php* to take advantage of this:

```
$return_rows = true;
if (preg_match("/^(CREATE|INSERT|UPDATE|DELETE|DROP)/i",
               trim($query_text))) {
  $return_rows = false;

}
```

No more *strtoupper*, and a new "i" at the end of the expression. With this change, the sort of query shown in Figure 5-1 will happily be recognized as DROP, which returns no result rows.

FIGURE 5-1

Even though you're not adding functionality with these regular expressions, you're definitely improving your code. You're searching for what you want in the original $query_text, instead of changing $query_text to work with your search. That's the way it should be: search an unchanged input string whenever possible.

So what about trimming whitespace? Well, you really don't need to trim *$query_string*; instead, in your regular expression, you just want to ignore leading spaces.

But think about that further: when you're searching, are you truly ignoring something? No. That may be what the result is, but what you actually want to say is something like this:

1. Begin by matching any number of spaces—including the case where there are no spaces.

2. Then, after some indeterminate number of spaces, look for (CREATE|INSERT| UPDATE|DELETE|DROP).

So while you're ignoring those spaces in your particular situation—figuring out if the query is a *CREATE*, or *UPDATE*, or whatever—you're really just doing another type of matching.

Now, you know how to match a space: you just include it in your regular expression. So /^ Mr. Smith/ requires an opening space. "Mr. Smith" would not match, but " Mr. Smith" would.

WARNING Laying out type in books can be tricky. In the examples above, be sure you notice that the first "Mr. Smith" has no leading space, the second " Mr. Smith" did have a space, and the regular expression, /^ Mr. Smith/ also had a space after the ^.

But that requires a space. How can you say that more than one space is okay? That's when you need +. + says, "The thing that came just before me can appear any number of times."

```
// Matches
echo "Matches: " . preg_match("/^ (MR|DR). sMiTH$/i",
                              " Dr. Smith") . "\n";
// Does NOT match
echo "Matches: " . preg_match("/^ (MR|DR). sMiTH$/i",
                              "    Dr. Smith") . "\n";
// Matches
echo "Matches: " . preg_match("/^ +(MR|DR). sMiTH$/i",
                              "    Dr. Smith") . "\n";
```

The first and second expressions look for exactly one space, and so the first entry matches, but the second—with multiple leading spaces—doesn't. But the third expression accepts any number of spaces, so once again matches.

But try this:

```
// Does NOT match
echo "Matches: " . preg_match("/^ +(MR|DR). sMiTH$/i",
                              "Dr. Smith") . "\n";
```

Uh oh. Apparently "any number of spaces" for + really means, "any non-zero number of spaces." If you are okay with nothing, or any number of characters, use *.

```
// Matches
echo "Matches: " . preg_match("/^ *(MR|DR). sMiTH$/i",
                              "Dr. Smith") . "\n";
```

So now you can look for spaces within your *$query_text* in *run_query.php*, and avoid touching the input string at all, even temporarily:

```
$return_rows = true;
if (preg_match("/^ *(CREATE|INSERT|UPDATE|DELETE|DROP)/i",
               $query_text)) {
  $return_rows = false;
}
```

Searching for Sets of Characters

Take a look at Figure 5-2. Will your current version of *run_query.php* handle what's typed in this text box?

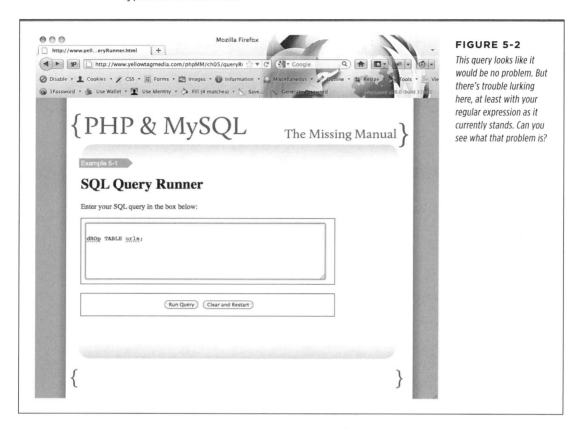

FIGURE 5-2

This query looks like it would be no problem. But there's trouble lurking here, at least with your regular expression as it currently stands. Can you see what that problem is?

There might be leading spaces—it's not possible to tell just looking at the illustration, or even if you were looking at an actual browser. But even if there isn't leading space, there's something else here: a return. Your clever, endearing users have done something you'd probably never think about: hit Enter a few times before typing in their SQL.

Suddenly, your regular expression doesn't match this as a DROP, despite your handling leading spaces and issues with capitalization. That's because Enter produces some special characters: usually either \n, or in some situations, \r\n, or, just to keep things interesting, occasionally just \r.

NOTE These are all just varying flavors of new line characters. \n is called the line feed character, and \r is called a carriage return. In general, Windows uses \r\n, Unix and Linux use \n, and Macs (in particular older, pre-OS X Macs) use \r.

Fortunately, there aren't nearly as many cross-system problems with these characters as there were just a few years ago. You can pretty safely use \n to create a new line, but when you're search, you need to account for all the variations.

So what can you do? Well, it's easy to account for multiple characters like this: \n* will match any number of new lines, and \r* will match any number of carriage returns. But what about \r\n? \r*\n* would match that, but what about spaces? You could do \r*\n* * and match Enter followed by spaces, but if you start to think about spaces and then Enters and then more spaces...and more Enters...it gets tricky again.

Of course, the whole point of regular expressions was to get away from that sort of thing. And, you can: you can search for any of a set of characters. That's really what you want: accept any number (including zero) of any of a set of characters, a \r, a \n, or a space. You don't care how many appear, or in what order, either.

FREQUENTLY ASKED QUESTION

Back to Square One?

It may seem like all this regular expression work has just gotten you back to where you began: a search for CREATE or INSERT or UPDATE anywhere within *$query_text*. If you're ignoring all the leading spaces, isn't that just the same as *$location = strpos($query_text, "CREATE");* and all its if-based brethren?

It may look like that at first glance, but you're worlds away from all those *if* statements. First, to restate the obvious, you've got a script you should be happy to show any of your programmer friends. You've used regular expressions, and used them well, so you don't have a litter box of conditions to sort through.

Second, your code is more sensible. It starts with the presumption that you'll return rows. Then, based on a condition, it may change that presumption. This is natural human logic: start one way, if something else is going on, go another way. That's a lot better than the sort of backward-logic of your earlier version of *run_query.php*.

But most importantly, you're still not searching anywhere within *$query_text* for those SQL keywords. You're searching anywhere within the string beginning with *the first non-space character*. So this sort of query...

```
SELECT *
  FROM registrar_activities
 WHERE name = 'Update GPA'
    OR name = 'Drop a class'
```

...still comes across as a SELECT, and isn't mistaken for a DROP, for example. And you did it without a lot of messy and obscure hard-to-read code.

You could do something like (\r/\n/)*, which is using the | to represent or again, and then the * applies to the entire group. But when you're dealing with just single characters, you can skip the | and just put all the allowed characters into a set, which is indicated by square brackets ([and]).

```
$return_rows = true;
if (preg_match("/^[ \t\r\n]*(CREATE|INSERT|UPDATE|DELETE|DROP)/i",
                $query_text)) {
  $return_rows = false;
}
```

This code handles spaces, the two flavors of new lines, and tosses in \t for tab characters. So no matter how many leading spaces, tabs, or new lines are input, your regular expression is happy to handle them. In fact, this sort of whitespace matching is so common that regular expressions can use \s as an abbreviation for [\t\r\n]. So you could simplify things further:

```
$return_rows = true;
if (preg_match("/^\s*(CREATE|INSERT|UPDATE|DELETE|DROP)/i",
                $query_text)) {
  $return_rows = false;
}
```

Try this out. Enter the SQL shown back in Figure 5-2, and submit your query. Your regular expression is just waiting to handle things. But wait...you'll probably get something like Figure 5-3. What's going on?

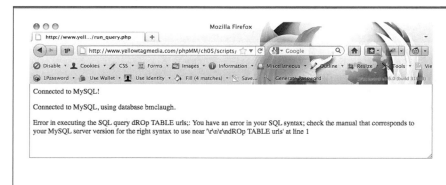

FIGURE 5-3

Just as you're getting your regular expression and search code bulletproof, there's a new error to deal with. This occurs before your search ever runs. But it definitely shows a problem: mysql_ query *did not seem to like those leading \r\n sequences.*

The problem here isn't your regular expression. It's really that you're trying to pass into *mysql_query* some queries that haven't been screened much for problems—like all those extra \r\ns at the beginning.

In fact, there are *lots* of queries that will create problems for *run_query.php*, regardless of how clean your regular expression code is. Try entering this query:

```
SELECT *
  FROM urls
 WHERE description = 'home page'
```

That seems simple enough, but it's still going to break your script. It doesn't matter if you have anything in the *urls* table or not; you'll still get an error (see Figure 5-4).

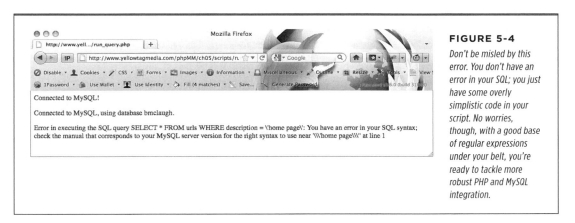

FIGURE 5-4

Don't be misled by this error. You don't have an error in your SQL; you just have some overly simplistic code in your script. No worries, though, with a good base of regular expressions under your belt, you're ready to tackle more robust PHP and MySQL integration.

Frankly, you could spend weeks writing all the code required to really handle every possible SQL query, make sure the right things are accepted and the wrong ones aren't, and to handle all the various types of queries.

But that's not a good idea. Just taking in any old SQL query is, in fact, a *very* bad idea. What's a much better idea is to take a step back, and think about what your users really need. It's probably not a blank form, and so in the next chapter, you'll give them what they need: a normal web form that just happens to talk to MySQL on the back end.

Regular Expressions: To Infinity and Beyond

It's not an overexaggeration to say you've just barely scratched the surface of regular expressions. Although you've got a strong grasp of the basics—from matching to ^ and $ and the various flavors of *preg_match*, from position and whitespace to + and * and sets—there are more than a few trees that have died to produce all the paper educating programmers about regular expressions.

But don't be freaked out or daunted, and don't stop working your PHP and MySQL skills until you've "mastered" regular expressions. First, mastery is pretty elusive, and even the best regular expression guys (and girls) dip into Google to remember how to get the right sequence of characters within their slashes. Practice makes perfect, so look for chances to use regular expressions. And, as you get better at PHP, you'll use them more often, and they'll slowly become as familiar as PHP itself, or HTML, or any of the other things you've been doing over and over.

Regular Expressions Aren't Just for PHP

As you're probably seeing, it does take some work to get very far with regular expressions. There are lots of weird characters both to find on your keyboard, and to work into your expressions. And it doesn't take long for a regular expression to start to look like something QBert might say: *SD)!!@8#.

But the world rewards you in more ways than you might realize. For instance, JavaScript also has complete support for regular expressions. Methods like *replace()* in JavaScript take in regular expressions, as do the *match()* methods on strings. So everything you've learned in PHP translates over, perfectly.

You also get some nice benefits in HTML5. You can use regular expressions in an HTML5 form to provide patterns against which data is validated. So your work in PHP is helping you out in almost every aspect of web programming.

In fact, there's hardly a serious programming language that doesn't support regular expressions. When you decide to learn Ruby and Ruby on Rails (and you should), you'll be swimming in regular expressions, and they're also hugely helpful as you move into using testing frameworks like Cucumber or Capybara or TestUnit. If all that sounds intimidating, relax! You've got regular expressions down, even before you've learned what lots of these languages are.

The moral of this story? What you're learning about SQL applies to more than MySQL, and what you're learning about regular expressions applies to more than PHP. Your skills are growing, so use them all over the place.

Generating Dynamic Web Pages

You've been building up quite a robust set of tools. You have PHP scripts to receive requests from your HTML forms. You have MySQL to store information from your users. You have regular expressions to massage information into just the formats you need, and some basic flow controls in PHP like *if* and *for* to let you build scripts that make decisions based on what information your users give you.

But at the end of the day, your goal in learning PHP and MySQL is probably to make dynamic and interesting web applications, and you've not done much of that yet. You've got a few interesting forms, but even those are pretty simple: take in some information and print it back out; accept a SQL query (and do that quite imperfectly).

Thankfully, you've got everything you need to start building pages that are built dynamically using your user's information and full-fledged web applications. You can get information from your users, store it in a database, and even do some basic data manipulation. It's time to put it all together into the web pages that folks expect: a place to enter their information, a place to see their information, and in most cases, a place to look at all related user information.

■ Revisiting a User's Information

On page 26, you built a form that took in a user's basic social media profile: a Twitter handle, a Facebook URL, and some basic contact information. That form is shown in Figure 6-1: it's simple and easy to use.

FIGURE 6-1

It turns out that you can design forms that interact and submit to PHP scripts the same way you create any other web page: you use HTML and hopefully CSS to create a clean, easy-to-understand page. Then get users to visit your page, fill out fields, and click buttons. It's the behind-the-scenes work that brings PHP and MySQL into the picture.

And here's where there's a surprising amount of work: getting from a simple form on the Web to a script that interacts with a database. You need to figure out, design, and create tables, interact with those tables, potentially deal with errors from your database, and the list goes on. Best get started!

> **NOTE** If you haven't already, copy over the HTML web form you created on page 26 to the directory you're working in. You can leave the file named as it is, but you may want to rename it as *create_user.html*. For reasons you'll see soon, this little change can really pay off as your site gets more complex.

There's really no reason to change this form. However, the script that accepts this information is pretty lame. It does nothing more than a little text manipulation and regurgitation (see Figure 6-2). That's where the work is: making the script *do something* with the user's information.

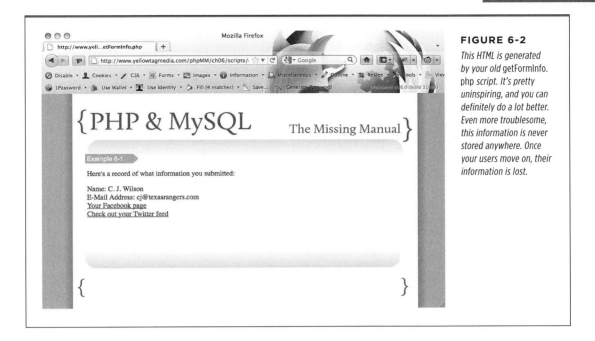

FIGURE 6-2

This HTML is generated by your old getFormInfo. php script. It's pretty uninspiring, and you can definitely do a lot better. Even more troublesome, this information is never stored anywhere. Once your users move on, their information is lost.

Planning Your Database Tables

Building web applications is a lot like working a tricky maze: sometimes the hardest part is figuring out where to start. Usually a web form needs a script to which it can submit data. But that script needs a table into which it can insert information. But where's the table? In a database you need to create or set up for web access. And then there's the table itself: it needs structure. And that's the way almost every form of every application goes: what starts out as a page that users see often ends up at a back-end structure that's invisible to everyone but you, the programmer.

It's always easiest to simply start with the information you want to store. You've actually already done some of this, when you created your entry form (look back at Figure 6-1). So here's basically what you're collecting from your users right now:

- First Name
- Last Name
- E-Mail Address
- Facebook URL
- Twitter Handle

It really is that simple: you just need these five bits of information. And each of these really are about a single "thing"—a user. So the simple conclusion is you need a table to store users, and each user has a first name, last name, email address, a Facebook URL, and a Twitter handle.

Now just translate this into a SQL *CREATE* statement, something you should have no problem doing:

```
CREATE TABLE users (
        user_id int,
        first_name varchar(20),
        last_name varchar(30),
        email varchar(50),
        facebook_url varchar(100),
        twitter_handle varchar(20)
);
```

> **WARNING** You may not want to dive into your MySQL command-line tool or your web form and run this command just yet. There are some important additions to be made before it's ready for prime time.

You may remember this SQL from page 81, but that was ages ago, when you had but a fragile understanding of databases. Now you know exactly what's going to be dropped into this table: information from the web form you've already got.

UP TO SPEED

One of These Things *Is* Like the Other

When you start talking with database people, you quickly encounter a lot of interchangeable terms.

A table has rows, and each entry in that table is a *row*. But you'll also hear a row called an *entry* in the table, as well as a *record*. These terms all mean the same thing, and even though it may be technically better to say a table has rows rather than entries or records, in real life people use these terms interchangeably.

In the same vein, the fields in a table like *first_name* or *last_name* are also called *columns*. And in those *fields* (or columns), you have *values*, or *information*, or for the technically stodgy, *data*. Lots of different terms, all with identical meaning.

You can help matters by not mixing and matching terms. Rows and columns go together; so do records and fields. A table that has rows has columns; a table with records has fields.

Above all, remember that, as with any other bit of language, context is king. It's more important you know what's an *int* and what's not than to be sure you say row instead of record. And not to confuse a complete entry with the individual *parts* of that entry. So a single entry, record, or row in the *users* table has multiple fields, columns, or pieces of information. Get that right, and you can solve the rest by listening carefully and asking the right questions.

Good Database Tables Have *id* Columns

There's one little detail worth noting, though: the table's *user_id* field. Think about the most common thing you do with databases. It's not creating new entries or user profiles; it's looking up and *accessing* that information.

Next, consider how do you search for information? You can look things up by a last name, and then find matching entries; or you can search by an email or Twitter handle, which are supposed to be unique for each user. In fact, you've probably often been asked to create a unique username (often at great pain; there aren't many "normal" names left on Twitter, except for *m97f-ss0*).

Databases are no different: they need something for which to look. And more than that, databases work well only when they can identify every individual row in a table by a unique piece of information. But there's more than that for a database: databases function better with numbers that text. The absolute preferred type of unique identifier—or ID—for a row in a table is a unique number.

That, then, is what *user_id* is about. It's a special value for each row that is unique, and that is numerical. It identifies each user as separate from all others, and lets your database do its thing quickly and well.

Auto-Increment Is Your Friend

There's a bit of a problem lurking in the SQL bushes here, though. If the point of the *user_id* field is to provide a unique identifier for each user, whose job is it to keep up with that unique ID? How do all the scripts (and there will be more than one or two before you're done with any large web application) make sure that no two users are entered into the *users* table with the same *user_id*?

This problem isn't trivial, because if you lose the ability to identify a user uniquely, things can go south fast. On the other hand, nobody wants to spend hours writing number generators for every table, or every web application they write.

The solution is not in your code, but in your database. Most databases, MySQL included, give you the ability to use *auto increment*. You specify this value on a field, and every time you add a row to that table, the field automatically creates a new number, incremented from the previous row you added. So if one script adds a new user and MySQL sets the *user_id* to 1029, and another script then adds a new user, MySQL simply adds one, gets 1030, and sets that up as the ID of the new user.

You can add this to your table *CREATE* statement like this:

```
CREATE TABLE users (
        user_id int AUTO_INCREMENT,
        first_name varchar(20),
        last_name varchar(30),
        email varchar(50),
        facebook_url varchar(100),
        twitter_handle varchar(20)
);
```

Much better. Now you don't have to worry about IDs. In fact, you don't have to do anything special to let MySQL know to fill in the *user_id* column. Every time you add a new row, MySQL also adds a new value to *user_id*.

■ IDS AND PRIMARY KEYS ARE GOOD BEDFELLOWS

Now that you've got *user_id* auto incrementing, you've actually done something else subtly in MySQL: you've defined *user_id* as the *primary key* in the *users* table. The primary key is a database term for that special, unique value that each table has.

> **NOTE** In some rather special cases, you might create a primary key out of multiple columns. That's somewhat unusual, though.

Primary keys are important because databases typically create an *index* on a table's primary key. An index is a database-level mechanism by which a database can find rows based on that index quickly. So if you have the *user_id* column indexed, you can find a row with a *user_id* of 2048 much faster than looking for a row with that same *user_id*, but on a table where *user_id* is *not* indexed.

An indexed field is like having a highly organized set of values that allow for quick searching. An unindexed field can still be searched, but then your database has to go through each value, one by one, until it finds the exact value you're searching for. It's the difference between looking for a book in a good library and looking for one in your great-great-grandfather's cluttered attic.

When you told MySQL to *AUTO_INCREMENT user_id*, you identified that field as special. In fact, MySQL won't let you set more than one field to *AUTO_INCREMENT*, because it's assuming you put that on a field to use it as a primary key.

But here's where you have to remember something—something that you might expect MySQL to do for you, but it won't. You have to tell MySQL that you want *user_id* to be the primary key:

```
CREATE TABLE users (
        user_id int AUTO_INCREMENT PRIMARY KEY,
        first_name varchar(20),
        last_name varchar(30),
        email varchar(50),
        facebook_url varchar(100),
        twitter_handle varchar(20)
);
```

This line makes explicit what is implicit with *AUTO_INCREMENT*: *user_id* uniquely identifies each user entry in your table. In fact, if you don't add this line, MySQL gives you an error. So suppose you have this SQL, without the *PRIMARY KEY*:

```
CREATE TABLE users (
        user_id int AUTO_INCREMENT,
        first_name varchar(20),
        last_name varchar(30),
        email varchar(50),
        facebook_url varchar(100),
        twitter_handle varchar(20)
);
```

If you were to run this query, MySQL will give you a weird error; Figure 6-3 shows that error in the phpMyAdmin console.

FIGURE 6-3

phpMyAdmin is a great tool for running queries. You can avoid spending lots of time in a text-based tool, you can browse your tables visually, and best of all, most Web hosting companies that provide MySQL and database services offer phpMyAdmin. That means if you learn it on one host, you can probably use the same tool on another host.

This error—the rather infamous #1075 if you've been around MySQL for long—tells you that since you've got an *AUTO_INCREMENT* column, you need to mark it with *PRIMARY KEY*. It would be nice if MySQL would take care of that for you, but alas, it's up to you. So add back in *PRIMARY KEY*, and you're *almost* ready to create this table for real, minus the errors.

Adding Constraints to Your Database

The purpose of a field like *user_id* is to allow for easy searching. Adding *AUTO_INCREMENT* (and setting the field as a primary key) helps, but there's something subtle that also happens behind the scenes when you create an *AUTO_INCREMENT* column: you're saying, "No matter what, this column will have a value." That's because MySQL is filling in that value.

But there are other fields that you also almost always want to fill in. First name and last name fields, for example. And you should probably require an email address, too. Users won't always have Twitter handles and Facebook URLs, so you can leave those off, but the rest is mandatory.

You could just let your PHP scripts and web pages deal with requiring this information. But is that really safe? What if someone else forgets to add validation on a web page? What if *you* forget, writing code on a coffee-high one day, typing away at 2 AM? Whenever you can validate, it's always a good idea to do so.

Once again, MySQL gives you what you need. You can require a value on a field by telling MySQL that field can't be null, which is just programmer-talk for "not a value":

```
CREATE TABLE users (
        user_id int NOT NULL AUTO_INCREMENT PRIMARY KEY,
        first_name varchar(20) NOT NULL,
        last_name varchar(30) NOT NULL,
        email varchar(50) NOT NULL,
        facebook_url varchar(100),
        twitter_handle varchar(20)
);
```

NOTE Even though MySQL handles auto incrementing and inserting values into *user_id*, it's still a good idea to make it *NOT NULL*. That makes it clear that the value in that column is required, regardless of how MySQL or any other code actually fills that value.

As with *AUTO_INCREMENT*, this change is quick, easy, and goes a long way to protecting the integrity of your information (or, to be more accurate, your user's information!).

DESIGN TIME

To Null or Not to Null

Although the *users* table makes figuring out which columns should be *NOT NULL* fairly easy, that's not always the case. In fact, even with *users*, there's ambiguity: are you sure you want to require an email address? It's possible that someone might not have one (although why email-less folks are surfing the Internet is a mystery), or you may have users concerned with you spamming them, and they don't want to enter an email address. Are you *sure* you want to require that as part of a user's information?

It might surprise you, but making a column *NOT NULL* is one of the most important decisions you'll make with regard to an individual table. This is particularly true if you decide *not* to make a column *NOT NULL*. Every record added might have a null value there, and if you decide down the line, "Oops, I really did need that value," you're stuck for all the old entries that don't have it. You can't ever un-ring that bell.

However, don't get too trigger-happy with *NOT NULL*, thinking that it's just safer to use it frequently and be sure you've got more data, rather than less. Users can get pretty upset when they have to fill out 28 fields just to use your site. Even mega-sites like Facebook and Twitter require only minimal information: usually a name, email, username, and password.

In general, the rule of thumb is to require only what you absolutely have to; but to absolutely require that information. That's a tongue twister, but a useful one. Think long and hard, make a decision, and then realize that you'll always upset someone. Your goal is to please most of your users most of the time; if you can pull that off while still getting the information from them you need, you're well on your way to Web stardom and Internet fame (whatever that's worth!).

And one last subtle bit of help: you're working at the table level with *NOT NULL*, not the application level. In other words, you're essentially saying, "This column can't be null *if (and only if) there's an entry in this table*." So you may decide that users don't have to enter an address, but *if* they enter an address, street, city, and country are required. Thinking along these lines—what data is essential for this particular table, rather than your entire app—will help you lock down your database with good, useful data, and still not go crazy with *NOT NULL*.

You should have a pretty useful SQL statement, so go ahead and create your *users* table. Log into MySQL using your command-line tool, the web form you built earlier, or another web tool like phpMyAdmin, and create the table. You're about to need it.

WARNING   You may need to DROP a previous version of the table. You can simply use *DROP TABLE users;* if you get an error trying to create the table. That should clear out any existing version of the table you've got. And be sure you're in the right database when you run your CREATE statement.

■ Saving a User's Information

You've had a table before, and now you've got a version of the *users* table that's a little sturdier, with *AUTO_INCREMENT* and validation of values in a few key fields. And your web form grabs exactly the information you need to stuff into that table. All that's left is tying these things together with PHP, and you have almost everything you need for that, too.

You can start with a new script, or use your old version of *getFormInfo.php* as a starting point. Either way, your first task is to get the user's entered information and do a little text manipulation to get the values just like you want:

```php
<?php

$first_name = trim($_REQUEST['first_name']);
$last_name = trim($_REQUEST['last_name']);
$email = trim($_REQUEST['email']);
$facebook_url = str_replace("facebook.org", "facebook.com", trim($_
REQUEST['facebook_url']));
$position = strpos($facebook_url, "facebook.com");
if ($position === false) {
  $facebook_url = "http://www.facebook.com/" . $facebook_url;
}

$twitter_handle = trim($_REQUEST['twitter_handle']);
$twitter_url = "http://www.twitter.com/";
$position = strpos($twitter_handle, "@");
if ($position === false) {
  $twitter_url = $twitter_url . $twitter_handle;
} else {
  $twitter_url = $twitter_url . substr($twitter_handle, $position + 1);
}

?>
```

Call this script *create_user.php*, and save it in your *scripts/* directory, either in your site root or under your *ch06/* examples directory. You should also update the action in your *create_user.html*'s *form* to submit to this newly named script.

You've written this code before, and because you haven't changed your form, it still works. Now you just need to update it so it stores this information in your new *users* table.

NOTE For some extra credit, see if you can convert this script, *create_user.php*, to use regular expressions instead of the *strpos* function to update these variables. If you think you've got things into great shape using regular expressions, tweet a link to your code to *@missingmanuals* and see what cool swag you might win.

Building Your SQL Query

First, you can use your existing database connection script to make connecting easy:

```php
<?php

require '../../scripts/database_connection.php';

// Get the user's information from the request into variables

?>
```

WARNING You may have some echo statements left in *database_connection.php* from an earlier version of the examples. If you do, remove them now so they won't disrupt the seamless experience you'll be giving your users.

With a database connection ready for use, you've got to turn all that information into the *INSERT* statement you want, so you can drop the information into your database.

Rather than just diving into your code, though, start with a sample statement. For example, pick a set of random values (maybe your own), and build the SQL to do what you want:

```sql
INSERT INTO users (first_name,
                   last_name,
                   email,
                   facebook_url,
                   twitter_handle)
           VALUES ("Brett",
                   "McLaughlin",
                   "brett.m@me.com",
                   "http://www.facebook.com/bdmclaughlin",
                   "@bdmclaughlin");
```

NOTE You can use your MySQL tools to test this SQL until it works, and is formatted just right.

This statement now becomes a sort of template: you basically want this statement, but you need to replace your sample values with your user's request information. Since you've already got those values, this task isn't too hard:

```
$insert_sql = "INSERT INTO users (first_name, last_name, " .
                    "email, facebook_url, twitter_handle) " .
           "VALUES ('{$first_name}', '{$last_name}', '{$email}', " .
                "'{$facebook_url}', '{$twitter_handle}');";
```

NOTE You may not need to break this code up into as many separate lines, connected by the periods, as was necessary to fit it on this page.

In this example, you're creating a new string that has the SQL query. You can then pass that query to *mysql_query*, and run against your database. The one gotcha here is that you must make sure each value you send to the database and that will go into a text field in the *users* table is surrounded by quotes. Using single quotes lets you use double quotes around the entire query, and to use curly braces (*{ }*) to drop your variables right into the query string (page 102).

Inserting a User

Now it's time add a user to your database, and it's the easiest (and often the most fun) line of SQL-invoking PHP to write:

```
<?php

// Handle user request

$insert_sql = "INSERT INTO users (first_name, last_name, email, facebook_url,
twitter_handle) " .
           "VALUES ('{$first_name}', '{$last_name}', '{$email}', " .
                "'{$facebook_url}', '{$twitter_handle}');";

// Insert the user into the database
mysql_query($insert_sql);

?>
```

Great! You're not quite done, though. You've got to account for the possibility of an error. For example, what if you forgot to add the *users* table first? What if you have a *users* table, but without a *facebook_url* column, or a misnamed or misspelled column?

There's really a lot of work to do when it comes to error reporting, so for now, take a really simple (and probably way *too* simple) approach:

```php
<?php

// Handle user request

$insert_sql = "INSERT INTO users (first_name, last_name, email, facebook_url,
twitter_handle) " .
                "VALUES ('{$first_name}', '{$last_name}', '{$email}', " .
                    "'{$facebook_url}', '{$twitter_handle}');";

// Insert the user into the database
mysql_query($insert_sql)
  or die(mysql_error());

?>
```

Using the *die* method (page 111) isn't ideal, but it's at least functional, and at least gives you some kind of report on error.

At this point, you can try out your page, albeit a little clumsily. So visit your web page, and fill out some sample values, as in Figure 6-4.

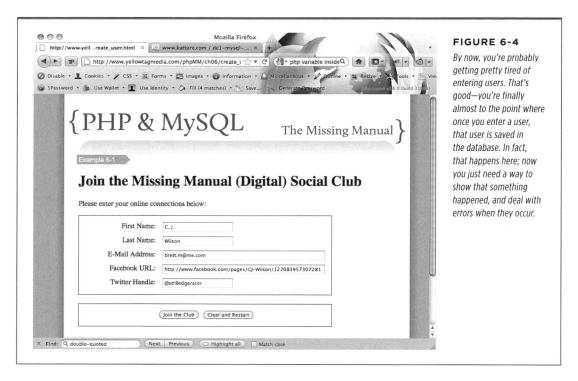

FIGURE 6-4

By now, you're probably getting pretty tired of entering users. That's good—you're finally almost to the point where once you enter a user, that user is saved in the database. In fact, that happens here; now you just need a way to show that something happened, and deal with errors when they occur.

Now submit your page, and your new code will run. It will construct a SQL statement using your values, connect to the database, and insert the data using *mysql_query*. Hopefully, your *die* statement *won't* get run.

Assuming you don't get an error, you'll get almost nothing back. That's rather disappointing, but something did happen—especially if you *didn't* get an error message.

NOTE If you still have the HTML section of *getFormInfo.php* copied into *create_user.php*, you might get back some output from your form submission.

To find out what happened in your database, fire up a SQL tool and enter this query:

```
SELECT user_id, first_name, last_name
  FROM users;
```

You should get back something like this:

```
+---------+------------+-----------+
| user_id | first_name | last_name |
+---------+------------+-----------+
|       1 | C. J.      | Wilson    |
+---------+------------+-----------+
1 row in set (0.00 sec)
```

If you're using phpMyAdmin, you can browse to your *users* table and check out any data that might be inside of it, as shown in Figure 6-5.

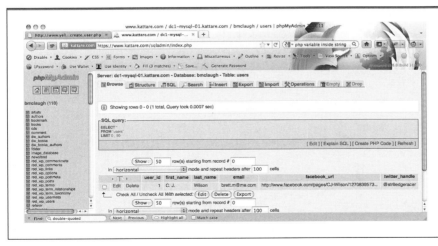

FIGURE 6-5

You can see here that the entry in users has not only the data pulled from the web form, but also an auto-generated (and auto incremented) id: in this case, 1. As you have more and more users, that number will continue to increment, although you can't count on it being sequential.

Name Follows Function

When you've got only a few web pages here and there, names are really not that big of a deal. Whether you name a page *getFormInfo.html* or *create_user.html* is pretty close to irrelevant; you can see all your files in a single directory listing or window of your FTP client.

But in even medium-sized web apps, you'll have a lot more files than that. In fact, if you start to do the testing you should be doing, you can easily have hundreds of files. At that point, your names really need to be meaningful.

But there's more to meaning than just description. Many of your forms and scripts will pertain directly to a single table in your database, and in fact doing one specific thing with

regard to that table, like creating a user via the *users* table. In these cases, you make it really easy on yourself and others who'll work on your code by naming your files according to function. So while your form may get a user's social networking information, it ultimately creates a user, and *create_user.php* is a descriptive, simple, clear name.

On top of all that, you'll soon be learning about CRUD: the idea that for any type of information, like a user, you CReate, Update, and Delete that information. Mapping your HTML pages and scripts to those basic actions (*create_user*, *update_user*, and so on) really helps you see what you have...and what you don't.

A First Pass at Confirmation

At this point, you've got a user (or as many as you created via your web form), but *your* user—the person using your web application—sees nothing but a blank screen. Time provide some feedback so your users know what's going on after they complete the form.

As a starting point, you can go back to the code from your older script, *getFormInfo. php*, from page 27:

```php
<?php

// Get the user's information from the request array

// Connect to the database and insert the user

?>

<html>
 <head>
  <link href="../../css/phpMM.css" rel="stylesheet" type="text/css" />
 </head>
 <body>
  <div id="header"><h1>PHP & MySQL: The Missing Manual</h1></div>
  <div id="example">Example 6-1</div>
  <div id="content">
```

```
<p>Here's a record of what information you submitted:</p>
<p>
  Name: <?php echo $first_name . " " . $last_name; ?><br />
  E-Mail Address: <?php echo $email; ?><br />
  <a href="<?php echo $facebook_url; ?>">Your Facebook page</a>
  <br />
  <a href="<?php echo $twitter_url; ?>">Check out your Twitter feed</a>
  <br />
</p>
</div>

<div id="footer"></div>
</body>
</html>
```

This page is better than nothing, but you can see some things to fix right away. First, you're not printing the user's Twitter handle; you're printing out the URL to that handle. While that's handier for clicking, it doesn't represent what was entered into the database. So you've got a tough choice:

- You can print what was entered into the database, the value in *$twitter_handle*. That's what was inserted, but it doesn't have much value in a web page, and it's simply letting your users know what's in your database. Do your users really care about your database structure?

- You can print the URL, which is better for clicking, but doesn't directly connect to what's in the database. It's a modification of the database value, which is OK, but might not be appropriate right on the heels of a form that's explicitly focused upon adding a user to the database.

Now, this point is rather trivial when you consider that it's only a Twitter handle. But the same issue comes up with whether you show the first and last names, or combine them together as this code does now:

```
Name: <?php echo $first_name . " " . $last_name; ?><br />
```

You can see the greater issue here: what exactly do you show your users? Do you show them the literal values as they're stored in the database, or do you massage your values so they're a little more readable for humans?

Users Are Users, Not Programmers

As the previous example suggests, you *always* want to show your users things that make sense to them. Very rarely will your users care about the columns in your database, or the value of the primary key, or whether you store their Twitter handle with or without the @ sign. Focus on what your users *want* to see, not what your database literally contains.

But there's something else going on here: what's the *source* for the information you're showing? Implied in this idea of showing a user what makes sense to them is the idea that you, the wise programmer, take information from the database, work with it to get it into the right format, and then show that massaged information to the user.

But in this first pass at a confirmation, are you showing what's in the database? Not at all; you're just spitting back out what the user gave you. What if something *did* happen when that information was inserted into your database table? You'd never know it. By showing the user their own information, you could be masking what really got dropped into the database.

So what do you do? You want to show users something that makes sense to them, but you also want to show those values based on the database, rather than just regurgitating a form, since that doesn't show any problems in the database.

Well, hopefully, you do both! Suppose you had a way to pull the user's information from the database, perhaps using a SQL *SELECT*, and then based upon that information—information from the database, problems or not—construct something the user can see and read and that makes sense.

One solution would be, after inserting the user, to reload that same information, for example like this:

```php
<?php

// Get the user's information from the request array

// Connect to the database and insert the user

$get_user_query = "SELECT * FROM USERS WHERE ..."
mysql_query($get_user_query);

// Load this information and ready it for display in the HTML output

?>

<!-- HTML output -->
```

> **WARNING** The *$get_user_query* in this code is intentionally incomplete. Those three dots won't really work; you'd need to include a *WHERE* piece that locates the user that was just added.

This code gets you the user from the database, and it still lets you modify those values as needed for good human-readable display. You still have to figure out how to find the particular user that just got inserted, but that's something you'll learn how to handle later in this chapter.

With this code, you do a bunch of text manipulation on the request information, and then you need to process it again with the response from the database. But is that the best way to go about it?

Not really. Think about your application as a whole: Is there any other place you might want to display a user? Absolutely—every good application has a place where a user can check out her own profile. To provide that functionality, you would need to take the code in the back part of *create_user.php* and then copy it into a *show_user. php* script later. But that's not good; remember, you really, really, *really* don't want the same code in more than one place. That's actually why you've got the very cool *database_connection.php* script you can use over and over.

What you really need is another script, one that shows user information. That way, you can simply throw users from *create_user.php*, which creates users, to this new script, and let it figure out what to do in terms of a response. So leave *create_user. php* incomplete for now, and you can come back and fix it up later.

■ Show Me the User

So here's the task: you need a page that shows a user's information, in a way that makes sense to the user. So this page is going to pull information from the *users* table, but it's not a form; there's no need (at least, not yet) to do anything but display information.

Now, you could dive right into your PHP, but most of the work here isn't code; it's getting a good user profile page built. So save yourself some PHP madness, and start with HTML.

And as a bonus, most web servers are configured to take a request for a file ending in *.php* and create HTML output, which is handed to a user's browser. So you can create HTML, drop it into a file ending in *.php*, and when you start adding actual PHP, you're ready to go. Your web server will send the HTML in that file to a requesting web browser, and your user's (or you) see HTML output.

Mocking Up a User Profile Page
Figure 6-6 shows a pretty solid-looking profile page. It shows the basics of each user's contact information, as well as some helpful additions: a short bio and a picture of the user.

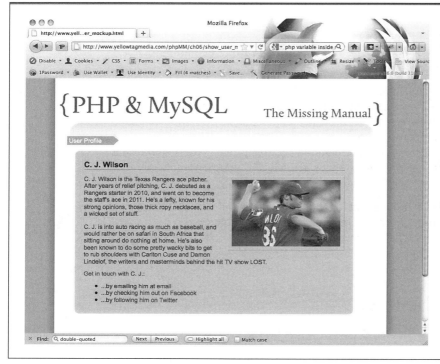

FIGURE 6-6

*Sometimes the best PHP
doesn't begin with PHP at
all. Creating HTML pages is
work, and often involves
lots of tweaking, not to
mention all the rules in
your CSS you'll need to
create. By starting with
a plain old HTML page,
you can get the look and
feel of things just right.
Then, when you're ready
to start writing your PHP,
you don't have much
HTML work left; you can
just drop in your database
values in the right spots,
and know your page will
turn out great.*

Here's the HTML for this page; with CSS, it stays pretty simple.

```
<html>
 <head>
  <link href="../css/phpMM.css" rel="stylesheet" type="text/css" />
 </head>

 <body>
  <div id="header"><h1>PHP & MySQL: The Missing Manual</h1></div>
  <div id="example">User Profile</div>

  <div id="content">
    <div class="user_profile">
      <h1>C. J. Wilson</h1>
      <p>
        <img src="images/cj_wilson.jpg" class="user_pic" />
        C. J. Wilson is the Texas Rangers ace pitcher. After years of
        relief pitching, C. J. debuted as a Rangers starter in 2010, and
        went on to become the staff's ace in 2011. He's a lefty, known
```

```
      for his strong opinions, those thick ropy necklaces, and a wicked
      set of stuff. </p>
    <p>C. J. is into auto racing as much as baseball, and would rather
      be on safari in South Africa that sitting around do nothing at home.
      He's also been known to do some pretty wacky bits to get to rub
      shoulders with Carlton Cuse and Damon Lindelof, the writers
      and masterminds behind the hit TV show LOST.</p>
    <p class="contact_info">Get in touch with C. J.:</p>
    <ul>
      <li>...by emailing him at
        <a href="wilson@texasrangers.com">wilson@texasrangers.com</a></li>
      <li>...by
        <a href="http://www.facebook.com/pages/CJ-Wilson/127083957307281">
        checking them out on Facebook</a></li>
      <li>...by <a href="http://www.twitter.com/str8edgeracer">following
        them on Twitter</a></li>
    </ul>
    </div>
  </div>
  <div id="footer"></div>
  </body>
</html>
```

> **NOTE** The bio and picture here are new, and not things you should already have in your *users* table. They're just nice touches for a user's profile page. Just a name and a few links for email and Twitter was pretty sparse.
>
> Don't worry, though. You'll be adding a profile picture and bio to your database soon, and then this page really will be something your app can display.

Now, even though this page is pretty straightforward, it's really even simpler than this. Go ahead and imagine (or type) this page not with placeholder text, but with variables in the place of the dummy text. So wherever the user's first name goes, simply envision *$first_name*, and then *$last_name, $email*, and so on. The result is pretty clean:

```
<html>
<head>
  <link href="../css/phpMM.css" rel="stylesheet" type="text/css" />
</head>

<body>
  <div id="header"><h1>PHP & MySQL: The Missing Manual</h1></div>
  <div id="example">User Profile</div>

  <div id="content">
    <div class="user_profile">
      <h1>$first_name $last_name</h1>
```

```
    <p><img src="$user_image" class="user_pic" />
      $bio</p>
    <p class="contact_info">Get in touch with $first_name:</p>
    <ul>
      <li>...by emailing them at
        <a href="$email">$email</a></li>
      <li>...by
        <a href="$facebook_url">checking them out on Facebook</a></li>
      <li>...by <a href="$twitter_url">following them on Twitter</a></li>
    </ul>
    </div>
  </div>
  <div id="footer"></div>
 </body>
</html>
```

> **WARNING** This example is helpful to think through, but it's not valid HTML or PHP. So don't try and view this code in a browser...you won't get anything useful, and it certainly won't work as a PHP script. Still, you should see that almost everything on the page really just represents information in the database, all in a very user-friendly format.

This example shows why it's a good idea to focus on your HTML first, rather than diving right into PHP. When you start designing your page, you'll often think of things you really need—like a bio (*$bio*) and a picture (*$user_image*), neither of which your *users* table has yet.

So with this simple mockup, you've figured out several important things:

1. You're missing some key information in your *users* table. You really need a bio, which is just a long chunk of text, and a way to load an image of the user.

2. Once you update your table, you've got to update your *create_user.html* and *create_user.php* form and code to let users enter that information, and then save the new information to your database.

3. Finally—and this is great news—with those changes, you can build a pretty nice looking user profile page.

So what do you do first? Well, the database is usually the centerpiece of things, so you need to update your *users* table.

Changing a Table's Structure with *ALTER*

There are two pieces of information missing from *users*: a bio, and an image. For now, don't worry about the image yet. That takes a little bit of work, and you can always drop a placeholder in and come back to that. But the bio...that's pretty easy.

First, you need to change your table's structure by adding a column. That's not hard at all; the SQL *ALTER* command lets you do just that:

```
ALTER TABLE users
     ADD bio varchar(1000);
```

WARNING Be sure you type *ALTER* and not *ALTAR*; the first is a SQL command, and the second is a place to make sacrifices. Either way, *ALTAR* will definitely not get your table in the shape you want.

This command really is as simple as it looks. You give SQL the table to *ALTER*, and then tell it what alteration you want. In this case, you want to add a column, so you use ADD, give it the new column name, and a type.

Of course, there are implications here: is it okay for a user to leave a biography blank, or should the *bio* column be *NOT NULL*? (It's probably okay if it's left blank, so *NOT NULL* really isn't required.) How in the world does information get into this column for new users? (Well, you need to update your *create_user* HTML web form, and the script that does the database work. That's up next.) Can you alter a table any time you want? Yes—databases are nothing if not flexible.

FREQUENTLY ASKED QUESTION

What Happens to the Old Rows in a Table When a New Column is Added?

Although it's easy to add a column to a database with *ALTER*, and it's often relatively painless to update your forms to let your users get information into those columns (and show the results, if you've already got a *show_user* script), there's something left that *can* be a pain: dealing with old data that suddenly has a new column.

Take the *users* table, and imagine it didn't have one or two recent entries, but thousands of users from the last five years. Now, with your alteration, every one of those users has a glaring empty spot: their bio. Most databases happily leave the column blank, meaning you'll get *NULL* every time you try and pull something out of the new *bio* column.

Getting *NULL* isn't a big deal in this case. You could probably call user bios a "new feature," throw together a press release, and spin the oversight as a brand-new version, improved and usable by a whole new generation of bio-loving potential users. Existing users can log in and add a bio, which they couldn't do before.

Adding a new required column to a database can be awkward. Imagine the owners of a website deciding that using an email address as a username isn't a great idea. They probably altered their tables, adding a username column, but had to make it *NOT NULL*. After all, what's the point of a username without requiring that it exist, or you have users without one?

So now you have a legitimate problem: you now have tons of rows that are missing required data. So what do you do? Well, you can simply lock those users out, and the next time they try and access your site, build a mechanism that forces them to select a username. That's pretty typical, and even expected in these security-conscious days of the Web. But what if that's not tenable? Then you're allowing all those rows to be in an invalid state until a user logs in.

If that's a problem—and it often is—you may have to insert some sort of placeholder data into your table, like NEEDS_USERNAME, and simply query a user to see if that's his username value when he comes back to your site. It's not the most elegant solution, but it keeps your data valid. And that's ultimately the big issue with using *ALTER*: you potentially end up with data in an invalid state for some amount of time, or you have to insert "fake" data for a time to keep things running, although you know that data can't ultimately stay put. Neither solution is great, so you'll simply have to choose the lesser of these two evils. (Or come up with something else altogether, and let us know by tweeting us at @missingmanuals. We'd love to hear what you come up with.)

Building Your Script: First Pass

So with the new bio column in *users*, and an HTML mockup, you're ready to get down to the business of PHP. Go ahead and create a new script, and call it *show_user.php*. This script goes along nicely with *create_user.php*, and you can already imagine you'll later add scripts like *delete_user.php* and *update_user.php* to complete the package.

To begin, you actually don't need any PHP in this script at all. Instead, just drop in your HTML. Then, as you did earlier, you can replace all the places where there will be data from the database with PHP variable names. Here's what you should end up with:

```html
<html>
<head>
 <link href="../../css/phpMM.css" rel="stylesheet" type="text/css" />
</head>

<body>
 <div id="header"><h1>PHP & MySQL: The Missing Manual</h1></div>
 <div id="example">User Profile</div>

 <div id="content">
   <div class="user_profile">
     <h1>$first_name $last_name</h1>
     <p><img src="$user_image" class="user_pic" />
       $bio</p>
     <p class="contact_info">Get in touch with $first_name:</p>
     <ul>
       <li>...by emailing them at
         <a href="$email">$email</a></li>
       <li>...by
         <a href="$facebook_url">checking them out on Facebook</a></li>
       <li>...by <a href="$twitter_url">following them on Twitter</a></li>
     </ul>
   </div>
 </div>
 <div id="footer"></div>
</body>
</html>
```

Now there are definitely some things here that are a bit odd:

- Where's the PHP? There's no *<?php* or *?>* yet, and certainly no code.

- Those variables are definitely PHP, not HTML. An HTML page won't know what to do with them.

- Where does the database interaction occur? There's no SQL, no *SELECT* from the database, or anything.

- Which user is to be loaded? How does the script know which user to load?

These are all the right questions to be asking, so if you came up with a few of these, you're really getting your head around the big issues in PHP and web programming.

First, as to where the *<?php* and *?>* tags are: they're coming later, but that's really incidental. You can give a file the *.php* extension, and still put nothing but HTML within that file. In fact, type the URL to your script into your browser, and see what happens; Figure 6-7 is about right.

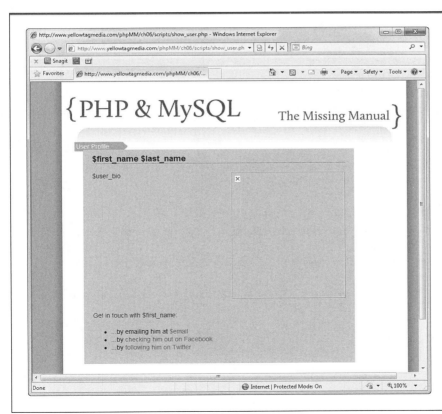

FIGURE 6-7

Starting with the HTML another good testing technique. At this stage, you don't have any real values in, so you can focus on how your page looks. Once you add PHP code, it's easy to get focused on your database interaction and formatting the actual strings and values in your variables. When you prototype before you get to your database interaction, you can make sure things look just right, and then just tweak things one more time once you drop in a real value for each variable.

At this point, in *show_user.php*, there's nothing but HTML inside the file, so your web server supplies that HTML to a user's web browser. The result is a nice-looking web page. Of course, there's still a handful of issues to deal with, like those variable names that are coming across as plain old text.

That's pretty easy, though. You can simply surround each variable with *<?php* and *?>*, which tells the browser, "Hey, treat this little bit as PHP." Then, you'll have to add *echo* because you want to output the value of the variable.

```html
<html>
 <head>
  <link href="../../css/phpMM.css" rel="stylesheet" type="text/css" />
 </head>

 <body>
  <div id="header"><h1>PHP & MySQL: The Missing Manual</h1></div>
  <div id="example">User Profile</div>
  <div id="content">
    <div class="user_profile">
      <h1><?php echo "{$first_name} {$last_name}"; ?></h1>
      <p><img src="<?php echo $user_image; ?>" class="user_pic" />
        <?php echo $bio; ?></p>
      <p class="contact_info">
        Get in touch with <?php echo $first_name; ?>:
      </p>
      <ul>
        <li>...by emailing them at
          <a href="<?php echo $email; ?>"><?php echo $email; ?></a></li>
        <li>...by
          <a href="<?php echo $facebook_url; ?>">checking them out
            on Facebook</a></li>
        <li>...by <a href="<?php echo $twitter_url; ?>">following them
            on Twitter</a></li>
      </ul>
    </div>
  </div>
  <div id="footer"></div>
 </body>
</html>
```

There's still a pretty obvious issue here: these variables have no values. You haven't defined them, and if you try and access this page now, you'll get very strange results (see Figure 6-8). But you're slowly moving toward a useful script.

The biggest problem here is you really don't know if this code works. Are there typos? Are there problems in the minimal PHP you have? It's a pain to move on to your database code when you're not sure that—even if you have the right values from the database—it'll work properly.

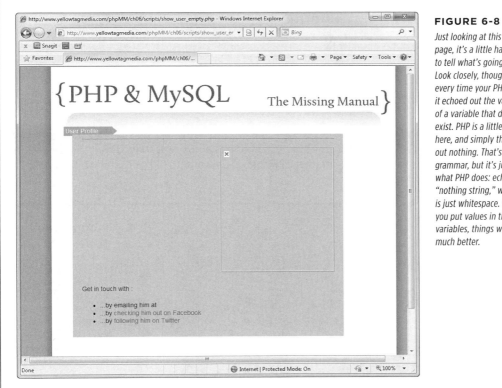

FIGURE 6-8

Just looking at this web page, it's a little hard to tell what's going on. Look closely, though: every time your PHP ran, it echoed out the value of a variable that didn't exist. PHP is a little loose here, and simply throws out nothing. That's bad grammar, but it's just what PHP does: echoes a "nothing string," which is just whitespace. Once you put values in those variables, things will look much better.

One easy way to test before getting much further is to simply create a small section of PHP before the HTML. In the *<?php* section, assign to each variable the sort of value you'd get from the database.

```php
<?php
$first_name = "C. J.";
$last_name = "Wilson";
$user_image = "/not/yet/implemented.jpg";
$bio = "C. J. Wilson is the Texas Rangers ace pitcher. After years of
        relief pitching, C. J. debuted as a Rangers starter in 2010, and
        went on to become the staff's ace in 2011. He's a lefty, known
        for his strong opinions, those thick ropy necklaces, and a wicked
        set of stuff. </p>
```

```
       <p>C. J. is into auto racing as much as baseball, and would rather
          be on safari in South Africa that sitting around do nothing at home.
     He's also been known to do some pretty wacky bits to get to rub
          shoulders with Carlton Cuse and Damon Lindelof, the writers
          and masterminds behind the hit TV show LOST.";
$email = "wilson@texasrangers.com";
$facebook_url = "http://www.facebook.com/pages/CJ-Wilson/127083957307281";
$twitter_url = "http://www.twitter.com/str8edgeracer";
?>

<html>
  <!-- All your HTML and inline PHP -->
</html>
```

Now you can actually visit your page, and see some useful results, as you see in Figure 6-9. You can see that your code is actually working, and now all you have left is to fill those variables with real values, and then figure out which user to look up in the first place.

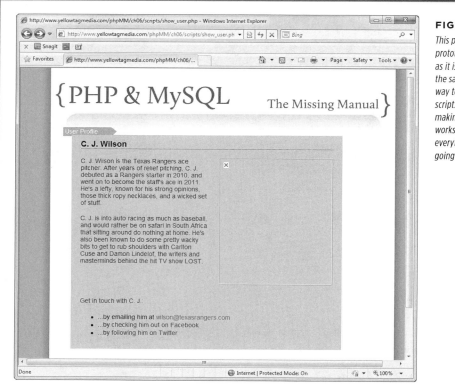

FIGURE 6-9

This page is still as much prototype and mock-up as it is working code. All the same, this is a good way to work up to a full script: piece by piece, making sure each step works independently of everything else that is going to be added later.

SELECT a User From Your Database

You've got your variables, and you've got your HTML. Now you need to get your user. That's pretty easy, as you've already used *SELECT* a few times:

```
SELECT *
  FROM users;
```

In fact, you can run that command now on your database, and get back all the rows you have:

```
+---------+------------+-----------+----------------+--------------
----------------------------------------------+----------------+------+
| user_id | first_name | last_name | email          | facebook_url
| twitter_handle | bio  |
+---------+------------+-----------+----------------+--------------
----------------------------------------------+----------------+------+
|       1 | C. J.      | Wilson    | brett.m@me.com | http://www.facebook.com/
pages/CJ-Wilson/127083957307281 | @str8edgeracer
 | NULL |
+---------+------------+-----------+----------------+------------------
----------------------------------------------+----------------+------+
1 row in set (0.03 sec)
```

> **NOTE** This output is intentionally left as a bit of a mess, because it's probably just what you see, too. The output of your *SELECT* is all the rows in the table, which won't fit in a normal command-line prompt, let alone the width of this page.

In this case, there's just a single user. So once you get this user, you can pull out the *first_name* and *last_name* values, the *email* value, and so on, and stuff them in *$first_name*, *$last_name*, and the rest of your variables.

But there's still one big question: how do you know *which* user to get? Obviously, in the table output here, there's just a single user. But what about when your new app is a hit and you have hundreds, or thousands, or even hundreds of thousands, of users? You need to select just one of those users for *show_user.php* to display... and how do you figure out that one?

To find out, think about how people will get to *show_user.php*. Here are a few:

- They get sent to this page after they've created a new user with *create_user. html* and *create_user.php*.

- They log in to your application and click a link like "My Profile" or "Update My Information."

- They select a particular user from a list of users, maybe all the users in the system, or all their friends, or all the users they're watching or following.

What's common in all these situations? Nobody ever goes to *show_user.php* directly by typing in a URL. In each case, they're selecting a user, or creating a user, or logging in as a user, and then some link is taking them to *show_user.php*.

As a result, in every reasonable situation, your code sends the user to *show_user. php*, and so your code is in control. If you need to, say, send some information to *show_user.php*, you can do it. All you do is send the unique ID of the user that *show_user.php* should load from the database, and display it.

So revisit those same scenarios again:

- A user is created by *create_user.php*, and the ID of that new user is handed off, along with your application user, to *show_user.php*.

- Clicking "My Profile" or "Update My Information" passes along the current logged-in user's ID to *show_user.php*.

- Selecting a user from a list—regardless of what's in that list—results in a link to *show_user.php* being followed, and the selected user's ID being passed to *show_user.php* at the same time.

In each case, your *show_user.php* script can get the passed-in ID, then look up the user by the passed-in ID, and finally display that user.

The beauty of this solution is not just that it's possible, because you have control over all the ways your users might get to *show_user.php*. It's also perfect because you can pass in the ID of the user to show as part of the request, and you've already pulled things out of the request before, using *$_REQUEST*.

Add this line to *show_user.php* now:

```php
<?php

$user_id = $_REQUEST['user_id'];

// Code to assign values to the page variables
?>

<html>
  <!-- All your HTML and inline PHP -->
</html>
```

Nothing new here; the only thing that's different from what you've done before is that you're pulling a request parameter with a new name: *user_id*.

Now you can finally add a *WHERE* clause to *SELECT*:

```sql
SELECT *
  FROM users
 WHERE user_id = $user_id;
```

So far, you've seen a few *WHERE* clauses (like the one on page 80), and they do just what you might expect: narrow a set of results based upon a match, or some other restriction. In this case, you're saying, "Give me everything (*) from the *users* table, but only for the records (rows) that have a *user_id* of the value in *$user_id*."

So if your sample user has a *user_id* of 1, and *$user_id* is 1, you'll get that sample user. If you don't have any rows that have a *user_id* of 1, then you'll get nothing back from the *SELECT*. And here's what's really cool: you made *user_id* a primary key (page 148) with *PRIMARY KEY*, which means that you'll never have more than one result returned. So you don't have to see how many values are returned, or do anything special to handle one row or multiple rows. You'll either get nothing back because there was no match, or you'll get just a single row back.

Put all this together, and you can make some really important additions to *show_user. php*:

```php
<?php

require '../../scripts/database_connection.php';

// Get the user ID of the user to show
$user_id = $_REQUEST['user_id'];

// Build the SELECT statement
$select_query = "SELECT * FROM users WHERE user_id = " . $user_id;

// Run the query
$result = mysql_query($select_query);

// Assign values to variables
?>

<html>
  <!-- All your HTML and inline PHP -->
</html>
```

This now connects to your database, builds the SELECT statement from the passed-in *user_id* request parameter, and runs the query. And all that's left is the one entirely new piece to this script: running through the actual result from a query, and getting information from that result.

Pulling Values From a SQL Query Result

You've got a *$result* variable, but what is that? You probably remember that it's a *resource*, a special type of variable that holds a reference to more information. So you can pass that resource to other PHP functions, and use it to get more information.

In the case of a *SELECT* query, what you really want are all the actual rows the query returned, and then for each row, you want the different values. That's exactly what you can use a resource for, so you're all set to finish off *show_user.php* and start accepting requests.

You begin by making sure that *$result* has a value; this is equivalent to making sure that *$result* is not false, which is returned when there's a problem with your SQL:

```php
// Run the query
$result = mysql_query($select_query);

if ($result) {
  // Get the query result rows using $result
} else {
  die("Error locating user with ID {$user_id}");
}
```

This *if* also (marginally) handles errors. If *$result* is false, something went wrong, which presumably means the user you were searching for using *$user_id* doesn't exist, or there was a problem finding that user. This code as it stands doesn't format the error very nicely, and in fact gives you little information about what actually caused the problem. That's okay, though; you'll fix up your error handling pretty soon, so this *if* is a decent short-term solution.

Now, you need a new PHP function: *mysql_fetch_array*. This function takes in a resource from a previously run SQL query. That's exactly what you have in *$result*:

```php
if ($result) {
  $row = mysql_fetch_array($result);

  // Break up the row into its different fields and assign to variables
} else {
  die("Error locating user with ID {$user_id}");
}
```

Here's where things get a little odd. Notice that your script, using the code above, stores the result from *mysql_fetch_array* in *$row*. That means *mysql_fetch_array* returns a single row from your SQL query—and that's correct.

But the actual name of the function suggests something else: that an *array* is returned (it's *mysql_fetch_array*, not *mysql_fetch_row*, isn't it?). So which is it? It's both. *mysql_fetch_array* does return an array; but it returns an array for a single row of the query associated with the result you pass into it.

So for *mysql_fetch_array($result)*, you're going to get back a *single* row of results, but that the *way* that row is returned is in the form of an array.

NOTE In case you're wondering, you certainly can get *every* row of results returned from a query, not just the first result row. You simply keep calling *mysql_fetch_array*, over and over, and it keeps returning the next row from the results. Eventually, *mysql_fetch_array* will return *false*, which means there are no more results.

Before long, you'll use *mysql_fetch_array* like this yourself, and it'll all make perfect sense. For now, know that every time you call this function, you'll get one row of results (or false if there are no rows left to return), and that row is an array of values.

Arrays are no problem for you, so getting back an array in *$row* is good news. In fact, *$row* is just like another array you know, the *$_REQUEST* array (page 46). And just like *$_REQUEST*, you have not just a list of values, but values that are keyed based on a name.

So when a request came in with a parameter named "first_name", you pulled the value for that parameter with *$_REQUEST['first_name']*. The exact same principle applies to *$row*. You can give it the name of a column returned in your SQL query, and you'll get the value for that column, in the specific row you're examining.

So once you've got *$row*, you can just grab all the columns you want, and stuff them into some variables:

```php
// Run the query
$result = mysql_query($select_query);
if ($result) {
  $row = mysql_fetch_array($result);
  $first_name    = $row['first_name'];
  $last_name     = $row['last_name'];
  $bio       = $row['bio'];
  $email         = $row['email'];
  $facebook_url  = $row['facebook_url'];
  $twitter_handle = $row['twitter_handle'];

  // Turn $twitter_handle into a URL
  $twitter_url = "http://www.twitter.com/" .
                 substr($twitter_handle, $position + 1);

  // To be added later
  $user_image = "/not/yet/implemented.jpg";
} else {
  die("Error locating user with ID {$user_id}");
}
```

> **NOTE** At the end of this *if*, you should add in the preceding code that creates a URL for the Twitter handle. It's the same code you used on page 42 to build this URL, although back then you weren't getting the user's Twitter handle from a database.
>
> Also add the code that fills in *$user_image* with a dummy value until you come back later to fix the user's image for real. You could also use a stock image for when there's no picture, like this:
>
> ```
> $user_image = "../../images/missing_user.png";
> ```
>
> There's a sample of an image like this in the downloadable examples for this chapter (page xvii) if you want to go this route for now.

At this point, you've got a fully functional script! In fact, other than figuring out how to use the *$result* resource with *mysql_fetch_array*, all this is pretty normal stuff and shouldn't be any problem for you at all.

Getting a User ID into *show_user.php*

At this point, you have to get a user ID into your script, so it can use that ID to look up a user, get his information, and display it. But before you start hacking all your other scripts together, it would be really nice to make sure *show_user.php* works. Who wants to spend a bunch of time on other scripts if there's a problem somewhere in *show_user.php*? That's no good.

Fortunately, there's an easy way to test your script. The *$_REQUEST* array has all the information passed into your script through its request—including extra information passed through the request URL itself. Now, remember, this isn't the ordinary way you'd either get information into *show_user.php*, or even access *show_user.php* in the first place. Instead, scripts like *create_user.php* or maybe a "My Profile" button would get your users to this script.

But for now, you're just testing. So why not go directly to the page, with a URL like *yellowtagmedia.com/phpMM/ch06/scripts/show_user.php*? And as long as you're there, you can feed that script request data with request parameters on the URL itself. You can simply add these to the URL, after a *?*. So the format is basically this:

```
[protocol]://[domain-name]/[location-of-file]?[request-paramaters]
```

So you might say *mysite.com/scripts/show_user.php?first_name=Lance*. Now you can grab *$_REQUEST['first_name']*, and you'd get back "Lance." You can stack these up, too; just separate the parameters with &. So you can go further and do *mysite.com/scripts/show_user.php?first_name=Lance&last_name=McCollum*.

> **NOTE** More formally, the file name (*show_user.php*) is the *path*. The information after that (*?first_name=Lance&last_name=McCollum*) is the *query string*.

You can see what to do next. Add the user ID of the user you created much earlier (or one of the users, if you inserted more than one), and try out *show_user.php*, with a URL like *yellowtagmedia.com/phpMM/ch06/scripts/show_user.php?user_id=1*.

You should get something back like Figure 6-10, which is a validation of all the work you've put into SQL and *show_user.php*.

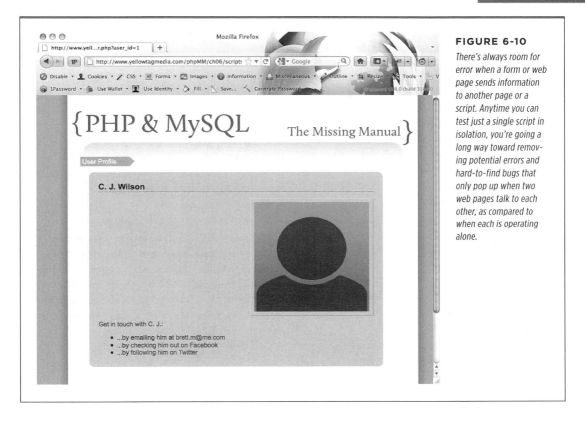

There's always room for error when a form or web page sends information to another page or a script. Anytime you can test just a single script in isolation, you're going a long way toward removing potential errors and hard-to-find bugs that only pop up when two web pages talk to each other, as compared to when each is operating alone.

WARNING Request parameters are case-sensitive, as is your PHP. So asking for *$_REQUEST['user_id']* will not match a request parameter named *USER_ID* or *user_Id*. Be careful your uppercase and lowercase letters all match up.

At this point, you've done just about everything you can to make sure *show_user. php* is going to behave. It's missing some information, like the user's pic and bio, but you can deal with the picture later, and the bio through updating *create_user. php*. Other than that, it's time to leave *show_user.php* alone and revisit the script that needs to send users *to* this one.

NOTE There *is* probably one more thing you could do: manually *INSERT* a user with a bio into your users table, and then try out *show_user.php* again. You might want to do that now, and really verify that *show_user. php* is just like you want it. You'll test that same bit of functionality in a little while once you update *create_user. php*, but there's really no such thing as too much testing.

DESIGN TIME

Is a *scripts/* Directory a Good Idea?

Storing all your scripts in a directory (or, technically, a sub-directory) called *scripts/* is a practice that largely dates back to older programming languages like Perl and CGI (something called the *Common Gateway Interface*, a way of calling external programs like server-side scripts). In those days, you'd have a really firm separation between client-side programs or views, and server-side programs. So a script never really did anything that resulted directly in a web page being displayed; they were just programs called by other processes.

But PHP really blurs the line between what's a script and what's a viewable page. The *show_user.php* script is actually a lot more HTML than it is PHP, and it's going to be common for a user to actually hit *show_user.php* directly. In other words, PHP is more than just a way to write scripts to which your forms submit behind the scenes. There will be lots of times where users click a link to a PHP page, rather than an HTML page, or even type in a PHP script's URL in their browser.

In fact, there are some pretty popular pieces of software that essentially handle *all* HTML within PHP. Wordpress (online at

wordpress.org and wordpress.com) is a hugely popular blogging and content management system that is built on PHP. In that system, the actual home page of your site is *index.php*, not *index.html*.

So at that point, does a *scripts/* directory make sense? No, it really doesn't. Your users don't care if they're getting a page from an HTML file or a PHP script, as long as it looks and acts the way they expect. And adding a scripts/ directory actually *increases* what your users have to know about your system, rather than making things more transparent.

So beginning in Chapter 7, this change will kick into gear. It's good that you've been thinking about the difference between what you've been doing as a web page creator with HTML, CSS, and JavaScript, and your new PHP skills. But now that you've moved beyond just submitting forms to PHP, it's time to blur the lines even further, and let many of your PHP scripts live alongside your HTML.

■ Redirection and Revisitation of Creating Users

All the changes you've made so far are great, but you're not done. You have a new bio column, but no place for users to enter that information when they sign up. You need *create_user.php* to deal with that information when it comes in from your sign-up form. And then there's getting a user from the sign-up form to *show_user.php*—and passing along the newly created user's ID as well. It seems like a lot, but with what you know, it'll be a breeze.

Updating Your User Signup Form

The first change is one of the easiest. Open up your original *create_user.html* page, and add a new form field so that your users can easily enter in a biography. Leave plenty of space: have you seen how much information people write about themselves on Facebook these days?

```
<html>
 <head>
  <link href="../css/phpMM.css" rel="stylesheet" type="text/css" />
 </head>

 <body>
  <div id="header"><h1>PHP & MySQL: The Missing Manual</h1></div>
  <div id="example">User Signup</div>

  <div id="content">
    <h1>Join the Missing Manual (Digital) Social Club</h1>
    <p>Please enter your online connections below:</p>
    <form action="scripts/create_user.php" method="POST">
      <fieldset>
        <label for="first_name">First Name:</label>
        <input type="text" name="first_name" size="20" /><br />
        <label for="last_name">Last Name:</label>
        <input type="text" name="last_name" size="20" /><br />
        <label for="email">E-Mail Address:</label>
        <input type="text" name="email" size="50" /><br />
        <label for="facebook_url">Facebook URL:</label>
        <input type="text" name="facebook_url" size="50" /><br />
        <label for="twitter_handle">Twitter Handle:</label>
        <input type="text" name="twitter_handle" size="20" /><br />
        <label for="bio">Bio:</label>
        <textarea name="bio" cols="40" rows="10"></textarea>
      </fieldset>
      <br />
      <fieldset class="center">
        <input type="submit" value="Join the Club" />
        <input type="reset" value="Clear and Restart" />
      </fieldset>
    </form>
  </div>

 <div id="footer"></div>
 </body>
</html>
```

While you're at it, you may as well let your users pick an image to use for their profile. You won't write any code in *create_user.php* to handle this, but it's coming soon, and doing it now will save you a trip back to *create_user.html* when you're ready to add images.

```
<html>
 <!-- head section -->

<body>
 <div id="header"><h1>PHP & MySQL: The Missing Manual</h1></div>
 <div id="example">User Signup</div>

 <div id="content">
  <h1>Join the Missing Manual (Digital) Social Club</h1>
  <p>Please enter your online connections below:</p>
  <form action="scripts/create_user.php" method="POST"
        enctype="multipart/form-data">
   <fieldset>
    <!-- Other fields -->

    <label for="user_pic">Upload a picture:</label>
    <input type="file" name="user_pic" size="30" />

   </fieldset>
   <!-- Buttons for submission and resetting the form -->

</body>
</html>
```

This HTML may look a little strange if you've never set things up to handle uploads before. You have to change the *form* tag a bit, as now you're actually uploading a file to a server, from your user's machine. So add the new *enctype* attribute with the value *multipart/form-data*. That addition lets any scripts receiving this form's input to expect more than just the values in the input fields, like the name of the file. A form like this also submits the data associated with those fields; in this case, that's the file that the user selects to upload.

Then you add a new input, of type *file*, which lets the user browse their hard drive, select a file, and upload it. This turns out to be almost boilerplate code, though, meaning that it's not specific to this use. Every time you let your users upload a file, you need to make this set of changes.

> **NOTE** If you want to start thinking ahead, the million-dollar question is, "*Where* do you store this image?" You must let the user upload the image; that's required for your scripts and code to work with it. But do you save the image on your server's file system, and reference it using a field in your *users* table? Or do you actually store the image itself in your database? Hot opinions are held here, and you'll develop one of your own in just a few chapters.

Save your changes here, and try hitting your form in a browser. You should get something like Figure 6-11; your updated form.

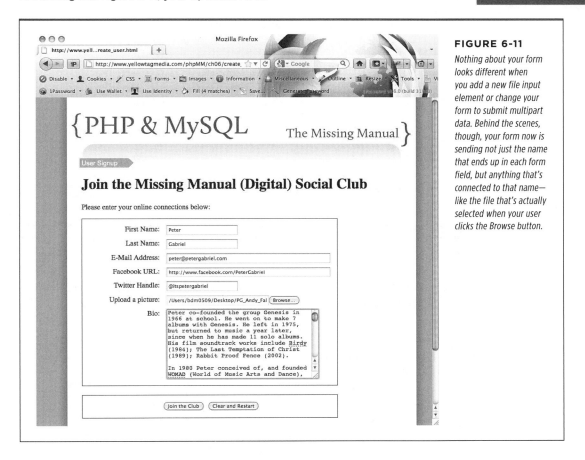

FIGURE 6-11

Nothing about your form looks different when you add a new file input element or change your form to submit multipart data. Behind the scenes, though, your form now is sending not just the name that ends up in each form field, but anything that's connected to that name— like the file that's actually selected when your user clicks the Browse button.

Go ahead and fill out values if you like, although without changes to *create_user. php*, you'll get a new user without their bio.

Updating Your User Creation Script

You can guess what you need to do to *create_user.php*. Simply grab the new bio request variable, add it to your *INSERT* statement, and you're good to go:

```php
<?php

require '../../scripts/database_connection.php';

$first_name = trim($_REQUEST['first_name']);
$last_name = trim($_REQUEST['last_name']);
$email = trim($_REQUEST['email']);
$bio = trim($_REQUEST['bio']);
```

```
// And other request variables follow...

$insert_sql =
  "INSERT INTO users (first_name, last_name, email, bio,
                      facebook_url, twitter_handle)
  " .
  "VALUES ('{$first_name}', '{$last_name}',
                      '{$email}', '{$bio}' " .
                      "'{$facebook_url}', '{$twitter_handle}');";

// Insert the user into the database
mysql_query($insert_sql);
?>
```

That's it. Now you can submit your new form, and get a new column—*bio*—with values happily dropped into your database.

> **WARNING** Be sure you've run the *ALTER TABLE* statement that adds the *bio* column to your *users* table before trying this out.

You can try this out, by filling out *create_user.html*, and hitting Submit. Then try this *SELECT* statement:

```
SELECT first_name, last_name, bio
  FROM users;
Your result should speak for itself:
| first_name | last_name | bio
| C. J.      | Wilson    |NULL |
| Peter      | Gabriel   |Peter co-founded the group Genesis in
1966 at school. He went on to make 7 albums with Genesis. He left
in 1975, but returned to music a year later, since when he has made
11 solo albums. His film soundtrack works include Birdy (1984); The Last Temp-
tation of Christ (1989); Rabbit Proof Fence (2002).
```

> **NOTE** Your result will be different, based on what bio you entered for your test user. You can also see that old users—in this case, the C. J. Wilson entry—has *NULL* for the *bio*, since that user was created before there even was a *bio* column.

Next, you need to redirect your user over to the *show_user.php* script, and then somehow get the ID of the user you just created into that script as well.

The first of these is easy:

```php
<?php

// Everything else you've already done

// Insert the user into the database
mysql_query($insert_sql);

// Redirect the user to the page that displays user information
header("Location: show_user.php");
exit();
?>
```

The header function literally sends a raw HTTP (hypertext transfer protocol) header to your user's browser. You don't need to know particularly much about HTTP; just that it's the "language" of web traffic. (That HTTP is the same *http://* you put in front of most of your URLs in your browser's address bar.) So you're directly manipulating the location of your user's page.

In this case, you're changing the location from the current one to a new one: the *show_user.php* script. There are a few things that are critical to get this working correctly, though:

1. You must call *header* before any other output in your script. You can't *echo* out anything, you can't print out an *<html>* tag, or anything else. *header* goes first, or problems arise.

2. The location reference must be a URL, either relative or absolute. So you could put *http://www.google.com* as the location, or *../../scripts/database_connection. php*, or in this case, a script in the same directory as this one, *show_user.php*.

These are simple rules but they're also really important ones. Get them right, or expect *header* to fail miserably.

All that's left now is that pesky user ID. You already know that *mysql_query*, which executes your *INSERT*, returns a resource, not a user ID. And the whole idea here was not to *SELECT* the user from the database, but leave that to *show_user.php*.

Making *show_user.php* get the user ID requires something that's one step removed from your current PHP knowledge: an incredibly handy PHP function called *mysql_insert_id*. You don't see this sort of function very often unless you're looking for, say, a function to get the ID of the last row *INSERT*ed into a database table with an *AUTO_INCREMENT* column.

Yes, that's the definition of *mysql_insert_id*. It's built exactly to do what you want to do: get an ID, without any additional *SELECT*s or work.

While you can pass into *mysql_insert_id* a resource, it automatically uses the last opened resource, which is perfect. Just add this after your *INSERT* is called via *myql_query*, and it'll automatically reference the resource returned from that call.

It returns ID of the user you want. You can even tag that onto the URL, just as when you were typing your URL manually:

```php
<?php

// Everything else you've already done

// Insert the user into the database
mysql_query($insert_sql);

// Redirect the user to the page that displays user information
header("Location: show_user.php?user_id=" . mysql_insert_id());
?>
```

That's it. Add this to *create_user.php*, and you're ready to try things out.

NOTE   You may be tempted to try something like this:

```php
("Location: show_user.php?user_id={mysql_insert_id()}");
```

Unfortunately, that won't work. While PHP is happy to insert variable values for variable names in curly braces, like this...

```php
("Location: show_user.php?user_id={$user_id}");
```

...it won't do the same for function calls.

Visit your user creation form and fill out some data. Submit the data, and you should be rewarded by not the output of *create_user.php*, but *show_user.php*, loading the user that was just created. Figure 6-12 shows what should be a fist-pumping moment.

Rounding Things Out with Regular Expressions (Again)

Your script is *almost* perfect. What's the remaining problem? Well, that output looks pretty awful with all that text running together. Is there some way you can add in a little formatting?

What probably happened in the example shown in Figure 6-12 is that the user hit a bunch of Enters between lines. But those don't show up in HTML. What you really need is a quick and easy way to replace those Enter key presses with HTML *<p></p>* tags.

What you need is a way to find certain characters—certain very specific characters—and replace them with certain other characters. You know how to do that, because you know that those Enters show up as \r or \n or some combination of the two, and you can use regular expressions to find and replace them.

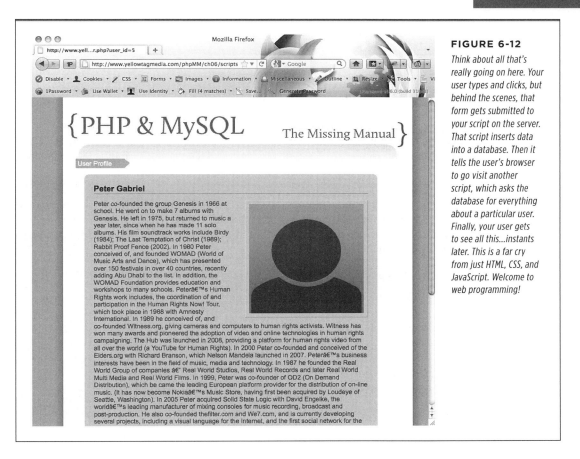

FIGURE 6-12

Think about all that's really going on here. Your user types and clicks, but behind the scenes, that form gets submitted to your script on the server. That script inserts data into a database. Then it tells the user's browser to go visit another script, which asks the database for everything about a particular user. Finally, your user gets to see all this...instants later. This is a far cry from just HTML, CSS, and JavaScript. Welcome to web programming!

Using *preg_match*, update *show_user.php* to change Enter presses into HTML *<p>* tags:

```php
<?php

// Database connection code

// SELECT the correct user

if ($result) {
  $row = mysql_fetch_array($result);
  $first_name     = $row['first_name'];
  $last_name      = $row['last_name'];
  $bio            = preg_replace("/[\r\n]+/", "</p><p>", $row['bio']);
```

```php
$email         = $row['email'];
$facebook_url  = $row['facebook_url'];
$twitter_handle = $row['twitter_handle'];

// Build the Twitter URL
}
?>

// HTML output
```

> **NOTE** Be sure you use *[\r\n]+*, and not *[\r\n]**. The * would match *no* occurrence, and you'd end up with
> *</p><p>* between every character in the user's bio. Not so good...the + makes sure that *\r* or *\n* (or both) appear
> *at least* once before replacing them with *</p><p>*.

You can see why regular expressions are so powerful. You didn't need lots of looping
and searching, and you don't have to figure out if the user entered *\r* or *\n* or *\r\n*
based on their platform. You just plug in the right regular expression, and you're
off to the races.

All this put together should give you a version of *show_user.php* like this:

```php
<?php

require '../../scripts/app_config.php';
require '../../scripts/database_connection.php';

// Get the user ID of the user to show
$user_id = $_REQUEST['user_id'];

// Build the SELECT statement
$select_query = "SELECT * FROM users WHERE user_id = " . $user_id;

// Run the query
$result = mysql_query($select_query);

if ($result) {
  $row = mysql_fetch_array($result);
  $first_name    = $row['first_name'];
  $last_name     = $row['last_name'];
  $bio           = preg_replace("/[\r\n]+/", "</p><p>", $row['bio']);
  $email         = $row['email'];
  $facebook_url  = $row['facebook_url'];
  $twitter_handle = $row['twitter_handle'];
```

```php
    // Turn $twitter_handle into a URL
    $twitter_url = "http://www.twitter.com/" .
                   substr($twitter_handle, $position + 1);

    // To be added later
    $user_image = "../../images/missing_user.png";
  } else {
    die("Error locating user with ID {$user_id}");
  }
?>

<html>
 <head>
  <link href="../../css/phpMM.css" rel="stylesheet" type="text/css" />
 </head>

 <body>
  <div id="header"><h1>PHP & MySQL: The Missing Manual</h1></div>
  <div id="example">User Profile</div>

  <div id="content">
    <div class="user_profile">
      <h1><?php echo "{$first_name} {$last_name}"; ?></h1>
      <p><img src="<?php echo $user_image; ?>" class="user_pic" />
        <?php echo $bio; ?></p>
      <p class="contact_info">
        Get in touch with <?php echo $first_name; ?>:
      </p>
      <ul>
        <li>...by emailing them at
          <a href="<?php echo $email; ?>"><?php echo $email; ?></a></li>
        <li>...by
          <a href="<?php echo $facebook_url; ?>">checking them out
            on Facebook</a></li>
        <li>...by <a href="<?php echo $twitter_url; ?>">following them
            on Twitter</a></li>
      </ul>
    </div>
  </div>
  <div id="footer"></div>
 </body>
</html>
```

Try things out, and you'll finally see not just your user's information, but a nicely formatted biography, as in Figure 6-13.

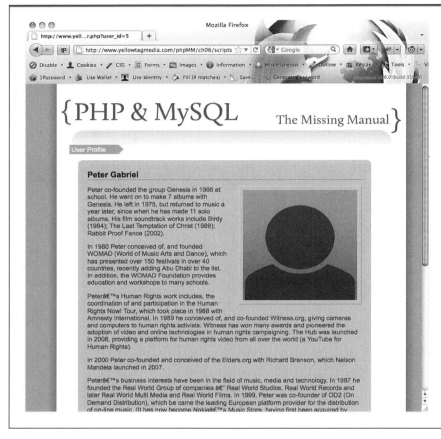

FIGURE 6-13

Here's another classic case how to be considerate to your users. Is it functionally correct to pull the user bio from the database and show it? Sure. Is it functionally correct to not insert weird HTML into the bio when you store it? Again, sure. But when you display that value, users don't care what's in your database. They care that it looks good.

Do My Field Names, Variable Names, and Table Column Names Have to Match?

You may have noticed that there's a continuous line from the name of a field in your HTML in *create_user.html* to your script, *create_user.php*, into other scripts like *show_user.php*, and then into your database table itself. So *first_name* is consistent in your HTML, PHP, and MySQL (and therefore your SQL, too). That's not required; you can call a field *firstName* and call a variable *user_firstName* and call a column *first_name*, and as long as you keep things straight, all your code will work just fine. So no, your names don't all have to match.

But maybe there's a better question: *should* your names match up across your HTML, PHP, and MySQL? Matching names give you consistency; you never have to think, "Now I know what I called that in my PHP, but what was the database column name again?"

Here's the flipside, though: there are some fairly standardized conventions for naming variables in different programming languages and database structures. The Java language favors less underscores, and more capitalization. So *firstName* would be preferred over *first_name*; the same is true in C++, although PHP and languages like Ruby prefer underscores over capitalization. SQL definitely favors underscores.

What this boils down to is a sort of conditional rule of thumb: *if* you can be consistent without messing up the conventions of the language within which you're programming, do it! Your code will easier to read, from the outermost HTML page to the innermost database table. Since PHP is one of the languages that likes underscores, use them, and keep things simple and consistent across your different pieces of your application.

From Web Pages to Web Applications

When Things Go Wrong (and They Will)

So far, you've got a growing, functioning set of scripts. You've got some web pages that interact with them, CSS to style both your static HTML pages and the HTML that your scripts output, and you can even go in and add some client-side JavaScript validation. Things are looking pretty good.

> **NOTE** Make that stronger: you *should* go in and add some client-side JavaScript validation.

But there's a monster lurking in the deep. While you've occasionally added a *die* or a conditional statement to make sure your queries return a result row, your code still assumes a perfect user. Someone who always types what you expect, never enters a phone number in the email field or spaces in the Facebook URL field; someone who never needs to go back and so never clicks the browser's Back button at an inopportune time; and never enters her information into the same form twice, furiously clicking "Add my information" instead of waiting on her lousy Internet connection.

Of course, nobody's *that* perfect—especially at a computer. The reality with web applications—and in fact any type of software—is that people always find ways to break your best-intended pages and forms and scripts. They supply bad information, leave out required fields, and make a general mess of anything that you've not planned on being messy.

> **NOTE** Once again, client-side JavaScript seems awfully valuable to mention here. You can reduce a lot of this sort of problem by validating your user's information *before* it gets sent to your scripts. For a lot more on how to do that, check out *JavaScript & jQuery: The Missing Manual* by David Sawyer McFarland (O'Reilly).

So what do you do? Well, so far, you've done something like Figure 7-1. Until now, this bare-bones error message has been fine. You're the only one using your system, and you're just testing things out, making sure your code is right. But it's a pretty poor way to handling errors in any kind of system that's going to make it out there in the Wild, Wild West of the Internet.

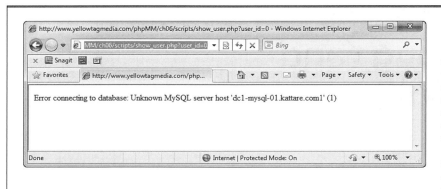

FIGURE 7-1

There's little that turns a user off more than an error message like this. It's cryptic, it reveals information about your system that it shouldn't, and worst of all for your user, it's ugly! On the Web, looks matter, and consistent looks matter a lot. Your errors should be reported as cleanly as possible, and in a format that's consistent with the look and feel of the rest of your site.

But it gets even worse. Try and visit the *show_user.php* URL again, and supply an ID of a user you know doesn't exist. Figure 7-2 shows that what should be an error is swallowed up by your script. You get an "empty" user profile, but it looks like nothing's wrong, even though the script received an invalid user ID.

So you have a lot of work to do here. First things first, though: what exactly should an error page have on it?

■ Planning Your Error Pages

When you were creating the page on which you show users, you began with HTML: mocking up a simple page, and then adding PHP as you needed it. There's no reason to abandon that approach here, as you're basically trying to do the same thing. You want a nice-looking page for displaying errors, and before you start digging into PHP, get things looking just right.

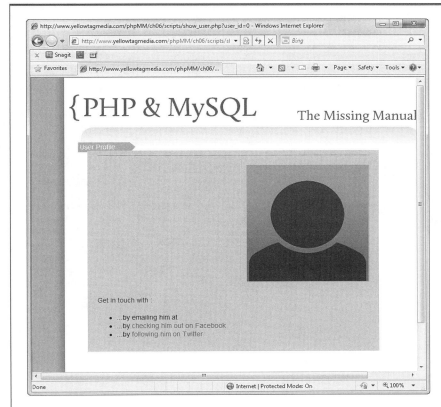

FIGURE 7-2

This "empty user" is actually a very nasty problem, because doesn't look like there's a problem. The show_user.php script loads up its HTML regardless of whether a SQL error occurred. Worse, because PHP is happy to simply echo out empty strings for variables without values, this page looks almost normal, except for all the missing information.

So first things first: create a new HTML page, and call it *show_error.html*. You can begin with the same structure you've been using for all your other pages:

```html
<html>
<head>
<link href="../css/phpMM.css" rel="stylesheet" type="text/css" />
</head>

<body>
<div id="header"><h1>PHP & MySQL: The Missing Manual</h1></div>
<div id="example">Error Page</div>

<div id="content">
  <h1>Error Page</h1>
  <p>Error</p>
</div>
```

```
    <div id="footer"></div>

  </body>

</html>
```

This code creates an empty shell of an error page (see Figure 7-3), and it's time to get to work.

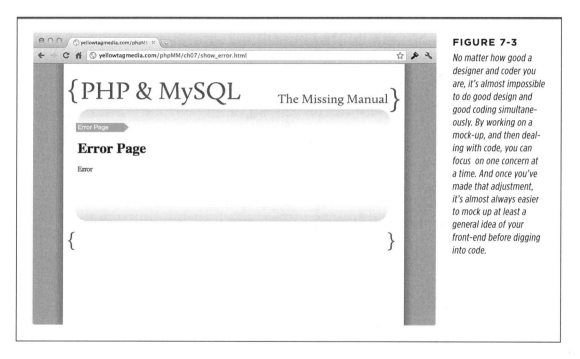

FIGURE 7-3

No matter how good a designer and coder you are, it's almost impossible to do good design and good coding simultaneously. By working on a mock-up, and then dealing with code, you can focus on one concern at a time. And once you've made that adjustment, it's almost always easier to mock up at least a general idea of your front-end before digging into code.

What Should Users See?

So here's your first question: what exactly goes on this page that helps your users? To answer this, consider the following two questions:

1. What information does your user need when an error has occurred?

2. In what tone does that information need to be communicated?

■ TELL YOUR USERS THAT A PROBLEM HAS OCCURRED

The answer to the first question should be pretty obvious. Something has gone wrong; your user needs an explanation. But even in that, there's nuance. Should you print out an errors that looks like this, the sort of thing MySQL might kick back to one of your scripts?

```
#1054 - Unknown column 'firstname' in 'field list'
```

Almost certainly not. Unless your user is a MySQL or PHP programmer, this message isn't helpful at all. You need to translate that into human language:

```
We're sorry, we couldn't locate the user's first name.
```

That's much more readable, but it may provide *too* much information, giving the user undue cause for concern: Why can't they find my first name? Is my record missing? Is my first name in the system? Uh oh, has my record been deleted? What's going on?!?

NOTE Does that reaction seem overly dramatic? Not necessarily, especially for users who don't really trust the Internet with their personal information in the first place.

So maybe that error needs to be just as readable, but a lot less specific:

```
We're sorry! There's been an error processing your request.
```

That's something most people can understand. Things go wrong, and something has here; Your job is simply to communicate that there was a problem, without alarming your user will all the gory details.

■ USE THE APPROPRIATE TONE FOR YOUR ERROR MESSAGE

You've figured out that, information-wise, your user really just needs to know that a problem has occurred. Details are probably irrelevant, and could even potentially create more worry, rather than less. But what about the tone?

This sounds pretty touchy-feely, and it is. After all, you're dealing with human users, and that means human emotions. Getting an error message is annoying enough; if your web application errors out, it's up to you to reduce the stress and frustration as much as possible. Otherwise, people will stop coming back.

It's not just what you say when a problem occurs, it's *how* you say it. A stern, bland error message isn't as comforting as a colloquial, conversational one. Sometimes you can even add in a little humor. Check out Figure 7-4 for a humorous way to turn a problem into a conversation point. You can almost bet that a user that lands on this page—error or not—is going to come back to the site.

Going full on with humor might be a little strong for your example site, but you can definitely make sure that you use conversational language. Just getting away from the stern, "Error 1282: An exception has occurred" goes a long way.

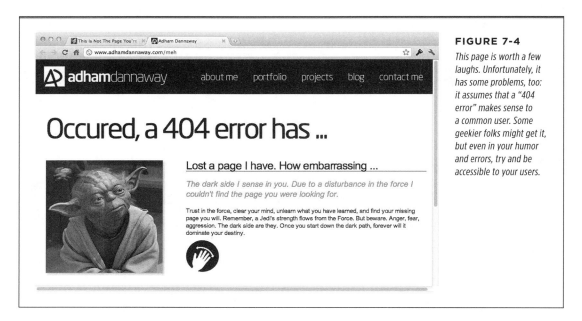

FIGURE 7-4

This page is worth a few laughs. Unfortunately, it has some problems, too: it assumes that a "404 error" makes sense to a common user. Some geekier folks might get it, but even in your humor and errors, try and be accessible to your users.

For example, make just a few conversational improvements to your error page mock-up, and notice how quickly this becomes a little more palatable when the inevitable error does occur:

```html
<html>
 <head>
  <link href="../css/phpMM.css" rel="stylesheet" type="text/css" />
 </head>

<body>
 <div id="header"><h1>PHP & MySQL: The Missing Manual</h1></div>
 <div id="example">Uh oh... sorry!</div>


 <div id="content">
   <h1>We're really sorry...</h1>
   <p><img src="../images/error.jpg" class="error" />...but something's
gone wrong. Don't worry, though, we've been notified that there's a
problem, and we take these things seriously. In fact, if you want to
contact us to find out more about what's happened, or you have any
concerns, just <a href="mailto:info@yellowtagmedia.com">email us</a>
and we'll be happy to get right back to you.</p>
```

```
    <p>In the meantime, if you want to go back to the page that caused
the problem, you can do that <a href="javascript:history.go(-1);">by
clicking here.</a> If the same problem occurs, though, you may
want to come back a bit later. We bet we'll have things figured
out by then. Thanks again... we'll see you soon. And again, we're
really sorry for the inconvenience.</p>

  </div>

  <div id="footer"></div>

  </body>

</html>
```

This message doesn't say much more than "Yes, we know a problem has occurred, and we're working on it." Everything else is about presentation: conversational words, an image to break up the cold page (which at the end of the day still *does* say, "Hey, sorry, something's broken"), and a contact link for email and another link to revisit the offending page.

Look at Figure 7-5; this message is a heck of a lot less annoying than the one in Figure 7-3, and took barely any more work to produce.

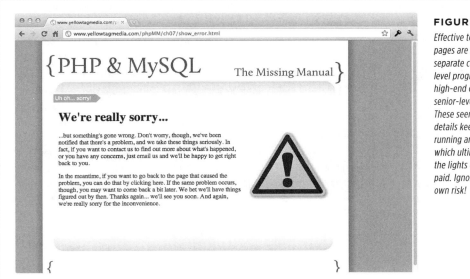

FIGURE 7-5

Effective testing and error pages are what often separate casual and mid-level programmers from high-end consultants and senior-level developers. These seemingly small details keep systems running and users happy, which ultimately keep the lights on and the bills paid. Ignore them at your own risk!

Know When to Say When

So you're a capable PHP programmer now, and you may have some clever ideas as to what could go on this error page. You could, say, grab the user's information from the database and personalize the page. You could set up a table that has error codes and a helpful, easy-to-read error message associated with each error code. Then, when an error occurs, you could look up the error code and print out the corresponding error message from the database.

All these ideas (and anything else you can come up with) would make for a pretty slick error page. But they also require fairly complex programming in and of themselves. There's a database to connect to, and queries to execute. And every time you write a query, or connect to a database, you introduce the possibility of another error! So where do your users go when your error pages have errors?

As a rule of thumb, you want your error pages to rely on as little programming as possible. They shouldn't interact with databases, and they shouldn't be fancy. As nice as that might sound, if your error page can cause an error, you're in trouble.

POWER USERS' CLINIC

Over-Promise At Your Own Risk

Nowhere other than error pages is it easier to over-promise and under-deliver. If you tell a user that you're looking into their problem, you better really be looking into their problem. If you're going to supply a contact email, make sure it's a working email address (yes, lots of times error pages have outdated, defunct contact information), and that the email actually gets to someone who can fix the problem.

If your user thinks you're dealing with their issue, and he comes back in a few hours only to get the same error, all the clever images and language in the world won't keep her invested in your site. Furthermore, he'll be annoyed not just that something went wrong, but that you apparently lied about working on the issue.

If you're just getting started or have limited resources, you might do well to simply say that you get notified when errors occur and you usually fix problems within 24 or 36 hours, or within some time period to which you can commit. You might

also provide an email address for urgent issues...and then actually watch your email! Another option is to pre-format the email with a subject line you look out for, like "URGENT" or "ERROR." You can even set up a rule in your email program to highlight mails with that subject.

Whatever you do, make sure that your responsiveness matches what your error page promises, or you're going to have a lot more than a programming problem to deal with.

One more bit of advice as you begin working in large companies: never let the marketing team write error page text without supervision! Not to promote stereotypes, but Marketing's job is to sell and promote, and in an effort to make your company look good, they could over-sell your capability. Get someone good with words to help you in crafting your error page, but ultimately, you're probably the person fixing problems; make sure you can back up what your error pages promise.

■ Finding a Middle Ground for Error Pages with PHP

On one hand, you want your error pages to be dead simple: some text, an image or two, and static content. That way, nothing can go wrong, and your users get some level of reassurance and comfort. On the other hand, the error page in Figure 7-5 is awfully generic. It doesn't *say* very much. It would be nice to tell your users *something* about what actually went wrong, maybe like this:

```html
<html>
<head>
 <link href="../css/phpMM.css" rel="stylesheet" type="text/css" />
</head>

<body>
 <div id="header"><h1>PHP & MySQL: The Missing Manual</h1></div>
 <div id="example">Uh oh... sorry!</div>

 <div id="content">
   <h1>We're really sorry...</h1>
   <p><img src="../images/error.jpg" class="error" />...but something's
gone wrong. <span class="error_message">the username you entered couldn't
be found in our database.</span></p>
   <p>Don't worry, though, we've been notified that there's a
problem, and we take these things seriously. In fact, if you want to
contact us to find out more about what's happened, or you have any
concerns, just <a href="mailto:info@yellowtagmedia.com">email us</a>
and we'll be happy to get right back to you.</p>
   <p>In the meantime, if you want to go back to the page that caused
the problem, you can do that <a href="javascript:history.go(-1);">by
clicking here.</a> If the same problem occurs, though, you may
want to come back a bit later. We bet we'll have things figured
out by then. Thanks again... we'll see you soon. And again, we're
really sorry for the inconvenience.</p>

 </div>


 <div id="footer"></div>

</body>

</html>
```

The result, shown Figure 7-6, does seem to be a good compromise between a generic error page and one that's so tricked up with user-specific information that it becomes error-prone in itself. So how can you get this personalized error message in place, and still keep the programming minimal?

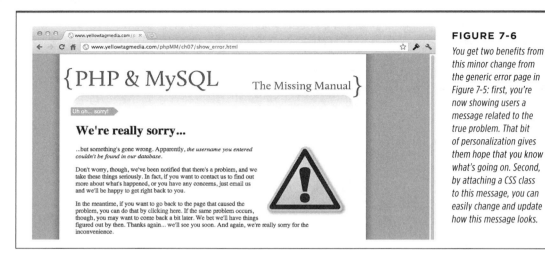

FIGURE 7-6

You get two benefits from this minor change from the generic error page in Figure 7-5: first, you're now showing users a message related to the true problem. That bit of personalization gives them hope that you know what's going on. Second, by attaching a CSS class to this message, you can easily change and update how this message looks.

Creating a PHP Error Page

Almost everything on the template for this error page is straight HTML. All that's dynamic—in other words, all that would change from request to request—is the actual error message. So this becomes a relatively easy exercise. As usual, you can start by putting in a variable for the error message, and just assume you'll come back and actually assign a value to that variable in a bit.

```
<html>
 <head>
  <link href="../css/phpMM.css" rel="stylesheet" type="text/css" />
 </head>

 <body>
  <div id="header"><h1>PHP & MySQL: The Missing Manual</h1></div>
  <div id="example">Uh oh... sorry!</div>

  <div id="content">
    <h1>We're really sorry...</h1>
    <p><img src="../images/error.jpg" class="error" />
      <?php echo $error_message; ?>
      <span></p>

    <p>Don't worry, though, we've been notified that there's a
    problem, and we take these things seriously. In fact, if you want to
    contact us to find out more about what's happened, or you have any
    concerns, just <a href="mailto:info@yellowtagmedia.com">email us</a>
    and we'll be happy to get right back to you.</p>
```

```
    <p>In the meantime, if you want to go back to the page that caused
    the problem, you can do that <a href="javascript:history.go(-1);">by
    clicking here.</a> If the same problem occurs, though, you may
    want to come back a bit later. We bet we'll have things figured
    out by then. Thanks again... we'll see you soon. And again, we're
    really sorry for the inconvenience.</p>

    </div>

    <div id="footer"></div>

    </body>

</html>
```

Save this file as *show_error.php*. And there's another wrinkle here: this error page will apply to all your scripts and HTML pages. So don't save it in a chapter 7 directory; put it in a *scripts/* directory in the root of your site, so it's easily accessible.

NOTE   If you want to follow along exactly with the book's structure, save this file in *phpMM/scripts/* where *phpMM/* is the root directory in this book's online examples (see page xvii).

Now you need to get the error message. What's the easiest way to do that? Better yet, what's the least error-prone way to do that? Well, probably by using request parameters and the *$_REQUEST* array.

```php
<?php
  $error_message = $_REQUEST['error_message'];
?>


<html>
  <!-- Existing HTML and PHP -->
</html>
```

What's so good about this approach? First, it's about as basic as PHP programming can be. You're not using any real calculation, but instead just pulling a value out of an array. Better still, it's not your own custom array, but one that PHP provides for you, and even fills for you, using information supplied in the request to *show_error.php*.

Testing out Your Faulty Solution

With all that in mind, try this page out in a browser. Visit your script's URL and add a request parameter. So you might use something like this in your URL:

```
http://www.yellowtagmedia.com/phpMM/scripts/
show_error.php?error_message=There's%20been%20a%20problem
%20connecting%20to%20the%20database.
```

NOTE This URL should all be on one line in your browser bar. Additionally, many browsers will convert spaces to the web-safe equivalent, that strange *%20*. That's a way of telling a browser "insert a space."

You should see something like Figure 7-7, which is a pretty nice looking error page without a lot of work.

FIGURE 7-7

One of the nicest things about any script that uses request parameters and $_REQUEST is that you can easily test these scripts with a little command-line magic. Just name your parameters on the command line, separate the first one from your script with a ?, and then separate multiple request parameters from each other with &.

The simplicity of using request parameters that are just plain text, passed from one page or script to another is the beauty of *show_error.php*. There's very little that can go wrong. That's what you want in an error page: elegance and simplicity.

You do need to make one fix, though: that back slash showing up before a single apostrophe is no good. You can get rid of that with a little regular expression magic. Replace all occurrences of a forward slash with...well, with nothing:

```
$error_message = preg_replace_all("/\\\\/", '',
                              $_REQUEST['error_message']);
```

PHP has an oddity in that you need to actually use four back-slashes to match a single back-slash. So \\\\ matches \, oddly enough. That's because you're sort of "fighting" the PHP escape mechanism—which uses a backslash.

Expect the Unexpected

Things are looking good. But once again, you're assuming that things go just the way you want. In fact, that's exactly the sort of thinking that leads people to ignore error pages. So if you need to deal with problems to the point that you're *creating* an error page, you better believe that problems can also occur when you're actually *on* the error page.

Thankfully, you've cut down on most of that with simplicity. But what about if there's not an *error_message* request parameter? Then you get something like Figure 7-8.

FIGURE 7-8

Apparently...well, apparently nothing. This page looks incomplete, which actually makes the user who landed here feel worse about their problem than they did when they first realized something went wrong.

Why is *show_error.php* still in a *scripts/* Directory?

In the last chapter, you should have started moving your scripts from nested *scripts/* directories into the main parts of your site. So you probably started having web forms like *create_user.html* right alongside *create_user.php* and *show_user.php*. That's because your HTML pages and your PHP pages are starting to be a lot more alike than they are different.

But here's *show_error.php*, still in a *scripts/* directory. So what gives? Well, *show_error.php* really isn't just another HTML page. It's something special—something used across your application. In fact, it's just like *database_connection.php*, which you should also keep in your main *scripts/* directory. These are really utilities, not pages that should live alongside other HTML pages.

Now, there's another natural question that follows along from this: won't you eventually end up with a giant mess? PHP files living alongside HTML...and then what? Images next to JavaScript next to CSS? It's a world gone mad, if you're not careful.

Ultimately, though, that's not the idea here. Rather, it's to move to organizing your files by function. So you might

have a directory called *users/* with all your user-related files: *show_user.php* and *create_user.php* and *create_user.html*. You might have other similar directories, like *groups/* and *social/* and the like.

When you begin to organize by function, your organization actually becomes meaningful. It tells you what things do, rather than what they are (CSS or PHP or whatever). In fact, down the line, you might even break things up further, separating code that's for displaying things from code that interacts with your database. That's still a bit off in the distance, but for now, be thinking "Function over format." It's more important that you have a group of user-related files together than that you have your PHP scripts together.

So store your utility scripts in *scripts/* for now. And yes, you could look at renaming *scripts/* something like *utilities/*, if you like. Go ahead, and organize well; when you have 50 or 100 files, you'll be grateful for the structure.

Now you're back to instilling confusion, and that's no good. There's an easy solution, though: just deal with the situation when there's no request parameter:

```php
<?php
  $error_message = preg_replace_all("/\\\\/", '',
                                    $_REQUEST['error_message']);
  if (!isset($error_message)) {
    $error_message = "something went wrong, and that's " .
                     "how you ended up here.";
  }
?>


<html>
  <!-- Existing HTML and PHP -->
</html>
```

You haven't seen *isset* before, but it makes a lot of sense: if the *$error_message* variable is set, or has a value, things are fine. If they're not (that's what the *!* means), then set *$error_message* to a conversational, albeit generic, message. *isset* returns true if a variable has been assigned something, and is not null. That's perfect in this case: even though you assign *$error_message* the value in *$_REQUEST['error_message']*, that value might be null, so *isset* does the trick nicely.

Your error page again, without anything on the URL, and you'll get a nice-looking page once again. Check out Figure 7-9 for what you should expect.

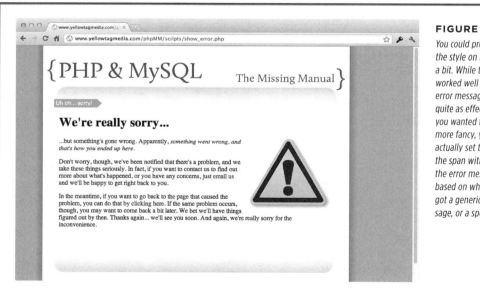

FIGURE 7-9

You could probably tweak the style on this page a bit. While the italics worked well for a specific error message, it's not quite as effective here. If you wanted to get a little more fancy, you could actually set the class on the span within which the error message prints based on whether you've got a generic error message, or a specific one.

Welcome to Security and Phishing

And now, welcome to a big fat ugly problem. By using a request parameter to pass information to your scripts, *anyone*—especially malicious users—can pass information to your script. They can put their own error message in as the value to the *error_message* request parameter...or they can put something in that's not an error message at all. And why is that a problem? Keep reading.

▇ PHISHING AND SUBTLE REDIRECTION

Putting actual information, like an error message, in a URL is a way of employing a type of Internet vandalism called *phishing*. Phishing is a technique that supplies to a user what appears to be a trusted URL, and gets that user to an untrusted website. So suppose you get an email with a link to a site that looks like this:

*http://yellowtagmedia.com/phpMM/ch07/show_error.php?error_message=
%3Ca%20href=%22http://www.syfy.com/beinghuman%22%3EClick%20Here%20
To%20Report%20Your%20Error%3C/a%3E*

You might just click on this. It's got lots of gibberish at the end, but you recognize the important part, the host name: *yellowtagmedia.com*. You've been reading *PHP & MySQL: The Missing Manual*, and all throughout that book, you've been seeing *yellowtagmedia.com* as a domain name. It's the author's domain, so you may think this is a perfectly fine site to visit. So you do, and you see something like Figure 7-10.

FIGURE 7-10

What's to be worried about here? It's a customized error page, just like the one you've built for your own machine. It's got an error message, and you can even apparently click through to report details about your problem. Looks like great customer service...right?

It's an error page, just like the one you've been creating. And, look, it's got a link on it. Might as well trust the link, too. It appears on a trusted page. So click the link, and you'd end up on a completely different site—probably one you didn't expect (see Figure 7-11).

Now, the SyFy channel's page for *Being Human* is hardly anything to lose sleep over, although *Being Human* really is a great show. But suppose that same link took you to a site that asks for your credit card, or that's full of illicit material that could get you fired when you accidentally land on that site at work, or even just a simple site that asks you to "reconfirm" your username and password: these are potential disasters.

FIGURE 7-11

How did you end up here? This is a classic example of phishing. You visit a site you trust (or think you trust), and end up on a site that you don't trust.

A clever and not-so-well-meaning coder could easily use the same CSS that's used on *yellowtagmedia.com* to ensure that site looks just like the initial error page, and most users would never know the difference.

■ THE DANGERS OF REQUEST PARAMETERS

The problem is that any old user can actually type in a request parameter. Look back at the URL that started all of this:

http://yellowtagmedia.com/phpMM/ch07/show_error.php?error_message= %3Ca%20href=%22http://www.syfy.com/beinghuman%22%3EClick%20Here%20 To%20Report%20Your%20Error%3C/a%3E

It's the *error_message* parameter that creates all the trouble. It allows...well, anything as a value. And when you take away all the escaping, this URL really amounts to this:

http://yellowtagmedia.com/phpMM/ch07/show_error.php?error_message=<a href="http://www.syfy.com/beinghuman">Click Here To Report Your Error</a>

So suddenly, a link to a non-trusted site gets dropped right into your trusted page. That's a big problem, and can create massive headaches for your users.

Unfortunately, fixing this is going to take a lot of PHP wizardry that you just don't have yet. Fortunately, it's coming...in about six chapters. So for now, use this approach to error handling, but know that it's not quite ready for primetime. You'll need to use something called *sessions*, detailed in Chapter 13, to avoid ever becoming part of a phishing scam.

> **NOTE** Your vulnerability to phishing is subtle, but it's there. It took a clever tech reviewer to reveal the potential problem. But that's the price of coding on the big bad InterWebs: You must always be aware of what a malicious bored teenager can do to your site if you're not careful. Thankfully, though, you're learning everything you need to combat and prevent those attacks. Just hang tight until Chapter 13, where you'll use sessions to make some small changes that completely shut down any phishing attempts.

■ Add Debugging to Your Application

You've taken care of your users in case of error, but what about taking care of your-self? You need to use your system too, which means you need to figure out what's going on, not just in your code, but on your front end. But the error pages you've put into place actually now *shield* you from what's really going on at the script level. Instead of seeing a technically accurate error that's ugly and unreadable to your users, you get a nice friendly error message. But that's no help to you!

So are you stuck digging through your code anytime something goes wrong, with no real lead on what happened? That's really not a good limitation to accept. A better approach would be to figure out a way to show the real errors that occurred, but to do it in a way that only you can see.

Turn on PHP Error Reporting

First, you need a way to report errors when they happen, especially if your program might normally act odd if that behavior went unreported. For example, consider this code fragment:

```
echo "Hello, {$first_name}\n\n";
$query = "SELECT * FROM users WHERE first_name = {$first_name}";
```

The results here radically change depending on whether or not there's actually a value in *$first_name*. You could get database errors, odd query results, and worse. Now, certainly, you could add some *isset* calls to avoid problems, but you'll often forget that sort of error prevention...at least until something goes wrong. What you need isn't a nice error message, but a report when bad things happen, *as they happen*. Then you can make the necessary fixes and avoid repeating these errors.

Here's where PHP offers help, though: you can turn on what's called *error reporting* within PHP itself. Typically, you do so through some of the low-level configuration files that PHP uses, but that's a more difficult a solution than your situation demands.

NOTE It may actually be more than just difficult. Most ISPs and web hosting companies won't let you anywhere near the configuration files for the web servers and PHP installations they host. That's a headache waiting to happen for them and their support staff.

So to see this in action, create a small script called *display_error.php*, and type this code:

```php
<?php

echo "Hello, {$first_name}\n\n";
$query = "SELECT * FROM users WHERE first_name = {$first_name}";
echo "{$query}\n\n";

?>
```

Obviously, there's the problem of *$first_name* not being defined. And although this script doesn't actually try and execute the query—which is going to be incomplete—it's pretty clearly a program where you'd want to know that something bad is going on.

But run this program, and you'll get this result:

```
$ php display_error.php
Hello,

SELECT * FROM users WHERE first_name =
```

Pretty lame, isn't it? PHP happily runs the program, ignoring the problems. That means you're not redirected to any error page, at least not until several lines later when you execute this query against your database. But by then, you're a few lines (or maybe a few *hundred* lines!) away from the real problem, the missing value in *$first_name*.

That's where PHP's *error_reporting* function comes in. Add this line into your *display_error.php* script:

```php
<?php

error_reporting(E_ALL);

echo "Hello, {$first_name}\n\n";
$query = "SELECT * FROM users WHERE first_name = {$first_name}";
echo "{$query}\n\n";

?>
```

The *E_ALL* constant is just a level of reporting. *E_ALL* reports every possible error. You can also use *E_ERROR*, *E_WARNING*, *E_PARSE*, and *E_NOTICE*, all of which report different things (and let different things pass by silently). You can get the whole scoop on these different levels at *www.php.net/manual/en/function.error-reporting.php*. In the simplest case, though, *E_ALL* absolutely lets you know when something might go wrong.

Now run the script again, and you get an entirely different result:

```
$ php display_error.php
PHP Notice:  Undefined variable: first_name in yellowtagmedia_com/phpMM/ch07/
display_error.php on line 5

Notice: Undefined variable: first_name in yellowtagmedia_com/phpMM/ch07/dis-
play_error.php on line 5
Hello,

PHP Notice:  Undefined variable: first_name in yellowtagmedia_com/phpMM/ch07/
display_error.php on line 6

Notice: Undefined variable: first_name in yellowtagmedia_com/phpMM/ch07/dis-
play_error.php on line 6
SELECT * FROM users WHERE first_name =
```

Suddenly, PHP is hyper-aware of potential problems, and it's letting you know about it. That's perfect for getting your application up and running; now you're going to be bugged about...well...potential bugs. That's a good thing.

WARNING Really, this reporting is a big for writing good code, but it's also a bit annoying. You're going to constantly get little nudges from PHP about your potential mistakes. Still, that's a small price to pay for knowing you've handled potential problems in your script.

■ SET ERROR REPORTING GLOBALLY

Now you're left with another subtle issue: you must remember to turn on error reporting. That's not something you want to have to do in every script, though. And you're going to have lots of basic procedures like error reporting that you want to apply to all your scripts.

The solution here is probably already apparent to you: you need another script, sort of like *database_connection.php*, that handles all this common behavior. Then, all your other scripts can make a single call to include that behavior, and it's taken care of. But you've already got a file like this: *app_config.php*, which *database_connection.php* uses for common constants like your database's name and password. That's actually exactly what you need here.

NOTE Yes, this does mean that you must still include this one common script, *app_config.php*, in all your other scripts, so there's still a level of "Remember to..." happening here. More on that in the box on page 210.

Go ahead and open up *app_config.php* in your core *scripts/* directory. It should live alongside *show_error.php* and *database_connection.php*. Add in the *error_reporting* directive to turn on error reporting for all your scripts:

```php
<?php

// Database connection constants

// Error reporting
error_reporting(E_ALL);

?>
```

Now you just need to add an include to all of your scripts:

```php
<?php

require '../scripts/app_config.php';

echo "Hello, {$first_name}\n\n";
$query = "SELECT * FROM users WHERE first_name = {$first_name}";
echo "{$query}\n\n";

?>
```

> **NOTE** If you're following along, you should remove the *error_reporting* directive from *display_error.php* (page 208), since that's now handled by *app_config.php*.

With that addition, you've now got error reporting in all of your scripts. That's a pretty helpful upgrade for a single-line addition to each of your scripts.

POWER USERS' CLINIC

Remembering (a Little Bit) is Part of Programming

So after all the talk about avoiding having to remember turning on error reporting, it seems like the solution is...remembering to include *app_config.php*? How does that make things easier?

Unfortunately, as a programmer, you're always challenged to remember to do certain things. That might be release a certain variable that takes up a lot of system resources, or closing a database connection, or logging out of a system...or including a certain file in every script you write. The key, though, is to *minimize* the number of things you have to remember.

That's the point of using *app_config.php*. By including this single file—one thing to remember—you can include all the common things your script needs. So if you later need to add to *app_config.php*, all your scripts immediately get those additions. (And you will make some additions to *app_config. php* really soon.) So include one thing, instead of two or three or ten, whenever possible.

■ TURN OFF ERROR REPORTING WHEN YOU GO TO PRODUCTION

Now you've got error reporting on, and you're getting a lot more information. But there's a problem: sometimes what is reported isn't an error, but the potential for an error. As an example, make sure you have *app_config.php* included in your *show_error.php* script:

```php
<?php
  require 'app_config.php';

  $error_message = preg_replace_all("/\\\/", '',
                                  $_REQUEST['error_message']);
  if (!isset($error_message)) {
    $error_message = "something went wrong, and that's how you ended up
here.";
  }
?>


<html>
  <!-- HTML and PHP -->
</html>
```

Now visit *show_error.php* in your browser, and *don't* put in anything for the error message. That's really not a problem for *show_error.php*, as that's something for which your code accounts. But look at Figure 7-12, and what may be a surprising output from the script.

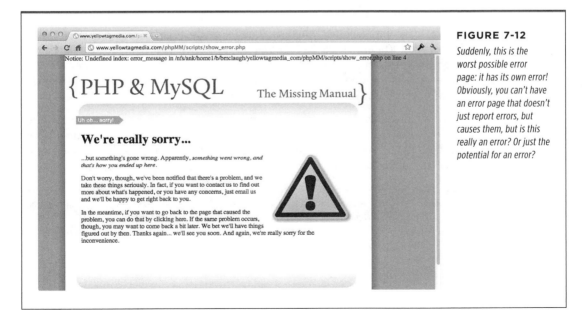

FIGURE 7-12

Suddenly, this is the worst possible error page: it has its own error! Obviously, you can't have an error page that doesn't just report errors, but causes them, but is this really an error? Or just the potential for an error?

Even though you handled the situation, it's still technically a potential problem that you assign *$error_message* a value (*$_REQUEST['error_message']*) that may be null.

There are two things you can do here, and both are good ideas. First, you can refactor this code to make sure you never directly access a potentially null value:

```php
<?php
  require 'app_config.php';

  if (isset($_REQUEST['error_message'])) {
    $error_message = preg_replace_all("/\\\\/", '',
                                  $_REQUEST['error_message']);
  } else {
    $error_message =
      "something went wrong, and that's how you ended up here.";
  }
?>


<html>
  <!-- HTML and PHP -->
</html>
```

PHP has no problem with you using a null value in *isset*. In fact, that's the purpose of *isset*: to help you avoid using an unexpected null value. So in that sense, the error reporting helped you improve your page. Reload the page, and the error message will be gone, and things should once again look more like Figure 7-9.

But beyond that, there's a bigger issue: even if this slight change made your code better, there may be times when you need your users to interact with your system before it's 100 percent perfect. Someone wise once said that "The perfect is the enemy of the good," and you could extend that to "The perfect web application is the enemy of the good web application." If you wait until your code is absolutely perfect, you'll probably never release it.

So what do you do? Well, suppose you could set the "mode" of your application. So you could run in "debug" mode, and errors would print, or you could run in "production" mode, and error reporting wouldn't be turned on. Then, you could simply run in debug mode until it's time to go live, and then switch to production mode.

NOTE You might even take this further: you could copy your code to a server, switch it to run in production mode, and then still run another copy in debug mode for you to work on and improve.

Setting up a debug mode is a breeze; and with *app_config.php*, you've already got a nice central place to configure this sort of thing:

```php
<?php

// Set up debug mode
define("DEBUG_MODE", true);


// Database connection constants


// Error reporting
if (DEBUG_MODE) {
  error_reporting(E_ALL);

} else {
  // Turn off all error reporting
  error_reporting(0);
}


?>
```

That's it; now you've got the ability to make a single change to *DEBUG_MODE*, and you get (or don't get) error reporting across your application.

Moving from *require* to *require_once*

If you follow your programming code carefully, you'll see that *database_connection.php* has this line at the top:

```php
require 'app_config.php';
```

So any script that does this...

```php
require '../../scripts/database_connection.php';
```

...also gets a sort of "automatic" require on *app_config.php*, also. So if you want to get the setup from *app_config.php* in a script that already requires *database_connection.php*, then you technically don't need to explicitly require *app_config.php*.

But—and it's a big but—you've now hidden a *dependency* in your code. So even though you're not requiring *app_config.php* explicitly, you're writing code that assumes that *app_config.php* has been loaded. So suppose you change a script to not use a database; the natural next step would be to remove the *require* for *database_connection.php*. Since your script no longer uses a database, requiring *database_connection.php* wouldn't make sense. But with that removal, you also lose *app_config.php*—a problem that doesn't show up until you realize that none of your helpful constants and error messages are defined.

For this reason alone, it's a good idea to be explicit in your requirements. Now, there's an obvious concern here: You'll require *app_config.php*, and then also *database_connection.php*, which in turn also requires *app_config.php*. You're requiring *app_config.php* twice in database-driven scripts. That turns out to be a problem, because it results in these constants being defined twice, which causes PHP to spit out an error:

```
// Database connection constants
define("DATABASE_HOST", "db.host.com");
define("DATABASE_USERNAME", "username");
define("DATABASE_PASSWORD", "super.secret.password");
define("DATABASE_NAME", "db-name");
```

Here's the error you'd see if you used a *require* on this file twice:

```
Notice: Constant DATABASE_HOST already defined in yellowtagmedia_com/phpMM/
scripts/app_config.php on line 4
Notice: Constant DATABASE_USERNAME already defined in yellowtagmedia_com/
phpMM/scripts/app_config.php on line 5
Notice: Constant DATABASE_PASSWORD already defined in yellowtagmedia_com/
phpMM/scripts/app_config.php on line 6
```

To get around this dilemma, you can use *require_once* instead of *require* in all your utility scripts. So in your main script—whichever script your main code lives—use the normal *require*:

```
// main script you're writing code
require '../scripts/app_config.php';
```

Then, in any utility scripts that also need *app_config.php*, use *require_once*:

```
// database_connection.php and any other utility scripts
require_once '../scripts/app_config.php';
```

require_once checks to see if the specified script has already been included (through *include* or *require*), and only include the script if it's not already been loaded. That ensures that you really only do get *app_config.php* loaded once.

But there's yet another problem: sometimes you have one script—like *create_user.php*—actually call another script—like *show_user.php*. In this case, you've got two scripts that probably both use *require*, and so you'll get errors about constants being redefined. Should you rethink and refactor *app_config.php*? Should you abstract out those constants into another file, or move them into *database_connection.php*?

Honestly, you can get around all of these issues by using *require_once* in all your scripts. This way, you ensure that *app_config.php* never gets loaded more than once. There's also another side effect: you're no longer trying to figure out which version of *require* to use. In fact, as a general rule, you should always use *require_once*, unless you have a specific need to require something multiple times. Which make sense, since you rarely require something more than once.

Now You See Me, Now You Don't

Unfortunately, you've done a lot of work, but you still haven't solved one core problem: you need a way to display more information about an error to you and your programmer buddies, without resorting to terrifying your users. But you've laid some groundwork; the *app_config.php* file you created has a *DEBUG_MODE*, and that seems to be the key ingredient.

What you need, then, is a way to print out additional error information if you're in debug mode. And just as with error reporting (through PHP's own error handling), you can simply turn this option off in production. In the same vein, you could always turn it on for a brief period if you had a problem, and then back off again once you'd used the error reporting to locate and fix any errors that are occurring.

So define a new function—call it *debug_print*—that only prints information if you're in debugging mode:

```php
function debug_print($message) {
  if (DEBUG_MODE) {
    echo $message;
  }
}
```

With this in *app_config.php*, you've now got this function available anywhere in your own code. All it does it selectively print a message; if debugging is turned on, it prints, and if not, *$message* never sees the light of day.

You've just created your first custom function! Nice work. Although there's lots more to learn about custom functions, notice how easy it is to create your own customized behavior for the rest of your application to use.

Now, you can add some additional information to your *show_error.php* page:

```php
<?php
  require 'app_config.php';

  if (isset($_REQUEST['error_message'])) {
    $error_message = preg_replace_all("/\\\/", '',
                                  $_REQUEST['error_message']);
  } else {
    $error_message = "something went wrong, and that's how you ended up
here.";
  }

  if (isset($_REQUEST['system_error_message'])) {
```

```
    $system_error_message = preg_replace("/\\\/", '',
                        $_REQUEST['system_error_message']);  } else {
    $system_error_message = "No system-level error message was reported.";
  }
?>
```

Then, down in your HTML, selectively print out this additional information:

```
<html>
 <head>
  <link href="../css/phpMM.css" rel="stylesheet" type="text/css" />
 </head>

 <body>
  <div id="header"><h1>PHP & MySQL: The Missing Manual</h1></div>
  <div id="example">Uh oh... sorry!</div>

  <div id="content">
    <h1>We're really sorry...</h1>
    <!-- Existing user-friendly error handling and printing -->
    <?php
      debug_print("<hr />");
      debug_print("<p>The following system-level message was received:
<b>{$system_error_message}</b></p>");
    ?>
  </div>

  <div id="footer"></div>
 </body>
</html>
```

Finally, then, you can put all this together. You've got an error page, you've got a means of printing information only if debugging is turned on, and you have *app_config.php* to tie things all together.

■ Redirecting on Error

You've got a pretty complex mechanism in place to deal with error messages as they crop up, and you've even got a way to report errors via PHP (with *error_reporting*) and a means of printing out errors for your programming benefit (with debug_print). But you've not gotten to actually use any of this! It's definitely time to rectify that situation.

Take a look at one of your simplest page/script combinations: *connect.html* and *connect.php*, from Chapter 4.

Updating Your Script to Use *show_error.php*

Here's the first place you really need to make changes:

```php
<?php

  require '../scripts/app_config.php';

  mysql_connect(DATABASE_HOST, DATABASE_USERNAME, DATABASE_PASSWORD)
    or die("<p>Error connecting to database: " .
          mysql_error() . "</p>");


  // And so on...
?>
```

So right now, if *mysql_connect* fails, the whole script just dies in a ball of flames. Not so great. Now, one way you could fix this would be to do something like this:

```php
  if (!mysql_connect(DATABASE_HOST,
                    DATABASE_USERNAME, DATABASE_PASSWORD)) {
    $user_error_message = "there was a problem connecting to the " .
                        "database that holds the information we need " .
                        "to get you connected.";
    $system_error_message = mysql_error();
    header("Location: ../scripts/show_error.php?" .
          "error_message={$user_error_message}&" .
          "system_error_message={$system_error_message}");
    exit();
  }
```

That uses your new error page in conjunction with PHP's redirect, supplies both a friendly and system-level error, and should work pretty well. For the sake of testing, type in a bad database host, like this:

```
if (!mysql_connect(DATABASE_HOST, DATABASE_USERNAME, "foo")) {
  // handle error
}
```

Now hit *connect.html* in your browser, submit the form to *connect.php*, and you should be rewarded with your error page, as in Figure 7-13.

FIGURE 7-13

This is just about all you could ask for in terms of handling errors. You get to see exactly what the user sees, plus you get error reporting at a programming level. Say goodbye to die... show_error.php *is a much better solution.*

NOTE Make sure that you have DEBUG_MODE set to true in *app_config.php* before you try this out, so you'll see both the user-friendly and developer-friendly errors.

This is perfect! In terms of seeing errors, you've got your users covered. Now, set *DEBUG_MODE* to false in *app_config.php*:

```
// Set up debug mode
define("DEBUG_MODE", false);
```

Try and hit *connect.html* and *connect.php* again, and this time, you should only see the user-facing error (check out Figure 7-14).

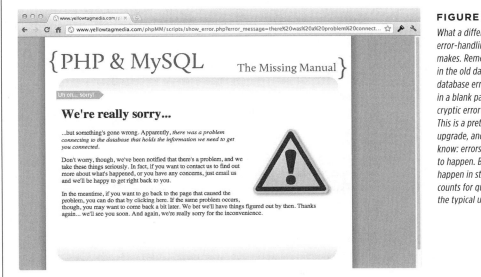

FIGURE 7-14

What a difference some error-handling work makes. Remember back in the old days when a database error resulted in a blank page with a cryptic error message? This is a pretty massive upgrade, and by now you know: errors are going to happen. But now they happen in style, and that counts for quite a bit with the typical user.

Simplify and Abstract

So are you done? Well, almost. The error printing is great, but take another look at the code in your main script, *connect.php*:

```php
if (!mysql_connect(DATABASE_HOST,
                   DATABASE_USERNAME, DATABASE_PASSWORD)) {
  $user_error_message = "there was a problem connecting to the " .
                        "database that holds the information we need " .
                        "to get you connected.";
  $system_error_message = mysql_error();
  header("Location: ../scripts/show_error.php?" .
         "error_message={$user_error_message}&" .
         "system_error_message={$system_error_message}");
  exit();
}
```

That's a lot of code to handle the problem. In fact, you've got a good bit more code dealing with the error than you do dealing with things going right. That's not always a bad thing, but in this case, it's just not necessary. Remember how this code originally looked?

```php
mysql_connect(DATABASE_HOST, DATABASE_USERNAME, DATABASE_PASSWORD)
  or die("<p>Error connecting to database: " . mysql_error() . "</p>");
```

That's pretty darn optimal—a line to do what you want, and then a line if there are problems. Now multiple that by all the different places your code can fail...that's a lot of error handling code.

So can you get your error handling to be that elegant? It's worth at try. Look closely at the code again, and notice how regardless of what the error is, parts of this will always be the same:

```php
if (!mysql_connect(DATABASE_HOST,
                   DATABASE_USERNAME, DATABASE_PASSWORD)) {
  $user_error_message = "there was a problem connecting to the " .
                        "database that holds the information we need " .
                        "to get you connected.";
  $system_error_message = mysql_error();
  header("Location: ../scripts/show_error.php?" .
         "error_message={$user_error_message}&" .
         "system_error_message={$system_error_message}");
  exit();
}
```

So the only thing that ever changes here is the actual error messages. The rest—the variable names, the header call, and the building of the URL—are always the same. So what about creating another function, a lot like *debug_print*, to handle all this?

Add this function to *app_config.php*, further expanding your utility script:

```php
<?php
  // Set up debug mode

  // Database connection constants

  // Error reporting

function debug_print($message) {
  if (DEBUG_MODE) {
    echo $message;
  }
}

function ($user_error_message, $system_error_message) {
  header("Location: show_error.php?" .
         "error_message={$user_error_message}&" .
         "system_error_message={$system_error_message}");
  exit();
}
?>
```

This script is really just a variation on what you did with *debug_print*. You've taken something that's essentially the same code, over and over, and put it into a nice handy, easy-to-reference custom function. The only change is the addition of exit. This ensures that regardless of how the calling script is structured, once the header redirects the browser to your error page, nothing else happens. The error page is shown, and PHP stops whatever else it might have planned to do.

Now, you can simplify *connect.php* by quite a bit:

```
if (!mysql_connect(DATABASE_HOST, DATABASE_USERNAME, "foo")) {
  handle_error("there was a problem connecting to the database " .
          "that holds the information we need to get you connected.",
          mysql_error());
}
```

This is a *lot* better, especially when you realize that this is easily a single line in a terminal or editor. But you can take this yet further:

```
mysql_connect(DATABASE_HOST, DATABASE_USERNAME, "foo")
  or handle_error("there was a problem connecting to the database " .
          "that holds the information we need to get you connect-
ed.",
          mysql_error());
```

Now you've dropped the *if*, and returned to the simple elegance of the *or die* you used to have... but with a much nicer function: your own *handle_error*.

redirect is Path-Insensitive

There's just one problem, and it looks like Figure 7-15.

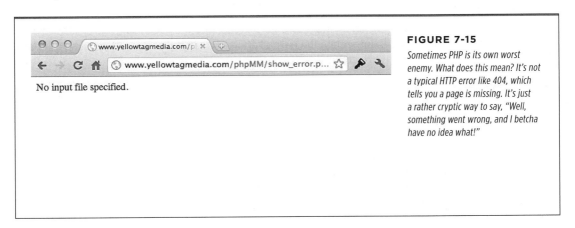

FIGURE 7-15

Sometimes PHP is its own worst enemy. What does this mean? It's not a typical HTTP error like 404, which tells you a page is missing. It's just a rather cryptic way to say, "Well, something went wrong, and I betcha have no idea what!"

You may see just this when you try out *connect.php* for yourself. While this reflects that something has gone wrong, it's sure not the *show_error.php* page on which you've worked so hard. But what is that?

It's actually a well-known error related to PHP. Most web servers are set to treat any URL request that ends in .php as PHP requests. That's good, as it means that you don't have to stash all your PHP scripts in one directory. But it's bad, because the web server doesn't actually see if the URL that ends in .php matches an actual file. It just hands the URL over to the PHP program. But if that URL isn't a pointer to a real file, PHP says, "I don't have anything to run." Or, more accurately, it says "no input file specified."

Yet the question remains: *why* are you getting this? It has to do with this little bit of code in *app_config.php*:

```php
function handle_error($user_error_message, $system_error_message) {
  header("Location: show_error.php?" .
        "error_message={$user_error_message}&" .
        "system_error_message={$system_error_message}");
}
```

In this code, the path to *show_error.php* is relative to *app_config.php*. Since *app_config.php* is in the same directory as *show_error.php*, there's nothing before the file name.

But this code is executed from your *connect.php* script, in (at least in the examples from the book) *ch07/*. So the path from *that* location to *show_error.php* is *../scripts/show_error.php*. And even though the *handle_error* function is defined in *app_config.php*, it's run from the *connect.php* script's context. The result? You're looking for *show_error.php* in the wrong place.

But if you change the path in *app_config.php* to work with *connect.php*, and you later have a different script in a different location, you're going to get this same issue all over again. So how is *handle_error* very utilitarian anymore?

What you need, once again, is a way to indicate a common property—the root of your site—and then relate the path of *show_error.php* to that with an absolute path, rather than using a relative path.

UP TO SPEED

Relative and Absolute Paths

A *relative path* is a path that references a file relative to the current file. This usually means that the path begins with either the file itself, like *show_error.php*, or a movement back a directory using the .. indicator. So relative paths look like *show_error.php* or *../scripts/show_error.php*. In both cases, your starting point is the current file indicating the path.

An *absolute path* is a path that is not related to the current file, but instead the root of your site. You can always tell an absolute path because they start with a /, indicating to begin looking for the indicated file at the root, or "base," of your website. So an absolute path would be something like */scripts/show_error.php*.

You can define your site root in *app_config.php* with a new constant:

```
// Site root
define("SITE_ROOT", "/phpMM/");
```

Now you can use that constant in *handle_error*. Here's the final version of *app_config. php*, with all the new constants and the completed *handle_error* and *debug_print* functions:

```php
<?php

// Set up debug mode
define("DEBUG_MODE", false);

// Site root
define("SITE_ROOT", "/phpMM/");

// Database connection constants
define("DATABASE_HOST", "database.host.com");
define("DATABASE_USERNAME", "username");
define("DATABASE_PASSWORD", "super.secret.password");
define("DATABASE_NAME", "database-name");

// Error reporting
if ($debug_mode) {
  error_reporting(E_ALL);
} else {
  // Turn off all error reporting
  error_reporting(0);
}

function debug_print($message) {
  if (DEBUG_MODE) {
    echo $message;
  }
}

function handle_error($user_error_message, $system_error_message) {
  header("Location: " . SITE_ROOT . "scripts/show_error.php?" .
         "error_message={$user_error_message}&" .
         "system_error_message={$system_error_message}");
}

?>
```

NOTE   You can't use the curly braces trick to insert constants into a string, so you've got to concatenate *SITE_ROOT* to your URL string in the call to header using the dot (.) operator.

Now, you should finally be able to see *show_error.php* via an error in *connect.php*, in all its glory! Check out Figure 7-16 for the result of all this work.

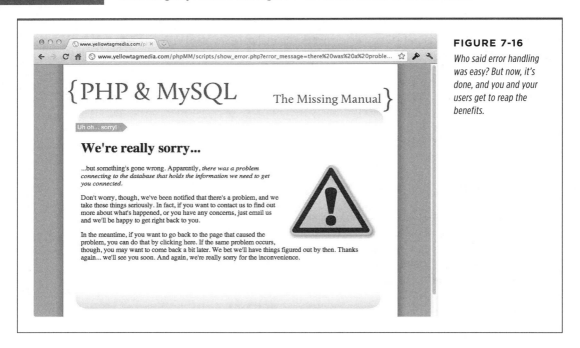

FIGURE 7-16

Who said error handling was easy? But now, it's done, and you and your users get to reap the benefits.

To finish up, take a blazing trip through all your scripts, and replace every bit of *die* and other error handling with calls to *handle_error*. And don't forget to update *database_connection.php* to use *handle_error*, too:

```php
<?php
  require 'app_config.php';

  mysql_connect(DATABASE_HOST, DATABASE_USERNAME, DATABASE_PASSWORD)
    or handle_error("there was a problem connecting to the database " .
            "that holds the information we need to get you connected.",
            mysql_error());

  mysql_select_db(DATABASE_NAME)
    or handle_error("there's a configuration problem with our database.",
                mysql_error());
?>
```

Seriously? 20+ Pages on Error Handling?

It seems hard to believe, doesn't it? You've not added any real new functionality to your web app. Of course, you've learned a bit more about constants, you've defined two custom functions, you've added a utility class, you've gotten a handle on *require* and *require_once*, and even added PHP's internal error reporting to your repertoire.

Still, error handling is usually something that books stick in the last chapter, figuring people won't mind if it's near the end and can be ignored. So why spend all this time on something that—hopefully—your users never see? Well, mostly because an application that doesn't handle errors simply isn't complete.

And, like it or not, when you're just starting out programming, or programming in a new language, you're going to make more mistakes.

Tests and error handling are the best two ways to catch mistakes early and then provide the simplest path toward fixing those mistakes. Now that you have robust error handling, you'll be surprised how often a big problem is turned into a small problem because you quickly see an error and can track it down...without wading through all your code, hopelessly wondering what really went wrong.

Handling Images and Complexity

Y ou've come to a real watershed moment in your programming career. Up until now, you've been using a lot of PHP constructs—from *if* statements to some basic functions to constants and even error handling—and have gotten familiar with the basic MySQL interactions you'll need in typical PHP scripts. With what you already know, you're ready to take on most of the basic programming problems you'll run across in a typical web application, as long as you're thinking on a single-page level.

In other words, if you've got a form that gathers information, you can handle that. You can grab information from a table, and put information into a table, too. No problems there; you can respond to errors, redirect users, and even distinguish between a good user experience and a bad one.

But you know that web applications are greater than the sum of their single-page interactions. Ten different pages that interact with ten different tables is a lot simpler than a complete web application that has ten pages, but also has those ten tables interacting, connecting to each other, and even relating information in one table to information in another. Then, add to that image handling (something you've got to dig into to finish your user form), some interaction with Facebook and Twitter, and letting users log in, and things just got a lot trickier.

And that's what's next: the jump from thinking about single forms and single scripts to thinking about entire systems. You're definitely ready to begin interacting with the file system—the place where your scripts and files and images live. You're ready to start thinking not just about a single table like *users* but working with multiple tables. And custom functions? No worries. You've already built two—*debug_print* (page 215) and *handle_error* (page 221)—so you should have no problem.

Along the way, though, the decisions get trickier. Complexity brings with it not just the question of "What do I do next?" but also "Of the two or three ways I *could* solve this problem, which one is the *best* way?" So get ready: you're diving into deeper programming waters, which tend to be mixed with as much critical thinking and philosophy as new PHP and MySQL language features.

NOTE Up till now, the changes to your code have become fast and furious. In fact, you may be a little unsure if you've got everything right. You can always hop online and visit *www.missingmanuals.com/cds/phpmysqlmm* to get the chapter-by-chapter examples, and make sure you're caught up and ready to keep programming.

■ Images Are Just Files

The big glaring omission in your work with users is that pesky profile image. You probably remember that the user's profile is pretty incomplete right now. The difference between your mock-up from Chapter 6 (shown in Figure 8-1) and where your code is (shown in Figure 8-2) is pretty easy to spot: it's all in that image.

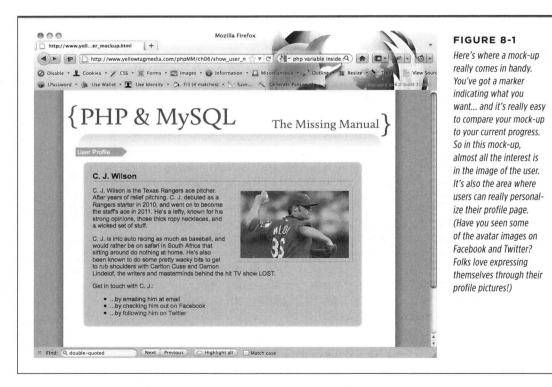

FIGURE 8-1

Here's where a mock-up really comes in handy. You've got a marker indicating what you want... and it's really easy to compare your mock-up to your current progress. So in this mock-up, almost all the interest is in the image of the user. It's also the area where users can really personalize their profile page. (Have you seen some of the avatar images on Facebook and Twitter? Folks love expressing themselves through their profile pictures!)

So it's obvious: you need an image for the user. That's pretty easy, right? Well, you've seen a thousand *img* tags in HTML by now:

```
<img src="images/cj_wilson.jpg" class="user_pic" />
```

The value of the *src* attribute may have gotten your attention. It's a reference to a file, but you don't have any image files yet. You've got the user's name and information in your *users* table, but there's no image on your web server to which you can point. That seems like a different sort of problem; you don't just need a string of text, like "Ryan Geyer" or "@trenspot," but an actual file, and then a reference to a file.

Your task now is to get something other than text information from a user, and then decide what do you do with that information once you've got it.

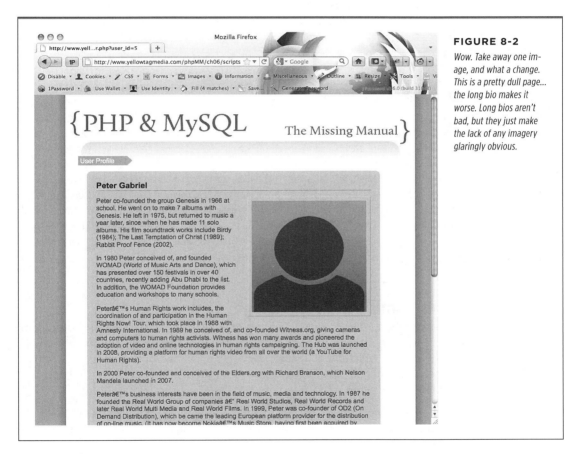

FIGURE 8-2

Wow. Take away one image, and what a change. This is a pretty dull page… the long bio makes it worse. Long bios aren't bad, but they just make the lack of any imagery glaringly obvious.

Files, File Systems, and Client Versus Server

This may be the first time you've had to get a clear under-standing of the difference between what's on your user's machine and what's on the web server. First, you know what a file is: it's just a collection of bits and bytes that your computer knows how to handle. Your scripts, HTML, CSS, and JavaScript are ultimately just text: characters strung together and interpreted by a web browser or the PHP program. In the case of PHP, your web server interprets that PHP, turns it into HTML and CSS and JavaScript for your browser, and then lets the browser take over. For the browser, it takes HTML and CSS and JavaScript—whether in a static file or returned by a web server that's processed a PHP script—and renders those to your user's screen.

Images, on the other hand, are binary data. The same bits and bytes that make up your text files are used to indicate location and color of pixels. And you need a different type of interpretation to read a binary file. Fortunately, web brows-ers are perfectly capable of taking an image file—be it a JPEG (.jpg), GIF (.gif), or PNG (.png)—and displaying it. Still, the process of getting a binary file is a bit different.

When users type in the URL of your web application into their browser, they're running your program, which lives on a web server somewhere and is available via the Internet. They're running that program using their web browser, which is a pro-gram that lives on *their* computer. And there's a big difference between what's on their computer, and what's on your web server. So your web server can't reach into their computer and grab images, for example. To see one of their images in your program, users have to upload that image to your web server.

Of course, most users don't know how to upload a file using a program like FTP. Why should they? They just want to use programs, not write them or learn lots of weird command-line tools. (They just haven't seen the geeky yet beautiful light of programming!) So it's up to you to get their file from their computer onto your file system. A *file system* is just a fancy word that means your own web server's system of files. It can also mean your user's computer. Another way to put this is that your user's computer is a client—a machine that is accessing your program. And your program runs on the server. So the interaction is called a *client-server* interaction. Your job, then, is to get an image file from the client to the server. Then, your server can give your PHP scripts access to that image file to be used in your programs...and of course, most importantly, in the user profile page.

HTML Forms Can Set the Stage

In this situation, HTML does much more than play a bit part to your PHP program. You need to make sure that the HTML form is working and is set up correctly to help your users upload their images. Not only does that form need to give the user a place to select an image, but it needs to set up the process by which that image is uploaded correctly.

Copy *create_user.html* from your Chapter 6 examples folder (page xvii) into the directory where you're working now. Here's how things were left (page 178); there are several steps already in place for uploading an image:

```
<html>
 <head>
  <link href="../css/phpMM.css" rel="stylesheet" type="text/css" />
 </head>
```

```
<body>
 <div id="header"><h1>PHP & MySQL: The Missing Manual</h1></div>
 <div id="example">User Signup</div>

 <div id="content">
   <h1>Join the Missing Manual (Digital) Social Club</h1>
   <p>Please enter your online connections below:</p>
   <form action="create_user.php" method="POST"
        enctype="multipart/form-data">
     <fieldset>

       <label for="first_name">First Name:</label>
       <input type="text" name="first_name" size="20" /><br />
       <label for="last_name">Last Name:</label>
       <input type="text" name="last_name" size="20" /><br />
       <label for="email">E-Mail Address:</label>
       <input type="text" name="email" size="50" /><br />
       <label for="facebook_url">Facebook URL:</label>
       <input type="text" name="facebook_url" size="50" /><br />
       <label for="twitter_handle">Twitter Handle:</label>
       <input type="text" name="twitter_handle" size="20" /><br />
       <label for="user_pic">Upload a picture:</label>
       <input type="file" name="user_pic" size="30" />
       <label for="bio">Bio:</label>

       <textarea name="bio" cols="40" rows="10"></textarea>
     </fieldset>

     <br />

     <fieldset class="center">

       <input type="submit" value="Join the Club" />
       <input type="reset" value="Clear and Restart" />
     </fieldset>

   </form>

 </div>

 <div id="footer"></div>

</body>

</html>
```

NOTE   You also should change the action of the form to reflect that you're no longer using a *scripts/* directory. This HTML is in the *ch08/* example directory in the book's downloadable examples.

The key parts here are the *enctype* attribute on the *form* tag, and the "file" *input* type for the *user_pic*. These lines set up the form to upload not just text, but also a binary image file.

Figure 8-3 shows that the page already lets users select an image. But there's something else this HTML needs: a size limit on the image. You've gotten that email from a friend that's 22MB and has a picture of a cat blown up to 100 times its normal size, right? You want to avoid that in your forms. No 22MB cat images; a single megabyte or two is plenty for any reasonable profile picture.

NOTE   MB stands for *megabyte*, which is one million bytes. That's what the *mega* prefix represents: 1,000,000 of something. To get an idea of sizes, a 20 or 30 page Word document is only about 1 MB. So a 20MB image is a *large* image.

In general, the only reason you'd want image files that big is for high-end photography sites or image sharing sites like Flickr (*www.flickr.com*) that really value tons of detail. You don't need anything like that for a simple profile picture.

You can limit the size of an uploaded file by adding a hidden *input* element, and give it the name "MAX_FILE_SIZE." For the *value*, just give the maximum size of the uploaded image you'll allow, in bytes. So if you wanted to allow a 1MB image, that's 1,000,000 bytes. Here's the HTML to allow a 2MB image:

```
<input type="hidden" name="MAX_FILE_SIZE" value="2000000" />
<label for="user_pic">Upload a picture:</label>

<input type="file" name="user_pic" size="30" />
```

WARNING   Make sure you put this *input* before the *input* that's a "file" type. You should also avoid any comments in the *value* attribute. Just count those zeroes carefully, or you'll be back to shockingly large cats again. (And for those concerned, no felines were harmed in the making of this book.)

The form doesn't look any different with this *input* element, but now you're ready to let users upload an image, and actually do something with that image (see Figure 8-3).

Try it: select an image, and then click "Join the Club." Even though there's no PHP script waiting to receive this information, you'll see your browser slowly uploading... something. Check out Figure 8-4 for Chrome's response: a bit-by-bit indication of how things are going.

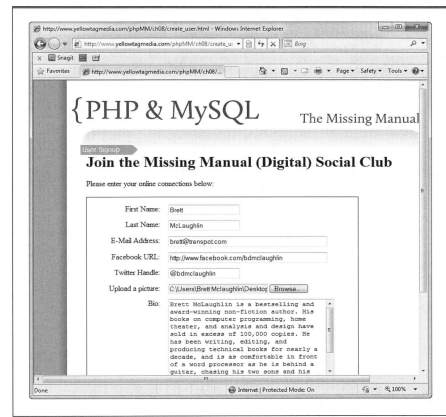

FIGURE 8-3

With much of your HTML already in place, a lot of the changes you're starting to make are invisible just by looking at the web page. Nothing looks different about this form. But it's imposing limits on what your users can do—limits that you've set. That's a good thing.

FIGURE 8-4

It's hard to imagine just how much the web browser does for you. Here's a case where, just by using the input file type, you get a progress indicator, network connections, and an image upload...all for free. Now you've got time to write great PHP.

Uploading a User's Image to Your Server

So now you've got to get that image and do something with it. Start by copying your old version of *create_user.php* into your current directory. Your script should look like this:

```php
<?php

require_once '../scripts/app_config.php';
```

```php
require_once '../scripts/database_connection.php';

$first_name = trim($_REQUEST['first_name']);
$last_name = trim($_REQUEST['last_name']);
$email = trim($_REQUEST['email']);
$bio = trim($_REQUEST['bio']);
$facebook_url = str_replace("facebook.org", "facebook.com", trim($_
REQUEST['facebook_url']));
$position = strpos($facebook_url, "facebook.com");
if ($position === false) {
  $facebook_url = "http://www.facebook.com/" . $facebook_url;
}

$twitter_handle = trim($_REQUEST['twitter_handle']);
$twitter_url = "http://www.twitter.com/";
$position = strpos($twitter_handle, "@");
if ($position === false) {
  $twitter_url = $twitter_url . $twitter_handle;
} else {
  $twitter_url = $twitter_url . substr($twitter_handle, $position + 1);
}

$insert_sql = "INSERT INTO users (first_name, last_name, email, " .
                              "bio, facebook_url, twitter_handle) " .
             "VALUES ('{$first_name}', '{$last_name}', '{$email}', " .
                     "'{$bio}', '{$facebook_url}', '{$twitter_handle}');";

// Insert the user into the database
mysql_query($insert_sql);

// Redirect the user to the page that displays user information
header("Location: show_user.php?user_id=" . mysql_insert_id());
exit();
?>
```

NOTE You need to make a few changes to get your script to this point. Update the path to *app_config.php* and *database_connection.php*, and use *require_once* instead of *require*.

■ SETTING UP SOME HELPER VARIABLES

First, you need to add some basic information you'll use for getting at the file, and for storing it. Add these variables to the top of your page:

```php
<?php

require_once '../scripts/app_config.php';
require_once '../scripts/database_connection.php';
```

```
$upload_dir = SITE_ROOT . "uploads/profile_pics/";
$image_fieldname = "user_pic";


$first_name = trim($_REQUEST['first_name']);
// Other variables

// Get request information

// Insert into MySQL
?>
```

Pretty basic stuff. That constant in *app_config.php* you defined, *SITE_ROOT*, comes in handy. Using it, you can define a directory in which you want to save uploaded files. Go ahead and create that directory on your web server, using a Terminal, command-line tool, or your FTP program. So if your *SITE_ROOT* is just */*, then create */uploads/profile_pics*. If your *SITE_ROOT* is *yellowtagmedia_com/phpMM*, you'd create *yellowtagmedia_com/phpMM/uploads/profile_pics*.

Now, you need to add an array of potential errors, like this:

```
$upload_dir = SITE_ROOT . "uploads/";
$image_fieldname = "user_pic";

// Potential PHP upload errors
$php_errors = array(1 => 'Maximum file size in php.ini exceeded',
                    2 => 'Maximum file size in HTML form exceeded',
                    3 => 'Only part of the file was uploaded',
                    4 => 'No file was selected to upload.');
```

You've used arrays before, but here you're doing something new. You're creating a new array with the *array* keyword, and then defining the values that go in that array.

Since an array is basically a list of values, you could do something like this just as easily:

```
// Potential PHP upload errors
$php_errors = array('Maximum file size in php.ini exceeded',
                    'Maximum file size in HTML form exceeded',
                    'Only part of the file was uploaded',
                    'No file was selected to upload.');
```

With this array, each value is automatically numbered, starting at 0. So *$php_errors[0]* would have the value "'Maximum file size in php.ini exceeded'", for instance.

WARNING Don't forget: almost every programming language you'll ever work with starts counting at 0, rather than 1 (see the box on page 37).

So then what are those numbers and funny arrows (=>)? Well, PHP arrays are *associative arrays*. That's why you can say, for example, *$_REQUEST['user_pic']*. The *$_REQUEST* array doesn't just have values, but it actually has an *association* between those values (the information in an HTML form, usually) and the name of the fields in which those values appeared.

You can think of the mapping between the field name *user_pic* and the value of that field—something like *profile_pic.jpg*, for example—as being defined like this:

```
$_REQUEST = array('user_pic' => 'profile_pic.jpg');
```

> **NOTE** PHP is actually doing things in a much trickier way—that's why you can define any form field you want, of any type you want, with any name you want, and PHP handles it. Still, what ends up happening boils down to a simple creation of an associative array, with field names associated with, or mapped to, field values.

So back to your array of PHP errors:

```
// Potential PHP upload errors
$php_errors = array(1 => 'Maximum file size in php.ini exceeded',
                    2 => 'Maximum file size in HTML form exceeded',
                    3 => 'Only part of the file was uploaded',
                    4 => 'No file was selected to upload.');
```

This array takes numbering into your own hands, rather than letting PHP define its own numbers. So *$php_errors[1]* is now "'Maximum file size in php.ini exceeded", rather than letting the 0-based numbering of PHP assign that same string value to *$php_errors[0]*.

But why in the world would you want to mess with PHP's numbering? It's generally a bad idea, because you're essentially messing with behavior that all PHP programmers expect. In this case, though, it's for a worthy cause.

You see, PHP does more than give you a *$_REQUEST* array. When there are files involved, it gives you a *$_FILES* array. And that array, just like *$_REQUEST*, is keyed to your field. So *$_FILES[$image_fieldname]* is associated with the image uploaded (hopefully) from your form. (Remember, you defined *$image_fieldname* nearer the top of *create_user.php*.)

But there's more. *$_FILES[$image_fieldname]* is itself an array, with information about the file uploaded, and any errors that might have occurred in the process. One of those pieces of information is *$_FILES[$image_fieldname]['error']*. This field returns a number: 0 for "Everything went OK," and a number other than zero if there was a problem. The text in the array indicates what each non-zero number means:

```
1 => 'Maximum file size in php.ini exceeded'
2 => 'Maximum file size in HTML form exceeded'
3 => 'Only part of the file was uploaded'
4 => 'No file was selected to upload.'
```

Now renumbering the *$php_errors* array makes sense: you've got a map of error codes that *$_FILES[$image_fieldname]['error']* might return, and the human-readable errors that go with them.

So now you've got all the information you need; time to start using it.

■ DID THE FILE UPLOAD WITH ANY ERRORS?

You know what to do: check that particular piece of the *$_FILES* array and see if any errors occurred. If the value is non-zero, something went wrong, and you need to handle the problem. Luckily, you've got a handy-dandy function for just that: *handle_error*.

```php
<?php
// Require utility scripts
// Set up variables
// Get everything from the form aside from the image

// Make sure we didn't have an error uploading the image
($_FILES[$image_fieldname]['error'] == 0)
  or handle_error("the server couldn't upload the image you selected.",
               $php_errors($_FILES[$image_fieldname]['error']));


// Interact with MySQL
// Redirect to show_error.php
?>
```

So if the error field (*$_FILES[$image_fieldname]['error']*) is zero, things are great; just keep going. If it's non-zero, show an error to the user, and then use the error code to look up the exact problem in your *$php_errors* associative array, and hand it off for view if debugging is on.

> **NOTE** Now would be a good time to check *app_config.php*, and make sure you have *DEBUG_MODE* set to *true*.

There's also a new little wrinkle in here that you may have just skipped right over: This is basically an *if* statement without an *if*. PHP will evaluate this line...

```php
($_FILES[$image_fieldname]['error'] == 0)
```

...and if that line is true, it will continue. If the line isn't true, it runs the *or* part of the code, on the next line; in this case, that's *handle_error*.

So this line is essentially like writing this code:

```php
if ($_FILES[$image_fieldname]['error'] != 0) {
  handle_error("the server couldn't upload the image you selected.",
             $php_errors[$_FILES[$image_fieldname]['error']]);
}
```

Watch your square brackets ([ ]) and parentheses carefully here; it's really easy to get them mixed up and cause a hard-to-find error.

But this code is a little longer, while the code without the *if* is just a little clearer. Every bit of complexity you can save helps, so this is a nice trick to add to your growing PHP toolkit.

You can actually check your code in action at this point. Visit *create_user.html* and find an image file that's bigger than 2 MB. Look for a photo in iPhoto or something you've pulled straight off your camera. Select that image, and then try and submit your form. You should get something like Figure 8-5 back.

FIGURE 8-5

Here's one of those beautiful situations where a lot of hard work earlier pays off later. Rather than wading through your code or even writing custom PHP, you were able to quickly hand off an error to your handle_error *function and get a nice response. Now multiply that by the hundreds (thousands?) of times you'll use* handle_error, *and you'll start to see the value of having that utility function written early on in your PHP life.*

You might have noticed that even though the image was rejected, your browser still uploads the image—regardless of how big the image is, or what your maximum file size is. That's because it's only after the image is uploaded that the size comparison is made. Sort of a bummer, but that's a browser issue, and not something you can fix with PHP.

This page is the result of your code finding an error code, and that error code being matched up to an error in *$php_errors*—in this case, the image was larger than your HTML allowed.

■ IS THIS REALLY AN UPLOADED FILE?

The next thing you need to do is left out of more PHP instructions and books than you can imagine, but it's critical. At this point, despite whether or not you have a real file, what your program has to work with is a file *name*. And that name is controlled entirely by what your users put into their file input box. So if they're tricky, malicious, and thoroughly dishonest, they might try and put in a filename that does upload a file on their system, but also just so happens to match one of the special files on web servers that control things like, say, the passwords for users. (That file is usually */etc/passwd*).

You might think you must get your regular expressions on here and check for all kinds of fancy filename characters, but there's an easier way. PHP gives you a function called *is_uploaded_file* that ensures that for a given name, that name references a file uploaded with HTTP (the language of web browsers and HTML forms). In other words, if the supplied name targets a file on your web server, this function will return false, and you know that something's fishy.

So you want to do something like this:

```
// Make sure we didn't have an error uploading the image

// Is this file the result of a valid upload?
is_uploaded_file($_FILES[$image_fieldname]['tmp_name'])
   or handle_error("you were trying to do something naughty. Shame on you!",
               "Uploaded request: file named " .
               "'{$_FILES[$image_fieldname]['tmp_name']}'");


// Interact with MySQL
```

Breathing and Sleeping Matter

Any good programmer will tell you stories of at least a few all-night hacking sessions. And odds are, those stories will be tinged rosy, full of victories and excitement. But the truth of the matter is that fatigue slows the brain down, and no programmer is as effective on two hours of sleep as she is on six.

Bottom line: a tired brain isn't as useful as a rested one. And, because if you've been swimming in the pool of PHP programming for seven chapters before this one, now you're well into the deep end. Chances are that you're having to read at least a few things twice, and some of this new code introduces not just one or two new things, but three or four or five.

There's nothing at all wrong with this, but if you're getting worn out, nobody wins by you plowing ahead. Take a few hours off, ride your bike, jog a mile, or just set PHP aside for the night. You'll be stunned at how much clearer things seem after a bit of rest from programming. Don't think that rest and taking a few moments to breathe out of sight of the keyboard are a sign of weakness; rather, just the opposite.

This code uses another property of (*$_FILES[$image_fieldname]*): the temporary name of the file. So you get the name of the file as it currently stands, and make sure it's an uploaded file.

But there's a problem here: *is_uploaded_file* fires off an error if the file isn't uploaded. That sounds good, except that you've done a lot of work to handle errors your own way. You don't want *is_uploaded_file* to generate an error; you just want its return value, even if there's a problem.

You can tell PHP to run a function and suppress errors with @ directly before the function (for more, see the box below), and that's exactly what you need here:

```
// Is this file the result of a valid upload?
@is_uploaded_file($_FILES[$image_fieldname]['tmp_name'])
    or handle_error("you were trying to do something naughty. Shame on you!",
            "Uploaded request: file named " .
            "'{$_FILES[$image_fieldname]['tmp_name']}'");
```

Now, the function is run, and if there's a problem, *handle_error* takes over, rather than your script throwing out some unintelligible error of its own. One more hacker thwarted; so nice work in adding this in, and avoiding a nasty security hole.

POWER USERS' CLINIC

Suppress Errors at Your Own Peril

There's perhaps no more intriguing operator in PHP than @. With one keystroke, all the problems that might come about from a user entering invalid data, or a SQL query having an incorrect column, or even just a poorly formed URL can be banished. Your code can continue without having to check for every possible mistake your users, you, and your code might make, and that's a lot of potential mistakes.

But @ really is an atomic bomb waiting to turn your code into a smoldering slag heap. Use it frequently, and you'll quickly find that your code is riddled with potential problems. You'll never really be sure if your problem is something your user did, something you did, or a legitimate bug you need to fix.

Regardless of what's causing the error, if you've gotten around it with @, then you've got a legitimate bug. Make a rule for yourself: when you use @ (as in the very next line), pair it with an *or* and explicit error handling. You'll be much better for the discipline.

But there's an exception. (There always is, isn't there?) The exception in this situation is a high-volume, production website. Production sites often use @ because they simply *can't* crash or stop working. In those cases, you've usually got to go with some sort of hybrid solution. On the one hand, use @, but then pair it with *or* triggered by a flag, like the debugging flag discussed on page 215. So in "normal" mode, things run without spewing tons of errors (or perhaps by only logging those errors). Then, by flipping on the debugging mode, you start to see what's really going on, and can track down problems and fix them.

■ IS THE UPLOADED FILE REALLY AN IMAGE?

So you've got a file uploaded, and you know it's not some fake file with a name that points to a protected file on your server's file system. But there's one more step: make sure that file is an image. There's nothing preventing a user from accidentally uploading a Word document, or a malicious user uploading some JavaScript or an executable file.

Thankfully PHP, makes checking for image files pretty easy. You use the *getimagesize* function, which checks to see the size of a given image file. And, best of all, this function kicks out an error if it's given a non-image file. Perfect!

```
// Is this actually an image?
@getimagesize($_FILES[$image_fieldname]['tmp_name'])
  or handle_error("you selected a file for your picture " .
                  "that isn't an image.",
                  "{$_FILES[$image_fieldname]['tmp_name']} " .
                  "isn't a valid image file.");
```

■ MOVING THE FILE TO A PERMANENT LOCATION

You're almost to the big finish. You've got a valid HTTP upload that's an image. All that's left is to move this image from the temporary location that browsers use for uploaded files to someplace permanent. Here's where your variable from long ago comes into use:

```
$upload_dir = SITE_ROOT . "uploads/profile_pics/";
```

> **NOTE** Create this directory now if you haven't already.

At this point, it's important to know what's happened to your user's uploaded file. When the server uploads this file, it uses a preconfigured location for the file. It's also quite likely to use a name that isn't identical to what the user's file was originally called. Sometimes the name is completely changed, and other times something is prepended or appended to the name.

Additionally, the file isn't in a place you want to leave it. It'll often be stuck into some sort of temporary storage, and that storage is often cleared out every so often. So you need to not only assign the file a name, but you also need to move it somewhere more permanent—that's why you have *$upload_dir*.

Now, there are lots of different approaches to naming. You could come up with something related to the user who uploaded the file, but often, it's just easiest to give the file a unique numeric name. And the easiest way to do that is to get the current time, and create a file name based on that—an almost surefire way to end up with a unique filename.

> **NOTE** Take a look at the image names on a site like Flickr or Facebook. Unless users have renamed their images, the names are often just a string of letters and numbers.

So you need a unique name, and then you can finally move the file from its current location to a permanent one.

First, figure out a name for the soon-to-be permanent image:

```php
// Name the file uniquely
$now = time();
while (file_exists($upload_filename = $upload_dir . $now .
                                      '-' .
                                      $_FILES[$image_fieldname]['name'])) {
    $now++;
}
```

Step through this bit by bit, and it will make perfect sense:

1. Create a new variable called *$now* and assign it the current time, using PHP's *time* function.

2. Start a loop using *while*. So *while* a certain condition is true, keep doing the loop. As soon as that condition *isn't* true, stop looping.

3. As part of the *while* condition, assign a value to *$upload_filename*: the *$upload_dir* plus the current time, and then a dash (-), and then finally the name of the original file. So this is a combination of a part that will be unique (the time) and the user's file's original name (which is in *$_FILES[$image_fieldname]['name']*).

4. Then, to complete the *while* condition, pass that calculated file name to *file_exists*. If that file exists, then the *while* loop runs. If not, you have a unique file name, so the loop will not run (or, run anymore, if it's already been looping).

5. Within the loop, you must come up with a way to change the file name. Since the *while* loop is only going to run if you've got a file name that's already in use, just add to *$now*, and try again.

And here's the beauty of PHP: you can do all of that in just a few lines of code. So when this code finishes running, you've got a unique file name for the user's file.

Now, move the file from its old temporary location to the permanent one:

```php
// Finally, move the file to its permanent location
@move_uploaded_file($_FILES[$image_fieldname]['tmp_name'], $upload_filename)
  or handle_error("we had a problem saving your image to " .
                  "its permanent location.",
                  "permissions or related error moving " .
                  "file to {$upload_filename}");
```

You've put in a lot of work, but you finally have your file in a permanent location—and you know that file is a valid image. Try it for yourself. Visit *create_user.php*, select an image from your hard drive that's under your size limit, and upload it. Then navigate to that directory in your web browser. If you've got permissions set to view directories on your server, you'll see something like Figure 8-6.

Don't be disappointed if you can't see the directory, or you get a message saying that Directory Listings are denied. That's a common web server practice, and doesn't necessarily mean that something's gone wrong.

IMAGES ARE JUST FILES

FIGURE 8-6

Honestly, it's probably not a great thing if you can look at files like this. It basically means that anyone with a web browser can navigate your site's directory structure. So while this is great for debugging, it's not something you want to leave on, and you may want to email or call your web server provider or hosting company and ask them to turn off directory listings through the Internet.

Instead, open back up *create_user.php,* and make two changes. First, add an *echo* command to print out your file's location:

```
// Name the file uniquely
$now = time();
while (file_exists($upload_filename = $upload_dir . $now .
                                     '-' .
                                     $_FILES[$image_fieldname]['name'])) {
    $now++;
}

echo $upload_filename;
echo "<br />";
echo $_FILES[$image_fieldname]['tmp_name'];
```

Now comment out the redirect, so you can see this *echo:*

```
// Redirect the user to the page that displays user information
//header("Location: show_user.php?user_id=" . mysql_insert_id());
```

Upload an image again, and you'll get a path back from your *echo,* assuming things went well. Figure 8-7 is an example of the output you should expect.

Now (finally!) you can drop that file path into your URL bar, adding your domain name, and you should get a glorious image from your user's machine to your web server. Check out an example in Figure 8-8.

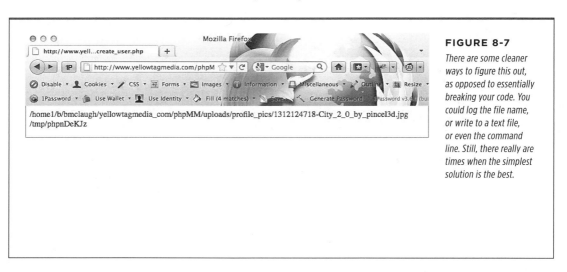

FIGURE 8-7

There are some cleaner ways to figure this out, as opposed to essentially breaking your code. You could log the file name, or write to a text file, or even the command line. Still, there really are times when the simplest solution is the best.

FIGURE 8-8

Yes! The image has landed. It's taken some work, but think about the best web applications out there: they all allow for custom images to be uploaded. Now you can do it, too. Nice work.

Storing the Image Location in the Database

It's taken some time, but you're finally ready to save this image—or at least its location—in your database table. You've already got a query built:

```
$insert_sql = "INSERT INTO users (first_name, last_name, email, " .
                        "bio, facebook_url, twitter_handle) " .
            "VALUES ('{$first_name}', '{$last_name}', '{$email}', " .
                " '{$bio}', " . '{$facebook_url}', " .
                "'{$twitter_handle}');";

// Insert the user into the database
mysql_query($insert_sql);
```

■ CREATING A NEW DATABASE COLUMN

All you need to do, then, is add a column in which you can store the image location. This is a matter of another *ALTER* command, something with which you're already comfortable:

```
ALTER TABLE users
        ADD user_pic_path varchar(200);
```

Go ahead and run this statement. You may want to *DESCRIBE* your users table just to make sure things took:

```
mysql> describe users;
+----------------+--------------+------+-----+---------+----------------+
| Field          | Type         | Null | Key | Default | Extra          |
+----------------+--------------+------+-----+---------+----------------+
| user_id        | int(11)      |      | PRI | NULL    | auto_increment |
| first_name     | varchar(20)  |      |     |         |                |
| last_name      | varchar(30)  |      |     |         |                |
| email          | varchar(50)  |      |     |         |                |
| facebook_url   | varchar(100) | YES  |     | NULL    |                |
| twitter_handle | varchar(20)  | YES  |     | NULL    |                |
| bio            | text         | YES  |     | NULL    |                |
| user_pic_path  | varchar(200) | YES  |     | NULL    |                |
+----------------+--------------+------+-----+---------+----------------+
8 rows in set (0.00 sec)
```

This *user_pic_path* field is just a text column, because all you're storing is the path to the image, rather than the image itself.

> **NOTE** If you're starting to get curious about what it would look like to store the actual image in your database, go ahead and nurture that curiosity. In the next section, that's exactly what you'll do (and work through whether or not that's a good idea).

■ INSERTING THE IMAGE PATH INTO YOUR TABLE

The update to the *INSERT* query isn't difficult at all, now:

```
$insert_sql = "INSERT INTO users (first_name, last_name, email, " .
                    "bio, facebook_url, twitter_handle, " .
                    "user_profile_pic) " .
           "VALUES ('{$first_name}', '{$last_name}', '{$email}', " .
                " '{$bio}', " . '{$facebook_url}', " .
                "'{$twitter_handle}', '{$upload_filename}');";
```

```
// Insert the user into the database
mysql_query($insert_sql);
```

Things are definitely starting to flow quickly now. With all your existing work already in place, adding a new column is pretty simple. But before you dive back into your HTML, there's one more thing left to do.

■ CHECKING YOUR WORK

This query should work...but how can you know? If you were just a PHP programmer, you'd have to try this code out and then either write a new script to select data from the users table, or jump right back into *show_user.php*. But why go to all that trouble? You know SQL and how to interact with MySQL.

First, create a new user, and use a name you've not used before. Then, jump back into your SQL command-line tool and check the results of your work for yourself. Just *SELECT* the user you just inserted, focusing on its picture path:

```
SELECT user_pic_path
  FROM users
 WHERE last_name = 'Roday';
```

You should see something like this:

```
mysql> select user_pic_path from users where last_name = 'Roday';
+------------------------------------+
| user_pic_path                      |
+------------------------------------+
| /yellowtagmedia_com/phpMM/uploads/profile_pics/1312127661-City_2_0_by_pince-
l3d.jpg |
+------------------------------------+
1 row in set (0.00 sec)
```

Perfect. The image is on your server, and now you've got the path to that image, indelibly stored in your database. *Now* you're ready to show your users their glorious image-selves.

If you've had any issues, you may want to check out the completed version of
create_user.php below. There have been a ton of additions, so just make sure
everything is right where it belongs:

```php
<?php

require_once '../scripts/app_config.php';
require_once '../scripts/database_connection.php';

$upload_dir = SITE_ROOT . "uploads/profile_pics/";
$image_fieldname = "user_pic";

// Potential PHP upload errors
$php_errors = array(1 => 'Maximum file size in php.ini exceeded',
                    2 => 'Maximum file size in HTML form exceeded',
                    3 => 'Only part of the file was uploaded',
                    4 => 'No file was selected to upload.');

$first_name = trim($_REQUEST['first_name']);
$last_name = trim($_REQUEST['last_name']);
$email = trim($_REQUEST['email']);
$bio = trim($_REQUEST['bio']);
$facebook_url = str_replace("facebook.org", "facebook.com", trim($_
REQUEST['facebook_url']));
$position = strpos($facebook_url, "facebook.com");
if ($position === false) {
  $facebook_url = "http://www.facebook.com/" . $facebook_url;
}

$twitter_handle = trim($_REQUEST['twitter_handle']);
$twitter_url = "http://www.twitter.com/";
$position = strpos($twitter_handle, "@");
if ($position === false) {
  $twitter_url = $twitter_url . $twitter_handle;
} else {
  $twitter_url = $twitter_url .
                 substr($twitter_handle, $position + 1);
}

// Make sure we didn't have an error uploading the image
($_FILES[$image_fieldname]['error'] == 0)
  or handle_error("the server couldn't upload the image you selected.",
                  $php_errors[$_FILES[$image_fieldname]['error']]);
```

```php
// Is this file the result of a valid upload?
@is_uploaded_file($_FILES[$image_fieldname]['tmp_name'])
  or handle_error("you were trying to do something naughty. " .
                  "Shame on you!",
                  "Uploaded request: file named " .
                  "'{$_FILES[$image_fieldname]['tmp_name']}'");

// Is this actually an image?
@getimagesize($_FILES[$image_fieldname]['tmp_name'])
  or handle_error("you selected a file for your picture that " .
                  "isn't an image.",
                  "{$_FILES[$image_fieldname]['tmp_name']} " .
                  "isn't a valid image file.");

// Name the file uniquely
$now = time();
while (file_exists($upload_filename = $upload_dir . $now .
                                      '-' .
                   $_FILES[$image_fieldname]['name'])) {
    $now++;
}

// Finally, move the file to its permanent location
@move_uploaded_file($_FILES[$image_fieldname]['tmp_name'],
                    $upload_filename)
  or handle_error("we had a problem saving your image " .
                  "to its permanent location.",
                  "permissions or related error moving " .
                  "file to {$upload_filename}");

$insert_sql = "INSERT INTO users (first_name, last_name, email, " .
              "bio, facebook_url, twitter_handle, user_pic_path) " .
              "VALUES ('{$first_name}', '{$last_name}', '{$email}', " .
              "'{$bio}', '{$facebook_url}', '{$twitter_handle}', " .
              "'{$upload_filename}');";

// Insert the user into the database
mysql_query($insert_sql);

// Redirect the user to the page that displays user information
header("Location: show_user.php?user_id=" . mysql_insert_id());
exit();
?>
```

■ Images Are For Viewing

Finally! It's time to show your users the fruit of all your hard work. They'll probably never realize how long you slaved to get one single image showing up—and protecting all their other information in the process—but you know, and sometimes that's enough.

Make sure you have a copy of *show_user.php* alongside *create_user.html* and *create_user.php*. You need to update *show_user.php* to select the user's picture path from the *users* table, and then display that picture.

> **NOTE** As with all scripts that you're updating, make sure you change *require* to *require_once*, include a reference to *app_config.php*, and update your paths to reflect you're not using chapter-specific *scripts/* directories. In any scripts that have HTML—like *show_user.php*—you should also check paths for things like CSS stylesheet and external JavaScript references.

SELECT the Image and Display It

This step turns out to be pretty easy. First, you've already got a *SELECT* that grabs everything for a particular user:

```
// Build the SELECT statement
$select_query = "SELECT * FROM users WHERE user_id = " . $user_id;
```

Next, you can just add a line grabbing the image path in the code you already have pulling information out of the result of running this SQL *INSERT*:

```
if ($result) {
  $row = mysql_fetch_array($result);
  $first_name    = $row['first_name'];
  $last_name     = $row['last_name'];
  $bio           = preg_replace("/[\r\n]+/", "</p><p>", $row['bio']);
  $email         = $row['email'];
  $facebook_url  = $row['facebook_url'];
  $twitter_handle = $row['twitter_handle'];
  $user_image    = $row['user_pic_path'];

  // Turn $twitter_handle into a URL
  $twitter_url = "http://www.twitter.com/" .
                 substr($twitter_handle, $position + 1);

} else {
  handle_error("there was a problem finding your " .
               "information in our system.",
               "Error locating user with ID {$user_id}");
}
```

NOTE   Take this opportunity to move from using *die* in the *else* block of your *if* statement to the much cooler *handle_error* function.

Be sure you remove this old code entirely:

```
// To be added later
$user_image = "../../images/missing_user.png";
```

Finally, you already have a place in this script's HTML that references the *$user_image* variable:

```
<div id="content">
  <div class="user_profile">
    <h1><?php echo "{$first_name} {$last_name}"; ?></h1>
    <p><img src="<?php echo $user_image; ?>" class="user_pic" />
    <!-- and so on... -->
```

So try things out. Hit your *show_user.php* page with an existing user's ID in your browser's address bar, or create a new user with a picture and let *create_user.php* redirect you. You should see something like Figure 8-9. Hardly the trumpets blaring and angels dancing you were hoping for.

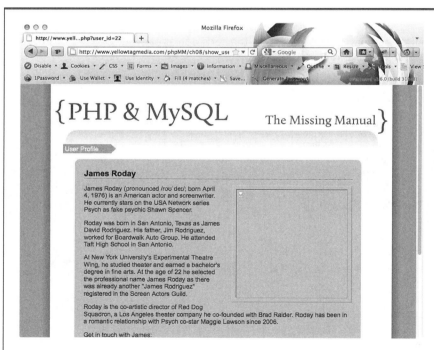

FIGURE 8-9

When you get an unexpected result like a missing image, start out by either viewing the source (under the View menu, or by right-clicking the page and selecting View Source) or using a plug-in like Firebug to inspect the offending element. That's almost always a good first step toward tracking down what's going wrong.

If you view the source for this page, and figure out what the image path being used is, you'll probably have something like Figure 8-10.

FIGURE 8-10

According to this HTML source, the img element has the correct absolute path to the image. But is this what paths in HTML pages should look like? How does the absolute path on a file system relate to the path on a web server?

Now, you checked earlier to make sure this is a valid image. So you know the path to the image isn't the problem...or is it?

Converting File System Paths to URLs

What you have is a path on your web server's file system, but what you need is a path that your web server recognizes. Every web server has something called a *document root*. That's the directory into which you place files so that they can be seen on the browser.

> **NOTE**   Old school programmers and HTML geeks will remember that *public_html/* used to be the almost universal standard for a document root.

Close out *show_user.php* and create a new script, called *test.php*. Type a single command between the opening and closing PHP syntax:

```php
<?php
echo "DOCUMENT ROOT: {$_SERVER['1G']}";
?>
```

$_SERVER is another one of those helpful associative arrays that PHP gives you. The *DOCUMENT_ROOT* key tells you your web server's document root.

> **TIP**   Visit *www.php.net/manual/en/reserved.variables.server.php* to see all the various things you can find out from *$_SERVER*.

Now hit this script with a browser. You'll get something like Figure 8-11. In this example, the root is */home1/b/bmclaugh/yellowtagmedia_com*. So what this means is that the web path */* is really mapping to the file system path */home1/b/bmclaugh/yellowtag-media_com*.

This test script gives you the sort of hook you need: a mapping that relates a file system path to an actual web path. And it's a pretty easy mapping, too. For any file path, you want to strip away everything from the beginning of the path up to and including *yellowtagmedia_com* (or whatever the end of your document root is).

FIGURE 8-11

According to this HTML source, the img element has the correct absolute path to the image. But is this what paths in HTML pages should look like? How does the absolute path on a file system relate to the path on a web server?

So now you need to put that into action. First, add a sample image path you're currently storing in your database to your *test.php* script:

```php
<?php
echo "DOCUMENT ROOT: {$_SERVER['DOCUMENT_ROOT']}";
$image_sample_path =
    "/home1/b/bmclaugh/yellowtagmedia_com/phpMM/" .
    "uploads/profile_pics/1312128274-james_roday.jpg";
?>
```

Now, you can use *str_replace*, a handy function you know quite well by now. You simply want to replace the file path equivalent of the document root with...nothing. You want to remove it:

```php
<?php
echo "DOCUMENT ROOT: {$_SERVER['DOCUMENT_ROOT']}";
$image_sample_path =
    "/home1/b/bmclaugh/yellowtagmedia_com/phpMM/" .
    "uploads/profile_pics/1312128274-james_roday.jpg";
$web_image_path = str_replace($_SERVER['DOCUMENT_ROOT'],
                             '', $image_sample_path);
?>
```

Finally, *echo* the result back out:

```php
<?php
echo "DOCUMENT ROOT: {$_SERVER['DOCUMENT_ROOT']}";
$image_sample_path =
    "/home1/b/bmclaugh/yellowtagmedia_com/phpMM/" .
    "uploads/profile_pics/1312128274-james_roday.jpg";
$web_image_path = str_replace($_SERVER['DOCUMENT_ROOT'],
                             '', $image_sample_path);
```

```
    echo "<br /><br />CONVERTED PATH: {$web_image_path}";
    ?>
```

Now hit your *test.php* again. Hopefully, you'll get something like Figure 8-12.

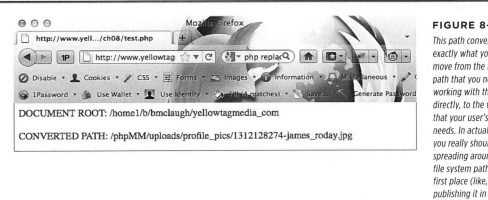

FIGURE 8-12

This path conversion is exactly what you want: a move from the file system path that you need when working with the image directly, to the web path that your user's browser needs. In actuality, you really shouldn't be spreading around your file system path in the first place (like, say, publishing it in a book?).

Take this path and drop it right into your browser, following the slash after your domain name. Then hit Enter and, if all is well, you'll see that image you've been after for so long. Figure 8-13 shows the magic in action.

FIGURE 8-13

Finally! Image uploading is a common, but tricky exercise... kind of like error handling. Just think how much has to go on to get one image into the right place, and easily viewable by your thousands (millions?) of users.

Now you can turn the code in *test.php* into...you guessed it: yet another helpful utility function. Open up your old friend *app_config.php*, and create a generic version of your code in *test.php*:

```
function get_web_path($file_system_path) {
  return str_replace($_SERVER['DOCUMENT_ROOT'], '', $file_system_path);
}
```

Pretty close, isn't it? Make sure you understand exactly what's going on here. This short bit of code:

1. Defines a new function, using *function*, that you can call from any script the requires or includes *app_config.php*.

2. Names the function: *get_web_path*.

3. Defines a single piece of information that the function gets from whatever script calls it: *$file_system_path*. This will be the complete path on the web server to the file that needs to be converted into a web path.

4. Takes *$file_system_path* and replaces the document root in the path with nothing (' ').

5. Returns the result of running *str_replace* using *return*.

The only thing new here is *return*. *return* is a part of the PHP language, and it does just what you'd expect: return something to the program or script that called this function. So if you passed in */usr/bbentley/web/images/profile.jpg*, and your document root was */usr/bbentley/web*, then the string */images/profile.jpg* would be returned from a call to *get_web_path*.

POWER USERS' CLINIC

Prototype with Simple Scripts

Some languages and frameworks, like Ruby on Rails in particular, offer a means to run commands within the context of your programming or web environment. This is sort of like a command-line-plus, where you get all the benefits of a running web server, logging, your scripts loaded, and even a few additional bells and whistles.

Unfortunately, PHP isn't one of those languages. When it comes to testing out a bit of new functionality, then, your choices are typically to either just start coding in one of your existing scripts, or to create a simple script like *test.php*, and work with it until you get your functionality figured out.

Although using a simple command-line script can seem like a bit of a drag compared to a nice CSS-styled web environment, it's often the better choice. You can test things and get your code just right without having to worry about HTML or interactions across scripts. Then, once you've got your code like you want it, it's easy to drop into your full-blown web scripting environment.

WARNING There is one fairly serious gotcha to this function. The function assumes you're sending it an absolute path, not a relative path. So *../../../web/images/profile.jpg* isn't going to match your document root in any form or fashion. Fortunately, the code that generates the path to an image uses absolute paths. That means that at least for your particular needs, this function works just fine.

Displaying Your User's Image: Take Two

To display your user's image, go back to *show_user.php*. This time, though, you're armed with a utility function. Use that function to convert the absolute path stored in your database into a web-safe path for viewing:

```php
if ($result) {
  $row = mysql_fetch_array($result);
  $first_name    = $row['first_name'];
  $last_name     = $row['last_name'];
  $bio           = preg_replace("/[\r\n]+/", "</p><p>", $row['bio']);
  $email         = $row['email'];
  $facebook_url  = $row['facebook_url'];
  $twitter_handle = $row['twitter_handle'];
  $user_image    = get_web_path($row['user_pic_path']);


  // Turn $twitter_handle into a URL
  $twitter_url = "http://www.twitter.com/" .
                 substr($twitter_handle, $position + 1);

} else {
  handle_error("there was a problem finding your " .
               "information in our system.",
               "Error locating user with ID {$user_id}");
}
```

It really doesn't get much easier than that. Fire up your browser, and try either creating a user again (with *create_user.php*) or visiting *show_user.php* and supplying a *user_id* parameter as part of the URL string. You should see *show_user.php* the way it's always been intended: resplendent with imagery, as seen in Figure 8-14.

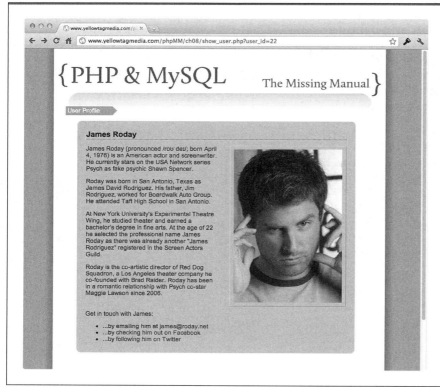

FIGURE 8-14

It's taken a while, but now you can be sure that you've got the most secure, well-built image-handling script around. (Well, okay, those guys from Facebook and Google+ might have a few additional tricks, but you're close.) Enjoy profile pictures for a moment, and then get ready for the next evolution.

A Few Quick Revisions to *app_config.php*

At this point, you've got a new tool: *$_SERVER['DOCUMENT_ROOT']*. And, really, you've got another tool based on that: your *get_web_path* function. This function is helpful in terms of cleaning up *app_config.php* right now. Currently, you've got your site root defined something like this:

```
// Site root
define("SITE_ROOT", "/phpMM/");
```

> **WARNING** Your exact value for *SITE_ROOT* is probably different. Still, you should have something that looks like a path from the root of your web directory to where all your site's files are hosted. It may be as simple as /, which is a pretty common site root.

But that's sort of misleading. That's a web path, not the site root. The site root is more like a file-system specific path. It's really the path on your hosting provider's machine to your site's root. So it might be something like */home1/b/bmclaugh/*

yellowtagmedia_com. Then, the web path happens to be */*, or */phpMM*, or whatever your particular directory structure from the root is.

But wait a second. You already *have* something that looks like that: *$_SERVER['DOCUMENT_ROOT']*. Not only that, but now with *get_web_path*, you can turn that into a web path, and then add the path from the root of your web server to your site. So if your *SITE_ROOT* was */phpMM*, then you really want something more like this:

```
// Site root - in actual filesystem path form
define("SITE_ROOT", $_SERVER['DOCUMENT_ROOT'] . "/phpMM/");
```

That's going to turn into the file system path to your web server, and then add the path from your web server to the files for this app, resulting in, for example, */home1/b/bmclaugh/yellowtagmedia_com/phpMM*. So now you've got a much cleaner setup. You're dealing with real files on a real file system, and then when you need to convert those files and their paths into the web domain, you use *get_web_path*.

To see how this works, check out your script in *handle_error*. Here's the version as you should have it now:

```
function handle_error($user_error_message, $system_error_message) {
  header("Location: " . SITE_ROOT . "scripts/show_error.php" .
         "?error_message={$user_error_message}" .
         "&system_error_message={$system_error_message}");
}
```

FREQUENTLY ASKED QUESTION

Why Not Store a Web Path in the Database?

Every single time you load an image from the database, you're going to have to call *get_web_path* on that image path—at least if you want to show the image on the Web. And since you're writing web applications, isn't that sort of the point? It might seem like you could just cut that conversion step out, and simply store the image in the database as a web path from the beginning.

There are a couple of reasons that's not a great idea, though. First, an absolute path is just that: it's absolute. Your web server software can change; your home directory can change; you can switch from PHP to Ruby to Perl and back to PHP; but short of you actually moving an image, it's absolute path remains unchanged. Most importantly, you can change the entire document root of your site, and an absolute path will still work.

So why is that so significant? Because you really might need to change the document root of your site at some point. And if you stored a web path in the database—a path related to your document root—and then your document root changed, all of your image paths would be invalid! You'd have to change every single one of them from being relative to your old document root to relative to your new document root. What a mess.

On top of that, a web path really is a relative path, even if it begins with a /. That's because it's relative to your document root. An absolute path is fixed in relation to a machine, regardless of that machine's software. And as a general rule, you want to store things in a database that are as absolute and fixed as possible. Given the choice between a piece of information in an absolute form and one in a relative form, always go for the absolute form. It's usually easy to change from one form to the other, so store the more "reliable" one. You won't regret it.

But *SITE_ROOT* isn't a web path anymore, and you do need a web path in this case. You're sending a redirect to the browser, and the browser speaks web paths, not file systems.

The remedy is simple, since you have the real path in place in *SITE_ROOT*. You just need to convert that to a web path:

```
function handle_error($user_error_message, $system_error_message) {
    header("Location: " . get_web_path(SITE_ROOT) .
        "scripts/show_error.php" .

        "?error_message={$user_error_message}" .
        "&system_error_message={$system_error_message}");
}
```

Now all your paths are based on real, actual files on the file system. Then, when you have to deal with web requests, you convert those real file paths to web paths. And of course, this was key in getting images to work, another bonus. So about those images...

And Now for Something Completely Different

Everything works now. Your users can upload images. You can get those images securely into a permanent location that you choose. You've got a way to store the location in a database and to convert that location into a URL that works with your website and your personal document root. And then, to top it all off, you can show your users their images when they visit *show_user.php*.

What else is there to do?

Suppose that you're using multiple web servers that share a single database. Are you really going to store the same image on each of those web servers?

Suppose you're using a temporary machine for a web server, or think you may change to a higher-end hosting solution as your business expands. Do you want to copy not just your site—which might only be 10 or 20 MB zipped up—but all of your user's images, perhaps 1 or 2 MB each? Probably not.

These are just a few reasons why the solution you've got in place might not be the best one for your particular web application. And there's another option, equally complex, but just as useful: you can store images not on the file system, but directly in your database.

You've got a solution that works...but there may be a better solution around the corner. That's a common situation in programming. In this case, there's a different solution, and it's in the next chapter. So turn the page, and see why you might just want your entire image stored in the database, rather than just the path to that image.

Binary Objects and Image Loading

Right now, you've got images on a file system, and paths to those images in a database. Then, in your web application, you convert that file system path to a web path, and display the image. This works, and actually works pretty well. In fact, you could run with that solution and likely never have any real issues...and then again, you might have a huge issue that crops up next week.

The real downside of this approach is that you don't have a self-contained solution. Images are on the file system, paths are in the database, and then you need some PHP to convert from the location of the image on your server to a path that users' browsers can interpret correctly. So you've created a real connection—sometimes called a *tight coupling*—between your file system, your PHP, and your database.

So how do you make things more self-contained? You'd have to take these pieces of information and put them all in one place. Obviously, you're committed to a database, so that becomes the logical place to consolidate your information. Instead of *some* of your information going into your database, it *all* goes into your database.

In this approach, you'd actually take the uploaded image and put it in your database, rather than just storing a reference to your image. But to do that, there's a lot more work to be done: you need not just a new column in your users table, but an entirely new table; you need a new data type; and you need more than just the *SELECT* and *INSERT* queries you've been using so far. But you may very well need just the type of solution, so time to get busy.

■ Storing Different Objects in Different Tables

Up until now, you've been working with one table: *users*. That's because you've been working with a single thing: a representation of one of your users. Everything in that table—the first and last name, the email address, and the Facebook URL and Twitter handle—are parts of that that user. Another way to think about it is that everything in the *users* table *describes* a user.

So now you come to the idea of storing an image—and information *about* that image, something you'll see is important when you go to storing an entire image within the database. This content no longer describes a user. In fact, while an image is related to a user—it's the image that a user wants to display when their profile is viewed—it's an object in its own right. It's its own "thing."

And once you come to that point—when you realize that you're dealing with a new object—then you need to create a new table. So you're going to create a new table, called *images*, that's going to not only store a user's image, but several key details about that image.

> **NOTE** If you think about it, this table is exactly the same as the *users* table. That table stores not just the user's name (equivalent to the image itself) but information about that user, such as their email address and Twitter handle. In the same way, you're going to store information about the image that helps define that image for when you need to use it.

- **Image ID.** Identifies this image, much like you have a *user_id* in the users table. It will also let you relate an image to the *users* table a bit later.

- **Image name.** Even though you're storing the data of the image, you still need a name by which you can refer to that image.

- **MIME type.** This information is important for telling a web server whether it needs to display a JPG, or a GIF, or PNG, or something else entirely.

- **File size.** Used by the browser for displaying the image.

- **Image data.** The raw bits and bytes that are turned into pixels and colors.

Translate this into SQL, and you get a new *CREATE* statement:

```
CREATE TABLE images (
    image_id    int          AUTO_INCREMENT PRIMARY KEY,
    filename    varchar(200) NOT NULL,
    mime_type   varchar(50)  NOT NULL,
    file_size   int          NOT NULL,
    image_data  mediumblob   NOT NULL
);
```

These items are all pretty straightforward, with the exception of a new column type: *mediumblob*. Hence, there are a few other blob types, and there are:

- *tinyblob*: Stores objects up to 256 bytes.

- *blob*: You can store objects up to 65 KB (kilobytes) in a blob column.

- *mediumblob*: Allows for up to 16MB of data.

- *longblob*: Here's the big one. You can store 4GB of data in a *longblob* column.

Blob stands for *binary large object*. It's a column built just for the type of information that makes up an image: information that's not a number or a string, but binary information.

DESIGN TIME

Planning for Growth and Describing Your Data

There's a fair bit of disagreement about which *blob* type you should use for a given column. Some argue that you should virtually always use *longblob*, while others argue that you should figure out the data you're aware of, and use the *blob* size that covers that size, and nothing more.

For those who argue for always using *longblob*, the thinking is that you're planning ahead. Because your database uses space as its needed by your actual information—and not the maximum size of a column—a *longblob* holding a 2MB image takes up just as much, and only as much, space as a *mediumblob* holding a 2MB image. If you use *longblob* all the time, you never have to change your column type as your storage needs change.

On the other hand, if you're only allowing images that are 2MB or smaller, then you best describe your data by using *mediumblob*. You're doing more than just choosing an arbitrary type; you're providing information about what goes in a column.

It's not a good idea to make everything a *varchar(255)* if you are only storing a first name because there's no first name that long; you lose a chance to say something about your data with that approach. The same is true for using a *longblob* if (and this is an important if) you've decided that you're only accepting images up to a size that would fit in a *mediumblob*.

Go ahead and create this table. Make sure it's in the same database as *users*. You should now be able to see both these tables in your database:

```
mysql> USE bmclaugh;
Database changed
mysql> SHOW tables;
+-----------------------------------+
| Tables_in_bmclaugh                |
+-----------------------------------+
| images                            |
| users                             |
+-----------------------------------+
2 rows in set (0.00 sec)
```

Inserting a Raw Image into a Table

It's time to revisit *create_user.php*. You're going to use a lot of your code, but there are also some changes to be made. Specifically, all the checks to ensure your user uploaded a valid image, that no errors were generated by the server or PHP, and that the file is an image via *getimagesize* are just fine.

Where things change is in the section of code that you used to move the temporary image into a final location. In this approach, the final location is the images table, so that code has to be replaced.

Here's the *create_user.php* script with the code you no longer need removed.

> **NOTE** You should make a backup of *create_user.php* before you start making changes. Consider copying it to *create_user.php.bak* or something similar, so if you want to go back to storing just an image's path, you can easily do that.

```php
<?php

require_once '../scripts/app_config.php';
require_once '../scripts/database_connection.php';

// The errors array and variables related to images stay the same
$upload_dir = SITE_ROOT . "uploads/profile_pics/";
$image_fieldname = "user_pic";

// Potential PHP upload errors
$php_errors = array(1 => 'Maximum file size in php.ini exceeded',
                    2 => 'Maximum file size in HTML form exceeded',
                    3 => 'Only part of the file was uploaded',
                    4 => 'No file was selected to upload.');

$first_name = trim($_REQUEST['first_name']);
$last_name = trim($_REQUEST['last_name']);
$email = trim($_REQUEST['email']);
$bio = trim($_REQUEST['bio']);
$facebook_url = str_replace("facebook.org", "facebook.com", trim($_
REQUEST['facebook_url']));
$position = strpos($facebook_url, "facebook.com");
if ($position === false) {
  $facebook_url = "http://www.facebook.com/" . $facebook_url;
}

$twitter_handle = trim($_REQUEST['twitter_handle']);
$twitter_url = "http://www.twitter.com/";
$position = strpos($twitter_handle, "@");
```

```php
if ($position === false) {
  $twitter_url = $twitter_url . $twitter_handle;
} else {
  $twitter_url = $twitter_url .
                 substr($twitter_handle, $position + 1);
}

// Make sure we didn't have an error uploading the image
($_FILES[$image_fieldname]['error'] == 0)
  or handle_error("the server couldn't upload the image you selected.",
                  $php_errors[$_FILES[$image_fieldname]['error']]);

// Is this file the result of a valid upload?
@is_uploaded_file($_FILES[$image_fieldname]['tmp_name'])
  or handle_error("you were trying to do something naughty. " .
                  "Shame on you!",
                  "Uploaded request: file named " .
                  "'{$_FILES[$image_fieldname]['tmp_name']}'");

// Is this actually an image?
@getimagesize($_FILES[$image_fieldname]['tmp_name'])
  or handle_error("you selected a file for your picture that " .
                  "isn't an image.",
                  "{$_FILES[$image_fieldname]['tmp_name']} " .
                  "isn't a valid image file.");

// Name the file uniquely
$now = time();
while (file_exists($upload_filename = $upload_dir . $now .
                                     '-' .
                   $_FILES[$image_fieldname]['name'])) {
    $now++;
}

// Remove the code that used move_uploaded_file to move the temporary image

// Remove the column name and value for user pics.
$insert_sql = "INSERT INTO users (first_name, last_name, email, " .
              "bio, facebook_url, twitter_handle) " .
              "VALUES ('{$first_name}', '{$last_name}', '{$email}', " .
              "'{$bio}', '{$facebook_url}', '{$twitter_handle}');";

// Insert the user into the database
mysql_query($insert_sql);
```

```
// Redirect the user to the page that displays user information
header("Location: show_user.php?user_id=" . mysql_insert_id());
exit();
?>
```

So this code is substantially the same. The big change is that now you need a new *INSERT* statement, and this statement doesn't insert into *users*, but into *images*.

Here's the beauty of this solution, though: you can get every bit of the information you need to put into images from the *$_FILES* array (which is actually an array of arrays). From here, writing the code is a piece of cake:

```
$insert_sql = "INSERT INTO users (first_name, last_name, email, " .
              "bio, facebook_url, twitter_handle) " .
              "VALUES ('{$first_name}', '{$last_name}', '{$email}', " .
              "'{$bio}', '{$facebook_url}', '{$twitter_handle}');";

// Insert the user into the database
mysql_query($insert_sql);

// Insert the image into the images table
$image = $_FILES[$image_fieldname];
$image_filename = $image['name'];
$image_info = getimagesize($image['tmp_name']);
$image_mime_type = $image_info['mime'];
$image_size = $image['size'];
$image_data = file_get_contents($image['tmp_name']);

$insert_image_sql = "INSERT INTO images " .
                    "(filename, mime_type, file_size, image_data) " .
                    "VALUES ('{$image_filename}', '{$image_mime_type}', " .
                    "'{$image_size}', '{$image_data}');";

mysql_query($insert_image_sql);

// Redirect the user to the page that displays user information
header("Location: show_user.php?user_id=" . mysql_insert_id());
?>
```

There's a lot going on here, and some of it's flat-out confusing, so take this piece by piece.

First, this code creates a new *$image* variable that's just for convenience:

```
$image = $_FILES[$image_fieldname];
```

This line makes it easier to deal with all the properties of an image. You don't have to keep typing *$_FILES[$image_fieldname]* over and over. This step isn't necessary, but it does make things much easier.

Next, you can get the name of the image from this array:

```
$image_filename = $image['name'];
```

getimagesize Doesn't Return a File Size

Here's where things start to get a little weird. *getimagesize* actually doesn't return a numeric file size of the uploaded image. Rather, it returns an array of information about the image, such as its MIME type (which you need), and the height and width of the image that you might use to display the image in an HTML page (which you currently don't need).

So you might think you should do something like this:

```
$image_size = getimagesize($image['tmp_name']);
```

But that's a problem on two counts: *getimagesize* returns an array, not a size; and the sizes that *getimagesize* returns in that array are height and width, not file size.

What you do need from the returned array, though, is the MIME type:

```
$image_info = getimagesize($image['tmp_name']);
$image_mime_type = $image_info['mime'];
```

Now, you still need the actual file size of the uploaded image. You get that from a property on the original image-related array:

```
$image_size = $image['size'];
```

file_get_contents Does What You Think It Does

Sometimes a function's name is a bit misleading, like *getimagesize*. Other times, a function is perfectly named; that's the case with *file_get_contents*. This function gets you the data in binary form from an object, which is just what you want for the *image_data* column in your *images* table:

```
$image_data = file_get_contents($image['tmp_name']);
```

INSERT the Image

Last but not least, you just need to build the *INSERT* query and run it:

```
$insert_image_sql = "INSERT INTO images " .
                    "(filename, mime_type, file_size, image_data) " .
            "VALUES ('{$image_filename}', '{$image_mime_type}', " .
                    "'{$image_size}', '{$image_data}');";


mysql_query($insert_image_sql);
```

WARNING   Hold off on running this code! Or, if you do, get ready for some weird errors. There are problems here, lurking in the dark corners of how MySQL handles data. So get your code to this point, but keep reading before you think you've done something wrong.

■ Your Binary Data Isn't Safe to Insert...Yet

So things look pretty good...but if you run the code from the previous section, you'll have some issues. First and foremost, that binary data has all sorts of weird characters on which PHP and MySQL are going to choke. There's actually always the possibility of running into characters that are a problem, but that's especially true—and almost always the case—when you're dealing with binary data.

Once again, though, there's a utility function for that.

> **NOTE** You've probably noticed that at almost every turn, there's a PHP utility function. That's one of the advantages of a language that's fairly mature. Well into version 4 and 5, PHP has settled and developed a pretty robust library of handy functions like *getimagesize* and the one you're about to use, *mysql_real_escape_string*.

mysql_real_escape_string escapes any special characters in the string you hand it. So you can pass in your *$image_data*, and then pass the result of *mysql_real_escape_string* to *mysql_query* through your *INSERT* statement. In fact, it's not a bad idea to use this function on any string data you pass in to MySQL:

```
$insert_sql = "INSERT INTO users (first_name, last_name, email, " .
                "bio, facebook_url, twitter_handle) " .
            "VALUES ('{mysql_real_escape_string($first_name)}', " .
                "'{mysql_real_escape_string($last_name)}', " .
                "'{mysql_real_escape_string($email)}', " .
                "'{mysql_real_escape_string($bio)}', " .
                "'{mysql_real_escape_string($facebook_url)}', " .
                "'{mysql_real_escape_string($twitter_handle)}');";

// Insert the user into the database
mysql_query($insert_sql);

// Insert the image into the images table
$image = $_FILES[$image_fieldname];
$image_filename = $image['name'];
$image_info = getimagesize($image['tmp_name']);
$image_mime_type = $image_info['mime'];
$image_size = $image['size'];
$image_data = file_get_contents($image['tmp_name']);

$insert_image_sql = "INSERT INTO images " .
                    "(filename, mime_type, file_size, image_data) " .
                "VALUES ('{mysql_real_escape_string($image_filename)}', ".
                    "'{mysql_real_escape_string($image_mime_type)}', " .
                    "'{ mysql_real_escape_string($image_size)}', " .
                    "'{mysql_real_escape_string($image_data)}');";

mysql_query($insert_image_sql);
```

NOTE   You don't need *mysql_real_escape_string* for the *$image_size*, since that's a numeric value. However, if you're constantly trying to remember whether or not input data is a string or a number, you're eventually going to make a mistake and not escape something you should.

To be safe, just escape everything. It's more consistent, and it's another layer of protection. The time it takes PHP to escape that one bit of data is trivial compared to the problems if malicious data goes unescaped.

Printing a String to a Variable

As natural as this code looks, it's got a pretty serious problem. While the curly braces surrounding a variable will allow that variable to be printed inside a string (so "*{$variable}*" prints the value of *$variable*), PHP draws the line at doing actual work inside the curly braces. So it won't interpret the call to *mysql_real_escape_string*.

There are two ways to get around this dilemma. The first is the easiest: you could just move the calls to *mysql_real_escape_string* up into the variable assignments, sort of like this:

```
// Insert the image into the images table
$image = $_FILES[$image_fieldname];
$image_filename = mysql_real_escape_string($image['name']);
$image_info = getimagesize($image['tmp_name']);
$image_mime_type = mysql_real_escape_string($image_info['mime']);
// and so on...
```

This method also looks okay, but it's not a good idea. Think about the function you're calling: it's specifically for getting values set up to work with MySQL. But what if you want to use *$image_filename* somewhere else in your script? You've turned this variable into a MySQL-specific version of the filename.

It seems like the original approach—converting the variable using *mysql_real_escape_string* as it's going into the actual SQL *INSERT* statement—is the right one. It allows the variable to just be the image filename, or the image MIME type, and then you convert that into a MySQL-friendly value when that's required.

So that seems to indicate there's a need for a way to perform calculations or run functions on values when you're constructing your SQL string...and there is. You typically do so using *sprintf*, which is a PHP function that prints to a string. In other words, you construct a string, using any calculations you need, and pass all the required information to *sprintf*. *sprintf* puts everything together and returns a string, which you can then assign to your variable, and boom, you're then ready to pass that variable into *mysql_query*.

This technique is a little different than anything you've done so far. Instead of just building the string up with string concatenation, you indicate the entire string you want to create, but every time you come to a spot in the string where you want to include the value of a variable, you put in a special *type specifier*. For example, you use *%s* for a string type:

```
$hello = sprintf("Hello there, %s %s", $first_name, $last_name);
echo $hello;
```

Suppose *$first_name* is "John" and *$last_name* is "Wayne". Running a script with these two lines would give you:

```
Hello there, John Wayne
```

sprintf replaces the first *%s* with the first value after the string, which is *$first_name*. Then it replaces the second *%s* with the second value after the string, *$last_name*. Finally, the whole thing—the string with the values inserted—is assigned to *$hello*.

What's great about *sprintf* is that you can perform calculations on variables before you pass them to *sprintf*. So even though this example is a bit silly, the following code is perfectly legal:

```
$hello = sprintf("Hello there, %s", $first_name . ' ' . $last_name);
echo $hello;
```

Of course, there are much better ways to use *sprintf*... like creating a query string and using *mysql_real_escape_string* in the process:

```
// This replaces the older assignment to $insert_sql
$insert_sql = sprintf("INSERT INTO users " .
                      "(first_name, last_name, email, " .
                      "bio, facebook_url, twitter_handle) " .
                "VALUES ('%s', '%s', '%s', '%s', '%s', '%s');",
                mysql_real_escape_string($first_name),
                mysql_real_escape_string($last_name),
                mysql_real_escape_string($email),
                mysql_real_escape_string($bio),
                mysql_real_escape_string($facebook_url),
                mysql_real_escape_string($twitter_handle));

// Insert the user into the database
mysql_query($insert_sql);
```

This code doesn't do anything noticeably different than your older version, because the data being inserted into users was probably not a problem in the first place. But now you can take this same approach and apply it to your insertion into *images*.

```
$insert_image_sql = sprintf("INSERT INTO images " .
                            "(filename, mime_type, " .
                            "file_size, image_data) " .
                      "VALUES ('%s', '%s', %d, '%s');",
                      mysql_real_escape_string($image_filename),
                      mysql_real_escape_string($image_mime_type),
                      mysql_real_escape_string($image_size),
                      mysql_real_escape_string($image_data));

mysql_query($insert_image_sql);
```

You can guess what *%d* means to *sprintf*: replace that type specifier with a decimal number, like 1024 or 92048. So this code builds up an *INSERT*, and executes it, and escapes your values in the process.

POWER USERS' CLINIC

sprintf is Your New Best Friend

Most PHP programmers use *sprintf* initially because it lets them do things like use *mysql_real_escape_string* on variables before they're inserted into a query string. But those same programmers find something else out, just like you will: using *sprintf* lets you write a lot more robust and flexible code.

Now you can do calculations on your data, escape values, and do pretty much anything else you want to your data as you're inserting into or selecting from your database. You no longer

have to calculate things, then assign the results of those calculations to a variable (or, even worse, a new variable, based upon some old variable), and then—and only then—use those variables as part of a SQL construction.

sprintf lets you do all that in a single step. In general, you should use *sprintf* as your default means of creating SQL strings that are executed as queries against your database.

Now try this script out. Head over to *create_user.php* once again, find a new friend to fill out the form, let them choose an image, and submit the form. Your new version of *create_user.php* should run, and you'll get to *show_user.php*.

Now, this time you *won't* see the user's profile, because that's not code you've written. But you should be able to dig into your new *images* table and see an entry for the uploaded image:

```
mysql> SELECT image_id, filename FROM images;
+----------+---------------------------+
| image_id | filename                  |
+----------+---------------------------+
|        4 | 220px-William_Shatner.jpeg |
+----------+---------------------------+
1 row in set (0.00 sec)
```

Now, you most definitely do not want to do a *SELECT* * here because you'll get MySQL's attempt to load your actual image data, which might be a few hundred KB, or a few *thousand* KB! But at least you can see that an image is indeed in your table.

You can also access your table use PhpMyAdmin if you've got that running, and get a little extra information about your entries in *images*. Figure 9-1 shows you what to expect.

Getting the Correct ID Before Redirecting

Unfortunately, there still is a problem. You may have noticed something like Figure 9-2 when you got your image insertion working.

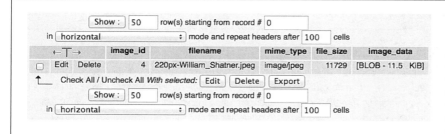

FIGURE 9-1

PhpMyAdmin reports BLOB columns—regardless of what type of BLOB you used—as BLOB and a size. In this case, you can see that the file size, at 11729 bytes, matches up with the size of the data in the BLOB column, which is 11.5KiB. This is a good way to make sure things are working: your script is correctly getting the size of the image it's inserting into your database table.

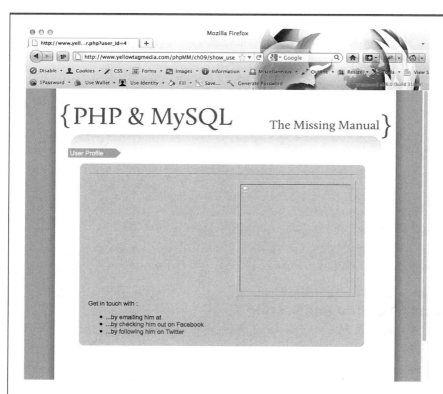

FIGURE 9-2

This screen is hardly what you want to see after all that work on getting images into your database. So what gives?

The missing image isn't as much of a mystery as it first seems. Here's the last bit of your code from *create_user.php*:

```
// This replaces the older assignment to $insert_sql
$insert_sql = sprintf("INSERT INTO users " .
                      "(first_name, last_name, email, " .
                      "bio, facebook_url, twitter_handle) " .
                      "VALUES ('%s', '%s', '%s', '%s', '%s', '%s');",
                      mysql_real_escape_string($first_name),
                      mysql_real_escape_string($last_name),
                      mysql_real_escape_string($email),
                      mysql_real_escape_string($bio),
                      mysql_real_escape_string($facebook_url),
                      mysql_real_escape_string($twitter_handle));

// Insert the user into the database
mysql_query($insert_sql);

$insert_image_sql = sprintf("INSERT INTO images " .
                      "(filename, mime_type, " .
                      "file_size, image_data) " .
                      "VALUES ('%s', '%s', %d, '%s');",
                      mysql_real_escape_string($image_filename),
                      mysql_real_escape_string($image_mime_type),
                      mysql_real_escape_string($image_size),
                      mysql_real_escape_string($image_data));

mysql_query($insert_image_sql);

// Redirect the user to the page that displays user information
header("Location: show_user.php?user_id=" . mysql_insert_id());
```

What's the problem? It's in that last line. Remember, *mysql_insert_id* returns the ID of the last INSERT query... which is no longer the INSERT for your *users* table, but your new INSERT for *images*. So the redirect to *show_user.php* is working, but it's sending the ID of the image inserted, rather than the user. You can fix that easily:

```
// This replaces the older assignment to $insert_sql
$insert_sql = sprintf("INSERT INTO users " .
                      "(first_name, last_name, email, " .
                      "bio, facebook_url, twitter_handle) " .
                      "VALUES ('%s', '%s', '%s', '%s', '%s', '%s');",
                      mysql_real_escape_string($first_name),
                      mysql_real_escape_string($last_name),
                      mysql_real_escape_string($email),
                      mysql_real_escape_string($bio),
                      mysql_real_escape_string($facebook_url),
                      mysql_real_escape_string($twitter_handle));
```

```
// Insert the user into the database
mysql_query($insert_sql);

$user_id = mysql_insert_id();

$insert_image_sql = sprintf("INSERT INTO images " .
                            "(filename, mime_type, " .
                            "file_size, image_data) " .
                "VALUES ('%s', '%s', %d, '%s');",
                mysql_real_escape_string($image_filename),
                mysql_real_escape_string($image_mime_type),
                mysql_real_escape_string($image_size),
                mysql_real_escape_string($image_data));

mysql_query($insert_image_sql);

// Redirect the user to the page that displays user information
header("Location: show_user.php?user_id=" . $user_id);
exit();
```

Try this script out again, and you should be back to what you expect: still a slightly broken version of *show_user.php*, but broken in the way you expect (see Figure 9-3).

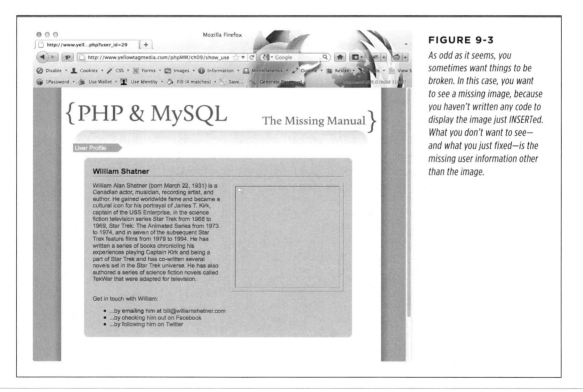

FIGURE 9-3

As odd as it seems, you sometimes want things to be broken. In this case, you want to see a missing image, because you haven't written any code to display the image just INSERTed. What you don't want to see— and what you just fixed—is the missing user information other than the image.

Connecting Users and Images

And it's here that things become sticky. You have two tables—*users* and *images*—but no connection between those tables. So when you go to load a user and display it by using *show_user.php*, how do you figure out which image in the *images* table you should display for a given user in the *users* table?

Clearly, there has to be some connection between these two tables. You've already got a unique ID for each entry in *users* (*user_id*) and in *images* (*image_id*), so that's a good starting place. But does a user reference an image, or does an image reference a user?

Here's the fundamental question you'll ask over and over when you're connecting two tables in a database: how are the two tables related? Better still, how are the two objects that your tables represent related?

Does a user have an image? Does a user have *lots* of images? In this case, a single user has a single profile image. So you have what is called a *one-to-one* (or *1-1*) *relationship*. One user is related to one image. So you can create a new column in your users table, and in that column, you can store the *image_id* of that user's profile image. You can make that change to your database like this:

```
mysql> ALTER TABLE users
    ->          ADD profile_pic_id int;
Query OK, 6 rows affected (0.11 sec)
Records: 6  Duplicates: 0  Warnings: 0
```

WARNING You've already made changes to your scripts to accommodate storing images in your database, rather than on your file system. With this *ALTER*, you're now making the same sort of changes to your database. These changes reflect a change in how your application works. So you want to back things up at this point in your database.

But backing up a script is a lot easier than backing up a database. You may want to give your hosting company a call and see if and how you can back up your database. Or, you can just figure out how to undo these changes if you go back to storing images on your file system.

Either way, you're going to get some PHP and MySQL practice switching between the two approaches. That's a good thing no matter what solution you end up using.

Foreign Keys and Column Names

The *profile_pic_id* column is setting up what's called a foreign key relationship. This column is a foreign key because it relates to the key in a "foreign" table: *images*.

In most databases, you not only define a column in your table that relates to the referenced table's primary key, you define a *FOREIGN KEY* at the database level. So your database actually knows that *profile_pic_id* is storing IDs that are in the images table's *image_id* column. But until recently, MySQL hasn't provided this feature.

Now, you can use foreign keys in MySQL, but you've got to use the MySQL InnoDB table engine. Doing so requires some extra setup, and not all hosting providers support InnoDB. Besides, programmers have been using MySQL without foreign key support for years, so if you code properly, you can work around this limitation. If you want to use InnoDB and foreign key support at the database level, start with this command on your tables:

```
ALTER TABLE [table-name]

    ENGINE = InnoDB;
```

Then Google "MySQL foreign keys" and you'll have a wealth of information at your fingertips.

Regardless of whether or not you use foreign keys through your programming, or you add support at the database level

by using InnoDB, naming your foreign key columns is a big deal. The typical practice here is to name the foreign key *[singular-table-name]_id*. So for a foreign key connecting users to images, you'd typically take the singular name of the table you're connecting to—"image" from *images*—and append "_id". So you'd get *image_id* for your foreign key column name.

So then why use *profile_pic_id* in users? Because you could very well store more than just profile pictures in *images*. You might store several images for a user, only one of which is a profile picture. You might keep up with user's candid photos, or icons for logging in, or images for companies to which your users connect.

In all these cases, then, *image_id* in *users* doesn't provide enough specificity. So in these cases—where you're not just setting up a foreign key, but actually setting up a foreign key *and* indicating a particular type of usage—using a different name makes sense. For instance, you could end up with a *profile_pic_id* column in *users*, and then perhaps a *company_logo_id* in a potential *companies* table, and who knows what other images you'll use? By using *profile_pic_id* now, you're indicating that you're relating to an image, and the specific purpose for which that image is being used.

Inserting an Image, then Inserting a User

Think carefully about what you have here. Once an image is in *images*, you need to get that image's ID, and insert that into a user's *profile_pic_id* column. But right now, your script inserts into *users* before inserting into *images*:

```
// This replaces the older assignment to $insert_sql
$insert_sql = sprintf("INSERT INTO users " .
                      "(first_name, last_name, email, " .
                      "bio, facebook_url, twitter_handle) " .
                  "VALUES ('%s', '%s', '%s', '%s', '%s', '%s');",
                  mysql_real_escape_string($first_name),
                  mysql_real_escape_string($last_name),
                  mysql_real_escape_string($email),
```

```
                     mysql_real_escape_string($bio),
                     mysql_real_escape_string($facebook_url),
                     mysql_real_escape_string($twitter_handle));

// Insert the user into the database
mysql_query($insert_sql);

$user_id = mysql_insert_id();

$insert_image_sql = sprintf("INSERT INTO images " .
                         "(filename, mime_type, " .
                          "file_size, image_data) " .
                    "VALUES ('%s', '%s', %d, '%s');",
                    mysql_real_escape_string($image_filename),
                    mysql_real_escape_string($image_mime_type),
                    mysql_real_escape_string($image_size),
                    mysql_real_escape_string($image_data));

mysql_query($insert_image_sql);

// Redirect the user to the page that displays user information
header("Location: show_user.php?user_id=" . $user_id);
exit();
```

Now, you could look up the ID of the user you inserted using *mysql_insert_id*, and store that in a variable. Then you could get the image ID using *mysql_insert_id* again. Finally, you could update the *profile_pic_id* column of the new user's row in *users*. That would work, and you'd end up with three different database interactions:

1. An *INSERT* to put the user's information into *users*.

2. An *INSERT* to put the image information into *images*.

3. An *UPDATE* to drop the new image's ID into *users*.

Now, these steps may not seem like much, but every interaction with your database takes time and resources. As a general principle, you want to interact with your database as few times as you need. That's not to say you don't work with a database; you just don't make three or four calls if you can pull off the same task with one or two.

In this case, you can actually reduce the number of MySQL interactions from three to two:

1. *INSERT* the image into the *images* table (and get the ID of that image in the process).

2. *INSERT* the new user into *users*, and use the image ID you just grabbed as part of the data you put into that INSERT.

Is this a big deal? Going from three MySQL interactions to two probably sounds pretty minor. Then again, you just cut your database interactions by a third! If you can make fewer calls, do it.

Go ahead and switch up your *INSERT* statements:

```php
// Get image data

$insert_image_sql = sprintf("INSERT INTO images " .
                            "(filename, mime_type, " .
                             "file_size, image_data) " .
                    "VALUES ('%s', '%s', %d, '%s');",
                    mysql_real_escape_string($image_filename),
                    mysql_real_escape_string($image_mime_type),
                    mysql_real_escape_string($image_size),
                    mysql_real_escape_string($image_data));

mysql_query($insert_image_sql);

// This replaces the older assignment to $insert_sql
$insert_sql = sprintf("INSERT INTO users " .
                        "(first_name, last_name, email, " .
                        "bio, facebook_url, twitter_handle) " .
                "VALUES ('%s', '%s', '%s', '%s', '%s', '%s');",
                mysql_real_escape_string($first_name),
                mysql_real_escape_string($last_name),
                mysql_real_escape_string($email),
                mysql_real_escape_string($bio),
                mysql_real_escape_string($facebook_url),
                mysql_real_escape_string($twitter_handle));

// Insert the user into the database
mysql_query($insert_sql);

// Redirect the user to the page that displays user information
header("Location: show_user.php?user_id=" . $user_id);
exit();
```

NOTE There's no additional code here. It's just a wholesale move of the insertion creation and *mysql_query* call related to a user from *before* the image-related code to *after* that code.

But, you can remove some code. Now that you've got the insertion into users second, you can go back to using *mysql_insert_id* in your redirection.

Now it's just a matter of getting the ID from your *images INSERT* and using it in the *users INSERT*. But you know how to do that: you can use *mysql_insert_id* to grab the ID of the row inserted into *images*, and then add that to your *INSERT* for *users*.

```
// Get image data

$insert_image_sql = sprintf("INSERT INTO images " .
                            "(filename, mime_type, " .
                             "file_size, image_data) " .
                    "VALUES ('%s', '%s', %d, '%s');",
                    mysql_real_escape_string($image_filename),
                    mysql_real_escape_string($image_mime_type),
                    mysql_real_escape_string($image_size),
                    mysql_real_escape_string($image_data));


mysql_query($insert_image_sql);

// This replaces the older assignment to $insert_sql
$insert_sql = sprintf("INSERT INTO users " .
                      "(first_name, last_name, email, " .
                      "bio, facebook_url, twitter_handle, " .
                      "profile_pic_id) " .
                "VALUES ('%s', '%s', '%s', '%s', '%s', '%s', %d);",
                mysql_real_escape_string($first_name),
                mysql_real_escape_string($last_name),
                mysql_real_escape_string($email),
                mysql_real_escape_string($bio),
                mysql_real_escape_string($facebook_url),
                mysql_real_escape_string($twitter_handle),
                mysql_insert_id());

// Insert the user into the database
mysql_query($insert_sql);

// Redirect the user to the page that displays user information
header("Location: show_user.php?user_id=" . mysql_insert_id());
exit();
```

NOTE Remember that because the ID of the image you're inserting into *profile_pic_id* is an *int*, not a string, you need to use *%d* as your type specifier for *sprintf*, and you don't need to include that value in single quotes.

Put everything together, and your updated version of *create_user.php* should look like this:

```php
<?php

require_once '../scripts/app_config.php';
require_once '../scripts/database_connection.php';

$upload_dir = SITE_ROOT . "uploads/profile_pics/";
$image_fieldname = "user_pic";

// Potential PHP upload errors
$php_errors = array(1 => 'Maximum file size in php.ini exceeded',
                    2 => 'Maximum file size in HTML form exceeded',
                    3 => 'Only part of the file was uploaded',
                    4 => 'No file was selected to upload.');

$first_name = trim($_REQUEST['first_name']);
$last_name = trim($_REQUEST['last_name']);
$email = trim($_REQUEST['email']);
$bio = trim($_REQUEST['bio']);
$facebook_url = str_replace("facebook.org", "facebook.com", trim($_
REQUEST['facebook_url']));
$position = strpos($facebook_url, "facebook.com");
if ($position === false) {
  $facebook_url = "http://www.facebook.com/" . $facebook_url;
}

$twitter_handle = trim($_REQUEST['twitter_handle']);
$twitter_url = "http://www.twitter.com/";
$position = strpos($twitter_handle, "@");
if ($position === false) {
  $twitter_url = $twitter_url . $twitter_handle;
} else {
  $twitter_url = $twitter_url . substr($twitter_handle, $position + 1);
}

// Make sure we didn't have an error uploading the image
($_FILES[$image_fieldname]['error'] == 0)
  or handle_error("the server couldn't upload the image you selected.",
                  $php_errors[$_FILES[$image_fieldname]['error']]);

// Is this file the result of a valid upload?
@is_uploaded_file($_FILES[$image_fieldname]['tmp_name'])
  or handle_error("you were trying to do something naughty. Shame on you!",
                  "Uploaded request: file named '{$_FILES[$image_fieldname]
```

```
['tmp_name']}'");

// Is this actually an image?
@getimagesize($_FILES[$image_fieldname]['tmp_name'])
  or handle_error("you selected a file for your picture that isn't an image.",
           "{$_FILES[$image_fieldname]['tmp_name']} isn't a valid image
file.");

// Name the file uniquely
$now = time();
while (file_exists($upload_filename = $upload_dir . $now .
                                      '-' .
                                    $_FILES[$image_fieldname]['name'])) {
    $now++;
}

// Insert the image into the images table
$image = $_FILES[$image_fieldname];
$image_filename = $image['name'];
$image_info = getimagesize($image['tmp_name']);
$image_mime_type = $image_info['mime'];
$image_size = $image['size'];
$image_data = file_get_contents($image['tmp_name']);

$insert_image_sql = sprintf("INSERT INTO images " .
                            "(filename, mime_type, file_size, image_data) " .
                            "VALUES ('%s', '%s', %d, '%s');",
                            mysql_real_escape_string($image_filename),
                            mysql_real_escape_string($image_mime_type),
                            mysql_real_escape_string($image_size),
                            mysql_real_escape_string($image_data));

mysql_query($insert_image_sql);

$insert_sql = sprintf("INSERT INTO users " .
                            "(first_name, last_name, email, " .
                            "bio, facebook_url, twitter_handle, " .
                            "profile_pic_id) " .
                      "VALUES ('%s', '%s', '%s', '%s', '%s', '%s', %d);",
                      mysql_real_escape_string($first_name),
                      mysql_real_escape_string($last_name),
                      mysql_real_escape_string($email),
                      mysql_real_escape_string($bio),
                      mysql_real_escape_string($facebook_url),
                      mysql_real_escape_string($twitter_handle),
                      mysql_insert_id());
```

```
// Insert the user into the database
mysql_query($insert_sql);

// Redirect the user to the page that displays user information
header("Location: show_user.php?user_id=" . mysql_insert_id());
exit();
?>
```

Try this code out by creating another user. Then, see what the last and highest inserted image ID is from your *images* table:

```
mysql> select image_id from images;
+----------+
| image_id |
+----------+
|        4 |
|        5 |
|        6 |
+----------+
3 rows in set (0.00 sec)
```

This should be the same ID that was inserted into your last inserted user in *users*:

```
mysql> select user_id, first_name, last_name, profile_pic_id from users;
+---------+------------+-----------+----------------+
| user_id | first_name | last_name | profile_pic_id |
+---------+------------+-----------+----------------+
|       1 | C. J.      | Wilson    |           NULL |
|       5 | Peter      | Gabriel   |           NULL |
|       7 | Bob        | Jones     |           NULL |
|      22 | James      | Roday     |           NULL |
|      30 | William    | Shatner   |              6 |
+---------+------------+-----------+----------------+
7 rows in set (0.01 sec)
```

Perfect! So now you can see that when an image gets inserted, the ID of that image gets dropped into *users*, and you've got a connection between a user and an image.

Joining Tables with *WHERE*

So how do you actually get an image when you have a user? Everything begins with a user ID. With that, you can select the user you want:

```
$select_query = sprintf("SELECT * FROM users WHERE user_id = %d",
                        $user_id);
```

This is just a *sprintf* version of code from *show_user.php*. Go ahead and make this change in your own version of *show_user.php*.

But you get more than just user information, now. You also get the *profile_pic_id* for that user. So you can use this ID to get the image for that user:

```
if ($result) {
  $row = mysql_fetch_array($result);
  $first_name    = $row['first_name'];
  $last_name     = $row['last_name'];
  $bio           = preg_replace("/[\r\n]+/", "</p><p>", $row['bio']);
  $email         = $row['email'];
  $facebook_url  = $row['facebook_url'];
  $twitter_handle = $row['twitter_handle'];
  $profile_pic_id = $row['profile_pic_id'];

  $image_query = sprintf("SELECT * FROM images WHERE image_id = %d",
                         $profile_pic_id);
  $image_result = mysql_query($image_query);

  // Turn $twitter_handle into a URL
  $twitter_url = "http://www.twitter.com/" .
                     substr($twitter_handle, $position + 1);

}
```

> **NOTE** You can remove any code in *show_user.php* that involves the profile image's file path, since you're no longer using that approach for dealing with images.

This code works, but it's actually turning what is potentially one step into two. What you're doing here is joining two tables: you've got a piece of information—*profile_pic_id* in *users* and *image_id* in *images*—that connects the two tables.

■ CONNECT YOUR TABLES THROUGH COMMON COLUMNS

You've also got a way to get only certain rows from a table: the *WHERE* clause. So putting this together, you can get a user from users and an image from images where the user's *profile_pic_id* matches the image's *image_id*:

```
SELECT first_name, last_name, filename
  FROM users, images
 WHERE profile_pic_id = image_id;
```

Run this in MySQL, and you should see a result like the following:

```
mysql> SELECT first_name, last_name, filename
    ->   FROM users, images
    ->  WHERE profile_pic_id = image_id;
+------------+-----------+----------------------------+
| first_name | last_name | filename                   |
+------------+-----------+----------------------------+
| William    | Shatner   | 220px-William_Shatner.jpeg |
+------------+-----------+----------------------------+
1 row in set (0.02 sec)
```

> **WARNING** Don't expect exactly the same actual data from your query result, unless you too have inserted Bill Shatner into your database, since you love him in brilliant shows like *Boston Legal*.

This is pretty spectacular stuff! You're connecting your tables together. In a single query, you've *joined* information in one table to corresponding information in another table. That's big stuff.

■ ALIAS YOUR TABLES (AND COLUMNS)

But as cool as this query is, it's a bit confusing. Take a look again:

```
SELECT first_name, last_name, filename
  FROM users, images
 WHERE profile_pic_id = image_id;
```

It's pretty obvious that *first_name* and *last_name* are columns from *users*. But unless you know your database structure, it's not immediately clear where filename comes from. (Of course, you *are* intimately familiar with your database, so you do know that *filename* is a column in *images*.)

The same is true with *profile_pic_id* and *image_id*. Both are column names, but which column belongs to which table?

You can make this clear, though, through using table prefixes on your columns. So you can convert this query to something a bit more obvious:

```
SELECT users.first_name, users.last_name, images.filename
  FROM users, images
 WHERE users.profile_pic_id = images.image_id;
```

You'll get the same result, but the query itself is a lot less ambiguous. Now, there's another important fact to keep in mind here: programmers are lazy. Yup, it's true; most programmers would rather type a single character—or at most two—if they can avoid typing five or ten. And SQL is happy to accommodate. You can alias a table by providing a letter or two after the table name, and then using that letter as your prefix in the rest of the query:

```
SELECT u.first_name, u.last_name, i.filename
  FROM users u, images i
 WHERE u.profile_pic_id = i.image_id;
```

Once again, there's nothing functionally different about this query, but it's now both clear and succinct: a programmer's best-case situation.

■ Show Me the Image

At this point, you've got all your data, and you can even get the image for a particular user. So all that's left is to actually show the image... right?

That's true. But you've got an entirely different situation than when you already had the image on a file system, and just needed to point at that file. In this case, you've got to load the actual raw image data from your database, and then somehow let the browser know, "Hey, this is an image, not just text. Display it like an image." That's not particularly difficult, but it is very much different from what you've been doing.

Displaying an Image

First, you need a script that can do the loading and displaying of an image. Then, once that's done, it's pretty simple to reference that display script in your *show_user. php*. So the script is the important piece, with all the new code.

Go ahead and create a new script, and call it *show_image.php*. You can start out with the basic script shell that all your scripts now have:

```
<?php

require '../scripts/app_config.php';
require '../scripts/database_connection.php';

?>
```

■ GAME PLAN YOUR SCRIPT

Now, what exactly needs to happen in this script? You can map out the basic steps:

1. Get an image ID from the request.

2. Build a *SELECT* query from the *images* table using that image ID.

3. Run the *SELECT* query and get the results.

4. Grab what should be the only row from those results.

5. Tell the browser that it's about to receive an image.

6. Tell the browser what kind of image it's about to receive.

7. Give the browser the image data.

With the exception of these last few steps, you're probably already whirring away, figuring out exactly what sort of code you need to write. But there's a lot of error handling that has to happen along the way, too:

1. Make sure an image ID was actually sent to the script.

2. Make sure the ID maps to an image in the *images* table.

3. Deal with general problems that occur loading or displaying the image data.

Again, though, none of this is particularly hard. So time to get to work.

■ GET THE IMAGE ID

First up, you need to get an ID to use for loading the image from the database. You can also do some initial error handling now: if there's no ID coming in as part of the request, something's gone wrong.

```php
<?php

require '../scripts/app_config.php';
require '../scripts/database_connection.php';

if (!isset($_REQUEST['image_id'])) {
  handle_error("no image to load was specified.");
}

$image_id = $_REQUEST['image_id'];

?>
```

Simple enough, and a lot like code you've written before, in *show_user.php*. And once again, *handle_error* makes dealing with problems if they do occur a piece of cake.

■ BUILD AND RUN A *SELECT* QUERY

Next up, you can use your new friend *sprintf* to construct a SQL query, and an older friend, *mysql_query*, to get a result set.

```php
<?php

// require statements

// Get the image ID

// Build the SELECT statement
$select_query = sprintf("SELECT * FROM images WHERE image_id = %d",
                        $image_id);
```

```
// Run the query
$result = mysql_query($select_query);
```

```
?>
```

Nothing new here, either.

■ GET THE RESULTS, GET THE IMAGE, AND DEAL WITH POTENTIAL ERRORS

Now you can grab the actual data from *$result*. In the past, you've done that in a few ways. Early on, you actually looped over all the rows returned from a query:

```
if ($return_rows) {
  // We have rows to show from the query
  echo "<p>Results from your query:</p>";
  echo "<ul>";
  while ($row = mysql_fetch_row($result)) {
    echo "<li>{$row[0]}</li>";
  }
  echo "</ul>";
} else {
  // No rows. Just report if the query ran or not
  echo "<p>The following query was processed successfully:</p>";
  echo "<p>{$query_text}</p>";
}
```

> **NOTE**   This code is from way back in Chapter 5. How to believe how much more advanced your PHP scripts have become in a few short chapters, isn't it?

You've also used an *if* statement if you expected only a single result:

```
if ($result) {
  $row = mysql_fetch_array($result);

  // Deal with the single result
} else {
  handle_error("there was a problem finding your information in our system.",
               "Error locating user with ID {$user_id}");
}
```

This statement assumes that as long as *$result* is valid, you've got a row. Further, it just ignores any rows other than the first, knowing that the SQL query that generated these results can only return a single row.

In *show_image.php*, you want something similar to this latter approach. But, it's possible to check and make sure you have a result without encasing everything in an *if*.

```php
<?php

// require statements
// Get the image ID
// Build and run the query

if (mysql_num_rows($result) == 0) {
    handle_error("we couldn't find the requested image.",
                 "No image found with an ID of " . $image_id . ".");
}

$image = mysql_fetch_array($result);

?>
```

This approach is cleaner because it keeps your code moving along once the error's been dealt with. (For more on why this sequence is more natural, check out the box below.)

DESIGN TIME

Sequential Code is Usually Clearer Code

There's almost always more than one way to accomplish any task in programming. In fact, there are usually multiple *good* ways to get a job done. But there's usually a *clearest* way and that's what you want to work toward. You want good, working code that's also clear and easy to understand.

Now, writing clear code gets harder as your code gets more complex. You often have multiple decision points (with *if* statements), error handling, loops, and all sorts of other constructs that take your code all over the place. Because of all this complexity, you want to make as much of your code as you can sequential. In other words, you want to be able to read that code more or less beginning to end, and be able to follow the flow.

With that in mind, take a look again at the earlier code from *show_user.php*:

```php
if ($result) {
    $row = mysql_fetch_array($result);

    // Deal with the single result
} else {
    handle_error(
```

```php
            "there was a problem finding your " .
            "information in our system.",
            "Error locating user with ID
            {$user_id}");
}
```

This code works, and it's even pretty solid. But is it sequential? Well... sort of. If there's a result, get that result, and work with it. If there's not, deal with errors.

But how do you really think about this? What's the *real* sequence?

First, you want to see if there's a result, and if not, handle the error. Then—and really, only after you're sure it's safe to carry on—you want to work with the results, and continue the program. So in this line of thinking, the *else* at the end handling the error is out of sequence. It's something you conceptually want to deal with *before* going on to work with the row.

That's why the newer sequence in *show_image.php*, where errors are handled and then results are used, is a better solution for your code's readability. Same functionality, but easier to understand and maintain.

■ TELL THE BROWSER WHAT'S COMING

Now you've got the information you want from *images*, but you can't just toss that to the browser. Well, you can, but the browser is going to be confused. It's used to dealing with HTML, but raw binary data is something else altogether.

There are a couple of things you have to let the browser know here:

- What kind of content is coming? This information is passed to the browser through a MIME type, and usually is something like *text/html* or *text/xml*, or in the case of images, *image/jpeg* or *image/gif* or *image/png*.

- If that type is binary—like images are—what size of information is coming? The browser needs to know so it can figure out when it's done receiving information.

Now, even though you may be wondering how to talk to the browser, you've already got the tools you need to do just that. Remember this line?

```
header("Location: " . SITE_ROOT . "scripts/show_error.php?" .
       error_message={$user_error_message}&" .
       system_error_message={$system_error_message}");
```

This code talks directly to the browser. It's sending a header, called *Location*, to the browser. The value of that header is a location, a URL, and the browser knows that when it gets a *Location* header, to go to the URL that's the value of that header.

So the header function in PHP is the mechanism by which you can speak directly to the browser. As for the two pieces of information you need to send—the content type and the size of that content—browsers have specific headers for both:

- *Content-type* lets you tell a browser what the MIME type is of the content you're about to send.

- *Content-length* lets you give a size—actually the "length" of a file—of the information you're about to send.

Now, you've got both of these pieces of information in your *images* table, in the *mime_type* column and the *file_size* column.

Put all this together, and you've got two lines of code to add to *show_image.php*:

```
<?php

// require statements
// Get the image ID
// Build and run the query
// Get the result and handle errors from getting no result

header('Content-type: ' . $image['mime_type']);
header('Content-length: ' . $image['file_size']);

?>
```

That's it. Now the browser expects a certain type of information (in your case, *image/
jpeg* or, in most cases, *image/gif*), it knows the size of the information and now it just
needs the actual information itself.

■ SEND THE IMAGE DATA

What's left? The easiest step of all:

```php
<?php

// require statements
// Get the image ID
// Build and run the query
// Get the result and handle errors from getting no result
// Tell the browser what's coming with headers

echo $image['image_data'];

?>
```

That's it. Now, this data is not a string of text; it's the raw binary information pulled
from a BLOB column in your images table, spit out bit by bit. But the magic isn't in
this line. The magic is you telling the browser that this is a certain kind of information, and a certain size. Those let the browser know, "This is an image coming. Treat
it like one."

Catching and Handling Errors

At this point, you've knocked out your list of things to do to show an image:

1. Get an image ID from the request.

2. Build a *SELECT* query from the *images* table using that image ID.

3. Run the *SELECT* query and get the results.

4. Grab what should be the only row from those results.

5. Tell the browser that it's about to receive an image.

6. Tell the browser what kind of image it's about to receive.

7. Give the browser the image data.

All done; excellent. And the script is short, too; clean and easy to follow. That's a
win by every account.

You've also taken care of most of your error handling:

1. Make sure an image ID was sent to the script.

2. Make sure the ID maps to an image in the *images* table.

3. Deal with general problems that occur loading or displaying the image data.

Hmmm. The first two are done, but what about those so-called general problems? What happens if, for example, there's an error sending the *Content-type* header? Or perhaps sending the *Content-length* header? And what about *echo*ing out the image data? Doesn't that seem like something can go bad? What if the image data is corrupt, or something happens in pulling data from the result set, or if the browser can't handle a particular type of image that your script tries to send?

In all these cases, you get an error that's unaccounted for. And when you have these general sort of errors—these errors that are beyond black-and-white, "I can check ahead of time and make sure there's no problem"—you have to deal with them.

The real problem here is that you can't pin these things down. You need a way to say, "While this entire chunk of code is running, if something general happens, do this..." And you've got a "do this" in *handle_error*. PHP provides a way to do just this with something called a *try/catch* block.

The *try* part of a *try/catch* block is a block that you put all your error-prone code into. So you're saying, "Try this code." The *catch* path of the *try/catch* block is run only if an error occurs. So if at any time within the *try* block, something goes wrong, the *catch* part of the block runs.

Not only that, but in the *catch*, an object gets handed off: an *Exception*. This *Exception* has information about what went wrong, so you can report on that...say to a custom function like *handle_error*.

To put this into place in *show_image.php*, first surround all your error-prone code with a *try* and curly braces, like so:

```php
<?php

require '../scripts/app_config.php';
require '../scripts/database_connection.php';

try {
  if (!isset($_REQUEST['image_id'])) {
    handle_error("no image to load was specified.");
  }

  $image_id = $_REQUEST['image_id'];

  // Build the SELECT statement
  $select_query = sprintf("SELECT * FROM images WHERE image_id = %d",
                          $image_id);

  // Run the query
  $result = mysql_query($select_query);

  if (mysql_num_rows($result) == 0) {
    handle_error("we couldn't find the requested image.",
```

```
                                    "No image found with an ID of " . $image_id . ".");
    }

    $image = mysql_fetch_array($result);

    header('Content-type: ' . $image['mime_type']);
    header('Content-length: ' . $image['file_size']);

    echo $image['image_data'];
}
?>
```

So now all this code is covered. Anything that goes wrong, the PHP interpreter will spit out an *Exception* object reporting the problem, and go to the *catch* block:

```
<?php

require '../scripts/app_config.php';
require '../scripts/database_connection.php';

try {
  // code that may cause an error
} catch (Exception exc) {
}
?>
```

You can see that this code almost looks like a function: the catch code gets control, and it gets an *Exception* object passed to it. *exc* is the variable name of the exception, so you can reference that exception if you need to.

NOTE The *exc* variable doesn't begin with a $ because it's typical for objects in PHP to not have names prefixed with the $ character. You'll learn more about PHP objects, but for now, realize that *exc* is a variable, just a different type of variable than you've worked with before.

Finally, you should do something useful in this *catch* block:

```
<?php

require '../scripts/app_config.php';
require '../scripts/database_connection.php';

try {
  // code that may cause an error
} catch (Exception exc) {
  handle_error("something went wrong loading your image.",
               "Error loading image: " . $exc->getMessage());
}
?>
```

This code should carry no surprises, except perhaps for that weird ->. Anytime there's an error, *handle_error* comes to the rescue. As usual, you pass *handle_error* a friendly string, and then some extra information for the programmers who might be looking on. In this case, that message comes from *exc*, and the *getMessage* method. An object in PHP doesn't have functions; it has methods. And you reference a method with ->.

> **NOTE**   Don't worry if that was totally confusing. You'll soon be an object pro, so just get the code down now, and trust that this, too, will all be old hat before much longer.

So when this code runs, it reports any error that might have occurred, and stops PHP from trying to continue on in the *try* block.

Here's what you should have for *show_image.php*:

```php
<?php

require '../scripts/app_config.php';
require '../scripts/database_connection.php';

try {
  if (!isset($_REQUEST['image_id'])) {
    handle_error("no image to load was specified.");
  }

  $image_id = $_REQUEST['image_id'];

  // Build the SELECT statement
  $select_query = sprintf("SELECT * FROM images WHERE image_id = %d",
                          $image_id);

  // Run the query
  $result = mysql_query($select_query);

  if (mysql_num_rows($result) == 0) {
    handle_error("we couldn't find the requested image.",
                 "No image found with an ID of " . $image_id . ".");
  }

  $image = mysql_fetch_array($result);

  header('Content-type: ' . $image['mime_type']);
  header('Content-length: ' . $image['file_size']);

  echo $image['image_data'];
} catch (Exception $exc) {
```

```
        handle_error("something went wrong loading your image.",
                "Error loading image: " . $exc->getMessage());
}
?>
```

So what's left? Just some testing to make sure things work.

Test, Test, Always Test

First, open up MySQL, and find an image that's been inserted. Make a note of that image's ID.

```
mysql> select image_id, filename from images;
+----------+----------------------------+
| image_id | filename                   |
+----------+----------------------------+
|        6 | 220px-William_Shatner.jpeg |
+----------+----------------------------+
1 row in set (0.03 sec)
```

Now, open up your browser, and type in the URL for *show_image.php*. But don't hit Enter! Well, you can, but you should get the error shown in Figure 9-4, because you didn't supply an ID.

FIGURE 9-4

It's not completely necessary, but it's probably a good idea to even test your errors out. In this case, by not specifying an image ID, you're verifying that errors are handled properly, and in particular that the case where no image ID is provided is handled.

Now, add the image ID to the URL like this: *show_image.php?image_id=6*. Put that (along with the rest of your domain name and path) and you should get something like Figure 9-5.

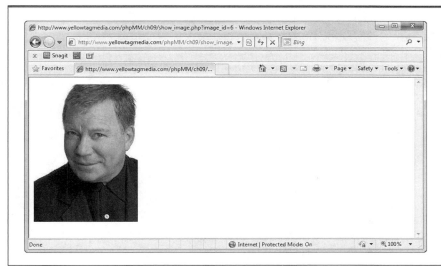

FIGURE 9-5

Here's what all this work is about: getting a browser to show an image. In fact, this is a lot like right-clicking an image on another web page, and selecting View Image. It shows you just the image, without any other text.

So now you've got William Shatner staring out at you, and that's actually a good thing.

Embedding an Image Is Just Viewing an Image

Finally, it's back to *show_user.php*. Remember, *show_image.php* was really a bit of a diversion. It's a necessary one, but the point isn't a script that displays an image. Instead, it's a script that displays a *user*, and that just happens to mean you have to show that user's image. But, you've got all the work done now to make this work, so *show_user.php* is back into the fold, ready to piece it all together.

All You Need is an Image ID

Your first thought might be to rewrite that SQL query that grabs an entry from *images* based on a user from *users*:

```
SELECT u.first_name, u.last_name, i.filename
  FROM users u, images i
 WHERE u.profile_pic_id = i.image_id;
```

But do you need to do this? No, because all that *show_image.php* requires is an image ID, and you have that in the *users* table, in *profile_pic_id*. You don't need to do a join on *users* and *images*.

So when you're getting the results from your SQL query, you just need to grab the profile image ID:

```php
<?php

require '../scripts/app_config.php';
require '../scripts/database_connection.php';

// Get the user ID of the user to show
// Build the SELECT statement
// Run the query

if ($result) {
  $row = mysql_fetch_array($result);
  $first_name    = $row['first_name'];
  $last_name     = $row['last_name'];
  $bio           = preg_replace("/[\r\n]+/", "</p><p>", $row['bio']);
  $email         = $row['email'];
  $facebook_url  = $row['facebook_url'];
  $twitter_handle = $row['twitter_handle'];
  $image_id      = $row['profile_pic_id'];

  // Turn $twitter_handle into a URL
} else {
  handle_error("there was a problem finding your information in our system.",
               "Error locating user with ID {$user_id}");
}
?>

<!-- HTML -->
```

> **NOTE** This line of new code replaces the older line where you grabbed the URL to the image, in the version where you stored just a path to the image in your *users* table.

A Script Can Be an Image *src*

With this ID, you're ready to deal with the missing image. But what's about to happen is going to seem a bit odd, so some explanation is in order.

Think about your standard, vanilla HTML *img* element:

```html
<img src="/images/roday.jpg" />
```

The *img* part tells the browser to expect an image. And the *src* tag tells the browser the location of that image. But that location is just going to trigger another browser request—in this case, to */images/roday.jpg*. And what does the browser get from that location? A bunch of bits that makes up the image *roday.jpg*.

But there's nothing magical about *roday.jpg*, or that URL. It's just a location, and as long as that location returns an image to the browser, the image is displayed. So it's perfectly okay to supply anything to the *src*, as long as that anything returns an image. You might supply it, let's say, a script that displays an image. You might just hand it something like this:

```
<img src="show_image.php?image_id=6" />
```

And since *show_image.php* with a valid ID returns an image, the browser happily displays that image in place of the *img* tag in your web page.

As a result, you can change your HTML to do just this:

```
<?php
  // Lots of PHP goodness
?>
<html>
 <head>
  <link href="../css/phpMM.css" rel="stylesheet" type="text/css" />
 </head>

 <body>
  <div id="header"><h1>PHP & MySQL: The Missing Manual</h1></div>
  <div id="example">User Profile</div>

  <div id="content">
    <div class="user_profile">
      <h1><?php echo "{$first_name} {$last_name}"; ?></h1>
      <p><img src="show_image.php?image_id=<?php echo $image_id; ?>"
              class="user_pic" />
        <?php echo $bio; ?></p>
      <p class="contact_info">
        Get in touch with <?php echo $first_name; ?>:
      </p>
      <ul>
        <!-- Connect links -->
      </ul>
    </div>
  </div>
  <div id="footer"></div>
 </body>
</html>
```

That's all there is to it! The *src* tag of your *img* is now a link to your script, with the right ID. So when you take all of *show_user.php* together, you should have something like this:

```php
<?php

require '../scripts/app_config.php';
require '../scripts/database_connection.php';

// Get the user ID of the user to show
$user_id = $_REQUEST['user_id'];

// Build the SELECT statement
$select_query = sprintf("SELECT * FROM users WHERE user_id = %d",
                        $user_id);

// Run the query
$result = mysql_query($select_query);

if ($result) {
  $row = mysql_fetch_array($result);
  $first_name     = $row['first_name'];
  $last_name      = $row['last_name'];
  $bio            = preg_replace("/[\r\n]+/", "</p><p>", $row['bio']);
  $email          = $row['email'];
  $facebook_url   = $row['facebook_url'];
  $twitter_handle = $row['twitter_handle'];
  $image_id       = $row['profile_pic_id'];

  // Turn $twitter_handle into a URL
  $twitter_url = "http://www.twitter.com/" .
                 substr($twitter_handle, $position + 1);
} else {
  handle_error("there was a problem finding your information in our system.",
               "Error locating user with ID {$user_id}");
}
?>

<html>
 <head>
  <link href="../css/phpMM.css" rel="stylesheet" type="text/css" />
 </head>

 <body>
  <div id="header"><h1>PHP & MySQL: The Missing Manual</h1></div>
  <div id="example">User Profile</div>

  <div id="content">
    <div class="user_profile">
      <h1><?php echo "{$first_name} {$last_name}"; ?></h1>
      <p><img src="show_image.php?image_id=<?php echo $image_id; ?>"
```

```
        class="user_pic" />
      <?php echo $bio; ?></p>
    <p class="contact_info">
      Get in touch with <?php echo $first_name; ?>:
    </p>
    <ul>
      <li>...by emailing them at
        <a href="<?php echo $email; ?>"><?php echo $email; ?></a></li>
      <li>...by
        <a href="<?php echo $facebook_url; ?>">checking them out
          on Facebook</a></li>
      <li>...by <a href="<?php echo $twitter_url; ?>">following
          them on Twitter</a></li>
    </ul>
  </div>
 </div>
 <div id="footer"></div>
 </body>
</html>
```

You can see the result in Figure 9-6.

Nice work. Who ever thought before you closed this chapter you'd be manually loading bits and bytes from a database and displaying them as an image on demand?

FREQUENTLY ASKED QUESTION

Aren't There Online Tutorials for Working with Images?

If you've spent much time on the Internet, you probably know what a force Google is. Spend five minutes on their search engine and you'll find at least 20 or 30 tutorials on image uploads in PHP, both for storing paths to the image in your database and for storing the images themselves in your database. Heck, there are even frameworks that take care of all this programming for you!

So why the heck is it worth you plowing through some of the trickiest PHP material you've run across yet, just to do this yourself? There are two very important reasons why this sort of code—and in fact this exact code—is important not only for you to type into your editor, but also to actually understand.

First, you can do *lots* of things using frameworks floating around on the Internet. And, truth be told, many of the frameworks, especially when you get them from reputable sources, do what your code would do, better, faster, and with greater efficiency. But that doesn't mean it's not important to understand what's going on. In fact, once you do understand

how this code works, you're *much* better prepared to make good choices about which frameworks to use, and why those frameworks might be better than writing your own...*after* you've written your own, and are ready to move to a more advanced usage.

And second, as you write more and more web applications, you'll often find your needs are more and more specific. So you need image uploading, but you need it with some particular wrinkle or tweak specific to your application. Maybe you only want to accept JPGs, and not GIFs; or you want to impose a server-side restriction on size, rather than relying on the HTML input field that sets a maximum size.

But if you have no idea how this sort of code works, then how can you possibly make adjustments like this? Whether it's your code or someone else's, you need to be able to make those sort of adjustments that personalize and specialize a piece of code. That requires knowledge, and knowledge comes from trying things out for yourself.

FIGURE 9-6

Wow, has this been a long time in coming. Just a few hundred lines of code ago, you were referencing an image on a file system. Cool, yes; but loading an image from a database? That was something else altogether. Now you've got a new script, a new approach, and yet another way to show a user's smiling face (or perhaps, her cat's face) in full color.

So Which Approach is Best?

So here you are, with two totally different approaches to getting users' images into your database (or at least the paths to those images). In fact, you've probably spent as much time working through this code as any other code you've run across in your PHP journey. Now, one question begs to be answered: which approach is best?

The best answer to that is, "It depends." Or maybe, "It's up to you." Those are frustrating answers, and probably completely unsatisfying. That's because the sort of questions you're getting into—storing images or handling errors or interacting with other frameworks and other people's code—you're not always going to have clear "right" answers.

Do you have a particularly small file system with which to work? Are you charged based on the space your web server's files take up? Is that charge greater or lesser than the charges you're assessed for the size of your database? Is your database locally accessible and blistering fast? Or is it a slow connection to another machine? These all have an effect; these all bear on your answer.

And still, at the end of the day, you sometimes have to say, "I'm not sure...I just like this approach better...or that approach better." That's okay. You may just need to pick something, try it out, and get moving. There are plenty of cases where the only real *wrong* solution is to wait around analyzing the options for hours (days! weeks!) instead of moving forward.

OK, If You Insist on an Answer...

If you're not sure, store your images on a file server, and store just the path to that image in your database. The reality is that while you can write good code that both stores an image in a database, and displays that image, it's a lot tougher to do things right. Every single time a *SELECT* runs against your *images* table and grabs the contents of the *image_data* column, you're selecting the entire size of that image's data. Say you have 100 rows each with an image of an average size of 1MB, then you've got 100MB of image data clogging up your network and database traffic.

So when in doubt, stick with a simple path in your database. So why go through an entire chapter on an alternative approach? Because now you have a handle on just what goes on with images, whether they're stored in the database or not.

FREQUENTLY ASKED QUESTION

So How Do I Get My Database Back In Order?

Going with images stored on the file system is the better solution, all things being equal. (To be clear, though, all things are *never* equal!) Since that's a good default option, the examples moving forward will assume that's your setup. So how do you get back to that solution?

First, you should have backed up your scripts. If you didn't, you may want to re-download the sample files from the Missing CD page, and use the versions that don't store images in the database.

Second, you need to remove the *profile_pic_id* column in your users table. Here's the SQL to make that change:

```
ALTER TABLE users
        DROP COLUMN profile_pic_id;
```

You can then delete the *images* table easily enough:

```
DROP TABLE images;
```

That's it. You're back in action.

10

Listing, Iterating, and Administrating

For quite a while now, you've been focusing on some pretty basic details: a user, his information, and as an extension of that information, his profile picture. It's been good. You've gotten pretty intimate with PHP and MySQL, figured out not just one but *two* ways to deal with one of the most common PHP issues: image loading—and you've managed to keep things looking good throughout. These aren't small accomplishments; they're very much big ones.

But it's still been a pretty focused view. Right now, as a user, you can get set up and specify some basic information. But what if you're not a user; what if you're you? If you want to see how many users are in your system; if you want to delete a malicious user; if you want to update a picture because it's not quite socially palatable; you have to do all that through your MySQL command line. That's okay, and you're certainly capable, but you probably already realize that in the big bad world of web applications, most administrators aren't keeping a MySQL terminal running in the corner of their screen.

Instead, they have administrative interfaces. With these interfaces, they can list all the users in a system. They can check some boxes here and there and mass delete users. They can see any user they want. And it's all through a nice clean web interface. You can give your web application the same nice features.

Granted, a web application where users supply their basic social profile isn't going to take down Facebook or Twitter or Google+ anytime soon. But whenever you start thinking about an administrative interface, you run into all sorts of interesting problems. You've got to use different types of SQL queries. You've got to mix together a lot more PHP and MySQL with your HTML, because you'll have to list every user from the database, one at a time. You'll have to deal with DELETE statements, and a lot more WHERE statements.

In other words, you'll take everything you know, and push further. There are not a lot of radically new techniques you need, but there are lots of important variations on what you already do know. So why wait any longer, or settle for MySQL as your admin interface? Time to get after a better, more visual way to keep up with your users.

> **NOTE** And if you're just salivating for something completely new and different, work through this chapter in anticipation of the next. There, you'll secure all these nice administrative pages, and then you'll need—and learn—a whole new bag of tricks.

■ Some Things Never Change

Where to begin? The same place you've begun in almost every other task: figuring out what you need, and roughing out the broad strokes of how things look and interact. You can start with a few bullet points, figure out the screens you're going to need, and throw together some mock-ups, either in HTML or even a tool like Photoshop.

Because your app is pretty straightforward, you don't need much right now:

- A form that lists all the users in the system
- A link to each user's profile page
- The ability to delete a user
- The ability to update or change a user's information
- A means of giving other users administrative privileges

That last one is going to take quite a bit of work, and create some unique headaches that you'll have to deal with, so save it for a bit later. (Later as in, the next chapter.) But the rest are very doable.

(User Interface) Brevity is Still the Soul of Wit

Now, you could build up a complex system of pages that let you manage all these interactions. *show_user.php* could figure out if you're an admin and selectively show a Delete button; you could build up a whole administrative menu, in fact. Then again, sometimes the simple things are the best things. On top of that, as a general rule, the Web rewards fewer clicks. If you *can* provide a single page that allows for the major required functionality, then you probably should *keep* things to just a single page.

In this case, you can do just that. You can list users in a simple sequence, turn the name of each user into a link to her profile page, and even add a delete button after each user. You'll have to deal with changing a user's information, but still, three items on one form is a good start.

So what should this look like? Figure 10-1 is a good place to begin.

FIGURE 10-1

No, this design isn't going to win any awards. The delete image needs to be better aligned, the little default bullets look cheesy, and as a whole, this page is in need of some serious help. But a lot of that can be handled later. Right now, this gives you some idea of what you need to get started, and that's all a mock-up has to be at this stage: a starting point, and a blueprint.

The HTML for this page is helpful. It's immediately apparent that there's a lot of duplication, and PHP is good at reducing duplication:

```html
<html>
 <head>
  <link href="../css/phpMM.css" rel="stylesheet" type="text/css" />
 </head>

 <body>
  <div id="header"><h1>PHP & MySQL: The Missing Manual</h1></div>
  <div id="example">Current Users</div>

  <div id="content">
   <ul>
    <li>
     <a href="show_user.php?user_id=30">William Shatner</a>
     (<a href="mailto:bill@williamshatner.com">bill@williamshatner.com</a>)
     <a href="delete_user.php?user_id=30">
       <img class="delete_user" src="../images/delete.png" width="15" />
     </a>
    </li>
```

```
    <li>
     <a href="show_user.php?user_id=22">James Roday</a>
     (<a href="mailto:james@roday.net">james@roday.net</a>)
     <a href="delete_user.php?user_id=22">
       <img class="delete_user" src="../images/delete.png" width="15" />
     </a>
    </li>
    <li>
     <a href="show_user.php?user_id=1">C. J. Wilson</a>
     (<a href="mailto:cj@texasrangers.com">cj@texasrangers.com</a>)
     <a href="delete_user.php?user_id=1">
       <img class="delete_user" src="../images/delete.png" width="15" />
     </a>
    </li>
   </ul>
  </div>
  <div id="footer"></div>
 </body>
</html>
```

Wish Lists are Good, Too

So far, you've gone directly from a mock-up to code. That's not altogether bad, but it does mean that when you get your mock-up created in code, anything you want to add is a bit of a mystery. Will it work well with the way you've built your pages and scripts? Or will you have to do some redesign to get your new ideas into your existing framework?

Obviously, you could spend some serious time with your mock-ups. You could get those little red Xs just right, and you could nail down spacing, and basically spend significant time in Photoshop. Of course, nothing in HTML and CSS ever looks just like a Photoshop mock-up, but still, you could get things pretty close.

The problem, though, is twofold. First, you're spending a *lot* of time on the front-end before you've done any code. Second, you're not even thinking about how decisions made as you implement your existing code might affect future decisions and functionality. So you are implementing code without any real foresight.

The answer? Just have a short list of future functionality you hope to implement. This doesn't need to be anything fancy; a text document or stickies (for the Agile development crowd) or even something on your iPad or iPhone sitting next to your workstation are all fine. Then, add or update that list as you go and features and functionality change. Hopefully, just having these "next version" features handy will help you think clearly about how decisions you make today might help you—or hurt you—when you get around to writing more code tomorrow, or next week, or next month.

So for now, here are just a few things that might be nice to add once the basic functionality is in place:

- Design a better user interface. So line up the different "columns" of data in a more intuitive fashion, as well as getting those delete "X" buttons to line up.

- Add in user profile pictures so you can get a little better graphical view of each user in the admin interface.

- Allow multiple users to be selected and deleted on one screen.

- Add a confirmation dialog box or pop-up when a user is selected for deletion to avoid accidental deletions.

You should add your own ideas to this list, but this is certainly a good starting point. Maybe you'll code these up, and maybe you won't, but now at least you can make decisions that will help these features, rather than hurt them.

NOTE Sometimes, no matter how well you plan ahead, current features require you to make decisions that are going to make wish list features harder down the road. That's okay. It's much more important you get the things you need to get done *now* completed on time.

■ Listing All Your Users

First things first: before you can add delete buttons and profile pictures and worry about alignment, you need a list of all your users. This isn't too hard, in terms of the SQL query you want to write. You could do something like this:

```
SELECT *
  FROM users;
```

But this is a bit of a brute force approach. There's some refinement you can make to improve performance, make your code clearer, and generally be a good PHP and MySQL citizen. So first things first: you should get that query into shape.

*SELECT*ing What You Need (Now)

The thing about *SELECT* * is that it gets everything in a table. Even worse, if you're joining tables, it gets everything in *all* the tables that are joined. Now, in the case of users, that's not awful. Here are all the columns you're going to grab with a *SELECT* *.

```
mysql> describe users;
+----------------+---------------+------+-----+---------+----------------+
| Field          | Type          | Null | Key | Default | Extra          |
+----------------+---------------+------+-----+---------+----------------+
| user_id        | int(11)       |      | PRI | NULL    | auto_increment |
| first_name     | varchar(20)   |      |     |         |                |
| last_name      | varchar(30)   |      |     |         |                |
| email          | varchar(50)   |      |     |         |                |
| facebook_url   | varchar(100)  | YES  |     | NULL    |                |
| twitter_handle | varchar(20)   | YES  |     | NULL    |                |
| bio            | text          | YES  |     | NULL    |                |
| user_pic_path  | varchar(200)  | YES  |     | NULL    |                |
| profile_pic_id | int(11)       | YES  |     | NULL    |                |
+----------------+---------------+------+-----+---------+----------------+
9 rows in set (0.10 sec)
```

NOTE Depending on how closely you've been following along, you may have the *user_pic_path* column, but not the *profile_pic_id*. In fact, that's probably where you want your database to be, so you don't have to worry about a foreign key with an *images* table that you're no longer using.

You can get rid of that column with this:

```
ALTER TABLE users
        DROP COLUMN profile_pic_id;
```

But look back again at Figure 10-1. You don't need all this information. Instead, you need *first_name*, *last_name*, the *user_id* for a hyperlink to *show_user.php*, and the user's *email*. So that *SELECT* * is grabbing several unnecessary columns: *facebook_url*, *twitter_handle*, *bio*, and *user_pic_path*.

Why is this a big deal? First, there's the principle of the thing: you should get the information you need, because...well...that's the information you need. Don't order everything on the menu when all you want is a hamburger. You'll end up carrying around way too much, and your arms will get tired.

NOTE Yes, that was a terrible analogy, but you get the idea.

Every time you select all the entries from the users table, you're getting one more row. And every column in that rows is space, bandwidth on your network, and resources. Suppose you have 100 users, or 1,000 users, or 10,000 users, and suppose they've all written 20-paragraph bios. Just by *not* selecting * (and thereby *not* selecting *bio*) from users, you're saving a lot of traffic and resource consumption. No, it won't change the nation's credit rating, but it will make a difference, especially over the life of your application.

So what do you need now? Just a few columns:

```
SELECT user_id, first_name, last_name, email
  FROM users;
```

That's all you need, so that's all you should SELECT.

Should I *SELECT* What I'll Need Later, Too?

Here's one of those situations where looking ahead creates a dilemma. It would be nice to add profile pictures of users to the admin page, and you already know there's a column with the path to those pictures in *users*: *user_pic_path*. So since you're going to want that down the line, should you go ahead and *SELECT* that column?

On the one hand, it would be nice to have a *SELECT* that's already set up for a future feature you know you want. On the other hand, you're not implementing that feature yet, so do you really want your code doing something halfway? It's not like you're also going to write the code to display a user's profile picture yet; it's just that you'd have the data when you *do* write that code.

In general, you should think about the implications of what you're doing on future features, but focus on writing code that solves current problems, not future ones. Think about how slippery a slope this can become. You might start selecting the bio because one day you want to excerpt that on the admin page; you might go ahead and select social information to build more links to contact the user. Before you know it, you're back to a *SELECT* * and grabbing way more information than you're using.

The good news is that you know it will be easy to add in grabbing a user's picture when the time comes. It's a simple change to your *SELECT*. But stop there, and focus on writing code for existing work. Leave future work for the future.

Here's another reason to do it this way: at some point in your programming career you'll have to start estimating your work. You'll have to know how long (in hours, or days) it will take you to implement this or that functionality. You typically bill at least partly based on these estimates, so it's important to be as precise as possible. If you start mixing current and future functionality in, your estimates stop making much sense. You end up overcharging, or worse, undercharging, because you're not doing one thing at a time.

Building a Simple Admin Page

So now you've got a good *SELECT* statement. It's time to create another script. But before you do that, there's another important decision to make: what will you call this script? *admin.php* might seem like a pretty good idea, but is that really thinking through the implications of that sort of choice?

Look back at the other script names you've used:

- *create_user.php* creates a new user
- *show_user.php* shows a user for a given user ID
- *app_config.php* configures your application
- *database_connection.php* connects to your database

Each of these names describes what the script does. That's very helpful, as it's clear immediately how to use these scripts, and even how they might interact. For example, *create_user.php* creates a user, and then should probably hand over control to *show_user.php*.

But what does *admin.php* do? What if you eventually need to add a form and script to let an admin change a user's password? That's administration, but doesn't belong on *admin.php*. The same is true for adding a user to a group, or updating the fields on a form. Those are all "admin-ing", but none of them involve this script.

In essence, this script lists all the users. To use the same naming scheme as other scripts, *show_users.php* is a better, more descriptive name.

So open up a new file, call it *show_users.php*, and begin by selecting all the users, with just the information you need:

```php
<?php

require_once '../scripts/app_config.php';
require_once '../scripts/database_connection.php';

// Build the SELECT statement
$select_users =
  "SELECT user_id, first_name, last_name, email " .
  "  FROM users";

// Run the query
$result = mysql_query($select_users);
?>
```

NOTE Since you're not inserting anything into the SELECT query, there's no reason to use *sprintf*. You can just create the query directly with a string.

You should also go ahead and set up the "shell" of the HTML page: the parts that you know won't be generated by your script:

```php
<?php
// Get all the users
?>

<html>
 <head>
  <link href="../css/phpMM.css" rel="stylesheet" type="text/css" />
 </head>

 <body>
  <div id="header"><h1>PHP & MySQL: The Missing Manual</h1></div>
  <div id="example">Current Users</div>

  <div id="content">
```

```
    <ul>
      <!-- All the users will go here, in <li> tags. -->
    </ul>
  </div>
  <div id="footer"></div>
  </body>
</html>
```

There's not much to see yet, but you can still test and make sure you don't have any errors in your PHP or HTML. Figure 10-2 shows the empty—but errorless—*show_users.php* in action.

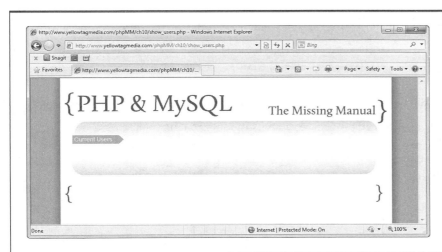

FIGURE 10-2

Even when there's nothing to see on a page, there may be things you don't want to see. Here, you can make sure that no errors occurred in connecting to your database or executing your SELECT statement. It's worth a few minutes to test at every stage of your development, and when you're creating a new script, test even more than that!

Iterating Over Your Array

Now you need to fill in an *<li>* for every user. You can build up the entire HTML string you need using *sprintf* again:

```
$user_row = sprintf(
  "<li><a href='show_user.php?user_id=%d'>%s %s</a> " .
  "(<a href='mailto:%s'>%s</a>) " .
  "<a href='delete_user.php?user_id=%d'><img " .
    "class='delete_user' src='../images/delete.png' " .
    "width='15' /></a></li>",
  // information to fill in the values);
```

NOTE There's not a significant advantage here to using *sprintf* over a string via quotation marks and curly braces with variables inside of them. Still, once you start using *sprintf*, you'll often find you use it almost everywhere you need to insert variables inside of strings. It becomes a default tool, and it's quite a handy tool at that.

That's a pretty big string, but ultimately, it should result in something like this:

```
<li><a href='show_user.php?user_id=1'>C. J. Wilson</a>
  (<a href='mailto:cj@texasrangers.com'>cj@texasrangers.com</a>)
   <a href='delete_user.php?user_id=1'><img class='delete_user'
      src='../images/delete.png' width='15' /></a></li>
```

So now all you need is to loop over each result from your query. But that's easy, you've done that before with code like this:

```
while ($row = mysql_fetch_row($result)) {
  echo "<li>{$row[0]}</li>";
}
```

And then of course you can get each piece of data in the returned query with this:

```
while ($row = mysql_fetch_row($result)) {
  echo "<li>{$row['col_name']}</li>";
}
```

This gets a specific value—whatever is associated with *col_name*—from *$row*.

So if you make that specific to your *users* table and the columns you know are being returned, and then insert *that* into your HTML, you end up with this:

```
<?php
  // Get all the users
?>
<html>
 <head>
  <link href="../css/phpMM.css" rel="stylesheet" type="text/css" />
 </head>

 <body>
  <div id="header"><h1>PHP & MySQL: The Missing Manual</h1></div>
  <div id="example">Current Users</div>

  <div id="content">
   <ul>
     <?php
       while ($user = mysql_fetch_array($result)) {
         $user_row = sprintf(
           "<li><a href='show_user.php?user_id=%d'>%s %s</a> " .
           "(<a href='mailto:%s'>%s</a>) " .
           "<a href='delete_user.php?user_id=%d'><img " .
             "class='delete_user' src='../images/delete.png' " .
             "width='15' /></a></li>",
           $user['user_id'], $user['first_name'], $user['last_name'],
           $user['email'], $user['email'], $user['user_id']);
         echo $user_row;
```

```
        }
      ?>
    </ul>
    </div>
    <div id="footer"></div>
  </body>
  </html>
```

NOTE　This HTML refers to a script that's not yet been written: *delete_user.php*. That's okay...it's coming up soon. So you're coding here in anticipation of what other work you know you've got to complete.

At first glance, this may seem a bit like a jump. That's a long *sprintf*, but take a second look. This is just putting a lot of things together, and it happens that this particular line of HTML is pretty long. Once you get past that, there's nothing here particularly tricky or difficult.

Your HTML is Getting Dangerously Cluttered

Something is subtly happening as you write more and more complex PHP. Early on, you had scripts that were all PHP, and perhaps used *echo* to throw out a few lines of text. Then, you started writing scripts that had a block of PHP at the beginning, and then a bunch of PHP at the end. Then there were scripts that inserted a little PHP here and there into the HTML at the end of the script.

Now, you've got *show_users.php*. There's a block of PHP, and then some HTML...and then it gets pretty messy. You've got PHP that does a pretty good bit of HTML printing. Now, you could probably write that same bit of output that spits out HTML and then has lots of tiny PHP bits inserted here and there, but it's basically the same issue. No matter how you cut it, you're going to end up with a real mixture of HTML and PHP.

And you've just found one of the real dangers of PHP: you're going to end up mixing your code and your markup pretty frequently.

As you start this sort of mixing, the separation between your code and your view—the markup that displays something to your user—becomes thin, if not nonexistent. It's very easy to just drop a big block of PHP in the middle of some HTML. Still, easy isn't good. As much as you can, keep the bulk of your PHP at the beginning of your script, and then just insert data as you need it.

Things are humming along, and you're ready to see how things look. Pull up *show_users.php* and make sure everything is where it belongs. Figure 10-3 shows you what you're going for.

This is still not a work of art, but it's a pretty significant step forward. Click on any of the users, and make sure you're taken to the correct *show_user.php* for that user, as shown in Figure 10-4.

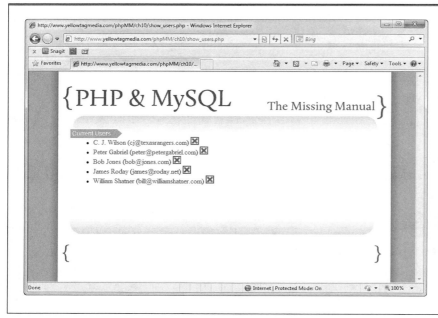

FIGURE 10-3

One of the things you'll do over and over in PHP apps is list things. Whether it's users or groups or products, listing is just one of those common tasks. So now's the time to make sure you understand how to iterate, or loop, over a list of results from SQL. Get that, and you've got the core to about a third of all the common things you'll ever do in PHP web apps.

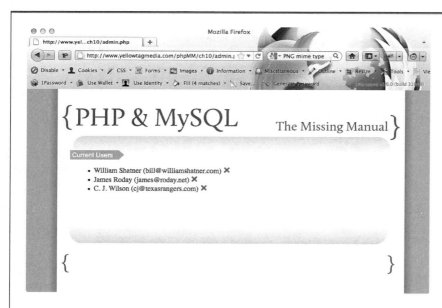

FIGURE 10-4

You're probably still getting used to scripts calling scripts which in turn build links to other scripts. Take your time, because you're going to be doing this a lot in your PHP programming career. Believe it or not, there are large-scale PHP apps that don't use any straight HTML files at all. Wordpress, for example, is 100 percent PHP.

Deleting a User

There are lots of times in programming where a new problem presents new challenges; new techniques that must be grasped; new language features that have to be absorbed. Those are fun times, but they can also be frustrating. Your pace slows to a crawl, and it's often at least a few hours—and sometimes a few days—before it seems like you make real progress. (This is also probably how and why programmers develop a stubbornness that drives those who spend much time with them absolutely nuts.)

Then there are times when you have tricks, knowledge, and experience to complete a new task. This is one of those simple cases: deleting a user.

Surveying the Individual Components

What's the query to delete a user? You already know:

```
DELETE FROM users;
```

Add to this query a *WHERE* clause to zero in on a particular user:

```
DELETE FROM users
    WHERE user_id = [some_user_id];
```

Nothing new here at all. To get that *user_id*, you can get it from whatever script calls your script. And that's what you've already got in place in *show_users.php*:

```php
<?php
  while ($user = mysql_fetch_array($result)) {
    $user_row = sprintf(
      "<li><a href='show_user.php?user_id=%d'>%s %s</a> " .
      "(<a href='mailto:%s'>%s</a>) " .
      "<a href='delete_user.php?user_id=%d'><img " .
         "class='delete_user' src='../images/delete.png' " .
         "width='15' /></a></li>",
      $user['user_id'], $user['first_name'], $user['last_name'],
      $user['email'], $user['email'], $user['user_id']);
    echo $user_row;
  }
?>
```

Once this code gets turned into HTML, you'll get this:

```
<a href='delete_user.php?user_id=22'>...</a>
```

This code should look quite similar to something you've done before, when you sent a *user_id* to the *show_user.php* script:

```
// Redirect the user to the page that displays user information
header("Location: show_user.php?user_id=" . mysql_insert_id());
```

NOTE This code was in *create_user.php* (page 181). The user got redirected after her information was stored in the database.

And once you've gotten a *user_id* and deleted the user, you can just redirect back to your *show_users.php* script, which will re-*SELECT* from users, and the deleted user will simply be gone. Perfect!

Putting It All Together

Now it's just a matter of retyping various bits from your other scripts, and changing a few things here and there. The result? *delete_user.php*, shown here:

```php
<?php

require_once '../scripts/app_config.php';
require_once '../scripts/database_connection.php';

// Get the user ID of the user to delete
$user_id = $_REQUEST['user_id'];

// Build the DELETE statement
$delete_query = sprintf("DELETE FROM users WHERE user_id = %d",
                        $user_id);

// Delete the user from the database
mysql_query($delete_query);

// Redirect to show_users to re-show users (without this deleted one)
header("Location: show_users.php");
exit();
?>
```

Real Programmers Cut and Paste

You've just written your first script that involves almost a complete reuse of code you've already written. But this code doesn't really belong in *app_config.php*, so it's not a case where you need to abstract out bits of code here and there and put them into utility functions, as was the case with handling errors or setting up database connections.

So at this point, if you've read many programming books, you're ready for a tongue-lashing, or at least some mild finger-wagging: don't cut and paste! Cutting and pasting code is evil; cutting and pasting code will lead to annoying, difficult-to-find mistakes; cutting and pasting will cause you to gain 10 pounds and hamper your sex life. Right? That's what computer book authors say at this stage of the game.

Of course, that's all ridiculous. Everyone knows that an extra margarita with your chocolate mousse cheesecake is what causes you to gain 10 pounds. But what you may *not* know is that despite all the warnings, every programmer that spends more than a few hours a day writing code knows the shortcut keys to copy, cut, and paste, and uses them liberally. Heck, if they're making their living coding, they probably know the shortcuts not just on the system, but on others, as well as the keys to do the same thing in *emacs* and *vi* and any other editor they might ever need to use. It's a key bit of functionality.

So then what's up with all the dire warnings? True, some of the worst bugs to track down are caused by cutting, copying,

and pasting code, and little inconsistencies are introduced as a result. In one bit of copied code a variable is called *$insert_sql* and in another its called *$insert_query*. Things go haywire, PHP doesn't always do a great job reporting what the problem is, and you're left to sort out the mess. But that's not a copying and pasting problem; that's an inconsistency-in-naming-variables problem.

So here's the real warning (or, rather, a few of them):

- Know that you're adding risk when you copy, cut, or paste. So be careful, and take your time.

- When possible, cut and copy from as few sources as possible. You're less likely to end up with matches between variable names and the like.

- Consider having two windows open (see Figure 10-5) or two tabs open (Figure 10-6) and moving between them, rather than copying, closing a file, opening the new file, and pasting. This setup makes it easier to compare, move back and forth between windows.

- Immediately test your code once you've pasted in other code. That way, you catch potential errors quickly and can track them down while you still remember which code you just dropped in.

That's it! Keep those things in mind, and don't be so afraid of cut and paste. They're important tools in your arsenal.

FIGURE 10-5

If you've got the screen real estate, there's nothing better than seeing two pieces of code side by side when you're cutting, copying, and pasting. You don't have to remember anything; it's all right there in front of you. And an editor like TextMate even gives you some nice visual clues like syntax highlighting. Your chances of making a mistake in this setup go way, way down.

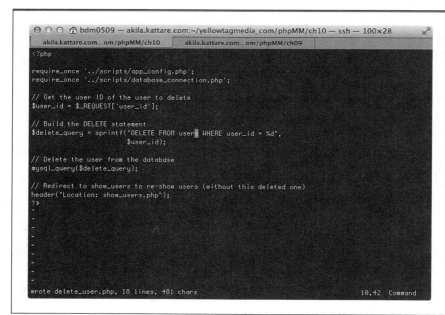

FIGURE 10-6

If you're pressed for screen space, or just like things a little more compact, using tabs in your editor (Terminal on the Mac is shown here) is a poor man's version of keeping two windows open. You still have to keep a bit more context in your head, but it's far better than closing one file, opening another, and so on. You can copy in one window, tab to the second window, and paste.

So try this thing out. You've already got *show_users.php* with the right links, so open it up, and pick an unlucky user to delete. Click the "X" icon, and you should get back something like Figure 10-7—which looks just like Figure 10-4, minus poor Peter Gabriel.

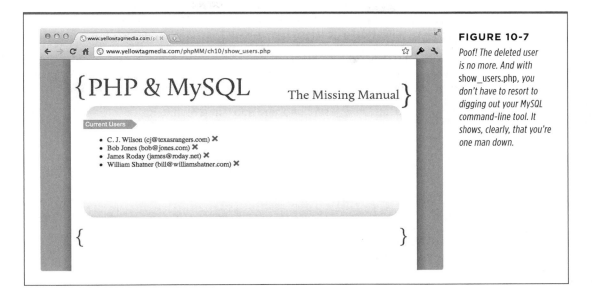

FIGURE 10-7

Poof! The deleted user is no more. And with show_users.php, *you don't have to resort to digging out your MySQL command-line tool. It shows, clearly, that you're one man down.*

Deleting Users Shouldn't Be Magical

The functionality you've got in place for deleting users is perfect. There are no hitches, no pauses, nothing but a quick request to *delete_user.php*, a deletion in your database, and a return to *show_users.php*.

And that perfection—that minimal pause and nothing else—is exactly why you're not done with deleting users.

Deletion is a big deal. You're trashing information, never to be heard from again. And you're doing it based on one click of the mouse, with no further warning or second thought. That's a problem.

In fact, think about your own web usage. Have you ever managed to delete anything with one click? For most of you, you're probably so inundated with "Are you sure?" and "You'll never get to use this file again" and even "Be careful! Your information will be gone forever!" that you may be a bit down on warnings. But they're an essential part of the process of deletion.

So you need to add a little more to the deletion process. What you're doing now is just pre-deletion. You've got to give the user a chance to rethink their decision before you pass things on to *delete_user.php*. So it's back to *show_users.php*.

■ START WITH A LITTLE JAVASCRIPT

When it comes to things like confirmation boxes, you're firmly in the world of browsers and clients. Although you could build some sort of PHP confirmation, it wouldn't be pretty. You'd essentially need to send a request to the server for deletion, the server would run a PHP script that creates a new HTML form and asks for confirmation, the browser would return that to the user, and the user would click "OK." Then another request would go to the browser, and you'd finally get to perform deletion.

Even if you use Ajax to avoid lots of page refreshing, you still have way too much server interaction for a simple confirmation. That's especially true because JavaScript offers you a built-in, all-client means of doing the same thing with *confirm*.

So open back up *show_users.php*, and add some JavaScript:

```php
<?php

// SELECT all users
?>

<html>
 <head>
  <link href="../css/phpMM.css" rel="stylesheet" type="text/css" />
  <script type="text/javascript">
    function delete_user(user_id) {
      if (confirm("Are you sure you want to delete this user?" +
                  "\nThere's really no going back!")) {
        window.location = "delete_user.php?user_id=" + user_id;
      }
    }
  </script>
 </head>
 <body>
   <!-- HTML body -->
 </body>
</html>
```

This script is pretty straightforward. You're just creating a function that asks for user confirmation before passing control over to *delete_user.php*. And there's a little extra work, as the *user_id* has to be passed to this function, which then shuffles it along to *delete_user.php* by using the JavaScript version of a redirect: *window.location*.

NOTE If this code freaks you out a bit, or if you're rusty on your JavaScript, check out *JavaScript: The Missing Manual* by David Sawyer McFarland. It's a solid JavaScript book that will break this and a lot more JavaScript down. In fact, it might be the perfect complement to a PHP book: it covers on the client side what you need for your server-side scripts to run smoothly and without error.

And while you're being freaked out, if you really feel unsettled by the use of JavaScript in this page—rather than it being referenced through an external JavaScript file—be sure to check out the box below.

FREQUENTLY ASKED QUESTION

Isn't It Evil to Not Use External JavaScript for Functions Like This?

Ahh, yes. Some of you are bothered by that last bit of code. It's okay to admit it. In fact, after being told that it's okay to cut and paste, and then seeing this code, you may be ready to throw this book out the window. (Or perhaps you're secretly rejoicing and ready to throw some *other* books out the window!)

What might you have seen that's so bothersome? How about the following:

```
<head>

  <link href="../css/phpMM.css"

        rel="stylesheet" type="text/css"
/>

  <script type="text/javascript">

    function delete_user(user_id) {

      // code for confirmation and redi-
rection

    }

  </script>

</head>
```

Almost as common as the scolding you'll get for copying and pasting is the admonition to never, ever use JavaScript in the head of your page like this. In fact, most books deal with the problem a bit like this:

1. Learn how to write a little JavaScript.

2. Learn how to write some pretty cool JavaScript.

3. Now that you're "advanced," get that JavaScript into external files!

4. Teach all your beginner JavaScript friends the same.

Sounds pretty good, and everybody loves a little dogma. But take a look at the source for pages like Amazon.com, or Google, or Apple. Every one of these Web giants has *<script>* tags that have code in the *head* of the page!

Is it conceivable that the book-writing world is made up of authors that are all better, cleaner, more organized coders than the high-paid folks at Apple and Amazon.com and Google?

Of course not. The truth is that there are plenty of times when you want JavaScript in your page. Most notably, this is true for JavaScript that is specific *to that page on which you're working.*

If you've got utility functions, like creating generic dialog boxes in jQuery (stay tuned for more on that) or handling validation for certain data types, put those things in a script file and reference it in all your pages. That's the same sort of thing that you've done with a site-wide CSS file, and on the server, with *app_config.php* and *database_connection.php.*

But *delete_user*, the JavaScript function you just wrote, is only useful for this one page! It doesn't belong in a site-wide utility script, and only adds to the clutter if that's where you put it. You could create external scripts for every page on your site, but what a mess that is!

Sometimes some well-placed JavaScript in the head of your page is *exactly* what you want. Not that you *should* have lots of JavaScript littering your page, stuck between *p* elements and in the crevices between adjacent *td*s. But don't be scared to write some JavaScript in your page. Just like copy-and-paste, it's there for you to use, albeit judiciously.

■ **FINISH WITH A CHANGE IN LINKING**

You've got your JavaScript in place, and now it's time for the big finish: just change the link that previously went directly to *delete_user.php* in your page to call your new JavaScript function:

```php
<?php
  while ($user = mysql_fetch_array($result)) {
    $user_row = sprintf(
      "<li><a href='show_user.php?user_id=%d'>%s %s</a> " .
      "(<a href='mailto:%s'>%s</a>) " .
      "<a href='javascript:delete_user(%d);'><img " .
        "class='delete_user' src='../images/delete.png' " .
        "width='15' /></a></li>",
      $user['user_id'], $user['first_name'], $user['last_name'],
      $user['email'], $user['email'], $user['user_id']);
    echo $user_row;
  }
?>
```

Beautiful! Try it out, and you'll finally get a handy warning before you flush William Shatner down the deletion black hole, as shown in Figure 10-8.

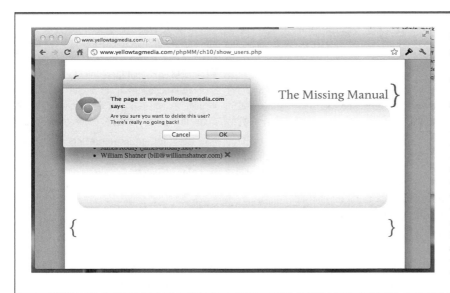

FIGURE 10-8

confirm is *right up there with* alert *as part of the grab bag of user intervention dialog boxes you get from JavaScript. In this case, it gives the user that one extra second or two to think about what they're doing. Yes, you're down on those awful Priceline commercials, but does that mean you need to actually delete Bill Shatner from your system? Sometimes you just want a little reminder to think these critical decisions through.*

■ Talking Back To Your Users

The addition of an alert confirmation box goes a long way on the front end of deletion. It gives users a chance to think twice about deleting a user, and to cancel the operation if they're dissatisfied or concerned. But that's only half of the equation; not only do you need to make sure deletion is the intent, but then you need to make sure that deletion was accomplished.

Obviously, for you the programmer, you've written code, you've run the code, you may have even gone back to the database and done your own manual *SELECT* to ensure that results were deleted in *delete_user.php*. And, of course, the user is gone in *show_users.php*. But that's from a programmer's point of view.

For a user, that's not enough. Just as she'll often want to confirm a deletion *before* the deletion goes through, she usually wants to know—beyond any shadow of doubt—that the deletion *has* gone through. So that means at the end of the process, she gets some sort of message that confirms what's just gone on. So your flow should look something like this:

1. A user selects another user to delete by clicking the red "X" in *show_users.php* next to that user.

2. The user confirms that deletion is intended.

3. *delete_user.php* handles the actual deletion of the selected user.

4. A message is supplied to the user saying something like, "Yup, they're gone, gone, gone."

5. *show_users.php* re-shows the users, minus the deletion.

So it's Step 4 here that's new, and requires a little thought and work.

redirect Has Some Limitations

Just looking at this flow, it seems like the natural place to handle confirmation is within *delete_user.php*. That's the script that handles deletion, and it's also before *show_users.php* re-shows all the users the post-deletion confirmation message applies.

So you might, for example, throw up a status message or pop up an alert box once deletion's complete. But take a look at the last line from *delete_user.php*:

```
header("Location: show_users.php");
```

Redirection in PHP is done using HTTP headers. So this line sends the browser a raw Location header. The browser gets the header, and moves the actual HTTP response to the URL specified. No big deal, and it works great.

But—and this is an important but—*header* can only be called before any output is sent from PHP. You can't use echo or HTML or blank lines in a file, or anything else. The browser can only get the headers, and then it shifts the request. So in reality, you can't send anything before calling *header*, and once you've called *header*, you're not supposed to send anything after. Of course, bugs are made when things that *shouldn't* happen *do* happen, and that's why every call to a *Location* header is followed by that little *exit()* statement to make sure nothing else tries to execute.

In other words, a script like *delete_user.php* can do work on the database and other PHP objects, but it can't do any output. It just deletes a user, and then redirects output to a view script, like *show_users.php*. So you've got to figure out a way to interact with *show_users.php*, and let that script handle letting the user know that a deletion's gone down.

Model-View-Controller (Well, Sort Of...)

You're starting to see an important web application pattern. This pattern is called the MVC pattern, which stands for "model-view-controller." In this pattern, you have three categories of operation: models, views, and controllers. In a strict MVC pattern, these three categories never overlap.

First, there's the *model*, which interacts with the database. The model represents—or models—your app's information. In your application, a script like *delete_user.php* uses MySQL directly. In a more formal MVC approach, you'd have PHP objects like *User.php* with methods like *delete()* or *remove()*. So you might write code like this:

```
User user_to_delete =
  User.find_by_id($user_id);
user_to_delete.delete();
```

You can see that the model part of MVC is what interacts with the database. For your code, you don't have a clear model, but you obviously are doing plenty of database interaction.

Second, there's the *view*, which shows information to the user. In your app, scripts like *show_user.php* and *show_users.php* are, to some degree, views. They're full of HTML and information. The reason they're only views "to some degree" is that they also share some controller behavior.

Controllers are the third category in an MVC architecture. A controller directs traffic. It uses the model to get information from the database or data store, and it passes that information

along to view classes or scripts that display that information. *delete_user.php* is a lot like a controller. Even though it directly accesses the database, rather than using a model, it does something, and then hands off control to a view, *show_users.php*.

In most PHP web applications, you won't have a strict MVC setup. In fact, it's quite a lot of work to go full-on MVC with PHP. You usually have a more hybrid approach, where mostly-controller scripts like *delete_user.php* hand off information to mostly-view scripts like *show_users.php*. But *delete_user.php* also has aspects of a model, in that it talks directly to the database. And *show_users.php* has aspects of a controller and a model, because it figures out what to show, and it grabs information directly from the database.

So if you can't do MVC in PHP, why the long diatribe? Two good reasons. First, you'll hear about MVC all the time, and you'll be a lot more popular at the geeky water cooler or your buddy's *Lord of the Rings* costume party if you can relate what you're doing on the Web to MVC, and what your friends might be doing. And second, if you can identify what your scripts do, you'll often be able to figure out more quickly how to do those things.

In the case of *delete_user.php*, when you see that it's mostly a controller. So it makes perfect sense to hand some information to a script that's mostly a view, like *show_users.php*, and let that script handle display of that information to the user.

So *delete_user.php* needs to provide a message—since it knows that deletion has occurred—but it's got to let something else handle the actual display. You can add a message to your redirect. Connect this new message to a new request parameter, *success_message*:

```
// Redirect to show_users to re-show users (without this deleted one)
$msg = "The user you specified has been deleted.";
header("Location: show_users.php?success_message={$msg}");
```

> **TIP** If you're already thinking that it might be nice to have an *error_message*, too, then you're very much on the right track.

Now, even before you go back to working on your view code in *show_users.php*, you can test this out. Visit *show_users.php*, delete a user, and then look closely at the browser bar when you're taken back to *show_users.php*. You should see the *success_message* request parameter with the value set to your message, as shown in Figure 10-9.

FIGURE 10-9

It's not just there for looks. You can see that the message that delete_user.php *appended to the URL sent to the browser contains a handy value: the exact text you'd want to see in a nice alert or status message. That's perfect: now you can have your view code handle displaying that message to your user, and you're in great shape.*

JavaScript *alert* Redux

So now you're back to *show_users.php*, and you've got an incoming message.

> **NOTE** Actually, you *potentially* have an incoming message. When *show_users.php* is called normally, it does not have a message. It's only when it's redirected to after deletion (or some similar operation) that it has information coming via request parameters.

What needs to happen when that message is received? Probably the easiest option is to go back to JavaScript, and use an alert dialog box. This is the equivalent of the confirmation dialog box you used before deletion, so it's certainly a nice symmetry.

■ AN ALL-JAVASCRIPT APPROACH

One approach would be to write a JavaScript function that you can add to *show_users. php*. JavaScript doesn't directly support reading request parameters, so you'd have to do a little parsing to get at them. You'd need something that uses regular expressions to pick apart the *window.location.href* property, which is the URL the browser has:

```
function get_request_param_value(param_name) {
  param_name = param_name.replace(/[\[]/,"\\\[").replace(/[\]]/,"\\\]");
  var regexS = "[\\?&]" + param_name + "=([^&#]*)";
  var regex = new RegExp(regexS);
  var results = regex.exec(unescape(window.location.href));
  if (results == null)
    return "";
  else
    return results[1];
}
```

WARNING You don't need to make much sense of this code. Heck, if this code made perfect sense to you, maybe *you* should be writing the chapters on JavaScript and regular expressions!

Now, all that said, if you wanted to take a few minutes to work through this code, line by line, you'd probably step up your JavaScript game significantly. It also demonstrates once again that while regular expressions might look pretty weird at first, they are an essential part of your programming toolkit. And just think: every bit of what you learned about regular expressions in this PHP book translates over to JavaScript.

You could then call this function like this to get at the *success_message* parameter (probably in another JavaScript function):

```
msg = get_request_param_value("success_message");
if (msg.length > 0) {
  // let the user know
}
```

So then—after uncrossing your eyes from all the forward and backslashes in *get_request_param_value*—you could issue an alert:

```
msg = get_request_param_value("success_message")
if (msg.length > 0) {
  alert(msg);
}
```

There's certainly nothing wrong with this approach. It works fine, and you'll get something like the message shown in Figure 10-10 if you add this code in to the head section between script tags in *show_users.php*.

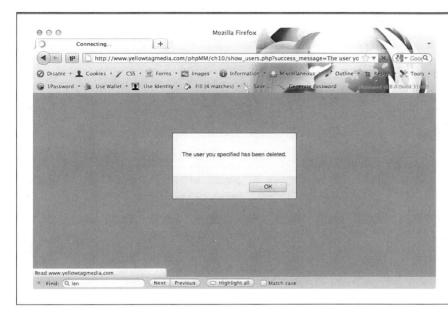

FIGURE 10-10

The gray background you see here is an artifact of where alert *is called. You'd probably want to improve the user experience further by not running the alert until the document loads. You can use the* window.onload *property, the onload event on body, or jQuery's various ways to run code on document load, and get a much better user experience.*

Before you start wondering how to piece all this together, though, there might just be a better way.

■ YOUR PHP CONTROLS YOUR OUTPUT

The all-JavaScript approach above makes a subtle but important assumption: that the page—the HTML, CSS, and JavaScript delivered to the user via his browser—has to make all the decisions about what to do, show, and how to act. So there's JavaScript that must figure out if the *success_message* parameter was passed along, JavaScript to parse the request URL and find the value of that parameter, and JavaScript that conditionally displays an *alert*.

But here's the thing: *show_users.php* isn't limited in the same way that the page that it outputs is. Just because the HTML and JavaScript that is ultimately output is unaware of whether or not there's a request parameter doesn't mean that your script that *generates* that output is unaware. In fact, it's trivial to get a request parameter in *show_users.php*; you've done it tons of times:

```
$msg = $_REQUEST['success_message'];
```

Now, in one line, you've eliminated all this JavaScript:

```
function get_request_param_value(param_name) {
  param_name = param_name.replace(/[\[]/,"\\\[").replace(/[\]]/,"\\\]");
  var regexS = "[\\?&]" + param_name + "=([^&#]*)";
  var regex = new RegExp(regexS);
  var results = regex.exec(unescape(window.location.href));
  if (results == null)
    return "";
  else
    return results[1];
}
```

That's a win by any measure of accounting.

NOTE   To be a little more balanced, it's probably not a bad idea to add a function like *get_request_param_value* to your basic JavaScript utilities, and have it around for situations where you don't have PHP generating your output.

But here's the big thing to sink your teeth into here: you're in control of what goes to the client. Your script can make decisions about what to output.

So in your PHP, you can do something like this:

```
// See if there's a message to display
if (isset($_REQUEST['success_message'])) {
  $msg = $_REQUEST['success_message'];
}
```

That's on the server. You haven't done any output yet. If you do have a message to show—and only if you have a message to show—you can simply add a few lines of JavaScript into your HTML output:

```
<script type="text/javascript">
  function delete_user(user_id) {
    if (confirm("Are you sure you want to delete this user?" +
              "\nThere's really no going back!")) {
      window.location = "delete_user.php?user_id=" + user_id;
    }   }

<?php if (isset($msg)) { ?>
    window.onload = function() {
      alert("<?php echo $msg ?>");
    }
<?php } ?>
  </script>
```

So put it all together, and here's the new-and-improved *show_users.php*:

```php
<?php

require_once '../scripts/app_config.php';
require_once '../scripts/database_connection.php';

// Build the SELECT statement
$select_users =
  "SELECT user_id, first_name, last_name, email " .
  "  FROM users";

// Run the query
$result = mysql_query($select_users);

// See if there's a message to display
if (isset($_REQUEST['success_message'])) {
  $msg = $_REQUEST['success_message'];
}
?>

<html>
 <head>
  <link href="../css/phpMM.css" rel="stylesheet" type="text/css" />
  <script type="text/javascript">
    function delete_user(user_id) {
      if (confirm("Are you sure you want to delete this user?" +
                  "\nThere's really no going back!")) {
        window.location = "delete_user.php?user_id=" + user_id;
      }
    }

<?php if (isset($msg)) { ?>
    window.onload = function() {
      alert("<?php echo $msg ?>");
    }
<?php } ?>
  </script>
 </head>

 <body>
  <div id="header"><h1>PHP & MySQL: The Missing Manual</h1></div>
  <div id="example">Current Users</div>
```

```
<div id="content">
  <ul>
    <?php
      while ($user = mysql_fetch_array($result)) {
        $user_row = sprintf(
          "<li><a href='show_user.php?user_id=%d'>%s %s</a> " .
          "(<a href='mailto:%s'>%s</a>) " .
          "<a href='javascript:delete_user(%d);'><img " .
            "class='delete_user' src='../images/delete.png' " .
            "width='15' /></a></li>",
          $user['user_id'], $user['first_name'], $user['last_name'],
          $user['email'], $user['email'], $user['user_id']);
        echo $user_row;
      }
    ?>
  </ul>
</div>
<div id="footer"></div>
</body>
</html>
```

NOTE   At this point, it's quite possible it's getting hard to keep up with all the changes to *show_user.php* and *show_users.php*, as well as *app_config.php*. If you find yourself getting some weird errors or unusual results, you may want to hop online to the Missing CD page (page xvii) and download the latest chapter's examples. That will get you a clean, current set of files that are up-to-date, and you can focus on new changes, rather than old debugging.

What you've done here is a really big deal when it comes to PHP programming. Instead of relying on your output to make complicated decisions, you're making most of the decisions in your PHP, and then tailoring your output as a result. So one script—depending on the decisions it makes—might push out two, three, four, even more variations of the same output.

First, take this thing for a test drive. If you've still got a browser up with a URL like *yellowtagmedia.com/phpMM/ch10/show_users.php?success_message=The%20 user%20you%20specified%20has%20been%20deleted*, then just reload that page to get the new changes to *show_users.php*. You should see a nice pop-up with the message passed through the URL, as in Figure 10-11.

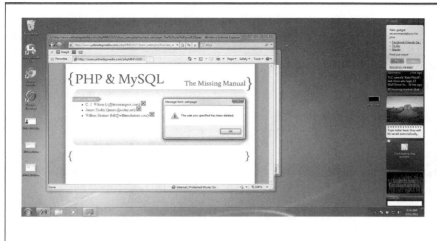

FIGURE 10-11

This piece of output looks a bit mind-bending. The output is fixed, and it shows an alert, and that alert is exactly equal to the specific message passed to this script, this one time it's being executed. Of course, that's all fixed because your PHP isn't fixed. It is running each time and creating slightly different versions of the output. Pretty cool...definitely truly dynamic programming.

Go ahead and view the source on this page to see what's so cool. Figure 10-12 shows that there's a "hard-coded" alert for the message passed along. Change the message in the request URL, and you'll see the HTML change to match.

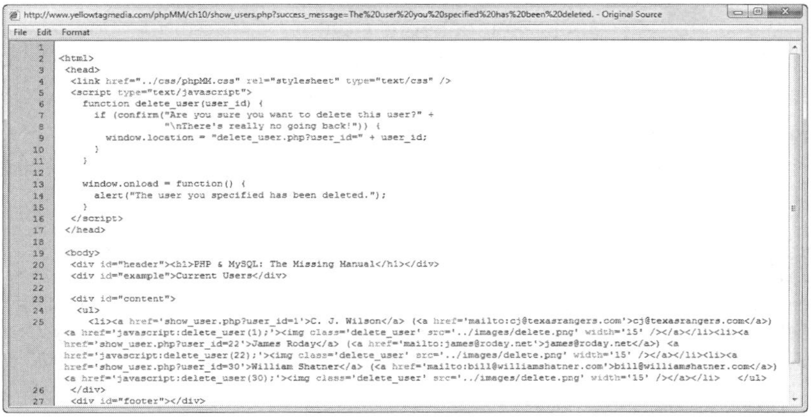

FIGURE 10-12

You'd never know that this source is perfectly matched to this particular message. It simply looks like there's an alert that triggers every time you access show_users.php. But that's not true; what is true is that every time you access show_users. php, you get a different variant of this basic HTML page.

Now delete all the request parameters from *show_users.php* in your URL bar, and hit the page again. The alert box should go away and so should the JavaScript in the HTML page that *show_users.php* generates. Figure 10-13 is the source from this page: the *window.onload* function has vanished.

FIGURE 10-13

Here's something to think about with this approach: how does bookmarking work? Since the request parameter for the message is part of the URL (or in this case, not part of the URL), bookmarking is going to attach a certain variant of that message to the bookmarked URL. That means you've got to think through what would happen if, say, someone bookmarked this page on a pass when a message was shown. Every time they pulled up the bookmark, they'd see a message again...and an inaccurate one at that.

alert Is Interruptive

You've got a pretty nice book-end of notifications now. A confirmation box gets a user's OK before deleting a user, and another alert lets them know once that deletion's done. So, from a functional point of view, you're ready to move on.

But now is one of those moments where you have to move a bit beyond web programming and start thinking about web designing...or better, web usability. Usability is just a high-dollar way of saying "What's the user experience like?"

NOTE You'll also often hear terms like UX (for user experience) and UI (user interface) in this discussion. To some degree, these terms aren't that different, although a UX designer might get ruffled if you confused him with a UI designer. Still, the basic goal is the same: create a natural, compelling online experience for a user. That experience includes not just functionality, but aesthetics, accessibility, and overall "feel" of a website or web application.

In terms of deleting a user, things are pretty solid. Although you might use something like jQuery to present a better looking dialog box, it makes perfect sense to interrupt the user to make sure they really want to delete a user. In effect, you're requiring a double-action: click once to select delete, and click once more to ensure that's the intention.

NOTE If you'd like a nicer jQuery-style dialog and confirmation box—and it's highly recommended that you do—check out jQuery UI and their dialog boxes at *www.jqueryui.com/demos/dialog*. In particular, look at the option for a Modal confirmation. It'll take you 10 minutes to download and install jQuery UI and another 5 to move from your *confirm* call to a call to the jQuery confirmation dialog.

But what about after deletion? Yes, you need to let the user know that deletion has occurred. But do you need to effectively shut them down until they click "OK"? Ideally, you'd let them know about deletion, but do it a little less interruptive.

And that's a general principle for web usability/design/whatever-you-want-to-call-it: if you're going to make the user take their hands off the keyboard and click a button, make sure it's worth it. In this case, there's a risk you're being annoying. "Why do I have to click again? I just clicked twice to delete the user in the first place!"

◼ Standardizing on Messaging

There's another issue that you may have already considered: is a success message the only type of message you may need to display? What if you have an error that doesn't rise to needing *handle_error*? What if you need a status message, perhaps something like "Please log in before attempting to delete a user."

NOTE Logging in before deleting a user? Hmmm...that does sound like a good idea. That just might be perfect topic for a Chapter 11, don't you think? Something to look forward to.

These are all similar cases: you want to tell the user something, but you don't want to interrupt their flow. You want to add content to the page, but JavaScript's *alert* and *confirm* aren't really the best choices.

And as an additional consideration, this would ideally be something that could be made generic. You don't want every script to have to output 5 or 10 lines of code. It would be nice to have your output do something like this:

```
<body>
  <?php display_messages($_REQUEST); ?>

  <!-- All the rest of the HTML output you want -->
</body>
```

Then, this function would just "take care of things," whatever that ends up meaning. So for a success message, you might get a banner-type of message across the top of a page, as shown in Figure 10-14.

FIGURE 10-14

This message won't win any design awards, but that's what good designers are for. They take rough ideas from programmers and give them subtle style and grace. The advancement here is in how nonintrusive this message is, though. It now communicates with the user, without causing them to click or confirm anything.

The HTML for success messages is pretty simple:

```
<div id="messages">
  <div class="success">
    <p>The user you specified has been deleted.</p>
  </div>
</div>
```

Errors could be shown in similar fashion, as in Figure 10-15.

> **NOTE**   You may have noticed that these rough mockups are done with *create_user.html*. That was simply the closest piece of HTML when it came to trying out a look for these messages. It's not relevant what page you use for testing these things out. Remember, the goal is to have every page automatically display, or not display, messages sent to it.

Here's the HTML for the error. It's identical to the success message with a different class on the inner *div*:

```
<div id="messages">
  <div class="error">
    <p>Your username and password were invalid.</p>
  </div>
</div>
```

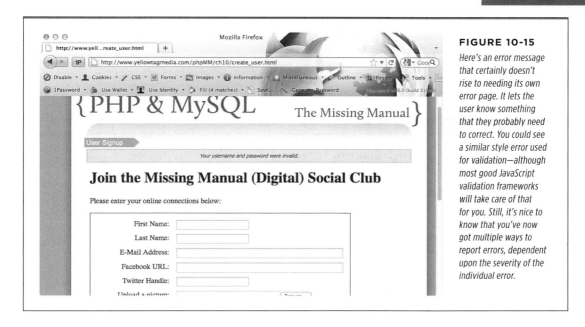

FIGURE 10-15

*Here's an error message
that certainly doesn't
rise to needing its own
error page. It lets the
user know something
that they probably need
to correct. You could see
a similar style error used
for validation—although
most good JavaScript
validation frameworks
will take care of that
for you. Still, it's nice to
know that you've now
got multiple ways to
report errors, dependent
upon the severity of the
individual error.*

Building a New Utility Function for Display

So once again, it's back to thinking generic. Rather than worrying about the specific
success message passed into *show_users.php* by *delete_user.php*, what's the more
general form of a success message?

It's something like this:

```
<div id="messages">
  <div class="success">
    <p>$msg</p>
  </div>
</div>
```

That's not real PHP, of course; you'd really want to do this:

```
<div id="messages">
  <div class="success">
    <p><?php echo $msg; ?></p>
  </div>
</div>
```

But that's not hard at all. You just need a new function that takes in the message:

```php
function display_success_message($msg) {
  echo "<div id='messages'>\n";
  echo " <div class='success'>\n";
  echo "  <p>{$msg}</p>\n";
  echo " </div>\n";
  echo "</div>\n\n";
}
```

FREQUENTLY ASKED QUESTIONS

What about *sprintf*? And why the *ns*?

There are probably about as many ways to write a function like *display_success_message* as there are letters in the alphabet. You could use *sprintf* to insert the message. You could combine the multiple *echo* calls into a single line (using *echo* or *sprintf*). You could output raw HTML and interrupt that HTML with PHP by using <*?php* and *?>*. And in each case, your solution would be just fine.

The *ns* are another curiosity. They're intended to make the viewed source a little cleaner. Without them, the output would look something like this:

```
<div id='messages'> <div class='success'>
<p>{$msg}</p> </div></div>
```

So it's just one big line of HTML. With the line feeds, the user sees nothing different. HTML doesn't care a bit about those feeds. But if you viewed the source, you'd see a much nicer bit of HTML:

```
<div id='messages'>
 <div class='success'>
  <p>{$msg}</p>
```

```
 </div>
</div>
```

So are the *ns* necessary? Not at all. Do they help the user? Nope. But they definitely do make debugging and readability a bit simpler. So should you use them, or not? And do they go with *echo*, or *sprintf*, or both?

You're at the place in your PHP journey where there's less right and wrong and more "style" and "personal preference." You can use *sprintf* everywhere, for queries and output and everything in between. You can use *echo* for output and *sprintf* for queries. Or, more likely, you'll use whatever comes to mind when you're writing the particular script you're writing.

The same is true with *n* and line feeds. Sometimes you'll work really hard so that the HTML output is nice and clean and easy to read. Other times, you'll realize that you could spend hours trying to get things to look good for that rare person who Views Source. (Then again, you're that rare person, so sometimes the effort makes perfect sense.)

So this function works well. But what about error messages? You could use something similar:

```php
function display_error_message($msg) {
  echo "<div id='messages'>\n";
  echo " <div class=error>\n";
  echo "  <p>{$msg}</p>\n";
  echo " </div>\n";
  echo "</div>\n\n";
}
```

But look closely: both of these are outputting the "messages" *div*. That's no good. You really need something that can handle both error types. Then that sort of "parent" function can pass the individual messages to smaller functions, each of which handles success and errors:

```
function display_messages($success_msg, $error_msg) {
  echo "<div id='messages'>\n";
  display_success_message($success_msg);
  display_error_message($error_msg);
  echo "</div>\n\n";
}

function display_success_message($msg) {
  echo " <div class='success'>\n";
  echo "  <p>{$msg}</p>\n";
  echo " </div>\n";
}

function display_error_message($msg) {
  echo " <div class='error'>\n";
  echo "  <p>{$msg}</p>\n";
  echo " </div>\n";
}
```

That looks better. Well, kinda... does anything bother you here? Does it seem like you might be seeing double?

Duplicate Code is a Problem Waiting to Happen

The problem here is a bit subtle, which is why it can be so nasty. Look how close these two functions are to each other:

```
function display_success_message($msg) {
  echo " <div class='success'>\n";
  echo "  <p>{$msg}</p>\n";
  echo " </div>\n";
}

function display_error_message($msg) {
  echo " <div class='error'>\n";
  echo "  <p>{$msg}</p>\n";
  echo " </div>\n";
}
```

That's a *lot* of code that's identical... all for just one change, the class of the *div* in each. And any time you see code that's this similar, be thinking "Uh oh. That's fragile code." So you really want to avoid this sort of thing.

Since there's so much repeated code, you can consolidate these functions:

```
function display_message($msg, $msg_type) {
  echo " <div class='{#msg_type}'>\n";
  echo "  <p>{$msg}</p>\n";
  echo " </div>\n";
}
```

This code is much better. It's clear, it's succinct, and, as explained in the box below, very DRY. In fact, take things even further and define the allowed message types as constants:

```
define("SUCCESS_MESSAGE", "success");
define("ERROR_MESSAGE", "error");

function display_messages($success_msg, $error_msg) {
  echo "<div id='messages'>\n";
  display_message($success_msg, SUCCESS_MESSAGE);
  display_message($error_msg, ERROR_MESSAGE);
  echo "</div>\n\n";
}

function display_message($msg, $msg_type) {
  echo " <div class='{#msg_type}'>\n";
  echo "  <p>{$msg}</p>\n";
  echo " </div>\n";
}
```

POWER USERS' CLINIC

Writing DRY Code

As you get further into programming, you're going to hear people start talking about DRY code, or "Drying up your code." Both of these expressions are using DRY as an acronym, which stands for "Don't Repeat Yourself." You've actually been doing a good job on that score. Remember way back in Chapter 4 when you moved some basic application-wide constants into *app_config.php*? You were making sure you didn't repeat those constants (or yourself) in multiple files. You put them in a single place, and then all your other scripts referenced that single place.

The same was true of you creating *database_connection.php*. Again, instead of repeating your connection code over and over,

you pulled that code out of multiple places and located it in a single place. That's DRYing up your code: making it DRY, and removing duplicate code whenever and wherever possible.

Now, in the case of *display_success_message* and *display_error_message*, things are at a bit more microscopic level. It's just three lines of code, right? Still, if you can write those three lines of code in one place and reference them in two, you've improved your overall project. You've made sure that if you need to change how messages are output, you've got one place to investigate, rather than two. This is good programming, it results in DRY code, and all your peers will think you're cool.

Beautiful! Now you don't have to remember the message type for an error was "ERROR" or "error" or "errors" or something else altogether. The constant handles that mapping for you.

So you can start to put this all together. Create a new script, and call it *view.php*. Then drop in all this code, along with a *require_once* for the obligatory *app_config.php*:

```php
<?php

require_once 'app_config.php';

define("SUCCESS_MESSAGE", "success");
define("ERROR_MESSAGE", "error");

function display_messages($success_msg, $error_msg) {
  echo "<div id='messages'>\n";
  display_message($success_msg, SUCCESS_MESSAGE);
  display_message($error_msg, ERROR_MESSAGE);
  echo "</div>\n\n";
}

function display_message($msg, $msg_type) {
  echo " <div class='{$msg_type}'>\n";
  echo "  <p>{$msg}</p>\n";
  echo " </div>\n";
}

?>
```

NOTE You're not actually using anything from *app_config.php* in *view.php*. Still, since that's where all your core information resides, it's probably a good bet that you'll need information from it sooner or later. Might as well *require_once* it now, so it's available.

View and Display Code Belongs Together

You've now got another script: *view.php*. This script belongs in your main *scripts/* directory, alongside *app_config.php* and *database_connection.php*. It also furthers you creating not only utility code, but nicely organized code. So while you could put *display_messages* and *display_message* in *app_config.php*, that's not good organization.

Taking time now to build out groups of functions in scripts that are nicely named is well worth that time. When you're writing a script like *show_users.php* that handles display, you immediately know you can include *view.php* and get helpful functions. On the other hand, in a script like *delete_user.php* that doesn't do any display, you can skip *view.php*. It's that simple.

NOTE Of course, this same principle is true of *database_connection.php*. If you don't need a database connection, you don't need to *require_once database_connection.php*. If you do, well then you do. It becomes very simple when you have scripts that are organized and named according to their function.

■ Integrating Utilities, Views, and Messages

You're finally ready to put all this together. Revisit *show_users.php*, and the less refined messaging that started this entire journey that led to *view.php*:

```
<head>
  <link href="../css/phpMM.css" rel="stylesheet" type="text/css" />
  <script type="text/javascript">
    function delete_user(user_id) {
      if (confirm("Are you sure you want to delete this user?" +
                  "\nThere's really no going back!")) {
        window.location = "delete_user.php?user_id=" + user_id;
      }
    }

<?php if (isset($msg)) { ?>
    window.onload = function() {
      alert("<?php echo $msg ?>");
    }
<?php } ?>
  </script>
</head>
```

Calling Repeated Code from a View Script

This code is no longer needed. So you can remove it, and then you should also add in the *require_once* for your new view-related function script:

```
<?php

require_once '../scripts/app_config.php';
require_once '../scripts/database_connection.php';
require_once '../scripts/view.php';

// and so on...

?>
```

WARNING It's nearly impossible to show deleted code in a book. "Look, there's some deleted code. What? You can't see it? That's because it's deleted!"

But be sure you do delete the PHP code interjected into the *head* section of the HTML output by *show_users.php* that pops up an alert message.

Now, you can add a call to your *display_messages* function in your HTML:

```
<body>
  <div id="header"><h1>PHP & MySQL: The Missing Manual</h1></div>
  <div id="example">Current Users</div>
  <?php display_messages($msg); ?>
```

Now, there's a bit of a problem here: *display_messages* takes two parameters: a success message and an error message. So there needs to be some means of passing in an empty message, and then *display_messages* needs to handle an empty message on the receiving end.

However the issue with errors is resolved, this should become a standard part of all your view HTML. Anytime you're displaying HTML, you want to allow messages to be handled. And where does that leave you?

You're back to repeat code! Every single view-related script has started out with the same basic HTML... although occasionally you've needed to insert some JavaScript, as in *show_users.php*:

```
<html>
 <head>
  <link href="../css/phpMM.css" rel="stylesheet" type="text/css" />
  <script type="text/javascript">
    function delete_user(user_id) {
      if (confirm("Are you sure you want to delete this user?" +
                  "\nThere's really no going back!")) {
        window.location = "delete_user.php?user_id=" + user_id;
      }
    }
  </script>
 </head>
```

And then you've got your body tag, the same header—more repeated code—and then a page title. And now, you've got messages to display. Here's another chance to take code that you've been typing into your scripts, over and over, and pull that repeated code out and drop it into yet more utility functions. *view.php* is about to get a lot bigger, and a lot more useful.

Flexible Functions are Better Functions

So there's now a bit of a list of interrelated things you have to deal with, most of which involves updates to *view.php*:

- *display_messages* should handle empty or nonexistent messages for the success and the error message. If either message isn't set, the *div* related to that message shouldn't be output.

- You need a new function—call it *display_header*—that handles outputting the head section of each page's HTML. This function should take in JavaScript that can be added into the document's head, but should also handle the case where there's no extra JavaScript needed.

- You need another new function—call this one *display_title*—that prints out the page title, the page's subtitle, which is passed in by each script, and any message, which also should be passed in by the calling script.

None of these functions are particularly difficult, so time to get back to work.

▣ USE DEFAULT ARGUMENT VALUES IN DISPLAY_MESSAGES

Returning to *view.php*, *display_messages* needs to be able to accept a non-value for a message. In PHP, this is handled by the special keyword *NULL*, which simply means "non-value."

> **NOTE** You'll see *NULL* in almost every language, although usually with slight variations. In Ruby, it's *nil*. In Java, it's *null*. PHP has *NULL*, as does C++. They always means the same thing, though: the absence of value.

Now, because *NULL* is a non-value, you can't compare it to a value. So this code doesn't make sense in PHP:

```
if ($value == NULL) // do something
```

What you need to use is another PHP helper, *is_null*. You pass a value to *is_null*, and PHP let's you know what you've got.

You can now update *display_messages*. If a message passed in is *NULL*, then there's no need to call the individual *display_message* for that type of message:

```
function display_messages($success_msg, $error_msg) {
  echo "<div id='messages'>\n";
  if (!is_null($success_msg)) {
    display_message($success_msg, SUCCESS_MESSAGE);
  }
  if (!is_null($error_msg)) {
    display_message($error_msg, ERROR_MESSAGE);
  }
  echo "</div>\n\n";
}
```

This script is almost perfect. There's just one thing missing: what if a script—like *show_users.php*—doesn't have a value to pass in for *$error_msg*? Or for *$success_msg*? In these cases, you want *display_messages* to have a default value. That's just a value to assign by default if nothing else is passed in.

You can assign a function's arguments default values like this:

```
function do_something(this_value = "default value") {
  // do something with this_value
}
```

So for *display_messages*, the default values should be NULL, or no value:

```
function display_messages($success_msg = NULL, $error_msg = NULL) {
  echo "<div id='messages'>\n";
  if (!is_null($success_msg)) {
    display_message($success_msg, SUCCESS_MESSAGE);
  }
  if (!is_null($error_msg)) {
    display_message($error_msg, ERROR_MESSAGE);
  }
  echo "</div>\n\n";
}
```

Now *display_messages* is finally ready for primetime and for usage by the other functions you need to add to *view.php*.

■ OUTPUTTING A STANDARD HEADER WITH *HEREDOC*

What's next? You need to deal with the standard HTML output for a page in your app. This is basically the opening *html*, the *title*, the *head*, and any page-specific JavaScript that needs to be added. But with *view.php* in place, your knowledge of functions, default arguments, and everything else you've already done, this should be a piece of cake.

You can create a new function, and since it's possible that some scripts need to pass in JavaScript to add to the head section, but others may not, using a default value for a function argument is the way to go again:

```
function display_head($page_title = "", $embedded_javascript = NULL) {
```

This code sets a default value for the *$page_title*, too. That's not completely necessary, but again, it's a bit of extra protection. Now if someone calling this function forgets to send in the title, the HTML output can be constructed regardless.

The body of this function is just some *echo* work and a conditional for the potential JavaScript:

```
function display_head($page_title = "", $embedded_javascript = NULL) {
  echo "<html>";
  echo " <head>";
  echo "  <title>{$page_title}</title>";
```

```
echo '  <link href="../css/phpMM.css" rel="stylesheet" type="text/css" />';
if (!is_null($embedded_javascript)) {
  echo "<script type='text/javascript'>" .
       $embedded_javascript .
       "</script>";
}
echo " </head>";
}
```

Notice that the link line uses single quotes around the HTML so that double-quotes can be used for the *href*, *rel*, and *type* attributes. Unfortunately, you're going to have to either use multiple quote styles like this, or escape a lot of your quotes with \" and \'. Neither solution is particularly pretty, so pick your own poison.

Of course, programmers aren't used to limitations like this, and you should immediately be thinking, "Wait a second. I'm a programmer. Why am I stuck with two bad solutions?" And truth be told, you're really not. What you need is a way to deal with multi-line strings, and PHP doesn't disappoint. In fact, multi-line strings are such a common issue in PHP that there are a couple of ways to deal with this issue.

The most common is to use something called *heredoc*. *heredoc* gives you a way to mark the beginning of a piece of text, and the end of a piece of text. Then, everything between that beginning and end is treated as text—without you needing to surround things in quotation marks.

You start a piece of *heredoc* with three less-than signs, and then a sequence that you'll use to mark the end of the string:

```
$some_text = <<<EOD
```

So here, you're saying, "I'm starting some text. And the text will end when you run across EOD."

> **NOTE** You can use any ending sequence you want. The most typical choices are EOD and EOT, though, so it's best to stick with these unless you have a good reason for going with a different sequence.

Now you can put as much text as you want in. You can use multiple lines, single quotes, double quotes, and even the *{$var_name}* syntax. It's all fair game:

```
<html>
 <head>
  <title>{$page_title}</title>
   <link href="../css/phpMM.css" rel="stylesheet" type="text/css" />
 </head>
```

And finally, end the text with your end sequence:

```
EOD;
```

So all together, you get this:

```
$some_text = <<<EOD
<html>
 <head>
  <title>{$page_title}</title>
   <link href="../css/phpMM.css" rel="stylesheet" type="text/css" />
 </head>
EOD;
```

WARNING   You *can't* indent the ending sequence. It has to be the first thing on a line, all by itself, with no spacing before it.

Just as dangerous is having whitespace after the ending sequence. There's no way to illustrate that, but even a single space after the closing semicolon will do you in.

The best way to recognize these things is to watch out for the dreaded "unexpected T_SL" error. That's usually PHP's ultra-cryptic way of letting you know that you've got whitespace where it doesn't belong: either before or after the ending sequence, in most cases.

Put all this together, and you can clean up the look of *display_head* quite a bit:

```
function display_head($page_title = "", $embedded_javascript = NULL) {
  echo <<<EOD
<html>
 <head>
 <title>{$page_title}</title>
 <link href="../css/phpMM.css" rel="stylesheet" type="text/css" />
EOD;
  if (!is_null($embedded_javascript)) {
    echo "<script type='text/javascript'>" .
         $embedded_javascript .
         "</script>";
  }
  echo " </head>";
}
```

You probably noticed that in this version of *display_head*, there was no need to assign the string created using *heredoc* to a variable. You can directly output the multi-line string, and save a step. The result is a hodgepodge of *echo*, *heredoc*, conditional logic, and potentially some JavaScript. But, it's getting increasingly easy to read, and that's a good thing.

■ UPDATING YOUR SCRIPT(S) TO USE DISPLAY_HEAD

Things are coming together. Now you can head back to *show_users.php* (and *show_user.php* if you like) and remove lots of HTML. Replace the HTML for the head of your document with a call to *display_head*. While you're at it, you may want to use a little more *heredoc* in the process, particularly in *show_users.php*, which sends some JavaScript to be embedded:

```php
<?php
// code to get all the user data
?>

<?php
  $delete_user_script = <<<EOD
function delete_user(user_id) {
  if (confirm("Are you sure you want to delete this user? " +
              "There's really no going back!")) {
    window.location = "delete_user.php?user_id=" + user_id;
  }
}
EOD;
  display_head("Current Users", $delete_user_script);
?>

<!-- Remaining HTML markup -->
</html>
```

> **NOTE** You could just as easily keep all the PHP that gets the users in the same *<?php/ ?>* block as the code that calls *display_head*. That's up to you. Some programmers like to keep the data gathering and the actual view display separate, and some prefer to avoid duplicating *<?php*. The choice is yours.

This uses *heredoc* so that creating a string of JavaScript to pass to *display_head* doesn't involve lots of escaping single or double quotes. In fact, you'll find that *heredoc* is almost as handy to have around as *sprintf*, and you'll use both liberally for outputting HTML or other long stretches of text.

There's still the issue of displaying messages, but before you get to that, try out your changes to *show_users.php*. You should see something like Figure 10-16.

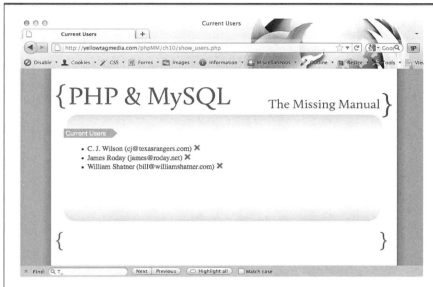

Standardize and Consolidate Messaging in the View

All that's left is messaging. You have a *display_messages* function, but it's not integrated into the HTML that's typically around those messages. Just as *display_head* output HTML with some potential embedded JavaScript, the first part of your page should output some standard HTML, the page title (again), and potentially success and error messages. So the final output should look a bit like this:

```
<html>
 <head>
  <title>Current Users</title>
  <link href="../css/phpMM.css" rel="stylesheet" type="text/css" />
  <script type='text/javascript'>function delete_user(user_id) {
  if (confirm("Are you sure you want to delete this user? " +
            "There's really no going back!")) {
    window.location = "delete_user.php?user_id=" + user_id;
  }
}</script>
 </head>
 <body>
  <div id="header"><h1>PHP & MySQL: The Missing Manual</h1></div>
```

```
<div id="example">Current Users</div>
<div id='messages'>
<div class='success'>
<p>The user you specified has been deleted.</p>
</div>
</div>


<div id="content">
  <!-- HTML content -->
</div>
</body>
</html>
```

This is a piece of cake now. Go ahead and create *display_title* in *view.php*:

```
function display_title($title, $success_msg = NULL, $error_msg = NULL) {
echo <<<EOD
 <body>
  <div id="header"><h1>PHP & MySQL: The Missing Manual</h1></div>
  <div id="example">$title</div>
EOD;
  display_messages($success_msg, $error_msg); ?>
}
```

How easy is that? You'd call this like so, say in *show_users.php*:

```
display_title("Current Users", $msg);
```

But you already know how messages come across: through request parameters, accessible via *$_REQUEST*. So why worry about whether they're set in your view or not? Just pass them in—even if the values are *NULL*—to *display_title*:

```
display_title("Current Users",
               $_REQUEST['success_message'], $_REQUEST['error_message']);
```

NOTE You can also remove the code in *show_users.php* that gets the *success_message* request parameter from *$_REQUEST* explicitly, as that's now handled by this new call to *display_title*.

Things are looking pretty good. *display_head* and *display_title* are both great, and you've already got calls to *display_head* in place.

But before you go adding in a call to *display_title* in all your scripts, take a moment to think about what you've done.

Why Not Pass *$_REQUEST* into display_title?

It may have occurred to you that you could pass the *$_REQUEST* variable wholesale into *display_title*. Then, *display_title* could pull out *$_REQUEST['success_message']* and *$_REQUEST['error_message']*. That's not a bad idea. It certainly would mean that your view scripts would not have to worry about which request parameter was which, or even if those particular request parameters came across.

The potential downside is that it does begin to tie your view code—the functions in *view.php* that basically spit out HTML—to how the data for that view is received. So now your view is interacting with the user's request itself, rather than letting a controller handle that and pass along information as needed.

As you can see yet again, trying to pull off a clean MVC architecture in PHP just isn't possible. You're going to constantly make choices that represent tradeoffs between a clean separation between view and controller, and ease of coding. In this case, you can leave things the way they are—and let *view.php* just output information—or let *view.php* do a little more work and pass it *$_REQUEST*.

Build a Function to Call Two Functions

Now, remember, the idea here was to create another function—*display_title*—to handle outputting the starting portion of every HTML page's body. But now that you have that function, there are a few things to think about:

- The HTML from *display_title* will *always* directly follow the HTML output from *display_head*.

- The title used in *display_head* should typically match the title used in *display_title*.

So if this HTML always follows the HTML from *display_head*, and the title in both is the same, why is this two calls? In your scripts, you'd always have something like this:

```php
<?php

// Code like crazy

?>


<?php display_head($title, $javascript);  ?>
<?php display_title($title,
                $_REQUEST['success_message'], $_REQUEST['error_message']);
?>

 <!-- More HTML -->
</html>
```

But is this necessary? Why do you need two calls here? Wouldn't this be cleaner?

```php
<?php

// Code like crazy

?>
```

```php
<?php page_start($title, $javascript,
                 $_REQUEST['success_message'], $_REQUEST['error_message']) ?>

<!-- More HTML -->
</html>
```

Not only is this a simpler call, but now you don't need to pass in *$title* twice. It goes in a single time and gets applied across all the opening HTML.

Now you don't need to start messing around with *display_title*, *display_head*, or *display_messages*. Instead, just build a function for your script to call that handles all the smaller functions:

```php
function page_start($title, $javascript = NULL,
                    $success_message = NULL, $error_message = NULL) {

  display_head($title, $javascript);
  display_title($title, $success_message, $error_message);
}
```

> **NOTE** Put this in *view.php*, along with all your other display functions.

Perfect! Now one call from a view script takes care of all of this.

Just Pass that Information Along

What's left? Removing calls to *display_head*; avoiding another call to *display_title*; and finally, one call to rule them all.

> **NOTE** Yes, that was *Lord of the Rings* humor. But 350 pages into programming PHP, you deserve a nerdy joke.

In fact, take a look at the new, improved *show_users.php*. This script is shorter, and a lot clearer. Even with the bit of indentation clutter that *heredoc* introduces, this is a pretty sleek script:

```php
<?php

require_once '../scripts/app_config.php';
require_once '../scripts/database_connection.php';
require_once '../scripts/view.php';

// Build the SELECT statement
$select_users =
  "SELECT user_id, first_name, last_name, email " .
  "  FROM users";

// Run the query
$result = mysql_query($select_users);

// Display the view to users
  $delete_user_script = <<<EOD
function delete_user(user_id) {
  if (confirm("Are you sure you want to delete this user? " +
              "There's really no going back!")) {
    window.location = "delete_user.php?user_id=" + user_id;
  }
}
EOD;
  page_start("Current Users", $delete_user_script,
             $_REQUEST['success_message'], $_REQUEST['error_message']);
?>
  <div id="content">
   <ul>
     <?php
       while ($user = mysql_fetch_array($result)) {
         $user_row = sprintf(
           "<li><a href='show_user.php?user_id=%d'>%s %s</a> " .
           "(<a href='mailto:%s'>%s</a>) " .
           "<a href='javascript:delete_user(%d);'><img " .
             "class='delete_user' src='../images/delete.png' " .
             "width='15' /></a></li>",
           $user['user_id'], $user['first_name'], $user['last_name'],
           $user['email'], $user['email'], $user['user_id']);
         echo $user_row;
       }
     ?>
   </ul>
  </div>
  <div id="footer"></div>
 </body>
</html>
```

At this point, take it out for a spin. Make sure error messages work. Make sure success messages work. Change your other scripts to also use *page_start*. Heck, add more functions to *view.php*. Maybe you want a *page_end* that outputs the closing *div*, the footer, and some contact text. You could add a sidebar function.

The thing is, with this modular approach, you can do anything you want...except for controlling just who gets to delete users. That's a problem for the next chapter.

DESIGN TIME

Two Functions Are Better Than One...Kinda

One of the things you've seen over and over is this idea of moving smaller and smaller bits of code into their own functions. So you've got a little bit of HTML in a function in *view.php*. You've got *database_connection.php* doing database connection, and even though it doesn't define a custom function, it's basically called like a function through *require_once*. The same has been true a number of times: take small pieces of behavior or functionality and put them into small, easy-to-call functions.

So it might be easy to think that the goal is lots of individual function calls. That's partially true. What is true is that you want lots of building blocks that you can assemble into bigger useful pieces. But when it comes to using those functions, do you really want to make 20 or 30 individual calls?

Probably not.

Instead, you'll likely want to make as few function calls as you need in your scripts, at least in the ones with which the user interacts. So it's preferable to call something like this...

```
display_page($title, $javascript, $con-
tent);
```

...than this:

```
display_head($title, $javascript);

display_messages($msg);

display_content($content);

display_footer();
```

Of course, the way you get around this isn't to reverse field and throw all your code across ten functions into one. But it might be that you want one function that then calls these functions for you. That's still using building blocks, but it's reducing the number of things your top-level scripts need to do to get things working properly.

Just think about it: is it easier to remember to call *display_page*, and then have to look up the arguments to pass? Or is it easier to remember to call *display_head*, and then *display_messages*, and then *display_content*, and then... what was that next one again? Of course it's easier to make the one function call.

And that's why you want to move toward a hybrid of small functions with groupings or higher-level functions that assemble those small functions in useful ways. Your scripts should make simple calls, rather than lots of calls. And then those simple calls can do whatever is needed—even if that means calling lots of smaller functions behind the scenes.

The result should be simpler, easier-to-read code. But you'll also get a nice set of functions that you can combine in useful ways, and in a *variety* of ways.

Authentication and Authorization

There's something a little weird that happens at just about this point in your application design and creation. You have four, five, or maybe more core features in place. You have a few tables set up. You have a lot of the guts of your application built, and even though things are simple, you have a sense of where you're taking things.

And at this point, you add some new feature, like the ability to delete users. It seems like just another feature; just another user requirement to tick off the list. But wait a second…deleting users? Do you want to offer all your users that power? Of course not. That's an administrative feature.

NOTE   You might even remember that an early candidate for the name of *delete_user.php* was *admin.php* (page 325).

But what's an administrator? Obviously, in the non-digital world, it's just a person or group of people who are managing accounts, probably someone who has a few extra passwords stickied to their monitor. But in your application, there's no such thing as an administrator. Right now, anyone can hop over to *delete_user.php* and nuke poor Bill Shatner, or James Roday, or whatever other celebrities have signed up through *create_user.html* and its friends.

But it's worse than that! Because of that little red "x" appears when you go to *show_users.php*, someone you can just be viewing users, and boom, there you have it: a little red "x" that can delete data forever. And with nothing more than a confirmation box in the way, anyone can access this functionality.

So here's that moment in your application's life. You've added one piece of functionality, but it causes you to realize you need several other things...and you need them soon. Here's the quick list of problems that need to be solved for you and your users to have a sensible app:

- Viewing all users (you've got this; page 308)

- Deleting users (you've got this, with way too much freedom; page 313)

- A way to identify users on your system (you kind of have this, through *create_user. html*, from page 151, but there's no logging in right now)

- A way to indicate that a user is an administrator

- A way that users can log in and verify who they are (say, with a password)

- A way to only show certain functionality—like deleting a user—if a user is an administrator

Basically, your system needs *authentication*. Users should have to log in, and then your system should know whether a user is a certain type—like an admin. And then, based on that type, the user sees (or doesn't see) certain things. This selective display of resources—or even selectively not allowing access to a resource at all—is authentication's bed fellow, *authorization*.

So you authenticate, and let a system know who you are. And based upon who you are, you're authorized to see certain things. And of course, like so many things, these terms are often confused for each other, or even casually used interchangeably.

> **NOTE** There are people that would rather be tarred and feathered than mistake authentication for authorization, or the other way around. Then again, those people probably have separate drawers for every color of sock they have, so while it's good to know the difference, you don't have to sweat the details.

Back to authentication and authorization on your growing application: It's certainly not surprising that you need to add these features. You log in to almost every site you regularly visit online. Even YouTube and Google have logins, and of course there's Twitter and Facebook and a slew of other options. All of them use authentication to know who is who. It's time that your application joined the party.

■ Start with Basic Authentication

Authentication, like everything else, can be done simply, or with tremendous complexity. And, also like almost everything else, it's usually best to start with the basics and add in complexity as it's needed. Honestly, for a simple application, you don't need thumbprint readers and lasers scanning your users' faces. (Well, it might be fun, but it's not necessary. James Bond almost certainly isn't going to fill out your *create_user.html* form.)

Basic Authentication Using HTTP Headers

With authentication, the basics literally are basic authentication. *Basic authentication*, also known as *HTTP authentication*, is a means of getting a username and password in a web application through HTTP headers. You've already worked with headers a bit (page 181). Remember this bit of code?

```
function handle_error($user_error_message, $system_error_message) {
  header("Location: " . get_web_path(SITE_ROOT) .
         "scripts/show_error.php" .
         "?error_message={$user_error_message}" .
         "&system_error_message={$system_error_message}");
}
```

> **NOTE** *handle_error* is in *scripts/app_config.php*.

This code consists of nothing more than an HTTP header, the *Location* header, to send a redirect to the browser. You've also used the *Content-type* and *Content-length* headers in displaying an image:

```
header('Content-type: ' . $image['mime_type']);
header('Content-length: ' . $image['file_size']);
```

> **NOTE** This code was part of *show_image.php* from Chapter 9, used to display an image stored in the database (page 283).

With basic authentication, there are a couple of other HTTP headers you can send. The first doesn't have a key value, like Content-type or Location. You simply send this header:

```
HTTP/1.1 401 Unauthorized
```

When a browser gets this header, it knows that a page that's been requested requires authentication to be displayed. 401 is a special status code, one of many, that tell the browser something about the request. 200 is the code used to say "Everything is OK," for example, and 404 is the HTTP error code.

> **NOTE** You can read up on all the HTTP status codes at *w3.org/Protocols/rfc2616/rfc2616-sec10.html*.

It's one thing to tell the browser that access to a page is restricted. But that's not much help—how do you get that page *unrestricted*? The answer is to send a second header:

```
WWW-Authenticate: Basic realm="The Social Site"
```

This header lets the browser know that authentication needs to happen. Specifically, the browser should pop up a box and ask for some credentials.

The header here is *WWW-Authenticate*, and you tell it what type of authentication to require: basic. Then, you give a realm to which that authentication should be applied. In this case that's "The Social Site." So as long as different pages use this same realm, authentication to one of those pages applies to other pages in that same realm.

Basic Authentication is...Pretty Basic

To see how basic authentication works, try adding it to your *show_users.php* script. Enter these two header lines near the top of the script:

```php
<?php

require_once '../scripts/app_config.php';
require_once '../scripts/database_connection.php';
require_once '../scripts/view.php';

header('HTTP/1.1 401 Unauthorized');
header('WWW-Authenticate: Basic realm="The Social Site"');

// Build the SELECT statement
$select_users =
  "SELECT user_id, first_name, last_name, email " .
  "  FROM users";

// Remaining PHP

?>
```

> **NOTE** As usual, you might want to think about making a backup of this script, or copying all your scripts into a new *ch11/* directory. That way you've got all your older, working scripts to fall back to in case something goes wrong.

Now navigate over to *show_users.php*. You should see a nice pop-up window asking you to log in, like Figure 11-1. Well, it's not *that* nice...but it does the trick. Basic authentication, pure and simple.

> **WARNING** If your web server is using a *.htpasswd* file (popular particular on Apache web servers) to restrict certain directories from web access, you could have problems here. *.htpasswd* doesn't play very nicely with PHP's basic authentication sometimes. Your best bet would be to call your provider and simply ask them to not use any *.htpasswd* files on the directories in which you're working.

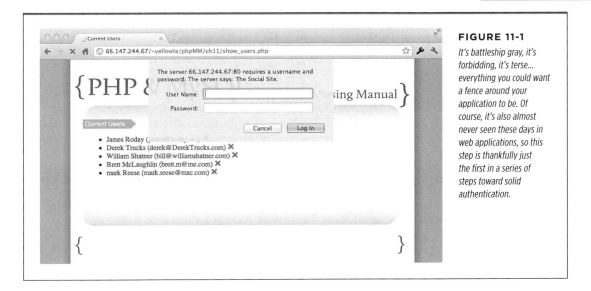

FIGURE 11-1

It's battleship gray, it's forbidding, it's terse... everything you could want a fence around your application to be. Of course, it's also almost never seen these days in web applications, so this step is thankfully just the first in a series of steps toward solid authentication.

The Worst Authentication Ever

There's a pretty gaping hole in your security, though. Navigate to *show_users.php* if you're not there already, and leave both the username and password fields blank. Then simply click "Cancel." What do you get? Figure 11-2.

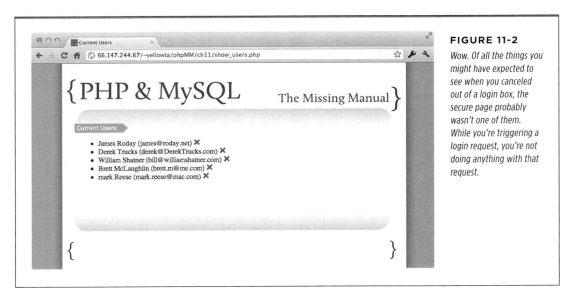

FIGURE 11-2

Wow. Of all the things you might have expected to see when you canceled out of a login box, the secure page probably wasn't one of them. While you're triggering a login request, you're not doing anything with that request.

As if that's not enough, enter in any username and password, and click Log In. There you go: Figure 11-2 again. In fact, spend some time trying to get *anything* other than the normal *show_users.php* page. You won't be able to.

Pretty poor security, isn't it? Obviously, something's not right. Canceling should *not* just take you on to the supposedly secure page. What you need to do is get the username and password entered in, check them against acceptable values, and then show the page. In every other case, the user should not get to see *show_users.php*.

Get Your User's Credentials

Unfortunately, try as you might, you'll never be able to check the username and password against any values—not without some changes to your script. That's because your code doesn't ever grab those values, let alone compare them against any other values that are OK for viewing the *show_users.php* page. There's clearly some work to do here.

Because HTTP authentication is defined in a standard way, though, it's easy for PHP to interact with users that enter their username and password into a basic authentication pop-up. In fact, PHP gives you access to both the username and password entered through two special values in a superglobal variable you've used before, *$_SERVER*:

- *$_SERVER['PHP_AUTH_USER']* gives you the user's entered username.

- *$_SERVER['PHP_AUTH_PW']* gives you the user's entered password.

> **NOTE** *$_SERVER* is used in *app_config.php* (page 256) to define the *SITE_ROOT* constant as well as in the *get_web_path* utility function.

Now, you might think your flow should go something like this:

1. At the beginning of a script, send the HTTP headers that trigger authentication.

2. Once the authentication code is complete, check *$_SERVER['PHP_AUTH_USER']* and *$_SERVER['PHP_AUTH_PW']* for values, and compare those values to some constants or a database.

3. Decide whether or not to let the user see the content your script normally outputs.

That makes a lot of sense, but turns out to be wrong...entirely wrong.

Here's what happens:

1. Your script gets called.

2. Authentication headers (that is, headers that say a user is unauthorized, and should be allowed to sign in) are sent.

3. Once the user enters in a username and password, the browser *recalls* your script, from the top once again.

So you need to check and see whether there are any available credentials *before* authentication headers are sent. And then, if there are credentials, check them against allowed values. Finally, if the credentials don't match or don't exist, *then* send the authentication headers.

Once again, then, *isset* (page 204) becomes your friend. Start with code like this:

```
if (!isset($_SERVER['PHP_AUTH_USER']) ||
    !isset($_SERVER['PHP_AUTH_PW'])) {
  header('HTTP/1.1 401 Unauthorized');
  header('WWW-Authenticate: Basic realm="The Social Site"');
}
```

But all this code does is pop up the login box if the username and password haven't previously been set. It still allows access to your page—through a couple of different ways. So you need to not just pop up a login box, but ensure that any preset usernames and passwords match an allowed set of values.

Cancel is Not a Valid Means of Authentication

Before you deal with checking usernames and passwords, though, there's something more pressing to deal with: even trickier than accepting any username and password is accepting a press of the Cancel button.

A Cancel press is easy to deal with, albeit a bit unintuitive. Here's your code right now:

```
if (!isset($_SERVER['PHP_AUTH_USER']) ||
    !isset($_SERVER['PHP_AUTH_PW'])) {
  header('HTTP/1.1 401 Unauthorized');
  header('WWW-Authenticate: Basic realm="The Social Site"');
}
```

The login box is prompted by the two calls to header:

```
header('HTTP/1.1 401 Unauthorized');
header('WWW-Authenticate: Basic realm="The Social Site"');
```

When a user clicks Cancel, your PHP continues to run, right from after the second header line:

```
header('HTTP/1.1 401 Unauthorized');
header('WWW-Authenticate: Basic realm="The Social Site"');
// This line is run if Cancel is clicked
```

So at its simplest, you could simply bail out of the script:

```
if (!isset($_SERVER['PHP_AUTH_USER']) ||
    !isset($_SERVER['PHP_AUTH_PW'])) {
  header('HTTP/1.1 401 Unauthorized');
  header('WWW-Authenticate: Basic realm="The Social Site"');
  exit("You need a valid username and password to be here. " .
      "Move along, nothing to see.");
}
```

So now if a user hits Cancel, the script runs the *exit* command—which is a lot like *die*—and bails out with an error message, as shown in Figure 11-3.

Get Your User's Credentials (Really!)

Now you can get back to seeing what your user actually supplied to the login box. Remember, the flow here isn't what you might expect. Once the user has entered in a username and password, your script is basically recalled. It's almost as if the server is giving you a free while loop, something like this:

```
while (username_and_password_are_wrong) {
  ask_for_username_and_password_again();
}
```

NOTE This script isn't running, working PHP. It's something called *pseudocode*. For more on what pseudocode is—and why it's your friend—check out the box on the next page.

Right now, you have an *if* that sees if the username and password have been set. If not, send the headers, and if Cancel is clicked, bail out.

```
if (!isset($_SERVER['PHP_AUTH_USER']) ||
    !isset($_SERVER['PHP_AUTH_PW'])) {
  header('HTTP/1.1 401 Unauthorized');
  header('WWW-Authenticate: Basic realm="The Social Site"');
  exit("You need a valid username and password to be here. " .
      "Move along, nothing to see.");
}
```

Pseudocode is Code Before You Write Code

Lots of times you'll find that you need a happy medium before writing full-on working code, syntactically accurate, debugged, ready to run; and scribbling a list down in a notebook. You want to think about the details of how things will work, without getting bogged down by minutiae.

This situation is the very type of thing for which pseudocode was designed. Like code, it typically uses the syntax of the language you're using. So you might use an *if*, a *while*, an *else*, and you'll probably throw in curly braces or angle brackets, if you're writing pseudocode that you'll eventually turn into PHP. That's why this...

```
while (username_and_password_are_wrong) {

  ask_for_username_and_password_again();

}
```

...is a great example of pseudocode that will later be PHP. But in the case above, it's not helpful to type out all the *$_SERVER* stuff, because it's long, full of little commas and apostrophes, and you already know the basic idea. So whether you're explaining to a coworker what you're doing, or just planning out your code, this is a perfectly good stand-in:

```
while (username_and_password_are_wrong) {
```

In your head, you may be translating that to something like this:

```
if (($_SERVER['PHP_AUTH_USER'] !=
      VALID_USERNAME) ||
    ($_SERVER['PHP_AUTH_PW'] !=
      VALID_PASSWORD)) {
```

And then what will you do once you make that determination? Something...you're not sure what yet. You know basically what has to happen, but the details are still up in the air. That leaves you with this:

```
ask_for_username_and_password_again();
```

It's clear, it's understandable, but it's not bogged down by intricacy. It's pseudocode. It's great for getting an idea going, or communicating about code. It's also great in a situation like this, where something tells you the way you're doing things might need to change. And if change is coming, the less work you put into a solution that isn't permanent, the better.

In an *else* part of this script—yet to be written—you could check the username and password against the acceptable values. If they match, go on and display the output from *show_users.php*. If not...well, you actually want to re-send the headers that cause the browser to prompt the user to log in again. So you want something like this:

```
if (!isset($_SERVER['PHP_AUTH_USER']) ||
    !isset($_SERVER['PHP_AUTH_PW'])) {
  header('HTTP/1.1 401 Unauthorized');
  header('WWW-Authenticate: Basic realm="The Social Site"');
  exit("You need a valid username and password to be here. " .
      "Move along, nothing to see.");
} else {
  if (($_SERVER['PHP_AUTH_USER'] != VALID_USERNAME) ||
      ($_SERVER['PHP_AUTH_PW'] != VALID_PASSWORD)) {
    header('HTTP/1.1 401 Unauthorized');
    header('WWW-Authenticate: Basic realm="The Social Site"');
```

```
        exit("You need a valid username and password to be here. " .
            "Move along, nothing to see.");
    }
}
```

Technically, the *if* block is supplying an incorrect message to *exit*. That *exit* deals with the case where the user hit Cancel, rather than entering a wrong username and password. As a rule, though, you want to provide minimal information to users on security failures, so a generic "one size fits all" message is the better approach here.

Given that, you can consolidate things a bit. Whether the user has never attempted to log in, or incorrectly entered their username or password, the script needs to send HTTP headers to force authentication. It's only if the user has entered information, and it matches the appropriate values, that the rest of the page's action should be taken, and the output should be displayed. So what you want is this:

```
if (!isset($_SERVER['PHP_AUTH_USER']) ||
    !isset($_SERVER['PHP_AUTH_PW']) ||
    ($_SERVER['PHP_AUTH_USER'] != VALID_USERNAME) ||
    ($_SERVER['PHP_AUTH_PW'] != VALID_PASSWORD)) {
  header('HTTP/1.1 401 Unauthorized');
  header('WWW-Authenticate: Basic realm="The Social Site"');
  exit("You need a valid username and password to be here. " .
      "Move along, nothing to see.");
}
```

NOTE Go ahead and add this code to your version of *show_users.php*.

So now go up to the top of *show_users.php*—make sure it's before your new *if* statement—and add in a few new constants:

```
<?php

require_once '../scripts/app_config.php';
require_once '../scripts/database_connection.php';
require_once '../scripts/view.php';

define(VALID_USERNAME, "admin");
define(VALID_PASSWORD, "super_secret");

if (!isset($_SERVER['PHP_AUTH_USER']) ||
    !isset($_SERVER['PHP_AUTH_PW']) ||
    ($_SERVER['PHP_AUTH_USER'] != VALID_USERNAME) ||
    ($_SERVER['PHP_AUTH_PW'] != VALID_PASSWORD)) {
  header('HTTP/1.1 401 Unauthorized');
  header('WWW-Authenticate: Basic realm="The Social Site"');
  exit("You need a valid username and password to be here. " .
```

```
            "Move along, nothing to see.");
    }
```

Try visiting *show_users.php* again, and entering in "admin" and "super_secret" as the username and password (as in Figure 11-4. You should be greeted with the normal *show_users.php* view (Figure 11-5). Otherwise, you'll just get the authentication pop-up over and over (as shown back in Figure 11-1).

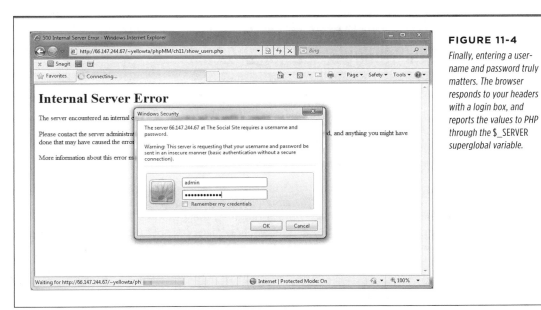

FIGURE 11-4

Finally, entering a username and password truly matters. The browser responds to your headers with a login box, and reports the values to PHP through the $_SERVER superglobal variable.

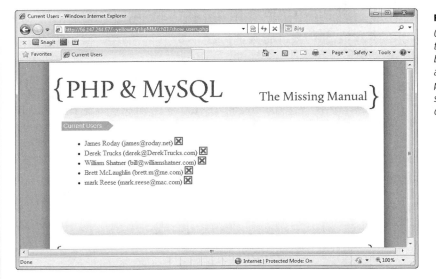

FIGURE 11-5

Once you've made it through security, you're back to seeing users again. And that's the point: authentication is separate from the core content of your pages.

Abstracting What's the Same

So here you are again, with some code in *show_users.php* that probably doesn't belong in *show_users.php*. Why is that? Because the same authorization and authentication you have in *show_users.php* belongs in every other script that should require logging in—like *delete_user.php*. You don't want to write that code over and over; it becomes just like other repeated code you now have in *app_config.php* and *database_connection.php*: you should take it out of individual scripts and place it someplace where all your scripts can use it.

Another Utility Script: *authorize.php*

Fire up your editor once more, and this time create *authorize.php*. You can start by adding in that valid username/password combination:

```php
<?php

define(VALID_USERNAME, "admin");
define(VALID_PASSWORD, "super_secret");

?>
```

At this point you'd usually write a function, maybe *authorize* or *get_credentials* or something like that. But is that really what you want? Do you want to have to *require_once authorize.php*, and then explicitly call a function?

More likely, you want to identify scripts that require authorization with a single line:

```php
require_once "../scripts/authorize.php;"
```

Then, ideally, the authorization would all just magically happen for you.

FREQUENTLY ASKED QUESTION

Isn't an Infinite Number of Login Attempts Bad?

Yes. Absolutely. And that's exactly what you're providing in *show_users.php* right now: the opportunity to try, over and over and over, to get a valid username and password. Truth be told, the sample code and patterns you'll see all over the Web for using basic authentication look just like what you've got in *show_users.php*.

There certainly are ways to get around this problem, but they're not as easy as you might wish. Since the browser is making multiple requests to your script, you'd have to figure out a way to pass the number of requests that have been made to your script...from your script. Yeah, it gets a little tricky.

There are ways to detect multiple requests, and you'll learn about them (although for a much better purpose) in the next chapter on sessions. For now, realize that the basic authentication approach is temporary anyway, and all this code is a starting point, not a stopping point.

Given that, then, you don't want a function that has to be called. You just want some PHP code, in the main part of *authorize.php*. That way, by requiring *authorize.php*, that code runs, handles authentication, and your script doesn't have to do anything to get the benefits of authentication and authorization.

In a lot of ways, authorization here is like having JavaScript inside a set of *<script>* tags with no function:

```
<script type="text/javascript">
  dashboard_alert("#hits_count_dialog");
  $("#hits_count_dialog").dialog("open");
  query_results_tables();
</script>
```

As soon as a browser hits that JavaScript, it runs it. The same is true of PHP outside of a function. So you can drop your authorization code right into *authorize.php*:

```
<?php

define(VALID_USERNAME, "admin");
define(VALID_PASSWORD, "super_secret");

if (!isset($_SERVER['PHP_AUTH_USER']) ||
    !isset($_SERVER['PHP_AUTH_PW']) ||
    ($_SERVER['PHP_AUTH_USER'] != VALID_USERNAME) ||
    ($_SERVER['PHP_AUTH_PW'] != VALID_PASSWORD)) {
  header('HTTP/1.1 401 Unauthorized');
  header('WWW-Authenticate: Basic realm="The Social Site"');
  exit("You need a valid username and password to be here. " .
      "Move along, nothing to see.");
}

?>
```

Now, any script that has a *require_once* for *authorize.php* will cause *authorize.php* to be processed, which in turn will run the authorization code. That, in turn, will ensure that either users are logged in, or are forced to log in. So things look pretty nice.

Go ahead and remove this code from *show_users.php* and add in a *require_once* for *authorize.php*:

```
<?php

require_once '../scripts/app_config.php';
require_once '../scripts/authorize.php';
require_once '../scripts/database_connection.php';
require_once '../scripts/view.php';
```

```
// Authorization code is no longer in this script

// Build the SELECT statement
$select_users =
  "SELECT user_id, first_name, last_name, email " .
  "  FROM users";

// and so on...
?>
```

Now you can hit *show_users.php* again and get a nice login box. But that's not all this change buys you. Add a similar line into *delete_user.php*:

```
<?php

require_once '../scripts/app_config.php';
require_once '../scripts/authorize.php';
require_once '../scripts/database_connection.php';

// and so on...
```

Now, close out your browser, so any passwords are lost. Then, re-open your browser and navigate directly to *delete_user.php*. You'll be greeted with a login box (see Figure 11-6). What's significant about this? Most obviously, it took a single line of PHP to add security to another page.

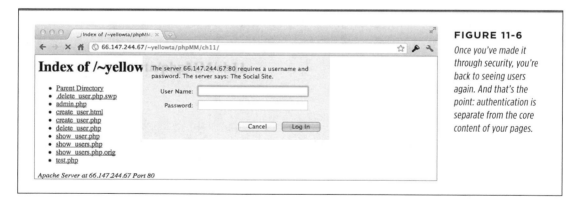

FIGURE 11-6

Once you've made it through security, you're back to seeing users again. And that's the point: authentication is separate from the core content of your pages.

But there's more! If you've logged in, close your browser again and head over to *show_users.php*. As you'd expect, you'll have to login. Do so, and then click the Delete icon on one of your users. This will take you to *delete_user.php*, and the PHP in *authorize.php* will be triggered. But because you've already logged in to the realm identified as "The Social Site", you're not prompted to login again. Remember your code that specifies a realm:

```
header('WWW-Authenticate: Basic realm="The Social Site"');
```

Any page that uses this realm will effectively "share" credentials with other pages in the same realm. So since you logged in to access *show_users.php*, and that realm is identical to the realm for *delete_user.php*, your delete request goes through without a problem (Figure 11-7 shows the result—no login box in sight).

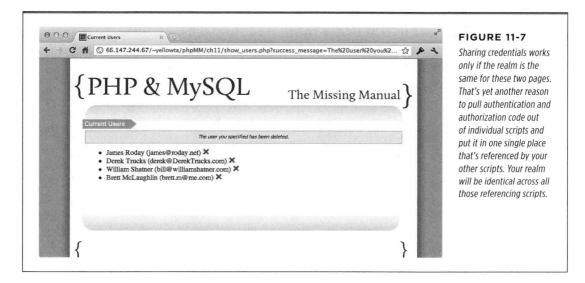

FIGURE 11-7

Sharing credentials works only if the realm is the same for these two pages. That's yet another reason to pull authentication and authorization code out of individual scripts and put it in one single place that's referenced by your other scripts. Your realm will be identical across all those referencing scripts.

There's still a pretty glaring problem, though...

Passwords Don't Belong in PHP Scripts

At this point, it's easy to forget that behind every good script lies a great database. (Or something like that.) It's simply a horrible idea to have a PHP script—even if it's a utility script like *app_config.php* or *authorize.php*—that has a few constants defining allowable usernames and passwords. That's very much the job of a database.

Databases are typically more difficult to access than your scripts, because your scripts are to some degree Web-accessible. Your database, on the other hand, is generally at least a layer further removed from the typical Web user. Additionally, your database and SQL require structural knowledge to be very useful. Scripts are just files that can be browsed, and often the information in those files is just text. The list could go on, but suffice it to say that a database is a safer place for passwords than *authorize.php*.

> **NOTE** You can do a few things to make your scripts—especially utility ones—less accessible from the Web. And you can certainly make bad decisions that make your database *more* accessible from the Web. But in their default states, scripts are meant to be accessed by a browser, and raw database columns and rows aren't, apart from a healthy authentication system in place by default.

And then there's yet another key reason to get your passwords into a database: you already are storing user information! So you can connect that information to a password by adding a column. And, as you'll see soon, groups of users aren't far away, either. So before you get too comfortable, you need to dig back into MySQL and improve that authentication situation.

Updating the *users* Table

The first thing you need to do is update *users*. It's been a while, so here's what you should have at this point:

```
mysql> describe users;
+----------------+--------------+------+-----+---------+----------------+
| Field          | Type         | Null | Key | Default | Extra          |
+----------------+--------------+------+-----+---------+----------------+
| user_id        | int(11)      | NO   | PRI | NULL    | auto_increment |
| first_name     | varchar(20)  | NO   |     |         |                |
| last_name      | varchar(30)  | NO   |     |         |                |
| email          | varchar(50)  | NO   |     |         |                |
| facebook_url   | varchar(100) | YES  |     | NULL    |                |
| twitter_handle | varchar(20)  | YES  |     | NULL    |                |
| bio            | text         | YES  |     | NULL    |                |
| user_pic_path  | text         | YES  |     | NULL    |                |
+----------------+--------------+------+-----+---------+----------------+
8 rows in set (0.02 sec)
```

There's nothing wrong here, but there are some omissions: most notably a username and a password. Those are the two essential pieces of information that your basic authentication requires.

Add both columns to your table:

```
mysql> ALTER TABLE users
    ->         ADD username VARCHAR(32) NOT NULL
    ->      AFTER user_id,
    ->         ADD password VARCHAR(16) NOT NULL
    ->      AFTER username;
```

NOTE The *AFTER* keyword tells MySQL exactly where to add a column. Using *AFTER* helps avoid important columns—and username and password are certainly important columns—from getting stuck at the end of a table's structure. You can leave it off, but it tends to make for more organized tables, especially when you're using *DESCRIBE*.

You should make sure these changes are in place now:

```
mysql> describe users;
+----------------+--------------+------+-----+---------+----------------+
| Field          | Type         | Null | Key | Default | Extra          |
+----------------+--------------+------+-----+---------+----------------+
| user_id        | int(11)      | NO   | PRI | NULL    | auto_increment |
| username       | varchar(32)  | NO   |     | NULL    |                |
| password       | varchar(16)  | NO   |     | NULL    |                |
| first_name     | varchar(20)  | NO   |     |         |                |
| last_name      | varchar(30)  | NO   |     |         |                |
| email          | varchar(50)  | NO   |     |         |                |
| facebook_url   | varchar(100) | YES  |     | NULL    |                |
| twitter_handle | varchar(20)  | YES  |     | NULL    |                |
| bio            | text         | YES  |     | NULL    |                |
| user_pic_path  | text         | YES  |     | NULL    |                |
+----------------+--------------+------+-----+---------+----------------+
10 rows in set (0.03 sec)
```

Deal with Newly Invalid Data

As was the case when you added columns before, you now actually have a table full of invalid rows. Since both username and password are required (*NOT NULL*), and none of the existing rows have values in those columns, all your table's rows are in violation of that table's rules.

You can fix the invalid rows with some more SQL. So, for example, to update James Roday, you'd use something like this:

```
mysql> UPDATE users
    ->    SET username = "jroday",
    ->        password = "psych_rules"
    ->  WHERE user_id = 45;
```

You can confirm these changes were made, as well:

```
mysql> SELECT user_id, username, password, first_name, last_name
    ->    FROM users
    ->   WHERE user_id = 45;
+---------+----------+-------------+------------+-----------+
| user_id | username | password    | first_name | last_name |
+---------+----------+-------------+------------+-----------+
|      45 | jroday   | psych_rules | James      | Roday     |
+---------+----------+-------------+------------+-----------+
1 row in set (0.00 sec)
```

You should make similar changes to your own *users* table so that all the users you've added have a username and password.

Isn't a Non-Email Username So 2006?

It seems like every time you turn around, a new social website is popping up...a site that you simply *must* join. And more and more of those sites are using email addresses as your login. There's a lot to like about this approach, too.

- Most people remember their email address more readily than one of 50 different usernames floating around.

- Email addresses like *tommy.n@dbc.org* are a lot more readable (and typeable) than a username like *tn1954a*.

- It's less information to store in your database.

So if that's the way the username-wind is blowing, why create a username column in users? Why not just use the email address?

First, a lot of people have just as many email addresses as they have usernames these days. With Gmail, Apple's MobileMe (now iCloud), at least one business email, and perhaps a personal domain or two, it can be pretty ridiculous.

Second, plenty of people don't like using their emails as their username. A username seems more anonymous, while an email is an actual way to get something into your inbox. It might seem odd, but lots of people are fine with supplying an email as part of sign-up, but they don't want to be reminded that tons of sites have that piece of information. Typing it into a login box isn't the greatest way to avoid that reminder.

And perhaps most important, if an email is the username, how do you retrieve a user's password? Typically, with a username system, you require a user to supply their username when a password is lost as some sort of verification. When the user's email *is* their username, what do you request for verification?

Even though there's nothing horribly wrong with using an email address as a username, it's still probably best to require a username. Besides, with fantastic programs like 1Password (*www.agilebits.com/products/1Password*), it's not that hard to manage multiple logins anymore. (And seriously, although it might seem a bit pricey at $59.99, go buy 1Password *today*. It's a Web-life changer.)

You Need to Get an Initial Username and Password

So now you've got to go back...way back. Remember *create_user.html*? That was the rather simple HTML form that got you the user's initial information (page 18). But it needs some real improvement: a username and password field, to start.

Here's a significantly updated version of *create_user.html*, which adds—among a lot of other things—a field to get a username and two fields that combine to get a password from new users.

```
<html>
 <head>
  <link href="../css/phpMM.css" rel="stylesheet" type="text/css" />
  <link href="../css/jquery.validate.password.css" rel="stylesheet"
type="text/css" />
```

```
<script type="text/javascript" src="../js/jquery.js"></script>
<script type="text/javascript" src="../js/jquery.validate.js"></script>
<script type="text/javascript" src="../js/jquery.validate.password.js">
</script>

<script type="text/javascript">
  $(document).ready(function() {
    $("#signup_form").validate({
      rules: {
        password: {
          minlength: 6
        },
        confirm_password: {
          minlength: 6,
          equalTo: "#password"
        }
      },
      messages: {
        password: {
          minlength: "Passwords must be at least 6 characters"
        },
        confirm_password: {
          minlength: "Passwords must be at least 6 characters",
          equalTo: "Your passwords do not match."
        }
      }
    });
  });
</script>
</head>

<body>
 <div id="header"><h1>PHP & MySQL: The Missing Manual</h1></div>
 <div id="example">User Signup</div>
 <div id="content">
   <h1>Join the Missing Manual (Digital) Social Club</h1>
   <p>Please enter your online connections below:</p>
   <form id="signup_form" action="create_user.php"
         method="POST" enctype="multipart/form-data">
     <fieldset>
       <label for="first_name">First Name:</label>
       <input type="text" name="first_name" size="20" class="required" />
       <br />
```

```html
      <label for="last_name">Last Name:</label>
      <input type="text" name="last_name" size="20" class="required" />
      <br />
      <label for="username">Username:</label>
      <input type="text" name="username" size="20" class="required" />
      <br />
      <label for="password">Password:</label>
      <input type="password" id="password" name="password"
             size="20" class="required password" />
      <div class="password-meter">
        <div class="password-meter-message"> </div>
        <div class="password-meter-bg">
          <div class="password-meter-bar"></div>
        </div>
      </div>
      <br />
      <label for="confirm_password">Confirm Password:</label>
      <input type="password" id="confirm_password" name="confirm_password"
             size="20" class="required" /><br />
      <label for="email">E-Mail Address:</label>
      <input type="text" name="email" size="30" class="required email" />
      <br />
      <label for="facebook_url">Facebook URL:</label>
      <input type="text" name="facebook_url" size="50" class="url" /><br />
      <label for="twitter_handle">Twitter Handle:</label>
      <input type="text" name="twitter_handle" size="20" /><br />
      <input type="hidden" name="MAX_FILE_SIZE" value="2000000" />
      <label for="user_pic">Upload a picture:</label>
      <input type="file" name="user_pic" size="30" /><br />
      <label for="bio">Bio:</label>
      <textarea name="bio" cols="40" rows="10"></textarea>
    </fieldset>
    <br />
    <fieldset class="center">
      <input type="submit" value="Join the Club" />
      <input type="reset" value="Clear and Restart" />
    </fieldset>
  </form>
</div>

<div id="footer"></div>
</body>
</html>
```

In addition to the two new fields, this version of the form adds in jQuery, available from *www.jquery.com*. jQuery is a free, downloadable JavaScript library that makes almost everything in JavaScript a lot easier. In addition to the core jQuery library, there are two jQuery plug-ins: one for general validation and another specifically for password validation. You can download both of these plug-ins from *www.jquery. bassistance.de.*

NOTE If you're completely new to jQuery, you should pick up *JavaScript & jQuery: The Missing Manual.* You'll get up to speed on how to use jQuery, and discover a whole host of reasons—besides the nifty validation plug-ins now used by *create_user.html*—that it's worth your time to learn.

FIGURE 11-8

The new version of create_user.html looks largely the same. It does add a password strength bar, although that's not apparent until the user tries to enter a password. Most importantly, this form adds a username and two places to enter a password: an initial entry and a place to confirm that entry. Make sure these fields are the "password" type to hide the user's typing, too.

Save this updated version of *create_user.html* and check it out. The initial page looks the same (see Figure 11-8), but now you get validation of most of the form fields (shown in Figure 11-9) and a nice password strength indicator, too (check out Figure 11-10).

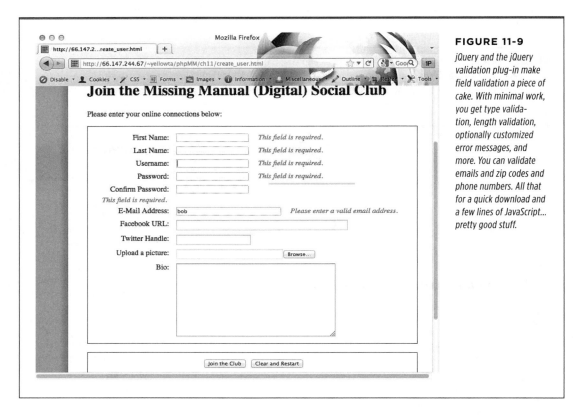

FIGURE 11-9

jQuery and the jQuery validation plug-in make field validation a piece of cake. With minimal work, you get type validation, length validation, optionally customized error messages, and more. You can validate emails and zip codes and phone numbers. All that for a quick download and a few lines of JavaScript... pretty good stuff.

Now you're getting the right information from your users. It's time to update your PHP to do something with this.

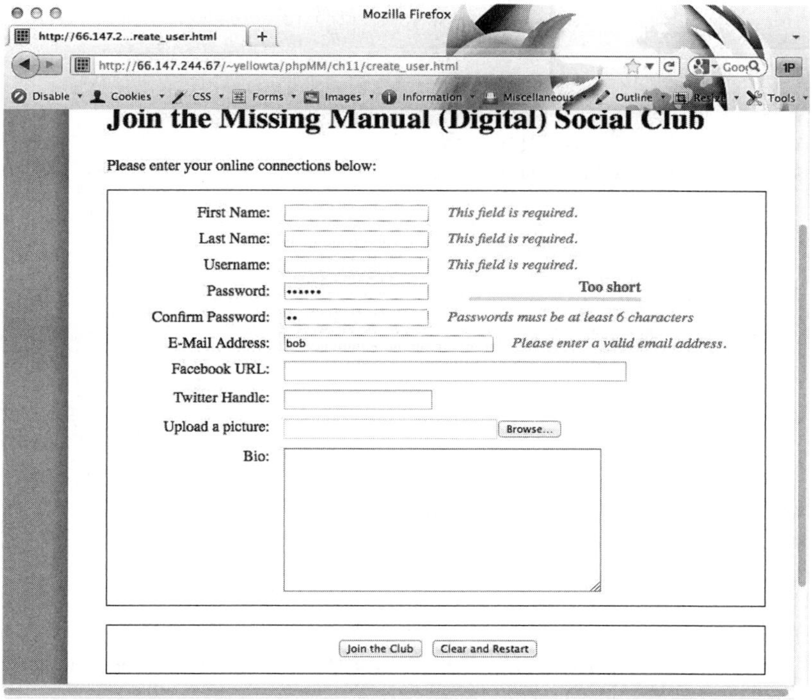

FIGURE 11-10

The password validator is an add-on for the jQuery validation plug-in, and adds a strength indicator that requires "strong" passwords. It's a nice feature, and best of all, doesn't increase your work load at all. You get all this "for free" before data ever makes it to your PHP scripts.

Inserting the User's Username and Password

Now you can update *create_user.php* as well. This update is simple, and certainly requires a lot less work, although the result of these changes is pretty significant.

```php
<?php

require_once '../scripts/app_config.php';
require_once '../scripts/database_connection.php';

$upload_dir = SITE_ROOT . "uploads/profile_pics/";
$image_fieldname = "user_pic";
```

```php
// Potential PHP upload errors
$php_errors = array(1 => 'Maximum file size in php.ini exceeded',
                     2 => 'Maximum file size in HTML form exceeded',
                     3 => 'Only part of the file was uploaded',
                     4 => 'No file was selected to upload.');

$first_name = trim($_REQUEST['first_name']);
$last_name = trim($_REQUEST['last_name']);
$username = trim($_REQUEST['username']);
$password = trim($_REQUEST['password']);
$email = trim($_REQUEST['email']);
$bio = trim($_REQUEST['bio']);
$facebook_url = str_replace("facebook.org", "facebook.com", trim($_
REQUEST['facebook_url']));
$position = strpos($facebook_url, "facebook.com");
if ($position === false) {
  $facebook_url = "http://www.facebook.com/" . $facebook_url;
}

$twitter_handle = trim($_REQUEST['twitter_handle']);
$twitter_url = "http://www.twitter.com/";
$position = strpos($twitter_handle, "@");
if ($position === false) {
  $twitter_url = $twitter_url . $twitter_handle;
} else {
  $twitter_url = $twitter_url . substr($twitter_handle, $position + 1);
}

// Make sure we didn't have an error uploading the image
($_FILES[$image_fieldname]['error'] == 0)
  or handle_error("the server couldn't upload the image you selected.",
                  $php_errors[$_FILES[$image_fieldname]['error']]);

// Is this file the result of a valid upload?
@is_uploaded_file($_FILES[$image_fieldname]['tmp_name'])
  or handle_error("you were trying to do something naughty. Shame on you!",
                  "Uploaded request: file named '{$_FILES[$image_fieldname]
['tmp_name']}'");

// Is this actually an image?
@getimagesize($_FILES[$image_fieldname]['tmp_name'])
  or handle_error("you selected a file for your picture that isn't an image.",
                  "{$_FILES[$image_fieldname]['tmp_name']} isn't a valid image
file.");
```

```
// Name the file uniquely
$now = time();
while (file_exists($upload_filename = $upload_dir . $now .
                                      '-' .
                             $_FILES[$image_fieldname]['name'])) {
    $now++;
}

// Finally, move the file to its permanent location
@move_uploaded_file($_FILES[$image_fieldname]['tmp_name'],
                    $upload_filename)
  or handle_error(
     "we had a problem saving your image to its permanent location.",
     "permissions or related error moving file to {$upload_filename}");

$insert_sql = sprintf("INSERT INTO users " .
                      "(first_name, last_name, username, " .
                      "password, email, " .
                      "bio, facebook_url, twitter_handle, " .
                      "user_pic_path) " .
                    "VALUES ('%s', '%s', '%s', '%s', '%s',
                         '%s', '%s', '%s', '%s');",
                    mysql_real_escape_string($first_name),
                    mysql_real_escape_string($last_name),
                    mysql_real_escape_string($username),
                    mysql_real_escape_string($password),
                    mysql_real_escape_string($email),
                    mysql_real_escape_string($bio),
                    mysql_real_escape_string($facebook_url),
                    mysql_real_escape_string($twitter_handle),
                    mysql_real_escape_string($upload_filename));

// Insert the user into the database
mysql_query($insert_sql);

// Redirect the user to the page that displays user information
header("Location: show_user.php?user_id=" . mysql_insert_id());
?>
```

NOTE Even though only a few lines have changed, this is a good chance for you to check your current version of *create_user.php* (along with *create_user.html*). Make sure they're current, especially since all the changes from Chapters 9 and 10 related to image handling. If you feel your code is hopelessly out-of-date, you can always re-download these scripts from the Missing CD page (page xvii).

As usual, try entering some sample data, and make sure you get something like Figure 11-11 as a validation that all your changes work. Also, make sure that you do not add *authorize.php* to your scripts list of *require_once* statements. You can hardly require users to log in to the form by which they tell your application about the username and password they want to use for those logins.

Shouldn't *create_user.php* Check the Requested Username?

Yes. It's a pretty big issue that in the current version of *create_user.php*, users are inserted into the database without checking the uniqueness of their usernames. Certainly, you could enforce that at the database level, but then you'd just get a nasty error.

In its simplest form, you could do a *SELECT* on the desired username, and if any users are returned, redirect the user to an error page using *handle_error*. That's pretty primitive, though. It completely shuts down any flow, and the user—if they don't bail from your application completely—will have to enter all their information into the user sign-up form again.

A better approach would be to convert *create_user.html* into a script, or even roll it into the current version of *create_user.php*. In either case, if the username is already taken, the user should be redirect back to the sign-up form, with all their previous information filled in, and a message should tell them

to try another password. Then, if you want to move into the deep end of the pool, do everything above, but do it with Ajax so that the sign-up page never reload.

So where's the code for creating this message? It's in your head and at your fingertips. At this stage of your PHP journey, you're ready to increasingly tackle problems like this yourself. Use a book or the Web as a resource for new techniques—like authentication in this chapter or sessions in Chapter 12—but you're plenty capable of working out new uses for things you already know on your own.

In fact, tweet a link to your solution to preventing multiple usernames to *@missingmanuals* on Twitter or post it on the Missing Manuals Facebook page at *www.facebook.com/MissingManuals*. Free books, videos, and swag are always available for clever and elegant solutions.

Connect *authorize.php* to Your users Table

At this point, there's just one glaring hole to plug: *authorize.php*. Right now, the only username and password accepted is this rather silly bit of constant work:

```
define(VALID_USERNAME, "admin");
define(VALID_PASSWORD, "super_secret");
```

But now *authorize.php* has a *users* table from which to pull users' usernames and passwords.

Fortunately, connecting *authorize.php* to *users* isn't very hard. In fact, fixing up *authorize.php* involves only stringing together things you've already done. First, remove those two constants, and add in *require_once* for *database_connection.php*, which you'll need for interacting with the *users* table.

```
<?php

require_once 'database_connection.php';
```

```
// define(VALID_USERNAME, "admin");          DELETE THIS LINE
// define(VALID_PASSWORD, "super_secret");   DELETE THIS LINE

if (!isset($_SERVER['PHP_AUTH_USER']) ||
    !isset($_SERVER['PHP_AUTH_PW']) ||
    ($_SERVER['PHP_AUTH_USER'] != VALID_USERNAME) ||
    ($_SERVER['PHP_AUTH_PW'] != VALID_PASSWORD)) {
  header('HTTP/1.1 401 Unauthorized');
  header('WWW-Authenticate: Basic realm="The Social Site"');
  exit("You need a valid username and password to be here. " .
      "Move along, nothing to see.");
}

?>
```

Now, that big burly *if* needs to be trimmed some. The first portion still works; if the *$_SERVER* superglobal has no value for *PHP_AUTH_USER* or *PHP_AUTH_PW*, then headers should still be sent to the browser instructing it to pop up a login box. But now, there's no *VALID_USERNAME* or *VALID_PASSWORD* constant to which the user's values should be compared. So that part of the *if* has to go. Here's what should be left:

```
if (!isset($_SERVER['PHP_AUTH_USER']) ||
    !isset($_SERVER['PHP_AUTH_PW'])) {
  header('HTTP/1.1 401 Unauthorized');
  header('WWW-Authenticate: Basic realm="The Social Site"');
  exit("You need a valid username and password to be here. " .
      "Move along, nothing to see.");
}
```

NOTE Everything after the *if* is effectively an *else*, even though there's no *else* keyword. If the body of the *if* executes, it will call *exit*, ending the script. So it's only if there is a value for *PHP_AUTH_USER* and *PHP_AUTH_PW* in *$_SERVER* that the rest of the script runs.

The next thing the script needs to do is get anything the user entered—and if the script gets here, then the user *did* enter something—and compare it to values in the database. But that's something you've done a number of times. It's just more *sprintf* and *mysql_real_escape_string*, both of which you've used a ton:

```
<?php

require_once 'database_connection.php';

if (!isset($_SERVER['PHP_AUTH_USER']) ||
    !isset($_SERVER['PHP_AUTH_PW'])) {
  header('HTTP/1.1 401 Unauthorized');
  header('WWW-Authenticate: Basic realm="The Social Site"');
```

```
    exit("You need a valid username and password to be here. " .
        "Move along, nothing to see.");
}

// Look up the user-provided credentials
$query = sprintf("SELECT user_id, username FROM users " .
                " WHERE username = '%s' AND " .
                "        password = '%s';",
            mysql_real_escape_string(trim($_SERVER['PHP_AUTH_USER'])),
            mysql_real_escape_string(trim($_SERVER['PHP_AUTH_PW'])));

$results = mysql_query($query);

?>
```

There's nothing particularly new here. And you know how to get the results. But this time, before worrying about the actual values from the response, the biggest concern is seeing if there are any results. If a row matches the username and password provided, then the user is legitimate. (Or, at a minimum, they've borrowed someone else's credentials. And "borrowed" is being used pretty loosely there.)

So the first thing to do is to see if there are any results. If not, then the script has reached the same place as the earlier version, when the username and password weren't valid. That means sending those headers again:

```
if (mysql_num_rows($results) == 1) {
  // Everything's ok! Let this user through
} else {
  header('HTTP/1.1 401 Unauthorized');
  header('WWW-Authenticate: Basic realm="The Social Site"');
  exit("You need a valid username and password to be here. " .
      "Move along, nothing to see.");
}
```

> **NOTE**   Move to the head of the class if you're bothered that the code that sends these headers here is identical to the code earlier in the script (page 379). Before moving on, go ahead and create a function that outputs those headers, takes in a message to pass to *exit*, and then call that function twice in *authorize.php*.

Now there's just one more thing to do, and it's a bit of a nicety. Since the user's just logged in, go ahead and let any script that calls *authorize.php* have access to the user that's just logged in:

```
if (mysql_num_rows($results) == 1) {
  $result = mysql_fetch_array($results);
  $current_user_id = $result['user_id'];
  $current_username = $result['username'];
```

```php
  } else {
    header('HTTP/1.1 401 Unauthorized');
    header('WWW-Authenticate: Basic realm="The Social Site"');
    exit("You need a valid username and password to be here. " .
        "Move along, nothing to see.");
  }
```

So now the entire script, new and certainly improved, looks like this:

```php
<?php

require_once 'database_connection.php';

if (!isset($_SERVER['PHP_AUTH_USER']) ||
    !isset($_SERVER['PHP_AUTH_PW'])) {
  header('HTTP/1.1 401 Unauthorized');
  header('WWW-Authenticate: Basic realm="The Social Site"');
  exit("You need a valid username and password to be here. " .
      "Move along, nothing to see.");
}

// Look up the user-provided credentials
$query = sprintf("SELECT user_id, username FROM users " .
                 " WHERE username = '%s' AND " .
                 "       password = '%s';",
             mysql_real_escape_string(trim($_SERVER['PHP_AUTH_USER'])),
             mysql_real_escape_string(trim($_SERVER['PHP_AUTH_PW'])));

$results = mysql_query($query);

if (mysql_num_rows($results) == 1) {
  $result = mysql_fetch_array($results);
  $current_user_id = $result['user_id'];
  $current_username = $result['username'];
} else {
  header('HTTP/1.1 401 Unauthorized');
  header('WWW-Authenticate: Basic realm="The Social Site"');
  exit("You need a valid username and password to be here. " .
      "Move along, nothing to see.");
}

?>
```

Test it out. Create a user (or add a username and password to an existing user in your database), and then close and re-open your browser to reset any saved credentials. Hit *show_users.php* or any other page in which you've required *authorize.*

php. You should get a login box, be able to enter in database values, and see the page you requested.

Passwords Create Security, But Should Be Secure

With your new database-driven login facility, there are lots of things that are new and possible. First and foremost, you could create groups in the database, and allow users access to certain parts of your application based on their group membership. So instead of letting just anyone access *show_users.php*, you only want users that are members of an admin group.

But before you do all that, take a second look at one of your recent SQL statements and the results:

```
mysql> SELECT user_id, username, password, first_name, last_name
    ->    FROM users
    ->  WHERE user_id = 45;
+---------+----------+-------------+------------+-----------+
| user_id | username | password    | first_name | last_name |
+---------+----------+-------------+------------+-----------+
|      45 | jroday   | psych_rules | James      | Roday     |
+---------+----------+-------------+------------+-----------+
1 row in set (0.00 sec)
```

Anything odd there? (Other than James Roday's lousy choice of password...sure, *Psych* is fantastic, but it's not exactly a hard-to-crack passcode.)

All the same, the more glaring issue is that the password just sits there in the database. It's plain old text. And even if you're new to the world of authentication and authorization, you probably have heard the term encryption. *Encryption* is simply taking a piece of information—usually something secure like a password—and making it unreadable for the normal mortal. The idea is that other than the user who "owns" a password, nobody—even you, the all-wise all-knowing programmer—should see a user's password in normal text.

So what you need is a means of encrypting that password into something unreadable. And, you know what's coming: PHP has a function for that.

Encrypt Text with the *crypt* Function

First, you've got to convert the password into something that's non-readable. You can do that using PHP's crypt function. *crypt* takes a string (and an optional second parameter you'll need shortly), and produces what looks a bit like gibberish:

```
$encrypted_password = crypt($password);
```

To see this in action, make the following change to *create_user.php*:

```
$insert_sql = sprintf("INSERT INTO users " .
                      "(first_name, last_name, username, " .
                      "password, email, " .
                      "bio, facebook_url, twitter_handle, " .
                      "user_pic_path) " .
              "VALUES ('%s', '%s', '%s', '%s', '%s',
                      '%s', '%s', '%s', '%s');",
              mysql_real_escape_string($first_name),
              mysql_real_escape_string($last_name),
              mysql_real_escape_string($username),
              mysql_real_escape_string(crypt($password)),
              mysql_real_escape_string($email),
              mysql_real_escape_string($bio),
              mysql_real_escape_string($facebook_url),
              mysql_real_escape_string($twitter_handle),
              mysql_real_escape_string($upload_filename));
```

Now create a new user, allow *create_user.php* to save that user, and then check out that user in your *users* table:

```
mysql> SELECT user_id, username, password, last_name
    ->    FROM users
    ->  WHERE user_id = 51;
+---------+----------+------------------+-----------+
| user_id | username | password         | last_name |
+---------+----------+------------------+-----------+
|      51 | traugott | $1$qzifqLu4$0C88 | Traugott  |
+---------+----------+------------------+-----------+
1 row in set (0.00 sec)
```

That's quite an improvement. In fact, you should probably increase the size of the password field, as crypt adds a good bit of length to the originally entered password.

```
ALTER TABLE users
    CHANGE password
        password VARCHAR(50) NOT NULL;
```

NOTE   That doubled "password" field name is intentional. When you're changing a column, you first give the original name of the column. Then, you provide the new column name, the new column type, and any modifiers (like *NOT NULL*). In this instance, since the original name and new name are identical, you simply double "password."

Now, that gets the password *into* your database, but what about getting it out?

crypt is One-Way Encryption

crypt, by definition, is one-way encryption. That means that once a password has been encrypted, it can't be unencrypted. While that presents you some problems as a programmer, it's a good thing for your users. It means that even the admins of applications they use can't go digging into their databases and pulling out users' passwords.

If they try, they get only an encrypted version. And there's no special formula or magical command that lets them get at the original of those passwords. Users are protected; you're protected. If you can't get at an encrypted password, you can't be blamed for identity fraud, for example.

So then, how do you see if a user has entered a valid password if you can't decrypt their password value in the database?

Easy: you can encrypt their supplied password, and compare that encrypted value to the encrypted value in the database. If the encrypted values match, then things are good—and you still haven't had to look at what that user's real password is.

So you want something like the following code in *authorize.php*, where passwords are checked:

```
// Look up the user-provided credentials
$query = sprintf("SELECT user_id, username FROM users " .
                 " WHERE username = '%s' AND " .
                 "       password = '%s';",
            mysql_real_escape_string(trim($_SERVER['PHP_AUTH_USER'])),
            mysql_real_escape_string(
              crypt(trim($_SERVER['PHP_AUTH_PW'])))));
```

> **WARNING** Take your time with all those closing parentheses. It can get pretty hairy, and the last thing you want is a nasty hard-to-find bug because you're one parenthesis shy.

Now, you should be able to try things out. You're encrypting passwords on user creation, and you're encrypting the value to compare with that password on user login.

Unfortunately, try as you might, you're going to be stuck with Figure 11-11.

So what gives?

Encryption Uses Salt

Remember that briefly-mentioned second argument to *crypt*? It's called a *salt*. A salt is a key—usually a few characters—that is used in generating the one-way encryption used by functions like *crypt*. The salt helps ensure the randomness and security of a password.

FIGURE 11-11

No, it's not groundhog day. But no matter how many users you create, you'll never get past this forbidding login box. There's one thing missing, and it has to do with the inner workings of crypt.

So far, by not providing a salt, you've been letting *crypt* figure one out on its own. But unless the salt provided in two different calls to *crypt* is identical, the resulting encryption *will not match*. In other words, calling crypt on the same string two times without providing a salt will give you two different results.

Create a simple script called *test_salt.php*:

```php
<?php

$input = "secret_string";
$first_output = crypt($input);
$second_output = crypt($input);

echo "First output is {$first_output}\n\n";
echo "Second output is {$second_output}\n\n";

?>
```

Now run this script in your command line terminal:

```
yellowta@yellowtagmedia.com [~/www/phpMM/ch11]# php test_salt.php
X-Powered-By: PHP/5.2.17
Content-type: text/html

First output is $1$ciU1qEcc$XFT9G7FD/4K/L1Kl.bd.q/

Second output is $1$7cLtF/bc$Js6rEk5RHg4PujAkVOOSG1
```

That's not all. Run it again, and you'll get two different results from those two.

But with one change, things get back to what you'd expect:

```php
<?php

$input = "secret_string";
$salt = "salt";
$first_output = crypt($input, $salt);
$second_output = crypt($input, $salt);

echo "First output is {$first_output}\n\n";
echo "Second output is {$second_output}\n\n";

?>
```

Now run this updated version, and smile at the results:

```
yellowta@yellowtagmedia.com [~/www/phpMM/ch11]# php test_salt.php
X-Powered-By: PHP/5.2.17
Content-type: text/html

First output is sazmIw2D3KJ/M

Second output is sazmIw2D3KJ/M
```

So you need to ensure that both calls to crypt in your application's scripts use the same salt. Now you could just create a new constant, but there's an even better solution: use the user's username itself as the salt! You could completely lose your scripts—and any constant that defines a salt—and your authentication would still work.

The user's username always stays with the password, so you're essentially ensuring that the username and password are truly a united combination.

First, update *create_user.php* (yes, one more time!) to use the user's supplied username as a salt:

```php
$insert_sql = sprintf("INSERT INTO users " .
                      "(first_name, last_name, username, " .
                      "password, email, " .
                      "bio, facebook_url, twitter_handle, " .
                      "user_pic_path) " .
                "VALUES ('%s', '%s', '%s', '%s', '%s',
                        '%s', '%s', '%s', '%s');",
                mysql_real_escape_string($first_name),
                mysql_real_escape_string($last_name),
                mysql_real_escape_string($username),
                mysql_real_escape_string(crypt($password, $username)),
```

```
mysql_real_escape_string($email),
mysql_real_escape_string($bio),
mysql_real_escape_string($facebook_url),
mysql_real_escape_string($twitter_handle),
mysql_real_escape_string($upload_filename));
```

Now, make the exact same change in *authorize.php*. Remember in this script, the username comes in through the *$_SERVER* superglobal:

```
// Look up the user-provided credentials
$query = sprintf("SELECT user_id, username FROM users " .
                " WHERE username = '%s' AND " .
                "       password = '%s';",
            mysql_real_escape_string(trim($_SERVER['PHP_AUTH_USER'])),
            mysql_real_escape_string(
              crypt(trim($_SERVER['PHP_AUTH_PW']),
                $_SERVER['PHP_AUTH_USER']))));
```

Now, finally, create a new user (hopefully you're not running out of friends yet!). Then, try and log in using that user's username and password.

And...finally. That same old *show_users.php* screen you say means a lot more than the ability to delete users. It means you've got a solid, working authentication system. Congratulations. Enjoy it...there's one more big hurdle left to overcome.

PHP & MYSQL: THE MISSING MANUAL

Cookies, Sign-ins, and Ditching Crummy Pop-ups

Yes, it's time to begin to wind down. You've gone from seeing PHP as some strange, cryptic set of angle brackets and dollar signs to building your own application, including integration with a MySQL database, authentication, redirection, and a pretty decent set of utility functions. And no, you're probably not going to sell your mini-application with its Twitter and Facebook sign-up to Google for a billion dollars or anything. But you should have a pretty good idea of how to think in PHP, and how scripts are structured to solve problems.

But before you can go twist and bend this app and your new skills to your own purposes, there are still some lingering issues that need to be handled. A few of these are nice-to-haves, and some are downright necessities if you're going to spend your career writing web applications.

Here are just a few things that your application needs to round out both the app and your skills:

- A better login screen. Nobody likes a bland gray pop-up; they want a branded, styled login form.

- Better messaging indicating whether a user is logged in or not.

- A way to log out.

- Two levels of authentication: one to get to the main application, and then admin-level authentication to get to a page like *show_users.php* and *delete_user.php*.

- Some basic navigation—and that navigation should change based on a user's login and the groups to which they belong.

These are almost all related to the idea of logging in, and that's no accident. Whether it's a good-looking login screen or the ability to group users, you'll probably spend as much time on the authentication and authorization of your web applications as you do anything else. Even if you have boilerplate code to get a username and password, most web pages are built using components that are only selectively accessible. In other words, a web application shows users different things and gives users different functionality based upon their login.

Get a handle on how to store user credentials, move users around your site, and the issues that underlie keeping up with a user's information. Yeah, you're ready to take your programming into the real world.

Going Beyond Basic Authentication

Right now, your authentication uses the browser's built in HTTP capabilities. Unfortunately, as useful as HTTP authentication is, it leaves you with a pretty lame visual; check out Figure 12-1 for the sad reminder.

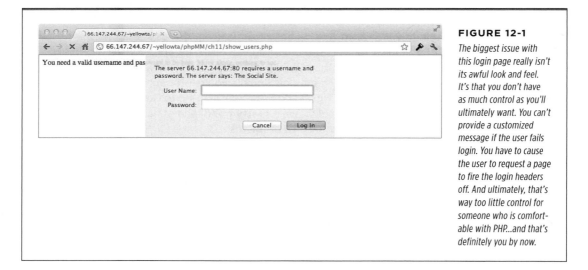

FIGURE 12-1

The biggest issue with this login page really isn't its awful look and feel. It's that you don't have as much control as you'll ultimately want. You can't provide a customized message if the user fails login. You have to cause the user to request a page to fire the login headers off. And ultimately, that's way too little control for someone who is comfortable with PHP...and that's definitely you by now.

Now, keep in mind: other than signing up initially or seeing a generic home page, this is the doorway to much of your application. So any work you do with a top-tier designer, any nice CSS and color scheming, or any clever HTML5 and SVG is all lost because it's hidden behind that annoying gray pop-up. Even worse, when the user doesn't get in, they *keep* getting that annoying pop-up.

But changing that takes more than changing one thing. It's going to take a complete reworking of how users access your site.

Starting with a Landing Page

Any site that requires a login has to give you somewhere to land before you hit the login page. So to build out your site, you need something simple and effective as a central location for your users to begin. From this starting point they should be able to login, or create a new login.

Here's a simple version of just that. Call it *index.html* so it can eventually be your site's default landing page:

```html
<html>
 <head>
  <link href="../css/phpMM.css" rel="stylesheet" type="text/css" />
 </head>

 <body>
  <div id="header"><h1>PHP & MySQL: The Missing Manual</h1></div>
  <div id="content">
    <div id="home_banner"></div>
    <div id="signup">
      <a href="create_user.html"><img src="../images/sign_me_up.png" /></a>
      <a href="signin.html"><img src="../images/sign_me_in.png" /></a>
    </div>
  </div>

  <div id="footer"></div>
 </body>
</html>
```

You can see what the page looks like in Figure 12-2.

Signing users up is pretty easy: just point them over to *create_user.html* and let the work you've already done take effect. But that link to *signin.html* creates a new set of questions to answer. First and foremost: what exactly needs to happen there to sign a user in?

Taking Control of User Sign-ins

Obviously, there needs to be a form into which a user can enter information. And the way things have been going, that form should submit to a script, which checks the username and password. Already, that's different from what you've got: currently, authentication happens as a sort of side effect of requesting a page that requires *authorize.php*. So there's not an explicit login form—but now there needs to be.

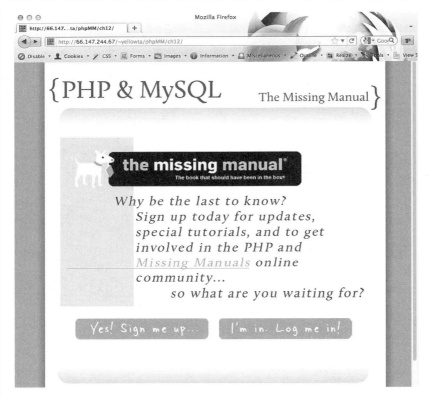

FIGURE 12-2

No, you probably shouldn't submit this site for any Web 2.0 design awards. Still, it gets the basic point across: you want users to either sign up or log in. A sign-up page, you've got...but logging in? That's going to require a new page or two, some PHP, and the death of that HTTP authentication login box.

Then, this script that receives information from the form login has to check the user's credentials. That's easy; *authorize.php* already does that, and even though it currently uses *$_SERVER*, that's easy to change to accept input from a sign-in form. But now here's another wrinkle: if the credentials aren't good, then the sign-in form needs to be shown again...preferably with the user's original input for username, or at a minimum, a message stating that there was an error logging in.

> **NOTE** There is nothing as frustrating as a login form that sits staring blank-faced at you, never telling you that it's received your credentials and they were rejected. User feedback is critical in any good login system.

So here's the basic flow:

1. Sign-in form (HTML): Takes in the user's username and password. Submits them to...

2. Authentication script (PHP): Verify the user's username and password against the database. If there's a match take them to a secure page, like the user's profile (*show_user.php*), and let him know he's logged in. If his credentials are not valid, take him back to...

3. Sign-in form (HTML)

And here's a problem: how can an HTML form display an error message on a particular condition? Or pre-fill out a username field?

Having that sign-in form as HTML really limits you, not on its initial display, but in the situation where there's a login failure. It's then that you want PHP on your side.

The obvious solution is to convert the sign-in page to PHP, and you'd end up with a flow like this:

1. Sign-in form (PHP this time): Takes in the user's username and password. Submits to...

2. Authentication script (PHP): Verify the user's username and password against the database. If there's a match take them to a secure page, like the user's profile (*show_user.php*), and let them know they're logged in. If their credentials are not valid, take them back to...

3. Sign-in form (PHP): Now this form can display a customized error and reload the user's username.

But why not take it even further? There are all just steps in a login process. So what if instead of two scripts, you had a single script that submitted to itself, and either redirects the user on successful login, or re-shows itself on an unsuccessful login? (If the idea of a script submitting to itself sounds like something you'd see in *Inception*, check out the box on page 394.)

By the way, you'll need to make a quick change to your site's new home page before you forget. Since you're using a script not just for processing logins, but creating the login page itself, do that now before you're neck deep into PHP:

```html
<html>
 <head>
  <link href="../css/phpMM.css" rel="stylesheet" type="text/css" />
 </head>

 <body>
  <div id="header"><h1>PHP & MySQL: The Missing Manual</h1></div>
  <div id="content">
    <div id="home_banner"></div>
```

```
        <div id="signup">
          <a href="create_user.html"><img src="../images/sign_me_up.png" /></a>
          <a href="signin.php"><img src="../images/sign_me_in.png" /></a>
        </div>
      </div>

      <div id="footer"></div>
    </body>
  </html>
```

PHP Loves to Self-Reference

Up until now, you've had a pretty strong distinction between forms—created in HTML files—and the scripts to which they submit—PHP. But you've pretty much torn down that distinction in view pages. You've got lots of scripts that do some programmatic "stuff"—logging a user in, or getting all the current users, or looking up a particular user—and then outputting a bunch of HTML.

So then why not blow that distinction away in forms, too?

A script could output a form, and set the action of that form as... itself. Then, when the form is recalled, it would see if there's any submitted data. If so, it's receiving a form submission and can do what it needs to programmatically. There's no real magic here; just an *if* that directs traffic. Inside that *if*, you could even output a completely different page, perhaps letting the user know their data has been accepted.

And if there's no submission data, then it's just a normal initial request for the form, and so the form should be shown. But you get some nice benefits here, too. You can see if there might be error messages or existing data from a previous submission, and drop those values right into your form.

Using submitted data is extremely common in PHP, and something with which you want to get comfortable. Even though it's

a bit of a mind trip the first few times, you'll soon find that in a PHP-driven application, there are very few times where you're *not* going to use a PHP script. Forms, error pages, login pages, even welcome pages...you'll get hooked on having the ability to use PHP, and be hard-pressed to go back.

Now, there are a few of you—those of you who are partial to the MVC (Model-View-Controller) pattern—who are dying inside. HTML inside a script that submits to itself means you've completely eradicated a wall (or even a large overgrown hedge) between the model, the view, and the controller. But as you've already seen, you're not going to get a true MVC pattern working well in PHP. You can get an approximation, and don't shy away from that approximation. You're just not going to get the clean separation that's possible in languages like Ruby or Java (and you can still make just as big a mess in those languages, in case you were wondering).

Given that, you may want to simply accept that PHP is often going to cause you to sacrifice clean MVC on the altar of getting things done. Always, always, always...get things done.

From HTTP Authentication to Cookies

Before you can dive into writing this sign-in script—call it *signin.php*—there's another glaring issue to work out. How do you let the user log in? By abandoning that pop-up login form, you're taking logging in into your own hands.

Getting the username and password and checking them against the database isn't a big deal. You can and will do that in *signin.php*. But the big problem is keeping that information around. With HTTP authentication, the browser kept up with all your pages being in one realm, and whether or not the user was logged into that realm. So logging in and accessing *show_users.php* meant that a user did not have to log in to get to *delete_user.php*. They'd already done that for another page in the same realm.

And that's where cookies come into play.

NOTE At this point, about a thousand obligatory jokes related to baking and sweets and a million other things come into focus. It's a strange term, one that refers back to something called *magic cookies*. That was a term old-school Unix hackers used for little bits of data passed back and forth between programs.

In any case, it stuck, so if you're new to cookies in the programming world, feel free to snicker as you code the rest of this chapter.

■ WHAT IS A COOKIE?

A cookie is nothing magical. It's simply a means by which you can store a single piece of information. So a cookie has a name, a value—that single piece of information—and a date at which the cookie expires. When the cookie expires, it's gone; you can't get the value anymore.

So you could have a cookie with a name "username" and a value "my_username", and perhaps another cookie named "user_id" with a value of "52". Then, your scripts can check to see if there's a "username" cookie, and if so, assume the user's logged in. In the same manner, your login script can set a "username" cookie.

In other words, other than setting the cookie in the first place, you get the same sort of effect as you were getting with basic authentication. Of course, the creation of cookies is within your control, so you can create them with your own form, delete them with your scripts (say, on a user logout), and issue messages based on the status of cookies.

WARNING Although you can control the creation of cookies, your users can easily modify them, delete them, and even create cookies of their own. Because of that, they're not ideal for the sort of information you're storing in them here: secure usernames and the like.

That's why there's a Chapter 13—and have no fear, even though you'll change the manner in which you use cookies, everything you're learning here will be important in your final authentication solution. Besides, there are plenty of times when cookies are helpful, and they'll be a staple of your programming toolkit.

■ CREATE AND RETRIEVE COOKIES

You're almost ready to jump into scripting again—and that's where all the fun is. (It's certainly not as fun reading about code as it is writing code.) All that's left is to figure out to write cookies and then look them up and get their values. Thankfully, PHP makes working with cookies as simple as working with the superglobals you've already gotten used to: *$_SERVER* and *$_REQUEST*.

To set a cookie, you simply call *setcookie* with the cookie's name and value:

```
setcookie("username", "my_username");
```

Once a cookie's set, you get the value you just set with the *$_COOKIE* superglobal:

```
echo "You are signed in as " . $_COOKIE['username'] . ".";
```

That's it. It's that simple. Sure, there are some wrinkles here and there, and you'll add a bit of nuance to your cookie creation, but if you've got *setcookie* and *$_COOKIE* down, you're more or less ready to roll.

> **NOTE** One of those nuances you may already be thinking about is the expiration value of a cookie. You can pass that as a third value to *setcookie*, but don't worry, there's more to come on expiration soon.

■ Logging In with Cookies

You know what cookies are. You know the flow of the sign-in form. Now it's time to code. Create *signin.php* and start with the basic outline:

```php
<?php

require_once '../scripts/database_connection.php';
require_once '../scripts/view.php';

// If the user is logged in, the user_id cookie will be set
if (!isset($_COOKIE['user_id'])) {

  // See if a login form was submitted with a username for login
  if (isset($_REQUEST['username'])) {
    // Try and log the user in
    $username = mysql_real_escape_string(trim($_REQUEST['username']));
    $password = mysql_real_escape_string(trim($_REQUEST['password']));

    // Look up the user

    // If user not found, issue an error
  }

  // Still in the "not signed in" part of the if
```

```php
    // Start the page, and we know there's no success or error message
    //   since they're just logging in
    page_start("Sign In");
?>


<html>
  <div id="content">
    <h1>Sign In to the Club</h1>
    <form id="signin_form" action="signin.php" method="POST">
      <fieldset>
        <label for="username">Username:</label>
        <input type="text"  name="username" id="username" size="20" />
        <br />
        <label for="password">Password:</label>
        <input type="password"  name="password" id="password" size="20" />
      </fieldset>
      <br />
      <fieldset class="center">
        <input type="submit" value="Sign In" />
      </fieldset>
    </form>
  </div>
  <div id="footer"></div>
 </body>
</html>

<?php
} else {
  // Now handle the case where they're logged in
  // redirect to another page, most likely show_user.php
}
?>
```

> **NOTE** Did you notice that *database_connection.php* is required—for logging the user in—but *app_config.
> php* isn't? You can include *app_config.php*, as there's a good change you'll need it at some point, but you may
> also remember that *database_connection.php* actually requires *app_config.php* itself. So if you require *data-
> base_connection.php*, you get a *require_once* for *app_config.php* for free.

This script is far from complete, has several problems, but is still a lot of code. Take
it piece by piece.

Is the User is Already Signed In?

Even if a user comes to your sign-in page explicitly, you shouldn't make them sign in.
So the first thing to do (other than a few *require_once* lines) is see if the "user_id"
cookie is set. If it's not, the user's not logged in, and everything flows from that.

```
<?php

require_once '../scripts/database_connection.php';
require_once '../scripts/view.php';

// If the user is logged in, the user_id cookie will be set
if (!isset($_COOKIE['user_id'])) {
```

Here's your first clue that cookies aren't much different than what you've already been using: you can use *isset* to see if it's already created, and you just pass in the cookie name. Piece of cake.

Is the User Trying to Sign In?

If the "user_id" cookie isn't set, the user's not logged in. So now you need to see if she's *trying* to log in. That would mean that you've got some request information. The user might have actually already filled out the HTML form (later in this script) and submitted that form back to this script.

But that's not the same as trying to access this script without any information. In that case, the user should just get the regular HTML sign-in form. So you can see if there's a submission by checking to see if there's anything in the *$_REQUEST* superglobal for "username", a field from the sign-in form:

```
// See if a login form was submitted with a username for login
if (isset($_REQUEST['username'])) {
  // Try and log the user in
  $username = mysql_real_escape_string(trim($_REQUEST['username']));
  $password = mysql_real_escape_string(trim($_REQUEST['password']));

  // Look up the user

  // If user not found, issue an error
}
```

If there's request data, then you can get the username and password that have been submitted, and (in a moment) look up the user and deal with any problems.

Before you do that, though, here's a nice change you can make. So far, you've been using *$_REQUEST* for everything. That takes in GET requests—which are requests where information is passed through the URL—and POST requests, like the ones that most of your forms have issued. But you already know that the only way information should get to this stage is by a submission from your own form, which will use a POST request.

You can replace *$_REQUEST* with a more specific superglobal, then: *$_POST*. *$_POST* only has request data from a POST request.

NOTE As you've probably already guessed, *$_POST* has a counterpart for GET requests: *$_GET*.

It's a good idea to begin moving toward the more specific $_POST when possible. POST data disallows parameters on the request URL, and is generally a bit more secure.

So make that small change to your script:

```
// See if a login form was submitted with a username for login
if (isset($_POST['username'])) {
  // Try and log the user in
  $username = mysql_real_escape_string(trim($_REQUEST['username']));
  $password = mysql_real_escape_string(trim($_REQUEST['password']));

  // Look up the user

  // If user not found, issue an error
}
```

FREQUENTLY ASKED QUESTION

$_REQUEST or $_POST: What's the Big Deal?

Ahh, yes, another quibble over which programmers can argue, demonize, and distort. No matter what you hear, there's just no functional difference between *$_REQUEST*, *$_GET*, and *$_POST*, in terms of getting request information. *$_REQUEST* will always have what's in both *$_GET* and *$_POST*, but if you know you've got a POST request, you don't gain or lose anything by using *$_REQUEST* over *$_POST*.

In fact, not only does *$_REQUEST* have the combined values from *$_GET* and *$_POST*, it has the contents of *$_COOKIE* in it too (at least by default). So technically, you could do this in *signin.php*:

```
// If the user is logged in, the user_id
cookie will be set
```

```
if (!isset($_REQUEST['user_id'])) {
```

So you could use *$_REQUEST* and totally ditch *$_GET*, *$_REQUEST*, and *$_COOKIE*. But think back to all the programming principles you've been getting a hold of: make your code clear and readable, be specific over being just generic, and think about what those who have to work with your code after you will see. For all those reasons, although *$_REQUEST* isn't bad, it's often helpful to use *$_GET* and *$_POST* and *$_COOKIE* when that's what you're dealing with.

In the case of *signin.php*, you know you're getting a POST request. Given that, use *$_POST* when you can. If you know you're getting a GET request, use *$_GET*. And if you're looking for a cookie, use *$_COOKIE*. Your code will be clearer and more specific...and you'll know exactly what it's intended to do.

Displaying the page

Whether the user got to this page by submitting incorrect credentials, or by not submitting credentials at all, he should see a form. So now you're ready to display some HTML.

NOTE If the user logs in successfully, your code will need to redirect them elsewhere. So that code block that checks usernames and passwords needs to eventually forward the user on to another location if his login is successful.

```
// Still in the "not signed in" part of the if
// Start the page, and we know there's no success or error message
//   since they're just logging in
page_start("Sign In");
?>

<html>
  <div id="content">
    <h1>Sign In to the Club</h1>
    <form id="signin_form" action="signin.php" method="POST">
      <fieldset>
        <label for="username">Username:</label>
        <input type="text"   name="username" id="username" size="20" />
        <br />
        <label for="password">Password:</label>
        <input type="password"   name="password" id="password" size="20" />
      </fieldset>
      <br />
      <fieldset class="center">
        <input type="submit" value="Sign In" />
      </fieldset>
    </form>
  </div>
  <div id="footer"></div>
  </body>
</html>
```

Don't miss that opening comment block; it's an important one. This code—including the HTML—is all still part of the opening *if* block:

```
// If the user is logged in, the user_id cookie will be set
if (!isset($_COOKIE['user_id'])) {
```

In other words, all this HTML is shown if and only if the user's not logged in.

There's another small improvement you can make here, in the same vein as using *$_POST* instead of *$_REQUEST*. Take a look at this line:

```
<form id="signin_form" action="signin.php" method="POST">
```

This tells the form to submit to the same script that's generating the form. Nothing wrong with it, but what if you rename *signin.php*? It might be a small possibility, but all the same, it's not unrealistic. (It wasn't that long ago that you moved away from calling a script *admin.php* and instead went with the more functionally named *delete_user.php* and *show_users.php*.)

Remember that PHP loves this script-submitting-to-script paradigm. In fact, just to make it a bit easier, you've got a property in *$_SERVER* that tells you the current script name. No, it's not there just for self-referential scripts, but it sure does help. Update *signin.php* to take advantage of *$_SERVER['PHP_SELF']*:

```
<form id="signin_form"
      action="<?php echo $_SERVER['PHP_SELF']; ?>"
      method="POST">
```

Now the form submits, literally, to itself. A small change, but a good one... and one you'll find yourself coming back to over and over again.

Redirecting as Needed

The only thing left—at least in this pseudocode version—is to redirect the user if she's logged in:

```
<?php
} else {
  // Now handle the case where they're logged in
  // redirect to another page, most likely show_user.php
}
?>
```

So now you've got the basic flow. But there's a ton missing. Time to dig in and start piecing this code into a usable form.

POWER USERS' CLINIC

Pseudocode with Comments and Real Code

It might seem strange to think of *signin.php* as it currently exists as pseudocode, but that's just what it is. It's certainly not a complete working script; there are holes through which you could drive a truck all over the place. But those holes are generally indicated with a helpful, clear comment. And although those comments don't do anything, they do remind you of *what* needs to be done, and *where* it needs to be done.

Truth be told, pseudocode is often best done just like this. You're not truly wasting time writing nonexistent function names like *check_the_user_credentials()*. But you're accomplishing the same goal with comments like:

```
// Look up the user
```

```
// If user not found, issue an error
```

Those comments are just as useful, and they can stay put as you write code under each comment that fills out the script's functionality.

Before you begin, though, you can already get a good idea of this flow. Right now, a non-logged in user will get the HTML output, without all the PHP that runs when there's a username coming in through a POST request. So Figure 12-3 is the default view, so to speak.

Try and submit the form—with a good or bad username—and you get the same form over again. Not so great...but still, this is a starting point. Now you can begin to tackle each individual piece of functionality.

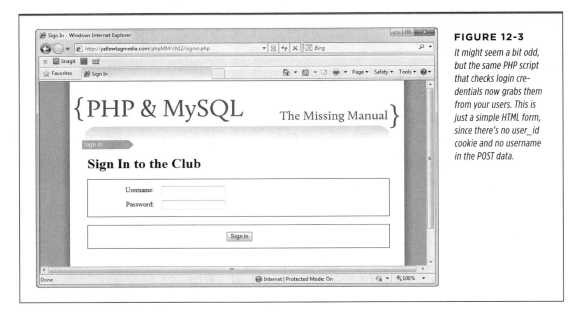

FIGURE 12-3

It might seem a bit odd, but the same PHP script that checks login credentials now grabs them from your users. This is just a simple HTML form, since there's no user_id cookie and no username in the POST data.

Logging the User In

The next bit of code is really a copy-paste-and-modify job from *authorize.php*. Here's where that script was left:

```
// Look up the user-provided credentials
$query = sprintf("SELECT user_id, username FROM users " .
                 " WHERE username = '%s' AND " .
                 "       password = '%s';",
            mysql_real_escape_string(trim($_SERVER['PHP_AUTH_USER'])),
            mysql_real_escape_string(
              crypt(trim($_SERVER['PHP_AUTH_PW']),
                    $_SERVER['PHP_AUTH_USER']))));

$results = mysql_query($query);

if (mysql_num_rows($results) == 1) {
  $result = mysql_fetch_array($results);
  $current_user_id = $result['user_id'];
  $current_username = $result['username'];
} else {
  header('HTTP/1.1 401 Unauthorized');
```

```
        header('WWW-Authenticate: Basic realm="The Social Site"');
        exit("You need a valid username and password to be here. " .
            "Move along, nothing to see.");
    }
```

Pretty good, although it all depends on HTTP authentication. Now you can drop
that into *signin.php*, change the successful block to set some cookies, and redirect
somewhere useful:

```php
<?php

require_once '../scripts/database_connection.php';
require_once '../scripts/view.php';

// If the user is logged in, the user_id cookie will be set
if (!isset($_COOKIE['user_id'])) {

  // See if a login form was submitted with a username for login
  if (isset($_POST['username'])) {
    // Try and log the user in
    $username = mysql_real_escape_string(trim($_REQUEST['username']));
    $password = mysql_real_escape_string(trim($_REQUEST['password']));

    // Look up the user
    $query = sprintf("SELECT user_id, username FROM users " .
                     " WHERE username = '%s' AND " .
                     "       password = '%s';",
                     $username, crypt($password, $username));

    $results = mysql_query($query);

    if (mysql_num_rows($results) == 1) {
      $result = mysql_fetch_array($results);
      $user_id = $result['user_id'];
      setcookie('user_id', $user_id);
      setcookie('username', $result['username']);
      header("Location: show_user.php");
    } else {
      // If user not found, issue an error
    }
  }

  // Still in the "not signed in" part of the if
  // Start the page, and we know there's no success or error message
  //   since they're just logging in
  page_start("Sign In");
?>
```

Open up *signin.php*, and you should get the login form (check out Figure 12-3 to make sure you're on the right page with the right HTML). Login with some valid credentials, and you should get logged in, have a cookie set, and be passed over to *show_user.php* (see Figure 12-4).

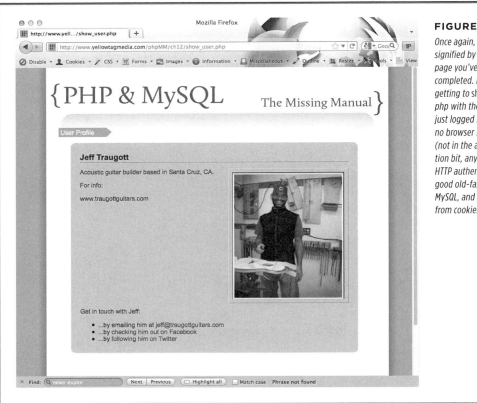

FIGURE 12-4

Once again, victory is signified by getting to a page you've long since completed. Here, it's getting to show_user. php with the user that just logged in. But there's no browser magic here (not in the authentication bit, anyway), and no HTTP authentication. Just good old-fashioned PHP, MySQL, and some help from cookies.

Did you notice anything odd in that last bit of redirection, though? Here's the line where the redirect is sent to the browser:

```php
if (mysql_num_rows($results) == 1) {
  $result = mysql_fetch_array($results);
  $user_id = $result['user_id'];
  setcookie('user_id', $user_id);
  setcookie('username', $result['username']);
  header("Location: show_user.php");
} else {
  // If user not found, issue an error
}
```

If no bells are ringing, check out *create_user.php* (page 182). That script creates a user and redirects him to *show_user.php*. Here's the relevant line:

```
header("Location: show_user.php?user_id=" . mysql_insert_id());
```

So here, additional information is sent: the *user_id* of the user to display, sent as a GET parameter within the request URL. But in *signin.php*, there's no *user_id* parameter. All the same, Figure 12-4 shows that things work.

show_user.php expects that information:

```
// Get the user ID of the user to show
$user_id = $_REQUEST['user_id'];
```

And this isn't the only place *show_user.php* requests user information. At the beginning of *signin.php*, there's this opening *if* statement.

```
// If the user is logged in, the user_id cookie will be set
if (!isset($_COOKIE['user_id'])) {
```

The *else* to this *if* is way down near the bottom of the script:

```
} else {
  // Now handle the case where they're logged in
  // redirect to another page, most likely show_user.php
  header("Location: show_user.php");
}
```

So here's another case where the user is sent to *show_user.php*, and there's no *user_id* parameter, but all the same, *show_user.php* continues to happily figure out which user should be shown, and display that user (see Figure 12-4).

So *how* does this work in *signin.php*? The answer lies in how *$_REQUEST* works, and what information it contains. For starters, flip to the box on page 399 and then come back. You are setting a cookie in *signin.php*, and that cookie is accessible through the *$_COOKIE* superglobal. But *$_REQUEST* also contains what's in *$_COOKIE*—along with what's in *$_POST* and *$_GET*. So this...

```
$user_id = $_REQUEST['user_id'];
```

...is just as good as this...

```
$user_id = $_COOKIE['user_id'];
```

...at getting the value in a cookie.

NOTE   The obvious question is, "Which should you use? *$_COOKIE* or *$_REQUEST*. As usual, it depends. Here, if you switch to *$_COOKIE*, you'll need to update *create_user.php*. It might be best to leave this as *$_REQUEST*, at least for now, as it makes *show_user.php* a little more flexible. It accepts request parameters and cookies, and that's a nice thing. Later, if you move to using only cookies, you can update *show_user.php* to use *$_COOKIE* and be more specific.

Blank Pages and Expiring Cookies

At some point in here, as you're trying things out, you may get a very strange response. You enter in *signin.php* in your URL bar. You hit Enter. And you get a blank page, as in Figure 12-5.

FIGURE 12-5

Nobody said that testing authentication wasn't a hassle. This blank screen means that your logging in and cookie setting is working...so why are you getting a blank screen? Any ideas?

You try it again. You try to reload. You try to clear your cache. Nothing! Finally, you restart your browser, and things start to behave. But no sooner have you signed in through *signin.php* before it's happening again. So what's up?

Actually, this is a sign that things are working *correctly*. Remember that in your script, the first conditional checks for a cookie:

```
// If the user is logged in, the user_id cookie will be set
if (!isset($_COOKIE['user_id'])) {
```

If this cookie is set, then the script jumps all the way down to this bit at the bottom of your file:

```
<?php
} else {
  // Now handle the case where they're logged in
  // redirect to another page, most likely
}
?>
```

But there's nothing there! So you get a blank browser. You can fix this (kind of) by setting up a default action for users that get sent to *signin.php* and yet are already logged in. In fact, it's the same thing you did earlier for a login: redirect them to *show_user.php*:

```
} else {
  // Now handle the case where they're logged in
  // redirect to another page, most likely
  header("Location: show_user.php");
}
```

Now, no more blank screen. *show_user.php* will pick up on the "user_id" cookie and show the currently logged in user. Good, right?

Sort of. It still leaves you in an endless loop. It's just that now you're looping on the nice looking *show_user.php* rather than a crummy-looking blank page. You'll need to completely close out your browser to stop the madness.

But that's normal behavior. Just as when you logged in via HTTP authentication, logging in here and setting a cookie, by default, sets that cookie to exist until the browser is closed.

> **NOTE** Calling *setcookie* with no value for the third parameter defaults it to "0", meaning the cookie expires at the end of the user's session, which is when the user closes their browser.

So if you need to get out of this loop, just close your browser out. Make sure you close the program, not just the current tab or window. That will cause the cookie—set with a default expiration value—to expire.

If you really want to set the cookie to last longer (or shorter), you can. Just pass in a third parameter to *setcookie*. That third parameter should be in the seconds from what Unix and Linux systems call the *epoch*, January 1, 1970, at 0:00 GMT. So you usually pass in *time*, which gives the current time—conveniently also in seconds since the epoch—and then add to that. So *time() + 10* would be 10 seconds in the future, as reckoned from the epoch.

Here are just a few examples of *setcookie* with an expiration time passed in:

```
// Expire in an hour (60 seconds * 60 minutes = 3600)
setcookie('user_id', $user_id, time() + 3600);

// This actually deletes the cookie, since it indicates an
//    expiration in the past
setcookie('user_id', $user_id, time() - 3600);

// The default: expire on browser close
setcookie('user_id', $user_id, 0);
```

You can also supply a time via *mktime*, which takes an hour, date, second, month, day, and year, and returns the number of seconds since the epoch (again). So...

```
setcookie('user_id', $user_id, mktime(0, 0, 0, 2, 1, 2021);
```

...would set a cookie to expire on February 1, 2021, GMT. That's a little far away, wouldn't you say? In general, the default value is perfectly reasonable. Most users are comfortable signing in again when their browser closes. In fact, many users would *not* be comfortable with their login lasting on and on, perpetually.

> **NOTE** The notable exceptions here are sites like Facebook and Twitter that don't contain a lot of valuable user information. Most financial sites like banks don't even wait for your browser to close; they'll expire your session every 10 minutes or so.

So close your browser, which will expire your cookies, and open up *signin.php* again for some more improvement.

Errors Aren't Always Interruptive

Now you've got a potential error with which you've got to deal. There's the *else* that is run when the user's username and password don't match what's in the database:

```
if (mysql_num_rows($results) == 1) {
  // set a cookie and redirect to show_user.php
} else {
  // If user not found, issue an error
}
```

Now, the typical error handling so far has been *handle_error*. But that's no good; you don't want to short-circuit the login process by throwing the user out to an error page. They'd have to get back to the login page, try again and potentially go to the error page yet again. That's no good at all.

What you need is a means by which you can show any errors without interrupting the overall application flow. When something goes badly wrong, *handle_error* makes perfect sense; a major error deserves to interrupt your application. But here, you need a non-interruptive way to show errors, other than *handle_error*.

But you *do* have another way to show errors: the *page_start* function in *view.php*. Right now, you're calling this function in *signin.php*, but without anything other than the page title:

```
page_start("Sign In");
```

But look back in *view.php*; here's the complete set of arguments this method takes:

```
function page_start($title, $javascript = NULL,
                    $success_message = NULL, $error_message = NULL) {
```

Normally, you've been passing in any request parameters as the values for *$success_message* and *$error_message*. But that's not a requirement. So you can create a new variable called *$error_message*, fill it with text as your script progresses, and then hand it off to *page_start* as the HTML output is begun.

Here's what you should do:

```
<?php

require_once '../scripts/database_connection.php';
require_once '../scripts/view.php';

$error_message = "";

// If the user is logged in, the user_id cookie will be set
if (!isset($_COOKIE['user_id'])) {
```

```
// See if a login form was submitted with a username for login
if (isset($_POST['username'])) {
  // Try and log the user in

  // Look up the user

  if (mysql_num_rows($results) == 1) {
    $result = mysql_fetch_array($results);
    $user_id = $result['user_id'];
    setcookie('user_id', $user_id);
    setcookie('username', $result['username']);
    header("Location: show_user.php");
  } else {
    // If user not found, issue an error
    $error_message = "Your username/password combination was invalid.";
  }
}

// Still in the "not signed in" part of the if
// Start the page, and pass along any error message set earlier
page_start("Sign In", NULL, NULL, $error_message);
?>

<!-- Rest of HTML output -->

<?php
} else {
  // Now handle the case where they're logged in
  // redirect to another page, most likely show_user.php
  header("Location: show_user.php");
}
?>
```

WARNING   Remember, this cookie-based solution is a step toward a final solution, not the final solution itself. In the next chapter, you'll add support for sessions, and move information like a username and user ID out of a user's cookie and onto the server.

Whatever you do, keep reading! You'll need the cookie skills you're learning here, but you'll add to those skills sessions in the next chapter. Woe to the PHP programmer who uses cookies—and only cookies—for authentication.

Now visit *signin.php* (or *index.html* and click the Sign Up button). Uh oh...Figure 12-6 reveals there's a problem somewhere.

FIGURE 12-6

That's a strange sight: an error-less error. This is an issue, sure...but this is probably the second screen all your users will ever see, so it's a big issue. Still, by now, you're probably already thinking about what the problem is, and how you'll fix it pretty quickly.

Problems pop up when you're writing applications all the time. You write a function ages ago—the code in *view.php* that shows an error—and then use it in a different way much later. That's when the bugs appear.

In this case, the problem is that you're calling *page_start* with *$error_message*, but in some cases, *$error_message* is blank. It's an empty string, "", and so nothing should be shown. Check out *view.php*, and find *display_message*:

```php
function display_messages($success_msg = NULL, $error_msg = NULL) {
  echo "<div id='messages'>\n";
  if (!is_null($success_msg)) {
    display_message($success_msg, SUCCESS_MESSAGE);
  }
  if (!is_null($error_msg)) {
    display_message($error_msg, ERROR_MESSAGE);
  }
  echo "</div>\n\n";
}
```

In this case, *$error_message isn't* null. It's an empty string. So the *if* lets it pass, and a blank error message is shown in a red box. Not so good.

The fix is trivial, though; just see if *$error_message* is not null, and that it's got a length greater than 0. While you're at it, make the same improvement to the handling of success messages:

```
function display_messages($success_msg = NULL, $error_msg = NULL) {
  echo "<div id='messages'>\n";
  if (!is_null($success_msg) && (strlen($error_msg) > 0)) {
    display_message($success_msg, SUCCESS_MESSAGE);
  }
  if (!is_null($error_msg) && (strlen($error_msg) > 0)) {
    display_message($error_msg, ERROR_MESSAGE);
  }
  echo "</div>\n\n";
}
```

Now you should see a proper sign-in form (Figure 12-7).

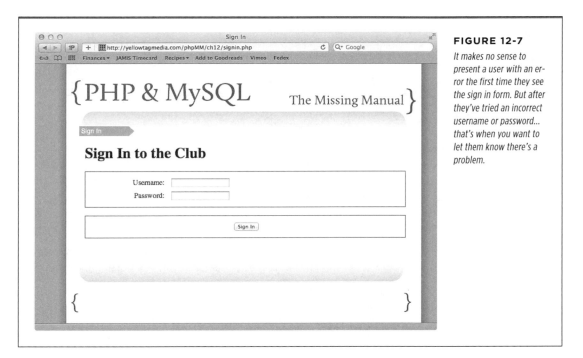

FIGURE 12-7

It makes no sense to present a user with an error the first time they see the sign in form. But after they've tried an incorrect username or password... that's when you want to let them know there's a problem.

Try and enter in an incorrect username or password, and you should see a nice, clear error—without pulling you our of the login process. Figure 12-8 shows this message, and users can immediately re-enter their information.

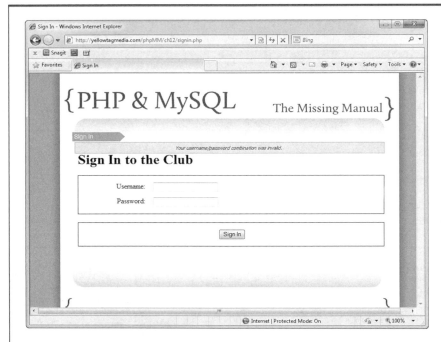

FIGURE 12-8

Now this is a solid non-interruptive error. It's impossible to miss, it creates a change that lets the user know something needs her attention, but it's not over the top. Now the user can try again... and again...and again.

An Option for Repeat Attempts

At this point, your sign-in page is functionally complete. However, there's one more option you can provide your users: reloading their username on login failure. Some sites do this reloading, and some don't. It's a matter of opinion, but as with most things, even if you choose not to implement this feature, you should know *how* to implement it.

If you need to display a username, that means the user's already submitted the form at least once before. So that places you squarely in this portion of *signin.php*:

```
if (isset($_POST['username'])) {
    // Try and log the user in
    $username = mysql_real_escape_string(trim($_REQUEST['username']));
    $password = mysql_real_escape_string(trim($_REQUEST['password']));

    // and so on...
}
```

The username's been sent, but logging in failed. So you've got the *$username* variable ready to display.

Now, move into the HTML. You can set the value of a form field with the value attribute, and you've got the attribute value in *$username*. So put that together, and you'll end up with something like this:

```
<label for="username">Username:</label>
<input type="text"  name="username" id="username" size="20"
       value="<?php if (isset($username)) echo $username; ?>" />
```

That's all there is to it. Enter in a username, submit the sign-in page, and you should see the sign in page with an error—and the username previously entered. Check out Figure 12-9 for the details.

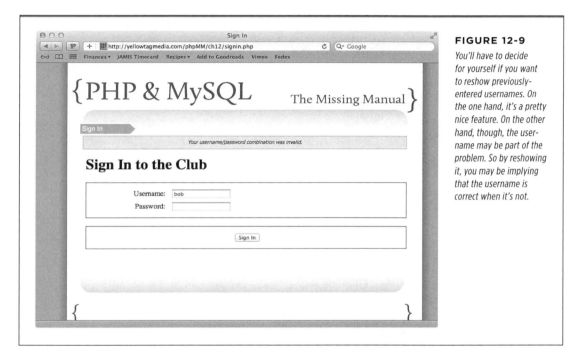

FIGURE 12-9

You'll have to decide for yourself if you want to reshow previously-entered usernames. On the one hand, it's a pretty nice feature. On the other hand, though, the username may be part of the problem. So by reshowing it, you may be implying that the username is correct when it's not.

▮ Adding Context-Specific Menus

Now, truly, menus and navigation deserve a lot more than a brief mention in a chapter. There's a ton of user interface design and usability to discuss; design principles; and the ever-raging argument over horizontal versus vertical menus. Still, these are all non-PHP issues. For you, PHP programmer extraordinaire, the concern is building out links and options that change based upon whether a user is logged in.

But you already have a sense of seeing whether a user is logged in. You can just check the "user_id:" cookie:

```php
if (isset($_COOKIE['user_id'])) {
  // show options for logged in users
} else {
  // show options for non-logged in users
}
```

That's all there is to it.

Putting a Menu Into Place

So back to *view.php*, which is where all the code that controls the header of your page lives anyway. Having some of your core view code tucked away in scripts that the rest of your pages can reference makes a huge difference in situations like this. The *display_title* function handles the first bits of a displayable page right now.

Find that function, and you can add a pretty simple *if*: if the "user_id" exists, show a profile link to *show_user.php* and a *signout.php* link (more on that in a bit). If they're not signed in, show them a Sign In link. And of course, you can add a Home link that shows regardless:

```php
function display_title($title, $success_message = NULL, $error_message = NULL)
{
echo <<<EOD
 <body>
   <div id="header"><h1>PHP & MySQL: The Missing Manual</h1></div>
   <div id="example">$title</div>
   <div id="menu">
     <ul>
       <li><a href="index.html">Home</a></li>
EOD;
   if (isset($_COOKIE['user_id'])) {
     echo "<li><a href='show_user.php'>My Profile</a>";
     echo "<li><a href='signout.php'>Sign Out</a></li>";
   } else {
     echo "<li><a href='signin.php'>Sign In</a></li>";
   }
echo <<<EOD
     </ul>
   </div>
EOD;
   display_messages($success_message, $error_message);
}
```

This code has two advantages. First, this menu is now available to all scripts through *view.php*. So you don't need to go rooting through all your files and insert new HTML and *if* statements to get a site-wide menu. And second, since you dropped this code into *display_title*, any of your scripts that already call *display_title* automatically get the menu code. Nothing to change in those at all.

And did you notice that, once again, the fact that *$_REQUEST* will return anything in *$_COOKIE* makes this script simple:

```php
if (isset($_COOKIE['user_id'])) {
  echo "<li><a href='show_user.php'>My Profile</a>";
  echo "<li><a href='signout.php'>Sign Out</a></li>";
} else {
  echo "<li><a href='signin.php'>Sign In</a></li>";
}
```

You're not worried about passing a user's ID into *show_user.php*, because there's a cookie set, and you've already seen that *show_user.php* is happy to grab that value through *$_REQUEST['user_id']*—just as if you'd explicitly passed in a user ID through a request parameter.

FREQUENTLY ASKED QUESTION

Does Anyone Actually Sign Out These Days?

It's true: unless people are on a financial site—their bank or perhaps a stock trading site—logging and signing out is largely never touched. Most Internet users are not very security conscious, and there's also just an expectation that a website will remember them when they return later. Signing out would prevent that, so why do it?

All the same, there are good reasons to add Sign Out capabilities to any app. First, if users are accessing your app on a public computer or shared laptop, you want to make sure they can

protect their credentials by signing out before letting anyone else use the computer. Second, just because most users aren't very security conscious doesn't mean that none are. Give someone the option to sign out, and if they don't take it, no big deal. If they do, they'll be glad your app supports the functionality they want.

And last but not least, you know how to create cookies. It would be a good thing to know how to delete them as well. So adding a sign out link forces you to get a handle on that, too.

To test this out, you should open up your various scripts that display HTML: *show_user.php*, *show_users.php*, and *signin.php*. Each should call *page_start*, rather than display HTML explicitly. Otherwise, you'll lose the menu code you just added to *page_start* in *view.php*. Here's what, for example, *show_user.php* should look like:

```php
<?php

require '../scripts/database_connection.php';
require '../scripts/view.php';

// Lots of PHP to load the user ID from a request parameter or
//   a cookie, look up that user, and set some values.
```

```
page_start("User Profile");
?>

    <div id="content">
      <div class="user_profile">
        <h1><?php echo "{$first_name} {$last_name}"; ?></h1>
        <p><img src="<?php echo $user_image; ?>" class="user_pic" />
          <?php echo $bio; ?></p>
        <p class="contact_info">
          Get in touch with <?php echo $first_name; ?>:
        </p>
        <ul>
          <li>...by emailing him at
            <a href="<?php echo $email; ?>"><?php echo $email; ?></a></li>
          <li>...by
            <a href="<?php echo $facebook_url; ?>">checking him out on
              Facebook</a></li>
          <li>...by <a href="<?php echo $twitter_url; ?>">following him
              on Twitter</a></li>
        </ul>
      </div>
    </div>
    <div id="footer"></div>
  </body>
</html>
```

Now sign in and head over to *show_user.php*.

NOTE   Actually, just signing in should automatically take you to *show_user.php*. Even better!

You should see something like Figure 12-10. There's a nice, simple menu on the right that now appears thanks to *start_page*, *display_title*, *view.php*, and the cookies you set in *signin.php*.

From HTML to Scripts

Something you might have noticed is that even once you've fixed up *show_user.php*, *show_users.php*, and *signin.php*, there are still pages left in your application. There's *index.html*, the initial page, as well as create_user.html. But these pages obviously don't get the benefit of *start_page* and *view.php*, because they're HTML, not PHP. For *index.html*, that probably makes sense. The only two places you want users to go is the sign-in page, or the sign-up page; both are clearly accessible through those big green buttons.

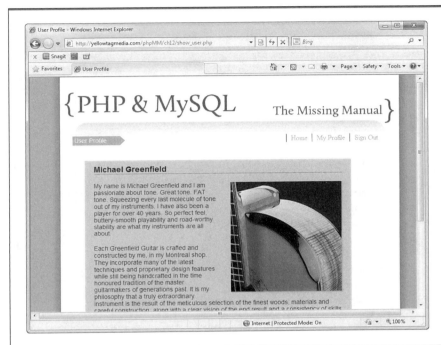

FIGURE 12-10

This particular menu is pretty simple. Still, it's easy to build this thing out now that you've got a basic mechanism for displaying it for authen- ticated users, and hiding it for others. You can add all the links and sublinks that your application needs, and as long as they're in the portion of the if in display_title that requires a cookie, you're good to go.

But that's not the case with *create_user.html*. Suppose someone clicks through to that form, and wants to return to the main page. Or, more likely, they may want to sign in, rather than sign up. That possibility becomes even more the case as you add other options to the menu, like an About page. So *create_user.html* needs that menu.

■ ANY HTML FILE CAN BE CONVERTED TO PHP

Converting *create_user.html* to be *create_user.php* is easy. But wait...*create_user. php* already exists. So, as a starting point, rename *create_user.html* to *signup.php*. That goes nicely with the wording on *index.html*, and it really is a form for signing up users.

```
[~/www/phpMM/ch12]# cp create_user.html create_user.html.orig
[~/www/phpMM/ch12]# mv create_user.html signup.php
```

NOTE   There's never a bad time to back things up, create copies of original files, and do the work of ensur- ing you can reverse any change you make. That can be accomplished through a full-fledged site-wide backup strategy, or just a duplicate of a file with a clear backup-related name.

Then, you can simply cut out the opening HTML and replace it with a PHP-driven call to *page_start*. You'll have to pass through all that inline validation JavaScript, but that's easy now; you can just use *heredoc*.

```php
<?php

require_once "../scripts/view.php";

$inline_javascript = <<<EOD
    $(document).ready(function() {
      $("#signup_form").validate({
        rules: {
          password: {
            minlength: 6
          },
          confirm_password: {
            minlength: 6,
            equalTo: "#password"
          }
        },
        messages: {
          password: {
            minlength: "Passwords must be at least 6 characters"
          },
          confirm_password: {
            minlength: "Passwords must be at least 6 characters",
            equalTo: "Your passwords do not match."
          }
        }
      });
    });
EOD;
page_start("User Signup", $inline_javascript);
?>

  <div id="content">
    <h1>Join the Missing Manual (Digital) Social Club</h1>
    <p>Please enter your online connections below:</p>
    <form id="signup_form" action="create_user.php"
        method="POST" enctype="multipart/form-data">
      <!-- Form content -->
```

```
     </form>
   </div>

   <div id="footer"></div>
  </body>
 </html>
```

Now is also a good time to update *view.php* to include the jQuery and validation scripts and CSS that *signin.php* needs. No reason to not make those available to all your site's pages:

```
function display_head($page_title = "", $embedded_javascript = NULL) {
echo <<<EOD
<html>
 <head>
  <title>{$page_title}</title>
  <link href="../css/phpMM.css" rel="stylesheet" type="text/css" />
  <link href="../css/jquery.validate.password.css" rel="stylesheet"
        type="text/css" />
  <script type="text/javascript" src="../js/jquery.js"></script>
  <script type="text/javascript" src="../js/jquery.validate.js"></script>
  <script type="text/javascript"
          src="../js/jquery.validate.password.js"></script>
EOD;
   if (!is_null($embedded_javascript)) {
     echo "<script type='text/javascript'>" .
          $embedded_javascript .
          "</script>";
   }
   echo " </head>";
}
```

Update your links in *index.html* to reference *signup.php* rather than *create_user.html*:

```
<div id="content">
  <div id="home_banner"></div>
  <div id="signup">
    <a href="signup.php"><img src="../images/sign_me_up.png" /></a>
    <a href="signin.php"><img src="../images/sign_me_in.png" /></a>
  </div>
</div>
```

Now you can check out the new page—and what should be a new menu. The results are shown in Figure 12-11. This is the "not logged in" version of the menu, so now you've tested both versions. Excellent.

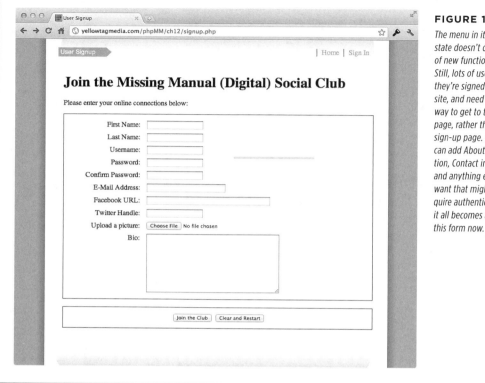

FIGURE 12-11

The menu in its current state doesn't offer a ton of new functionality. Still, lots of users forget they're signed up for a site, and need a simple way to get to the sign-in page, rather than the sign-up page. And you can add About information, Contact information, and anything else you want that might not require authentication, and it all becomes available to this form now.

■ CHALLENGE: BE SELF-REFERENTIAL WITH USER CREATION

Surely by now you realize that you don't *need* two scripts to handle user creation, right? You could create a single script that submits to itself. That would allow you to not only do the client-side validation already in place with jQuery and JavaScript, but check usernames and emails against the database, and return errors if there are duplicates.

But by this stage, you don't need to see another big long code listing. You can just do it yourself. So go ahead. Set this book down and get after combining *signin.php* and *create_user.php*. As always, there's swag to be had by tweeting your solution to *@missingmanuals* or hopping on Facebook at *www.facebook.com/MissingManuals*.

Log Users Out

You've got logging in working, but don't forget to add logging out. Whether you set your cookie's expiration value to a short one—even just a few minutes—or a long one, always allow users to control their own authentication. They should be able to log in when they want, and log out when they want.

Logging in involved setting a cookie name, value, and optionally a time for expiration:

```
setcookie('user_id', $user_id);             // Defaut expiration:
setcookie('username', $result['username']); // Log out on browser close
```

Logging out is much the same, inverted. Just set the cookie's value to an empty value, and set the expiration in the past:

```
// Expire the user_id cookie with a date a year in the past
setcookie('user_id', '', time()-(60*60*24*365));
```

In this case, the "user_id" cookie's value is set to nothing (an empty string), and the expiration date is set to a year in the past.

> **NOTE** Be sure you set the expiration well into the past. That way, if the system time on your server is off by a few minutes or even days, it doesn't affect your code. If the system time is more than a year off, then you have bigger issues.

Turning this into a script is awfully simple. Just expire the two cookies your app uses—"user_id" and "username"—and redirect the user back to a home page or sign in page.

```
<?php

setcookie('user_id', '', time()-(365*24*60*60));
setcookie('username', '', time()-(365*24*60*60));

header('Location: signin.php');
?>
```

To try it out, visit your app (after closing your browser and clearing any cookies), and sign in as a known user. You should be able to visit *show_user.php*, *show_users.php*, and delete users. That's all working as it should.

> **NOTE** Well, it's kind of working. Any old user shouldn't be able to see all the users and delete users, but you'll fix that shortly.

Now click the Sign Out link on the menu. You should be redirected to the sign-in page. You also can visit pages that require a user ID, and you'll not see your user's profile. That's good...but what happens isn't. Check out Figure 12-12.

So signing out appears to be working, but it's revealed a nasty hole in the app: pages that shouldn't be accessible at all *are* accessible. They just error out, which is arguably worse than just letting unauthorized users see them. No matter how you cut it, there's an issue to be resolved.

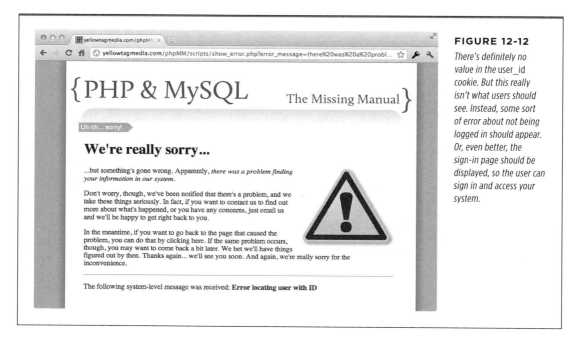

FIGURE 12-12

There's definitely no value in the user_id cookie. But this really isn't what users should see. Instead, some sort of error about not being logged in should appear. Or, even better, the sign-in page should be displayed, so the user can sign in and access your system.

Require the Cookie to Be Set

Fortunately, this isn't hard to fix. Earlier, *show_user.php* and other restricted scripts required *authorize.php*, which did all sorts of database work to see if a user could log in, all using basic HTTP authentication. But in that, you got a nice wall around your scripts.

By removing *authorize.php*, it became possible to have *signin.php* handle logins. But in the process, you tore out that wall around your other scripts. So you need the wall, but you still need to let *signin.php* handle authentication. That's not hard.

First, you can drastically simplify *authorize.php*. Chop it down to do little more than check for a valid cookie:

```php
<?php
if ((!isset($_COOKIE['user_id'])) ||
    (!strlen($_COOKIE['user_id']) > 0)) {
}
?>
```

If there's no cookie, or if the cookie has an empty value, just redirect the user to the sign-in page with a message that explains what's going on:

```php
<?php
if ((!isset($_COOKIE['user_id'])) ||
    (!strlen($_COOKIE['user_id']) > 0)) {
  header('Location: signin.php?' .
         'error_message=You must login to see this page.');
  exit;
}
?>
```

WARNING   The exit here is pretty important. Since this code will run and then pass control back to the calling script—*show_user.php* or *delete_user.php* or whatever else—then you need to make sure those scripts don't continue to try and run. Send the redirect headers and bail out of any further action.

Perfect. Now, you can add the *require_once* back in to *show_user.php*, *show_users.php*, and *delete_user.php*.

Try this out. Make sure you're signed out (*signout.php* via the menu's link makes this trivial now). Then try and access *show_user.php*. You get signs of progress, although things aren't yet perfect. Figure 12-13 is a good start, though.

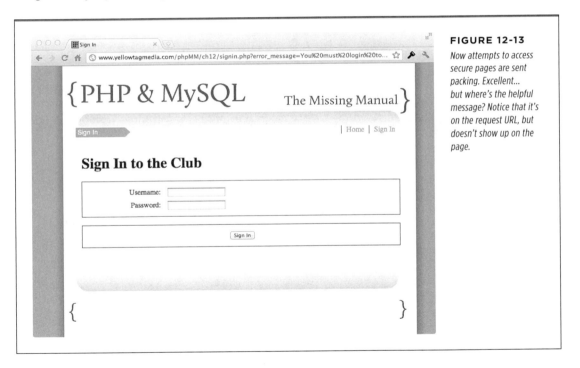

FIGURE 12-13

Now attempts to access secure pages are sent packing. Excellent... but where's the helpful message? Notice that it's on the request URL, but doesn't show up on the page.

So what gives? Well, there's nothing in *signin.php* that deals with a potential message on the request URL. But you've actually got the mechanics for this in place. Open up *signin.php*, and check out the opening section:

```
require_once '../scripts/view.php';

$error_message = "";

// If the user is logged in, the user_id cookie will be set
if (!isset($_COOKIE['user_id'])) {
```

This is great. And you've already got code to display *$error_message* as an error:

```
// Still in the "not signed in" part of the if
// Start the page, and pass along any error message set earlier
page_start("Sign In", NULL, NULL, $error_message);
```

So now you just need to see if there's a request parameter back up at the top:

```
<?php

require_once '../scripts/database_connection.php';
require_once '../scripts/view.php';

$error_message = $_REQUEST['error_message'];

// If the user is logged in, the user_id cookie will be set
if (!isset($_COOKIE['user_id'])) {
```

Piece of cake. Now, you can try things one more time. Hit *show_user.php* without a cookie set, and you should see something like Figure 12-14.

So what's left? Take a look back at your original list:

- A better login screen. Nobody likes a bland gray pop-up; they want a branded, styled login form. **(Done!)**

- Better messaging indicating whether a user is logged in or not. **(Done!)**

- A way to log out. **(Done!)**

- Two levels of authentication: one to get to the main application, and then admin-level authentication to get to a page like *show_users.php* and *delete_user.php*. **(Hmmm, nothing here yet at all.)**

- Some basic navigation—and that navigation should change based on a user's login and the groups to which they belong. **(Sort of done...)**

Pretty good. So take a quick breath, and it's time for the home stretch: group-based authentication, and the reason that cookies are cool, but maybe not your final authentication destination.

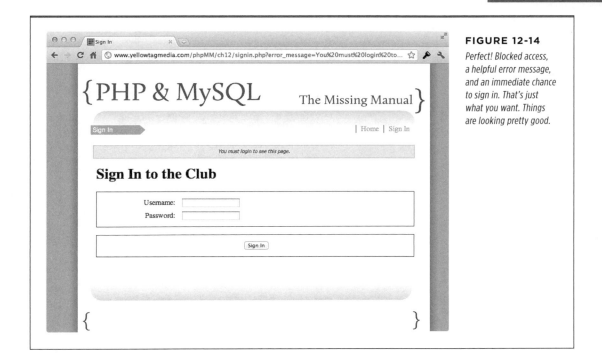

FIGURE 12-14

Perfect! Blocked access, a helpful error message, and an immediate chance to sign in. That's just what you want. Things are looking pretty good.

Authorization and Sessions

You have two big tasks left. Well, one and a half, as some of this work you've already done:

- Two levels of authentication: one to get to the main application, and then admin-level authentication to get to a page like *show_users.php* and *delete_user.php*.

- Some basic navigation—and that navigation should change based on a user's login and the groups to which they belong.

You've already got blanket authentication on that first item. That's handled through *authorize.php*. But now it's time to go further: *authorize.php* needs to be improved. It should take in a group (or, better, a list of groups) and only allow access if the user is in the passed in groups.

And on the second item, you've also got some work done. You've got menus that changed based on whether a user is logged in or not. Again, though, there are some needed improvements: if a user is in certain groups, they should see an option to administrate users, and get a link to *show_users.php* (in addition to the standard link to *show_user.php*).

And then...there's a problem with cookies. It's not a huge problem, but there are some very real concerns over a high-end application using cookies and only cookies for authentication. So there's that to consider.

Time's a wasting. You've got problems to fix.

◼ Modeling Groups in Your Database

First things first. Before you can look up the groups to which a user belongs, you've got to have some groups in your database. That, of course, means you need a table to store groups, and some means by which you can connect a user to a group. Not only that, you need to be able to connect one user to multiple groups.

So there are a few distinct steps here:

1. Create a table in the database to store groups.

2. Map a user to zero, one, or more groups.

3. Build PHP to look up that mapping.

4. Restrict pages based on any login, or a particular set of groups.

First things first: it all begins with a database table.

Adding a Groups Table

Creating a new table is a trifling thing for a PHP and MySQL programmer. You can easily create a new table, name it, give MySQL a few columns, specify which are *NOT NULL*, and you're quickly past database table creation.

```
mysql> CREATE TABLE groups (
    ->    id          INT         NOT NULL AUTO_INCREMENT PRIMARY KEY,
    ->    name        VARCHAR(30) NOT NULL,
    ->    description VARCHAR(200)
    -> );
Query OK, 0 rows affected (0.03 sec)

mysql> DESCRIBE groups;
+-------------+--------------+------+-----+---------+----------------+
| Field       | Type         | Null | Key | Default | Extra          |
+-------------+--------------+------+-----+---------+----------------+
| id          | int(11)      | NO   | PRI | NULL    | auto_increment |
| name        | varchar(30)  | NO   |     | NULL    |                |
| description | varchar(200) | YES  |     | NULL    |                |
+-------------+--------------+------+-----+---------+----------------+
3 rows in set (0.03 sec)
```

As usual, each group needs an ID and a name. The description column is optional—it's not *NOT NULL*, which is bad grammar but good database design—and that's all you need.

It's hard to do much testing without some actual group information, so go ahead and add a few groups into your new *groups* table:

```
mysql> INSERT INTO groups
    ->        (name, description)
    -> VALUES ("Administrators",
    ->        "Users who administrate the entire application.");
Query OK, 1 row affected (0.04 sec)

mysql> INSERT INTO groups
    ->        (name, description)
    -> VALUES ("Luthiers",
    ->        "Guitar builders. They make the instrument that make the mu-
sic.");
Query OK, 1 row affected (0.00 sec)

mysql> INSERT INTO groups
    ->        (name, description)
    -> VALUES ("Musicians",
    ->        "Play what you feel, they say. And they feel it.");
Query OK, 1 row affected (0.00 sec)
```

NOTE Create whatever groups you want for your own users. Just make sure you create an Administrators group. If you call that group something else, you'll want to change the later references in this chapter from "Administrators" to whatever name you use.

As usual, test before moving on:

```
mysql> SELECT id, name FROM groups;
+----+----------------+
| id | name           |
+----+----------------+
|  1 | Administrators |
|  2 | Luthiers       |
|  3 | Musicians      |
+----+----------------+
3 rows in set (0.01 sec)
```

The Many-to-Many Relationship

How do you connect users to groups? Before you can start worrying about SQL, you need to think clearly about how these two tables are related. Relationships help you determine in what manner tables are linked.

◼ ONE-TO-ONE, ONE-TO-MANY, MANY-TO-MANY

You've already seen an example of a one-to-one relationship. When you were storing actual images in your database, you had a single entry in *users* that was related to a single entry in *images*. So there was a *one-to-one relationship* between *users* and *images*.

With groups, that's not the case. You've already seen that a single user can be in zero groups, or one group, or many groups. For example, Michael Greenfield can be a luthier, a musician, and an administrator. And you might have another user who is in none of those groups.

So from that perspective, you have a *one-to-many relationship*. One user can be related to many groups. Many here doesn't have a strict literal meaning, either. It means something more like "as many as you want." So "many" can mean 0 or 1 or 1000, or anything in between or above.

However, that's only part of the story. Because you can flip things around, and look at it from the *groups* point of view. A group can have many users. So the Administrators group might have four, five, or twenty users. That means there's a one-to-many relationship on the groups-to-users side of things, as well as on the users-to-groups side.

What you have here is a *many-to-many relationship* between users and groups (or, if your like, between groups and users). One user can be in many groups; one group can have many users. It's a multi-sided relationship, which is a bit more complex to model at the database level, but just as important in the real world of data as a one-to-one relationship or a one-to-many relationship.

> **NOTE** A good example of a true one-to-many relationship is a user that might have a gallery of images. A user can have many images, but that user's images can't be related to multiple users. It really is a one (user)-to-many (images) relationship.

POWER USERS' CLINIC

Lots of Programmers Are Secretly Math Geeks

It's true: most programmers have at least a little love for math, often buried somewhere deep down. One proof of that is that many programming concepts share naming ideas from math.

So you may hear about one-to-one (1-to-1 or, sometimes, 1:1) relationships. And you'll also hear about one-to-many relationships. But just as often, you'll hear about a 1-to-N relationship. N is a mathematical term; it's usually written as lowercase n in math, but it's more often capital N in programming. And that N is just a stand-in for a variable number. So N could be 0, or 1, or some really large number.

In that light, then, a one-to-many relationship is the same as a 1:N relationship. It's just that 1:N is a shorter, more concise way to say the same thing. By now, you know programmers—like you—tend to favor short and concise. So on database diagrams you'll often see 1:N, which just tells you that you've got a one-to-many relationship occurring between two tables.

And then, of course, you've got N:N, which is just saying that many items in one table are related to many items in another. That said, an N:N relationship (and the many-to-many relationship that it represents) is really a conceptual or virtual idea. It takes two relationships at the database level in most systems to model an N:N relationship, as you'll see on the next page.

■ JOINS ARE BEST DONE WITH IDS

When you related a user to a profile image, you used an ID. So an image had its own ID, uniquely identifying the image. But it also had a *user_id*, which connected the image to a particular user in the *users* table. That made it easy to grab an image for a user with something like this:

```
SELECT *
  FROM images
 WHERE user_id = $user_id;
```

Or, you can join the two tables like this:

```
SELECT u.username, u.first_name, u.last_name, i.filename, i.image_data
  FROM users u, images i
 WHERE u.id = i.user_id;
```

In both cases, it's the IDs that are the connectors. This works fine in a one-to-one relationship, as it does in a one-to-many relationship. The "many" side just adds a column that references the ID of the "one" side. So many images all have a *user_id* column that references a user with the ID 51 (or 2931 or whatever else you have in *users*).

But with users and groups, you don't have a one-to-one or a one-to-many. You have a many-to-many. How do you handle that?

■ USING A JOIN TABLE TO CONNECT USERS WITH GROUPS

IDs are the key. And it's pretty simple to model a one-to-many relationship. The trick is modeling a many-to-many relationship, because connecting the IDs is a problem. You need a sort of matrix: a set of user IDs and group IDs that are connected.

Think about the many-to-many relationship. In its simplest form, it's really two one-to-many relationships; that's how you worked out that users and groups were related via a many-to-many relationship. You started with one side: users. Then you figured out it was one-to-many. Then, the other side: groups. Also one-to-many.

In the same way, you can construct a many-to-many relationship at the database level this way. You have a table like users that connects to an intermediary table. Call it *user_groups*, and suppose it has a *user_id* and a *group_id*. So a *user_id* might appear in two rows: in the first row along with the ID for the "Administrators" group, and again with the ID of the "Musicians" group. That gives you the one-to-many from *users* to *groups*.

But then you also have the one-to-many from groups to users. The ID for "Administrators" might appear in five different rows within *user_groups*, once for each of the five users to which that group relates.

Create this table to give this idea a concrete form:

```
mysql> CREATE TABLE user_groups (
    ->         user_id  INT NOT NULL,
    ->         group_id INT NOT NULL
    -> );
Query OK, 0 rows affected (0.03 sec)
```

This table becomes a bridge: each row connects one user to one group. So for "Jeff Traugott" with an ID of 51, and a group "Luthiers" with an ID of 2, you'd add this row to *user_groups*.

```
mysql> INSERT INTO user_groups
    ->         (user_id, group_id)
    -> VALUES (51, 2);
Query OK, 1 row affected (0.02 sec)

mysql> select * from user_groups;
+---------+----------+
| user_id | group_id |
+---------+----------+
|      51 |        2 |
+---------+----------+
1 row in set (0.00 sec)
```

On their own, the *users* and *groups* tables aren't connected. But this additional table establishes the many-to-many relationship.

Testing Out Group Membership

So to see if a user is in a group, you need to see if there's an entry with both the user's ID you want, and the group's ID you want, in *user_groups*.

```
mysql> SELECT COUNT(*)
    ->   FROM users u, groups g, user_groups ug
    ->  WHERE u.username = "traugott"
    ->    AND g.name = "Luthiers"
    ->    AND u.user_id = ug.user_id
    ->    AND g.id = ug.group_id;
+----------+
| COUNT(*) |
+----------+
|        1 |
+----------+
1 row in set (0.00 sec)
```

Bingo! Walk through this query slowly; it looks a little complex at first blush, but it's straightforward.

First, you can use *COUNT(*)* to return a count on the rows returned from the query. And then there are the three tables you'll need to involve: *users*, *groups*, and *user_groups*.

```
SELECT COUNT(*)
    FROM users u, groups g, user_groups ug
```

Then, you indicate the name of the user you want (using any column you want; first name, or last name, or username), and the name of the group you want. This will cause exactly one (or zero, if there's no match) row in both *users* and *groups* to be isolated.

```
SELECT COUNT(*)
    FROM users u, groups g, user_groups ug
  WHERE u.username = "traugott"
    AND g.name = "Luthiers"
```

Now, you need to connect those individual rows—each with an ID—to *user_groups*. This is just a regular join. You use the IDs in each table to match up with the ID columns in *user_groups*:

```
SELECT COUNT(*)
    FROM users u, groups g, user_groups ug
  WHERE u.username = "traugott"
    AND g.name = "Luthiers"
    AND u.user_id = ug.user_id
    AND g.id = ug.group_id;
```

So this connects zero or one row in *users* to *user_groups*, which is also connected to zero or one row in *groups*. The result? Either a single row with a *COUNT* value of 1, meaning that there's a connection from a user in *users* to the group in *groups* you indicated...

```
+----------+
| COUNT(*) |
+----------+
|        1 |
+----------+
```

...or a row with a *COUNT* value of 0, meaning there's no connection:

```
mysql> SELECT COUNT(*)
    ->    FROM users u, groups g, user_groups ug
    ->  WHERE u.username = "traugott"
    ->    AND g.name = "Administrators"
    ->    AND u.user_id = ug.user_id
    ->    AND g.id = ug.group_id;
```

```
+----------+
| COUNT(*) |
+----------+
|        0 |
+----------+
1 row in set (0.05 sec)
```

> **WARNING** Watch out! With this particular expression—using *COUNT*—you do get a single row each time. The important information is the *value* in the row, not that there *is* a row.

Now you just have to turn this into PHP code.

Checking for Group Membership

You've already got the makings of a good authentication scheme. You've replaced basic authentication with your own authentication scheme. And that's authentication: allowing a user in if she logs in. They authenticate in some manner that tells your system that the user really is who she says she is.

But now it's time to add authorization: the ability to only give access to certain pages based on more specific criteria. At its simplest, you do have some level of authorization through *authorize.php*: you only authorize users who are authenticated. But usually authorization goes a lot further than that. It's more granular; you can control access based on, say, group membership.

At this point, you've got the users. You've got the groups. You've got the connection between the two. So now *authorize.php* needs to be enhanced to work these groups into your authorization scheme.

authorize.php Needs a Function

Right now, *authorize.php* runs automatically when it's required by a script. So the code in *authorize.php* isn't in a function; it's just dropped into the body of the PHP file:

```php
<?php

if ((!isset($_COOKIE['user_id'])) || (!strlen($_COOKIE['user_id']) > 0)) {
  header('Location: signin.php?' .
         'error_message=You must login to see this page.');
  exit;
}
?>
```

That's worked fine up until now. But the times, they are a' changin'. You need a means by which you can pass a group—or a list of groups—to *authorize.php*, and then *authorize.php* has to run through those groups and see if there's a connection with the current user. That situation—a block of code that should take in a piece of information with which to work—screams "function." There are some other options, but they're less easy to understand and maintain. (If you're curious about those options, see the box on page 437.)

Go ahead and create a new function in *authorize.php*. Eventually, it should take an array of groups that allow access. For now, you can set a default value for the parameter the function takes and use that default value to keep the current functionality: allowing access to any authorized user.

```php
<?php

function authorize_user($groups = NULL) {
  // No need to check groups if there aren't cookies set
  if ((!isset($_COOKIE['user_id'])) ||
      (!strlen($_COOKIE['user_id']) > 0)) {
    header('Location: signin.php?' .
           'error_message=You must login to see this page.');
    exit;
  }
}
?>
```

Now jump back into *show_user.php*, and add an explicit call to this function. You don't need to pass in any group names. *show_user.php* should be open to any logged-in user.

```php
<?php

require '../scripts/authorize.php';
require '../scripts/database_connection.php';
require '../scripts/view.php';

// Authorize any user, as long as they're logged in
authorize_user();

// Get the user ID of the user to show
$user_id = $_REQUEST['user_id'];

// Build the SELECT statement

// and so on...
```

You should test this out. Since the default functionality should be just what you already have, make sure you can't access *show_user.php* without logging in first. Enter the URL into your browser, and you should see your sign-in page, as shown in Figure 13-1.

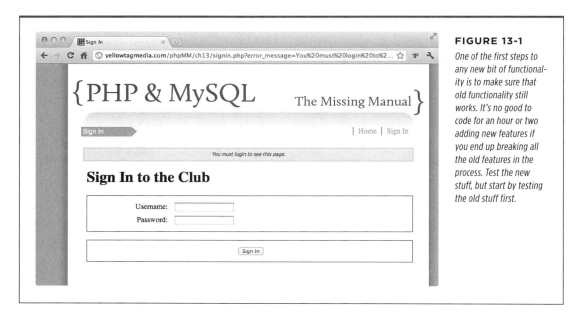

FIGURE 13-1

One of the first steps to any new bit of functionality is to make sure that old functionality still works. It's no good to code for an hour or two adding new features if you end up breaking all the old features in the process. Test the new stuff, but start by testing the old stuff first.

Taking in a List of Groups

Now it's time to get to the point of all this work. Start out by sending a list of groups—through a PHP array—to *authorize_user*. You can do this in *show_users.php* and *delete_user.php*, both of which should require the Administrators group for access.

```php
<?php

require_once '../scripts/app_config.php';
require_once '../scripts/authorize.php';
require_once '../scripts/database_connection.php';
require_once '../scripts/view.php';

// Only Administrators can access this page
authorize_user(array("Administrators"));

// Rest of the PHP code and HTML output
```

NOTE The change above is shown in *show_users.php*. Make the same change in *delete_user.php* so that it can't be directly accessed.

On Functions and Non-Functions

In *authorize.php*, you've got a function that takes in zero or more groups via a parameter. But that's just one way to handle the issue. There are other approaches: you could, for example, set a variable and then use that variable in the required file.

So, for example, take a simple script like this:

```php
<?php
$message = "hello\n\n";
require_once "print.php";
?>
```

You can call this script *test.php* if you're following along. And then suppose *print.php*, the references script, looks like this:

```php
<?php
echo $message;
?>
```

When *print.php* is required, it's like the code in *print.php* is inserted right in the place of the *require_once* line. That means that when you run this script, PHP essentially sees this:

```php
<?php
$message = "hello\n\n";
echo $message;
?>
```

Run *test.php*, and you'd get this result:

```
yellowta@yellowtagmedia.com [~/www/phpMM/
ch13]# php test.php
X-Powered-By: PHP/5.2.17
Content-type: text/html
hello
```

So you can "pass" information into a required script in this manner.

The problem with this approach isn't that it's not easy to implement, or that it has problems in implementation. The problem is that it's just not that clear.

Here's what the code would look like for authorization:

```php
$allowed_groups = array("Musicians", "Lu-
thiers");
require_once "../scripts/authorize.php";
```

There's nothing wrong here. It's simply unclear that the *$groups* variable is required before the *require_once* to *authorize.php*, and that in fact *authorize.php* makes use of that variable. So while an *authorize_user* function is a bit clumsy, it's clear and better than the alternative: code that's a little difficult to read unless you already know what it does.

Using an array is about the simplest means in PHP of getting a list to a function. Now, in *authorize.php*, you're getting either nothing, or a list of allowed group names. So you can start to do some work with those groups.

First, though, if the parameter passed to *authorize_user* is either an empty list or *NULL*, you should have the function bail out. No need to do any database searching in those two cases.

```php
<?php

function authorize_user($groups = NULL) {
  // No need to check groups if there aren't cookies set
  if ((!isset($_COOKIE['user_id'])) ||
      (!strlen($_COOKIE['user_id']) > 0)) {
    header('Location: signin.php?' .
```

```
                'error_message=You must login to see this page.');
      exit;
    }

    // If no groups passed in, the authorization above is enough
    if ((is_null($groups)) || (empty($groups))) {
      return;
    }
  }
?>
```

> **NOTE** The *empty* function takes just about any PHP type and figures out what "empty" means, and returns either *true* or *false*. For an array, *empty* returns true if there aren't any items in the array.

Telling PHP to *return* causes control to return to the calling script. That's allowing the script to run, which means letting the user see the page they requested.

Iterating Over Each Group

Now, back to the case where you *do* get a list of groups, as in *show_users.php* and *delete_user.php*. In those cases, *authorize.php* should loop over each group, and for each group, build a SQL query.

Start out by just looping over the *$groups* array. You can use a *for* loop, but in this case, there's a better choice: *foreach. foreach* lets you loop over an array and automatically assign a variable to the current item in the array:

```
$my_array = array("first", "second", "third");
foreach ($my_array as $item) {
  echo $item;
}
```

So for *$groups*, you could set the loop up like this:

```
foreach ($groups as $group) {
  // do a SQL search for the current $group
}
```

Now, think through what happens inside the loop. You want something similar to the original SQL you used to connect users to groups:

```
SELECT COUNT(*)
  FROM users u, groups g, user_groups ug
 WHERE u.username = "traugott"
   AND g.name = "Luthiers"
   AND u.user_id = ug.user_id
   AND g.id = ug.group_id;
```

But this code is *more* complex than what you need in *authorize.php* (page 364). First, you don't need the *users* table at all. That table is only part of the query to connect a *username* to a *user_id*. But your app already has the user's *user_id*. So things simplify to this:

```
SELECT COUNT(*)
  FROM user_groups ug, groups g
 WHERE g.name = mysql_real_escape_string($group)
   AND g.id = ug.group_id
   AND ug.user_id = mysql_real_escape_string($_COOKIE['user_id']);
```

> **NOTE** As usual, you'll want to use *mysql_real_escape_string* to make sure your database gets clean values. In fact, you might as well get into the habit: just use *mysql_real_escape_string* on pretty much anything that originates in your scripts and is sent to MySQL.

There's another improvement you can make, too. In the query above, you'd need to get the result row, and see if the value is 0 (no membership) or 1 (membership). But that's an additional step. What would be even better is to just check and see if there's a result at all. In other words, you want a query that only returns a result row if there's a match. So you can make another change:

```
SELECT ug.user_id
  FROM user_groups ug, groups g
 WHERE g.name = mysql_real_escape_string($group)
   AND g.id = ug.group_id
   AND ug.user_id = mysql_real_escape_string($_COOKIE['user_id']);
```

The particular column you select from *user_groups* doesn't matter; you could use *ug.group_id* as well. The point is that now, you either get a result when there's a match, or you get no result, so that's one less step your code needs to take.

Put all this together, and you end up with something like the following in your *foreach* loop:

```
foreach ($groups as $group) {
  // do a SQL search for the current $group
  $query = "SELECT ug.user_id" .
           "  FROM user_groups ug, groups g" .
           " WHERE g.name = '" . mysql_real_escape_string($group) . "'" .
           "   AND g.id = ug.group_id" .
           "   AND ug.user_id = " .
                 mysql_real_escape_string($COOKIE['user_id']) . "';";
  mysql_query($query);

  // Deal with results
}
```

This script works, and it doesn't require the *users* table. But you're constructing this string, over and over again. For every group, this string is recreated and that's wasteful.

Here's where *sprintf* becomes your friend (again). With *sprintf*, you can construct a single string, give it an escape character or two, and simply insert into the string values for each escape character. The string says unchanged, and you're only modifying the data within that string that's variable.

So you can construct the query string outside of the *foreach*, like this:

```
// Set up the query string
$query_string =
    "SELECT ug.user_id" .
    "  FROM user_groups ug, groups g" .
    " WHERE g.name = '%s'" .
    "   AND g.id = ug.group_id" .
    "   AND ug.user_id = " . mysql_real_escape_string($_COOKIE['user_id']);

foreach ($groups as $group) {
  // do a SQL search for the current $group

  // Deal with results
}
```

Then, within the *foreach*, use *sprintf* to supply the values to drop into the string for a particular group:

```
// Set up the query string
$query_string =
    "SELECT ug.user_id" .
    "  FROM user_groups ug, groups g" .
    " WHERE g.name = '%s'" .
    "   AND g.id = ug.group_id" .
    "   AND ug.user_id = " . mysql_real_escape_string($_COOKIE['user_id']);

foreach ($groups as $group) {
  // do a SQL search for the current $group
  $query = sprintf($query_string, mysql_real_escape_string($group));
  $result = mysql_query($query);

  // Deal with results
}
```

Note that in addition to using *sprintf*, this code assigns the current user ID—from *$_COOKIE*—to the string assembled outside of the loop. There's no need to feed that to *sprintf*, because it won't change as you loop.

Wouldn't All Those Queries Work?

Absolutely. As you've come to realize, though, there are solutions to problems, and then they are *better* solutions to problems. When you're working with databases, "better" usually means "faster," and "faster" usually means "less work for the database to do."

In the case of looking up a group and seeing if a user is a member, there's nothing functionally wrong with this query:

```
SELECT COUNT(*)
  FROM users u, groups g, user_groups ug
 WHERE u.username =
       mysql_real_escape_string($_
COOKIE['username'])
    AND g.name = mysql_real_escape_
string($group)
    AND u.user_id = ug.user_id
    AND g.id = ug.group_id;
```

But you're doing a *lot* more work than you need. There's an entire extra table involved (*users*) that you can cut out, because you already have the user's ID in a cookie.

You can cut down on dealing with results by moving from a *COUNT* in the SELECT—which will require you to always examine the results in a row—for a column in *user_groups*. Then you only need to see if there are rows returned; the values in those result rows become irrelevant.

And you can improve on general execution time by only creating a string once, and using *sprintf* to modify just a small part of that string every time you go to a new group. Again, this is a small improvement, but an important one that's easy to make.

All these small changes can add up to noticeable improvements in your app. It will simply "feel" more responsive. This is even more important because the authorization script is going to run every time a user hits your page. That means that a script that's sloppy or slower than it needs to be creates a lag in every single page access.

Most users don't like—and many won't put up with—slow-loading sites. This isn't a pause while you secure your user concert tickets or look up shipping information. It's simply them navigating to a new page. A little work on your script to keep things peppy makes a huge difference on their experience, especially as you have more and more users accessing your site, which means more and more hits against your database to verify group membership.

Allow, Deny, Redirect

With a solid query in place, it's time to deal with the results. You can check the number of rows, and know all you need: if no rows were returned, the user isn't a member of the group indicated by *$group*, and your loop should continue, going to the next *$group* in *$groups*.

If there is a row returned from a query, not only is the user in an allowed group, but *authorize_user* needs to stop. No need to keep looping over *$groups*; just return control to the calling script, so the PHP and HTML of that script can take over.

And then, the final case: all the groups have been checked, and there's never been a result row. That's the case when the *foreach* loop ends. If this is the case, it's not okay to send control back to the calling script, because that would be letting the user "in," and that's exactly the *opposite* of what should happen. It's also not appropriate to redirect the user back to the sign-in page. They are signed in, at least in most cases, and simply don't have the right level of permissions to access the current page.

So what's left? In the simplest case, just use *handle_error* one more time. You might want to build this out yourself, though. Perhaps you could redirect them to the last page they viewed and set an error message. Or you could build a customized page to allow the user to request permissions for a certain page. No matter how you cut it, though, you're going to be sending them somewhere else; the current page is never shown.

Here's a version of *authorize.php* that takes all this into account:

```php
<?php

require_once 'database_connection.php';
require_once 'app_config.php';

function authorize_user($groups = NULL) {

  // No need to check groups if there aren't cookies set
  if ((!isset($_COOKIE['user_id'])) || (!strlen($_COOKIE['user_id']) > 0)) {
    header('Location: signin.php?' .
           'error_message=You must login to see this page.');
    exit;
  }

  // If no groups passed in, the authorization above is enough
  if ((is_null($groups)) || (empty($groups))) {
    return;
  }

  // Set up the query string
  $query_string =
      "SELECT ug.user_id" .
      "  FROM user_groups ug, groups g" .
      " WHERE g.name = '%s'" .
      "   AND g.id = ug.group_id" .
      "   AND ug.user_id = " . mysql_real_escape_string($_COOKIE['user_id']);


  // Run through each group and check membership
  foreach ($groups as $group) {
    $query = sprintf($query_string, mysql_real_escape_string($group));
    $result = mysql_query($query);

    if (mysql_num_rows($result) == 1) {
      // If we got a result, the user should be allowed access
      //   Just return so the script will continue to run
      return;
    }
```

```
    }

    // If we got here, no matches were found for any group
    // The user isn't allowed access
    handle_error("You are not authorized to see this page.");
    exit;
  }
?>
```

It's been a long time coming, but you can finally try this out. Make sure you've got a user in users that is a member of Administrators (through *user_groups*), and one that's not. The former should be able to navigate to *show_users.php* without any problems; the latter should be kicked to the error page, as shown in Figure 13-2.

FIGURE 13-2

You should see this page as a first step toward authorization, rather than a last one. This setup is a bit clumsy, and you should come up with a better, less interruptive way to let users know they've ended up some-where they shouldn't be. Take them back to a page they can access, if possible. Full-page errors should be serious things, rarely shown without a lot of thought.

Group-Specific Menus

Right now, you can use *authorize_user* to check a user against a list of groups, and either reject access to a page, or allow the user to see a page. That means you have the logic to handle group-specific menus, but the actual implementation may take a bit of refactoring.

Take a look at your menu system as it stands, in *view.php*:

```
function display_title($title, $success_message = NULL, $error_message = NULL)
{
echo <<<EOD
```

```
  <body>
<div id="page_start">
  <div id="header"><h1>PHP & MySQL: The Missing Manual</h1></div>
  <div id="example">$title</div>
  <div id="menu">
    <ul>
      <li><a href="index.html">Home</a></li>
EOD;
  if (isset($_COOKIE['user_id'])) {
    echo "<li><a href='show_user.php'>My Profile</a></li>";
    echo "<li><a href='signout.php'>Sign Out</a></li>";
  } else {
    echo "<li><a href='signin.php'>Sign In</a></li>";
  }
echo <<<EOD
    </ul>
  </div>
EOD;
  display_messages($success_message, $error_message);
  echo "</div> <!-- page_start -->";
}
```

authorize_user isn't a function you can just drop in here; it either allows a user to see a page, or disallows him. It's not a fine-grained tool with which you can check group membership and get back a true or false value.

What you really want is something like the following:

```
function display_title($title, $success_message = NULL, $error_message = NULL)
{
echo <<<EOD
  <body>
<div id="page_start">
  <div id="header"><h1>PHP & MySQL: The Missing Manual</h1></div>
  <div id="example">$title</div>
  <div id="menu">
    <ul>
      <li><a href="index.html">Home</a></li>
EOD;
  if (isset($_COOKIE['user_id'])) {
    echo "<li><a href='show_user.php'>My Profile</a></li>";
    if (user_in_group($_COOKIE['user_id'], "Administrators")) {
      echo "<li><a href='show_users.php'>Manage Users</a></li>";
    }
    echo "<li><a href='signout.php'>Sign Out</a></li>";
  } else {
    echo "<li><a href='signin.php'>Sign In</a></li>";
```

```
    }
  echo <<<EOD
      </ul>
    </div>
EOD;
    display_messages($success_message, $error_message);
    echo "</div> <!-- page_start -->";
  }
```

> **NOTE** You'll also need to add a *require_once* for *authorize.php* to *view.php* for this code to eventually work.

Then, that function would check group memberships, and show the Manage Users link to Administrators. You've already got all the relevant code in *authorize_user.php*:

```
  // Set up the query string
  $query_string =
      "SELECT ug.user_id" .
      "  FROM user_groups ug, groups g" .
      " WHERE g.name = '%s'" .
      "   AND g.id = ug.group_id" .
      "   AND ug.user_id = " . mysql_real_escape_string($_COOKIE['user_id']);


  // Run through each group and check membership
  foreach ($groups as $group) {
    $query = sprintf($query_string, mysql_real_escape_string($group));
    $result = mysql_query($query);

    if (mysql_num_rows($result) == 1) {
      // If we got a result, the user should be allowed access
      //   Just return so the script will continue to run
      return;
    }
  }
```

It just needs to be adapted into a new function that takes in a user's ID and a group. That's pretty easy, though:

```
  function user_in_group($user_id, $group) {
    $query_string =
      "SELECT ug.user_id" .
      "  FROM user_groups ug, groups g" .
      " WHERE g.name = '%s'" .
      "   AND g.id = ug.group_id" .
      "   AND ug.user_id = %d";
```

```
        $query = sprintf($query_string, mysql_real_escape_string($group),
                                 mysql_real_escape_string($user_id));
        $result = mysql_query($query);

        if (mysql_num_rows($result) == 1) {
          return true;
        } else {
          return false;
        }
      }
```

Nothing here is new. It's just a new riff on an old hit: the code you've already got in *authorize.php*, in the *authorize_user* function.

Get this code in place, and then try it out. First, log in as a user that's not in Administrators. Visit a page like *show_user.php*, and your menu options should not have a Manage Users options (see Figure 13-3).

FIGURE 13-3

Ahh, the poor user who isn't a member of Administrators. They see no Manage Users option— but that's actually good. They don't see options that they can't access, and never feel poor at all. That's the heart of good authorization: as important as it is to "keep people out," it's equally important to just avoid showing options that aren't accessible.

Now sign out, and do exactly the same thing again, this time with an administrative user. Magically—at least from the non-PHP programmer's point of view—a new menu option appears. You can see the Manage Users link in Figure 13-4.

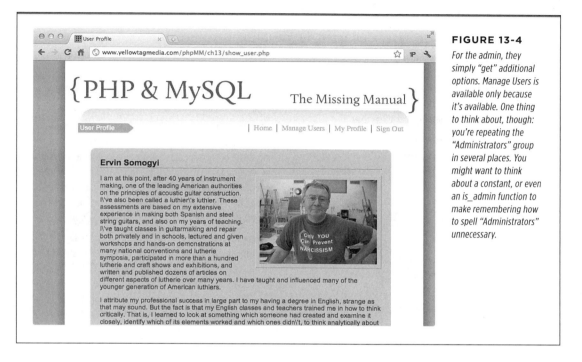

FIGURE 13-4

For the admin, they simply "get" additional options. Manage Users is available only because it's available. One thing to think about, though: you're repeating the "Administrators" group in several places. You might want to think about a constant, or even an is_admin function to make remembering how to spell "Administrators" unnecessary.

■ Entering Browser Sessions

So far, cookies have been the secret to much of your authentication and authorization success. But there are many programmers who really, really hate a cookie-only solution to storing a user's information. The biggest issue with cookies is that they are entirely client-side. That means that anything you store in a cookie lives in that cookie, on the client's computer.

In your case, that means the user's ID and username are stored on your computer. In fact, on most web browsers, you can easily look at your cookies. Log in to your app, and then view your cookies. On Firefox, for example, you can click Tools→Web Developer→Cookies→View Cookie Information. Figure 13-5 shows the cookies related to this app.

Shouldn't *authorize_user* Call *user_in_group*?

Major refactoring points if you thought of this question, or if it felt a bit like you might be duplicating code in *user_in_group*, and that bothered you. It's true; there's a lot similar about the code in *user_in_group* and the code that iterates over *$groups* and looks up each group within *authorize_user*.

One way to take advantage of *user_in_group* and remove this similar code would be to rework the *foreach* in *authorize_user*:

```
// Remove the initial query string
// before the loop


// Run through each group and
// check membership
foreach ($groups as $group) {
  if (user_in_group($_COOKIE['user_id'],
$group) {

    // Just return so the script
    // will continue to run
    return;
```

```
  }
}
```

This looks pretty good. There's a lot less code, and you've done some pretty nice refactoring.

But, you've actually gone back toward the original code in *authorize_user* from which you moved away. Now there's a query string created every time through the loop (hidden away within *user_in_group*). That string is being created over and over, and continually assigned the same user ID with each group in *$groups*. By moving away from that approach, you (if only in some small ways) sped up the performance of *authorize_user*.

And here's where you have to make a tough decision. Is the clean, refactored approach here worth the loss in speed that requires some nearly duplicate code? In the case of a bit of code that's potentially called on most, if not every page—*authorize_user*—it might be worth not refactoring. That little bit of improved speed times one hundred page views; one thousand; one million...it starts to seriously add up.

NOTE On Safari, cookies are under *Preferences*. Click the Privacy tab, and then the Details button. With Chrome, select *Preferences*, then Under the Hood, Content Settings and then All Cookies and Site Data In Internet Explorer, select View→Internet Options, click the General tab, and select "Settings" under Browser History. Then you can select View Files under "Temporary Internet Files and History Settings." All these options get you the same information, although in each case it looks a bit different.

This client-side storage is the main reason some developers don't like cookies. Whether the client computer is a public machine in a library, or a home machine, there's just something that seems pretty unsafe about leaving what amounts to a system-level value like a user ID on any old computer.

And that's an important issue. That user ID uniquely identifies a user in your database. On top of that, most applications that use cookies add additional information to a client's machine, rather than lessening it. You might speed up user and group searches by storing cookies with the user's groups (or the IDs of those groups) in cookies; you might store personal information you don't want to constantly look up in cookies.

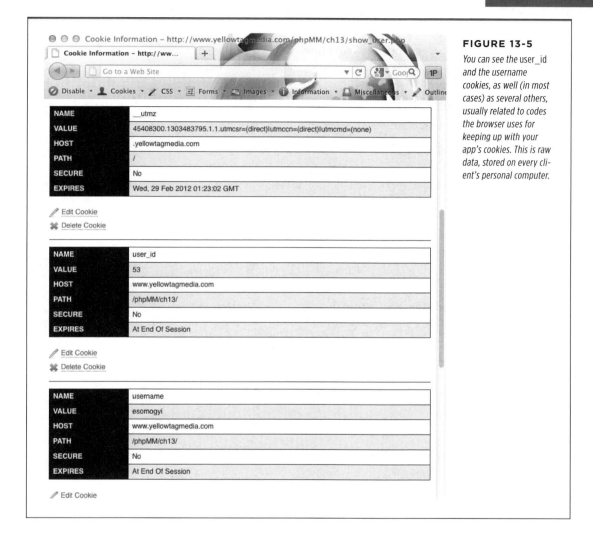

FIGURE 13-5

You can see the user_id and the username cookies, as well (in most cases) as several others, usually related to codes the browser uses for keeping up with your app's cookies. This is raw data, stored on every client's personal computer.

And all this information ends up living on your users' computers until those cookies expire. So what's a security conscious programmer to do?

Sessions are Server-Side

Sessions are generally considered the "answer" to cookies. Sessions are very similar to cookies in that they can store information. However, sessions have two big differences:

1. Sessions are stored on the server, rather than the client. You can't view session data from a browser because there's nothing to view, except perhaps a non-readable ID that connects a particular browser with a session.

2. Because sessions are stored on the server, they can be used to store much bigger chunks of data than cookies. You could store a user's profile picture on the server in a session, for example, and not worry about taking up space on a user's computer.

Because they don't store potentially sensitive information on the user's computer, a lot of programmers prefer sessions.

Sessions Must Be Started

The biggest change in dealing with sessions isn't lots of new syntax. In fact, you'll quickly see that changing from using cookies to sessions is pretty simple. But there is one significant difference: before you can do any work with sessions, you have to call *session_start*:

```
// Start/resume sessions
session_start();

// Now do work with session information
```

So, you might naturally think: call *session_start* in *signin.php*, and you're ready to roll. That's exactly where you should first call *session_start*:

```
<?php

require_once '../scripts/database_connection.php';
require_once '../scripts/view.php';

$error_message = $_REQUEST['error_message'];

session_start();

// Rest of PHP and HTML...
```

Calling *session_start* here kicks off the PHP machinery that makes sessions available.

From *$_COOKIE* to *$_SESSION*

Now, it gets easy: instead of using the superglobal *$_COOKIE*, you use the super-global *$_SESSION*. Yes, it's that simple:

```
<?php

require_once '../scripts/database_connection.php';
require_once '../scripts/view.php';
```

```
$error_message = $_REQUEST['error_message'];

session_start();

// If the user is logged in, the user_id in the session will be set
if (!isset($_SESSION['user_id'])) {
  // and so on...
```

And then there's one other small change. With sessions, you don't use *setcookie*. Instead, you directly set values in *$_SESSION*, providing a key and a value:

```
if (!isset($_SESSION['user_id'])) {

  // See if a login form was submitted with a username for login
  if (isset($_POST['username'])) {
    // Try and log the user in
    $username = mysql_real_escape_string(trim($_REQUEST['username']));
    $password = mysql_real_escape_string(trim($_REQUEST['password']));

    // Look up the user
    $query = sprintf("SELECT user_id, username FROM users " .
                " WHERE username = '%s' AND " .
                "       password = '%s';",
                $username, crypt($password, $username));

    $results = mysql_query($query);

    if (mysql_num_rows($results) == 1) {
      $result = mysql_fetch_array($results);
      $user_id = $result['user_id'];
      // No more setcookie
      $_SESSION['user_id'] = $user_id;
      $_SESSION['username'] = $username;
      header("Location: show_user.php");
      exit();
    } else {
      // If user not found, issue an error
      $error_message = "Your username/password combination was invalid.";
    }
  }
}
```

So now you use *$_SESSION* to retrieve values from the session, and *$_SESSION* to insert values into the session.

All the while, behind the scenes, all this information is stored on the server, rather than the client. Nice, right?

Sessions Must be Restarted, Too

But now there's something a little strange. Try and sign in using a good username/
password combination. You're not going to see what you expect. Instead, you'll
get the error about not being logged in, shown in Figure 13-6. So what's going on?

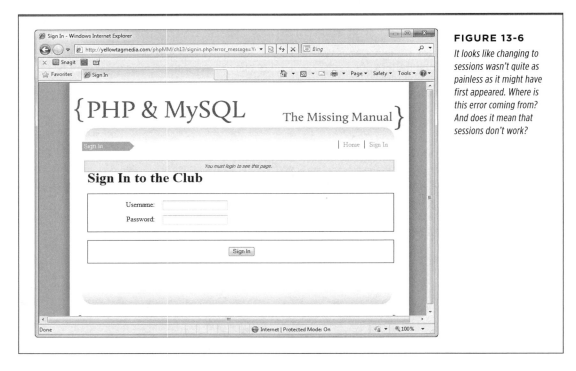

FIGURE 13-6

*It looks like changing to
sessions wasn't quite as
painless as it might have
first appeared. Where is
this error coming from?
And does it mean that
sessions don't work?*

Think carefully; you may even want to search through *signin.php*. Is this an error
related to sessions? Well, kind of. But it's generated by *show_user.php*, not *signin.
php*. In fact, it's really an issue in *authorize_user*, which lives in *authorize.php*; that
function is called at the beginning of *show_user.php*:

```php
<?php

require '../scripts/authorize.php';
require '../scripts/database_connection.php';
require '../scripts/view.php';

// Authorize any user, as long as they're logged in
authorize_user();
```

But that makes perfect sense. *authorize_user* is expecting to find a user ID in
$_COOKIE, which is exposed through *$_REQUEST*.

```php
<?php

require_once 'database_connection.php';
require_once 'app_config.php';

function authorize_user($groups = NULL) {

  // No need to check groups if there aren't cookies set
  if ((!isset($_COOKIE['user_id'])) || (!strlen($_COOKIE['user_id']) > 0)) {
    header('Location: signin.php?' .
           'error_message=You must login to see this page.');
    exit();
  }

// And so on...
```

But now this is another easy change. *$_COOKIE* just has to go to *$_SESSION*:

```php
<?php

require_once 'database_connection.php';
require_once 'app_config.php';

function authorize_user($groups = NULL) {

  // No need to check groups if there aren't cookies set
  if ((!isset($_SESSION['user_id'])) || (!strlen($_SESSION['user_id']) > 0)) {
    header('Location: signin.php?' .
           'error_message=You must login to see this page.');
    exit();
  }

// And so on...
```

Don't forget to make a similar change later in the function, when the query string used for group searching is constructed:

```php
// Set up the query string
$query_string =
    "SELECT ug.user_id" .
    "  FROM user_groups ug, groups g" .
    " WHERE g.name = '%s'" .
    "   AND g.id = ug.group_id" .
    "   AND ug.user_id = " . mysql_real_escape_string($_SESSION['user_id']);
```

This looks good. Unfortunately, you're going to get the exact same result. Sign in again, and you'll get Figure 13-7, yet another error. So now what's going on now?

NOTE You may get a different response, depending on your browser. You might see a timeout, or your browser may simply hang. In all these cases, it's not good.

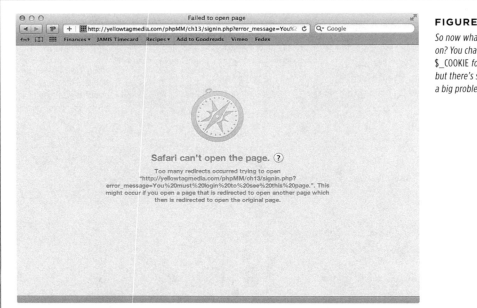

FIGURE 13-7

So now what's going on? You changed out $_COOKIE for $_SESSION, but there's still obviously a big problem here.

The secret is in the rather poorly named *session_start* function. That function sounds like it starts a new session. In that case, you should call it once—as you did—in *signin.php*. But PHP scripts each run on their own, without connection to any other script. So when *show_user.php* is called, it has no idea that a session was started back in *signin.php*.

In fact, there's no connection at all between two scripts; they're just two calls from a browser out there somewhere, hooked to the Internet with WiFi or an Ethernet cable. So how do two scripts—or a whole application's worth of scripts—share this session data? The truth is a bit surprising: calling *start_session* actually creates a cookie on the client. Yes, you're back to cookies!

But this cookie holds a fairly cryptic value (see Figure 13-8). This value refers to where a particular user's data is stored on the server. It's a way to say, "Look up this code in all the server's session data. Whatever's there...that's mine."

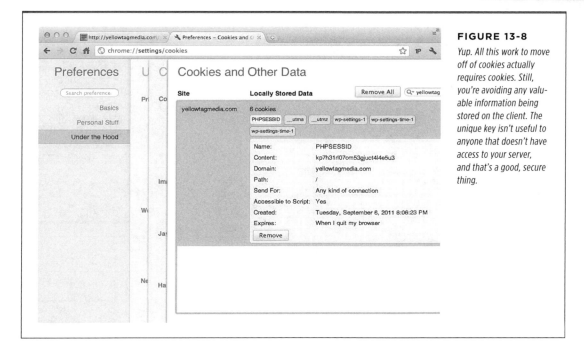

FIGURE 13-8

Yup. All this work to move off of cookies actually requires cookies. Still, you're avoiding any valuable information being stored on the client. The unique key isn't useful to anyone that doesn't have access to your server, and that's a good, secure thing.

Accordingly, *session_start* does a lot more than start a one-time session. It looks up a user's cookie, and if it's there, *restarts* the session that ID references. So every script that wants to use *$_SESSION* has to call *session_start*.

That means fixing the problem in *show_user.php* involves two things: first, you need to call *session_start* in *authorize.php*, to ensure that session data is available to *authorize_user* and the other functions in *authorize.php*.

```php
<?php

require_once 'database_connection.php';
require_once 'app_config.php';

session_start();

function authorize_user($groups = NULL) {
  // an so on...
}
?>
```

Try this script out, and you'll see an error pointing you to the second thing you've got to do. That error is a familiar one, shown in Figure 13-9.

FIGURE 13-9

You've seen this a few times, haven't you? What's going on in this particular case? For some reason, the code that looks up the user's ID isn't working, and kicking the user out with this error about their information not being found.

$_REQUEST Doesn't Include $_SESSION

Here's the line in *show_user.php* that's a problem:

```
// Get the user ID of the user to show
$user_id = $_REQUEST['user_id'];
```

This code worked because whether the user's ID was in *$_REQUEST*, *$_GET*, *$_POST*, or *$_COOKIE*, it didn't matter. All these bubble up to *$_REQUEST*. But now you're passing the user ID in a different superglobal, one not included in *$_REQUEST*: *$_SESSION*.

Not only that, you still have code in *show_users.php* that does pass the user ID in a request parameter:

```
$user_row = sprintf(
  "<li><a href='show_user.php?user_id=%d'>%s %s</a> " .
  "(<a href='mailto:%s'>%s</a>) " .
  "<a href='javascript:delete_user(%d);'><img " .
    "class='delete_user' src='../images/delete.png' " .
    "width='15' /></a></li>",
  $user['user_id'], $user['first_name'], $user['last_name'],
  $user['email'], $user['email'], $user['user_id']);
echo $user_row;
```

So you can't just switch *$_REQUEST* to *$_SESSION* and call it a day. Instead, you need to check both *$_SESSION* and *$_REQUEST* to cover all your bases:

```php
<?php

require '../scripts/authorize.php';
require '../scripts/database_connection.php';
require '../scripts/view.php';

// Authorize any user, as long as they're logged in
authorize_user();

// Get the user ID of the user to show
$user_id = $_REQUEST['user_id'];

if (!isset($user_id)) {
  $user_id = $_SESSION['user_id'];
}

// Look up user using $user_id
```

Now, if there's no user ID found in *$_REQUEST*, the *$_SESSION* is checked. And then, last but not least, you need to call *session_start* before you can do any work with the session:

```php
<?php

require '../scripts/authorize.php';
require '../scripts/database_connection.php';
require '../scripts/view.php';

session_start();

// Authorize any user, as long as they're logged in
authorize_user();

// Get the user ID of the user to show
$user_id = $_REQUEST['user_id'];

if (!isset($user_id)) {
  $user_id = $_SESSION['user_id'];
}

// Look up user using $user_id
```

Now...finally...you can get back to viewing user profiles.

You're now calling *session_start* twice in the *show_user.php* flow: once in *authorize.php*, pulled in through *require_once*. Then, again, in the body of *show_user.php*.

Still, that extra call doesn't do much beyond causing PHP to issue a notice, and there's no guarantee that other scripts that bring in *authorize.php* will also call *session_start*. So the duplicate in *show_user.php* won't always happen. It's a better bet to treat each script as self-contained. Use *session_start every time* you're working with sessions, even if it might have been called somewhere else.

Menu, Anyone?

All that's left is the menu. That still uses *$_COOKIE*, but you know exactly what to do now. First, add the all-important call to *session_start*:

```php
<?php

require_once 'app_config.php';
require_once 'authorize.php';

define("SUCCESS_MESSAGE", "success");
define("ERROR_MESSAGE", "error");

session_start();

// And then functions follow...

?>
```

Then, replace *$_COOKIE* with *$_SESSION* in *display_title*:

```php
function display_title($title, $success_message = NULL, $error_message = NULL)
{
echo <<<EOD
  <body>
<div id="page_start">
  <div id="header"><h1>PHP & MySQL: The Missing Manual</h1></div>
  <div id="example">$title</div>
  <div id="menu">
    <ul>
      <li><a href="index.html">Home</a></li>
EOD;
    if (isset($_SESSION['user_id'])) {
      if (user_in_group($_COOKIE['user_id'], "Administrators")) {
        echo "<li><a href='show_users.php'>Manage Users</a></li>";
      }
      echo "<li><a href='show_user.php'>My Profile</a></li>";
```

```
      echo "<li><a href='signout.php'>Sign Out</a></li>";
    } else {
      echo "<li><a href='signin.php'>Sign In</a></li>";
    }
  echo <<<EOD
      </ul>
    </div>
  EOD;
    display_messages($success_message, $error_message);
    echo "</div> <!-- page_start -->";
  }
```

Be sure and check your menu; when you're logged in, you should see "Sign Out" and "My Profile." When you're signed out, you shouldn't.

And Then Sign Out...

That leads you back to signing out. With cookies, you set the expiration value to a time in the past. With *$_SESSION*, you need to call *unset* on the session variable.

And, as odd as it may seem, you can't work with *$_SESSION*—even if that work is to unset values—without calling *session_start*. Here's what *signout.php* should look like:

```
<?php

session_start();

unset($_SESSION['user_id']);
unset($_SESSION['username']);

header('Location: signin.php');
exit();
?>
```

The cookies are gone, and once *signout.php* runs, so will your user's sessions variables.

And just like that—less than 20 lines of code changed—you've moved out of cookies and into sessions. Nice work. Your security-conscious users will thank you for it.

■ Memory Lane: Remember that Phishing Problem?

There's just one little annoyance left to which you should attend. Remember the phishing problem way back on page 205? It had to do with your use of *error_message* as a request parameter to *show_error.php*. *show_error.php* takes in the error message it displays from a request parameter:

```
if (isset($_REQUEST['error_message'])) {
  $error_message = preg_replace("/\\\\/", '', $_REQUEST['error_message']);
} else {
  $error_message = "something went wrong, and that's how you ended up
here.";
}
```

NOTE This code is in *scripts/show_error.php* (page 201).

And you saw that a URL like this…

http://yellowtagmedia.com/phpMM/ch07/show_error.php?error_message= %3Ca%20href=%22http://www.syfy.com/beinghuman%22%3EClick%20Here%20 To%20Report%20Your%20Error%3C/a%3E

…could create a page that looks like Figure 13-10. Seemingly safe, but actually, not so much.

FIGURE 13-10

Remember this example of a phishing scam (page 205)? Click on the innocent looking link, and you end up on a totally different website. Add in some CSS to match your site and a form to take in information, and your users are going to get scammed.

But now with sessions, you don't have to settle for this security hole. The problem is that you've been letting a request parameter handle the error message payload. But now, with sessions, you can remove those errors from view. This means that a hacker can't possibly force-feed in a bad request parameter because you're no longer using those parameters for that purpose.

Hop back over to *scripts/app_config.php*, and look at *handle_error*.

```php
function handle_error($user_error_message, $system_error_message) {
  header("Location: " . get_web_path(SITE_ROOT) .
         "scripts/show_error.php?" .
         "error_message={$user_error_message}&" .
         "system_error_message={$system_error_message}");
  header("Location: " . get_web_path(SITE_ROOT) . "scripts/show_error.php");
  exit();
}
```

That's the code that turns a PHP-supplied error into a request parameter. But now you can rework this using sessions:

```php
function handle_error($user_error_message, $system_error_message) {
  session_start();
  $_SESSION['error_message'] = $user_error_message;
  $_SESSION['system_error_message'] = $system_error_message;
  header("Location: " . get_web_path(SITE_ROOT) . "scripts/show_error.php");
  exit();
}
```

It's a simple change. In fact, it makes *handle_error* a lot clearer.

Now, open up *show_error.php* and make the accompanying change to pull values from the session:

```php
<?php
  require 'app_config.php';

  session_start();

  if (isset($_SESSION['error_message'])) {
    $error_message = preg_replace("/\\\/", '', $_SESSION['error_message']);
  } else {
    $error_message = "something went wrong, and that's how you ended up
here.";
  }

  if (isset($_SESSION['system_error_message'])) {
    $system_error_message = preg_replace("/\\\/", '',
                                    $_SESSION['system_error_message']);
  } else {
    $system_error_message = "No system-level error message was reported.";
  }
?>
```

> **NOTE** The HTML portion below the PHP stays exactly the same.

Now, update the problematic URL to reflect the new location of *show_user.php* (in your *scripts/* directory). So it might look something like this:

http://www.yellowtagmedia.com/phpMM/scripts/show_error.php?error_message=
%3Ca%20href=%22http://www.syfy.com/beinghuman%22%3EClick%20Here%20
To%20Report%20Your%20Error%3C/a%3E

> **NOTE** You should be able to replace the domain name, and update the path, but leave the file name and request parameters the same.

Now, visit that page in your browser. You should see a response like that shown in Figure 13-11.

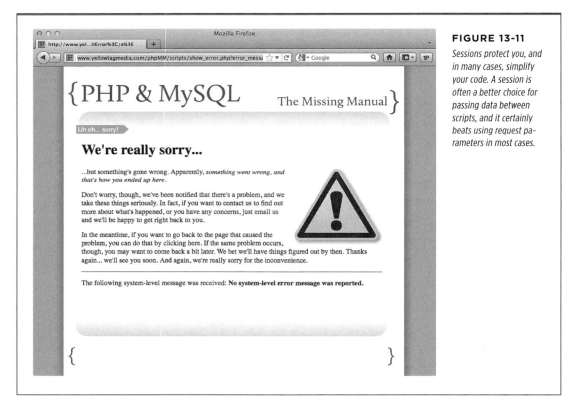

FIGURE 13-11

Sessions protect you, and in many cases, simplify your code. A session is often a better choice for passing data between scripts, and it certainly beats using request parameters in most cases.

Now, that phishing message is gone. Because the error message is stored in the session, it's resistant to someone coming along and controlling the message via the URL. It's a tiny change with huge implications for your users.

So Why Ever Use Cookies?

It's easy to think that sessions are the answer for everything. They're not, though. Probably the biggest limitation with sessions is that when the browser closes, the session's over. There's no way to get around this limitation. So if you want to offer users the ability to remain logged in across browser closings, sessions simply aren't an option. You've got to use cookies.

Second, just because cookies can be used poorly doesn't mean that they *have* to be used poorly. You can expire your cookies more frequently. You can store only very small bits of information in your cookies. And you can avoid storing much meaningful data in cookies. In fact, you may choose to do a few extra database lookups—even causing your app to run a little slower—to avoid storing much useful information on your users' machines.

Of course, like almost everything at this stage of the game, you're going to have to make a good decision for *your* application. But that's no problem. You know what you're doing now, and you know the tools at your disposal. Use them wisely, play around, and learn...always learn.

Index

Get even more for your money.

Join the O'Reilly Community, and register the O'Reilly books you own. It's free, and you'll get:

- $4.99 ebook upgrade offer
- 40% upgrade offer on O'Reilly print books
- Membership discounts on books and events
- Free lifetime updates to ebooks and videos
- Multiple ebook formats, DRM FREE
- Participation in the O'Reilly community
- Newsletters
- Account management
- 100% Satisfaction Guarantee

Signing up is easy:

1. Go to: oreilly.com/go/register
2. Create an O'Reilly login.
3. Provide your address.
4. Register your books.

Note: English-language books only

To order books online:
oreilly.com/store

For questions about products or an order:
orders@oreilly.com

To sign up to get topic-specific email announcements and/or news about upcoming books, conferences, special offers, and new technologies:
elists@oreilly.com

For technical questions about book content:
booktech@oreilly.com

To submit new book proposals to our editors:
proposals@oreilly.com

O'Reilly books are available in multiple DRM-free ebook formats. For more information:
oreilly.com/ebooks

O'REILLY®

Spreading the knowledge of innovators   oreilly.com

Have it your way.